HEALTHCARE
EMPLOYMENT GUIDE

Counseling on the New
Medical Realities

Bloomberg BNA Books Authored by the ABA Section of Labor and Employment Law

ADR in Employment Law

Age Discrimination in Employment Law

Covenants Not to Compete: A State-by-State Survey

The Developing Labor Law

Discipline and Discharge in Arbitration

Elkouri & Elkouri: How Arbitration Works

Employee Benefits Law

Employee Duty of Loyalty: A State-by-State Survey

Employment at Will: A State-by-State Survey

Employment Discrimination Law

The Fair Labor Standards Act

The Family and Medical Leave Act

How ADR Works

How to Take a Case Before the NLRB

International Labor and Employment Laws

Labor Arbitration: A Practical Guide for Advocates

Labor Arbitration: Cases and Materials for Advocates

Labor Arbitrator Development: A Handbook

Labor Union Law and Regulation

Occupational Safety and Health Law

The Railway Labor Act

Restrictive Covenants and Trade Secrets in Employment Law: An International Survey

Tortious Interference in the Employment Context: A State-by-State Survey

Trade Secrets: A State-by-State Survey

The Uniformed Services Employment and Reemployment Rights Act

Wage and Hour Laws: A State-by-State Survey

Workplace Data: Law and Litigation

For details on these and other related titles, please visit our Web site at **bna.com/bnabooks** or call **1-800-960-1220** to request a catalog. All books are available on a 30-day free-examination basis.

HEALTHCARE EMPLOYMENT GUIDE

Counseling on the New Medical Realities

James O'Reilly
Mary Ellen Keegan

Bloomberg BNA

Arlington, VA

Library of Congress Cataloging-in-Publication Data

Names: O'Reilly, James T., 1947- author. | Keegan, Mary Ellen, author.
Title: Healthcare employment guide : counseling on the new medical realities
 / by James T. O'Reilly and Mary Ellen Keegan.
Description: Arlington, Virginia : Bureau of National Affairs, Inc., [2017] |
 Includes bibliographical references and index.
Identifiers: LCCN 2017020393 (print) | LCCN 2017020577 (ebook) | ISBN
 9781682673188 (ebook) | ISBN 9781682673195 (alk. paper)
Subjects: LCSH: Health facilities--Law and legislation--United States. |
 Labor laws and legislation--United States. | Collective labor
 agreements--Health facilities--United States. | Medical
 personnel--Employment--United States. | Medical personnel--Legal status,
 laws, etc.--United States. | Group medical practice--Law and
 legislation--United States.
Classification: LCC KF3825 (ebook) | LCC KF3825 .O74 2017 (print) | DDC
 344.7304/1--dc23
LC record available at https://lccn.loc.gov/2017020393

Published by Bloomberg BNA
1801 S. Bell Street, Arlington, VA 22202
bna.com/bnabooks

ISBN 978-1-68267-319-5
Printed in the United States of America

This book is dedicated to

Ann Rick O'Reilly, R.N.
and
John R. O'Reilly, M.D.

Honoring their years of great service to the health of the
People of Western Massachusetts

and to

Tariq Shakoor, M.D.

Honoring his years of great service to the health of the
People of Ohio

PREFACE

This book confronts a growing problem for lawyers: We don't know how to "heal the healers."

The medical community—doctors, nurses, technicians, administrators, and hospital staff at all levels, among others—have been generous in allowing us to share in their many experiences with workplace conflict, subject to our guarantee of non-attribution. In dozens of texts on other subjects, we have been able to quote this regulator or cite to that court opinion, making clear the precise source of an observation. The hubristic competition among and about trial lawyers is familiar to all cable television viewers.

But medicine strives to appear "above all that," because trust in our doctors' ability to heal us begins with our simple trust in them. It has been a year-long effort to expose the conflicts among the hospital management suite, the medical regulatory bodies, the local medical societies, the various practices and beliefs of healthcare providers, and the unheralded nurses and technicians who actually operate the system.

The reader is encouraged to stay tuned for news reports on the budgets—both federal and state—from which quality and sufficiency of staff for healthcare sites will be determined. As this book was being finalized for print, in May 2017, epic developments occurred.

The Trump budget plans revealed a desire to sharply reduce Medicaid—the principal funding source for many elderly nursing home residents. The May 15, 2017, Supreme Court decision in *Kindred Nursing Centers Limited v. Clark* will block many liability lawsuits against those nursing homes which had included mandatory arbitration clauses in their admissions paperwork. Liability insurers are less concerned, and thus less demanding of the facility operator, since juries will not be able to weigh the errors or misconduct of the "care staff" and arbitration awards will be miniscule compared to the occasional windfall jury awards against facilities. To the extent that families expected an easy move of an elder into a Medicaid facility, and expected robust staffing with assurances of safe surroundings in these facilities, there may be more bad news ahead. To the extent that employee representatives had sought a strong bargaining posture, it may be eroded by some of these external events. So this remains a dynamic area indeed.

We thank those undisclosed sources who generously shared their inside stories with us.

Lorene Schaefer-Hooi of Atlanta, Georgia; Megan C. Phillips and Cori Casey Turner of Husch Blackwell, deserve our deepest gratitude for sharing their talents with our readers in this book.

The legal and commercial aspects of conflicts and developments have been explored with the expert assistance of law librarians Jim Hart, Lauren Morrison, Julie Koehne, and their colleagues at the University of Cincinnati and the Hamilton County Law Library in Cincinnati. The University of Cincinnati Harrison Medical Library team, led by Edith Starbuck, gave enormous help to our researchers on medical practice issues. Law graduates Marina Schemmel and Kellie Ann Kulka invested countless hours to produce excellent, in-depth research on legal issues. Kathryn Miller, Esq., aided our understanding of the complex immigration issues facing the medical recruiting community. Dr. Jabeen Taiba of the University of Cincinnati's College of Medicine engaged in valuable medical literature research. Erin Conklin of Northern Kentucky University's Salmon P. Chase College of Law investigated contractual issues in considerable depth. Xavier University's health services administration masters' program shared with us the wise and talented researching skills of Jennifer Terry, Anne Mitchell, and Katie Weiskircher, who will be among the best young administrators to improve the working environment which this text explores.

But none of the views expressed in this book are to be attributed to them; the authors alone bear that burden.

Professor O'Reilly thanks his family and friends for their long-suffering support of this seemingly endless quest to delineate our complex healthcare system, and to prescribe improvements. Ms. Keegan appreciates the encouragement and support of her husband, Tariq Shakoor M.D., whose high professional standards and deep devotion to the practice of medicine are an inspiration to his wife and to countless others. Ms. Keegan would also like to thank the hundreds of dedicated physicians from around the country who took time to be interviewed and to share their thoughts, experiences and concerns about the trends in physician employment. The authors also appreciate the enormous assistance of Nancy C. Elliott of the Washington state bar for her insights into these issues.

And we all thank Bloomberg BNA, and especially editor David Wagoner, for exceptional guidance. Please send comments and corrections for future editions to joreilly@fuse.net.

James T. O'Reilly
Mary Ellen Keegan
Cincinnati

May 2017

ABOUT THE AUTHORS

James O'Reilly is a veteran professor of law at the University of Cincinnati, currently teaching Public Health Policy and serving as Concentration Director of the Health Services Management program for the Department of Environmental Health at the UC College of Medicine. He is a graduate of the University of Virginia School of Law, and a graduate, with honors, of Boston College. This is his 51st textbook. His work has been quoted by the U.S. Supreme Court, and by numerous appellate and state supreme courts. He served as a labor arbitrator for the Ohio State Employment Relations Board for many years, and was one of the keynote speakers on that Board's celebration of its 25th anniversary. Professor O'Reilly has lectured internationally and served as an expert consultant to the European Commission on its "Better Regulation" project. He has also worked with Procter & Gamble Company as its Associate General Counsel as well as with numerous law firms, and served as Section Chair of the American Bar Association Section on Administrative Law & Regulatory Practice.

Mary Ellen Keegan is retired senior counsel for the General Electric Co. in Cincinnati, Ohio. She is a graduate of Seattle University School of Law. For more than twenty years she worked as in-house legal counsel for General Electric's Aviation Division, where she drafted, led and successfully concluded billions of dollars of U.S. and international business transactions, mergers and acquisitions, financings, and other sophisticated business transactions, year after year. Mary Ellen has lectured nationally and internationally on sophisticated business transactions. After marrying a gastroenterologist in 1993, she became keenly interested in the national healthcare delivery system, and most particularly, how it affected physicians on an individual and group level. She observed highly educated, bright, sleep-deprived, responsible, but ultimately vulnerable individuals being taken advantage of by insurance companies and large healthcare organizations. She has tracked the changes in healthcare delivery as it negatively impacts physicians and others in the U.S. healthcare system. Her vast business and transactions background has enabled her to consult and negotiate favorably for physicians with insurance companies and healthcare organizations.

INTRODUCTION: AN OVERVIEW OF HEALTHCARE EMPLOYMENT

Conflicts between workers and employers have been reported for millennia, including in biblical stories and in the comparable legends of other civilizations. Modern employment relationships feature these traditional disputes along with newer and often more intractable ones. And the greater the complexity of the relationship, the greater the potential for discord. Conflicts between U.S. healthcare institutions and their workers are no exception.

For attorneys who counsel physicians, nurses, and other health care workers in negotiations with their employer institutions, these uniquely modern and deeply historical bundles of conflicts present serious predicaments. The mantra of "Time is money!" that governs reimbursement by Medicaid, Medicare, and preferred provider organizations increases pressure on hospital managers to deliver electronically documented services, to as many patients as possible, in the time that is available on the computerized schedule.

Once, the American physician could listen, talk with, diagnose and recommend actions for patients; the solo doctor could communicate and manage diagnostic technologies with sufficient time and freedom to persuade her or his adult patients to follow thoughtful measures to improve their self-care. No more.

This text aims to help the busy lawyer aid the very busy medical client. We offer analysis of the "why" of healthcare employment conflicts and economics as well as the "how." In many ways, economic stresses predominate. Healthcare is a huge fraction of the U.S. economy. A large portion, perhaps one-fifth, of our gross domestic product is spent on healthcare programs and needs. Tens of millions of workers and their families depend on a viable compensation system for the services which are increasingly demanded. The need for solutions to our collective problems is evident.

The proper legal exercise of rights makes the expensive delivery system more equitable, but not necessarily more lucrative. Despite wildly increasing healthcare costs, doctors, surgeons, advanced practice registered nurses, and technology specialists will encounter novel legal problems in their quest for compensation that adequately rewards them for their services. Registered nurses, nurse aides, and the many operatives of the modern hospital staff are feeling squeezed, unable to earn the level of pay and benefits to which they are entitled.

Some noneconomic conflicts involve "whistleblower" safety or fraud situations. Other conflicts involve customary union debates with employers about the need for contract protection against further layoffs. Throw in patient disputes, and the cauldron of modern healthcare employment can reach a high boil.

With a growing, aging population, the demand for physicians has intensified, and communities around the country are already experiencing doctor shortages. A 2017 study conducted for the American Association of Medical Colleges predicts that by the year 2030, the United States will face a shortage of between 40,800-104,900 physicians. There will be shortages in both primary and specialty care, and specialty shortages will be particularly large.[1]

This book examines the modern landscape of healthcare employment, from janitor to surgeon, from urgent-care storefront to mega-chain hospital, from entrepreneur to local health department. The common element in our approach is to have counsel remain calm, factual and focused in offering viable solutions, despite the real drama and trauma experienced by your clients as they cope with the many destabilizing forces at work, including interpersonal conflicts. Healers with great medical skills can become unreasonable, emotional competitors when strikes are threatened, or when discipline charges are filed, or when whistleblower claims are sprung on unsuspecting management.

This text assists the legal advisor to help clients overcome crises within the healthcare employment context, illuminating paths and revealing patterns to facilitate a client's proper assertion of a well-presented legal position. We hope this book will provide guidance to healthcare employers for years to come.

---

[1] "New Research Reaffirms Physician Shortage," AAMC News, *American Ass'n of Medical Colleges*, https://news.aamc.org/press-releases/article/workforce_projections_03142017/. See also AAMC News, "GME Funding: How to Fix the Doctor Shortage," *American Ass'n of Medical Colleges*, https://news.aamc.org/for-the-media/article/gme-funding-doctor-shortage.

We welcome your comments, critiques, and suggestions. Please send them to Bloomberg BNA Editorial Offices, 1801 South Bell Street, Arlington, Virginia, 22202, or by e-mail to books@bna.com.

Professor James O'Reilly
Department of Environmental Health
University of Cincinnati College of Medicine
Cincinnati, Ohio
James.oreilly@uc.edu

June 2017

SUMMARY TABLE OF CONTENTS

PART III: HOW OTHER HEALTHCARE PERSONNEL INTERACT WITH EMPLOYERS

PART IV: ISSUES FOR ALL HEALTHCARE PERSONNEL

APPENDICES

DETAILED TABLE OF CONTENTS

PART II: PHYSICIANS' EMPLOYMENT ISSUES

Part 1

Introduction

CHAPTER 1

HEALTHCARE CONFLICTS AND PHYSICIAN DISSATISFACTION

I. OVERVIEW

This chapter delves into the root causes of strife among the physician members of the medical community. Unhappiness with the conditions of daily work appears to be a pervasive source of personal discontent, and legal conflicts (in particular, rocketing malpractice rates),[1] add to the burden. Multiple reviewers have investigated physician despondency and found no single answer. Rather, myriad reasons converge and result in widespread physician upset. To explore these reasons, we begin with a look at the polling data.

A. Most Practicing Physicians Would Rather Quit Medicine

Why would there be such stark conflict in such a rewarding profession? What could cause the sharpening conflicts that physicians are experiencing today? Why and what indeed.

---

[1] *See* Abigail Zuger, M.D., *Dissatisfaction with Medical Practice*, 350 NEW ENGLAND J. OF MED. 69, Jan. 1, 2004.

A recurring theme in this chapter will be the loss of autonomy within the medical profession. Overwhelmed with oversight, paperwork and documentation, and battered by changes in funding and payment programs and requirements (not to mention legislative developments), many doctors readily express their dislike for the conditions of today's medical practice. And their dislike is leading them straight toward the exit doors.

According to a 2012 Survey of American Physicians, six out of ten practicing physicians would quit if they could.[2] A 2016 Survey of American Physicians echoed that sentiment, with almost half (48%) of the 17,236 physicians responding to the survey indicating a plan to—immediately or within the next three years—either retire (14%), seek temporary locum tenens positions (11.5%), work non-clinical administrative jobs (13.5%), go part time (10%), do concierge medicine (9%), or otherwise significantly cut back on patient clinical work, rather than practice traditional full-time medicine. A full 46.8% plan to accelerate their retirement plans.[3]

B. Why are American Physicians Dissatisfied to the Point They Would Like to Quit?

Physicians want to leave medicine mainly because of the loss of professional autonomy, due to interference by third parties. That conclusion applies to physicians in every type of practice and geographic region, including employed physicians, private practice physicians, academic physicians and government physicians, all of whom are leaving, or want to leave, or want to significantly change their medical practice.

It is estimated that for every one hour a physician sees patients, the physician spends nearly two additional hours on documentation behind the scenes, out of the view of the patient. And much of that heavy paperwork ends up being completed when the physician

---

[2]John Commins, *6 in 10 Physicians Would Quit Today*, HEALTHLEADERS MEDIA (Sept. 26, 2012), http://www.healthleadersmedia.com/physician-leaders/6-10-physi cians-would-quit-today.

[3]MERRITT HAWKINS, 2016 SURVEY OF AMERICA'S PHYSICIANS: PRACTICE PATTERNS AND PERSPECTIVES (Sept. 21, 2016), http://www.merritthawkins.com/phy-sicians-foundation-survey.aspx. The biennial survey has been conducted since 2012 and is sponsored by the Physicians Foundation, a nonprofit organization that seeks to advance the work of practicing physicians and facilitate the delivery of healthcare to patients.

leaves the office and is at home, supposedly relaxing.[4] As one business health journalist for *Forbes* magazine wondered, "Is this really the best use of doctors' training and ability? Isn't this like telling LeBron James to spend the majority of his time manning the Cleveland Cavaliers ticket windows and phone lines?" [5]

The 2016 Survey of America's Physicians shows that a full 72 percent of the survey respondents did not like the way third parties intruded into and detracted from the quality of care they provide to their patients. In addition to their loss of clinical autonomy and the regulatory and paperwork burdens, other important survey results showed:

Physicians reported that they spend 21 percent of their time on nonclinical paperwork.

- 54 percent described their morale as very negative or somewhat negative.
- 49 percent said they always or often experience feelings of burnout.
- 49 percent would not recommend medicine as a career to their children.
- 63 percent are pessimistic about the future of the medical profession.
- 80 percent are over-extended or are at capacity.
- 48 percent said their time with patients is always or often limited.

Only 14 percent of physicians thought they had enough time to spend with their patients to provide the highest standard of patient care.

- 27 percent of physicians do not see Medicare patients, or limit the number they see.

---

[4]For the full report see Christine A. Sinsky, John W. Beasley, Greg E. Simmons, *Electronic Health Records: Design, Implementation, and Policy for Higher-Value Primary Care*, ANNALS OF INTERNAL MED., Sept. 6, 2016, available at www.annals.org/aim/article/1872852/electronic-health-records-design-implementation-policy-higher-value-primary-care.

[5]Bruce Y. Lee, *Doctors Wasting over Two-Thirds of Their Time Doing Paperwork*, FORBES, Sept. 7, 2016, available at https://www.forbes.com/sites/brucelee/2016/09/07/doctors-wasting-over-two-thirds-of-their-time-doing-paperwork/#2f4665915d7b.

- 36 percent of physicians do not see Medicaid patients, or limit the number they see.
- 66 percent of physicians surveyed do not believe hospital employment of physicians will enhance quality of care or decrease costs.

Even 50 percent of physicians who are themselves employed by hospitals do not see hospital employment of physicians as a positive trend.

As if the foregoing indicators weren't dismal enough, physician reimbursements have declined significantly. From 1995 to 2008 physician reimbursements, adjusted for inflation, declined more than 25 percent as health insurers and other payors decreased physician reimbursement rates.[6] At the same time, burgeoning regulatory and legislative changes in the form of Stark Law and Anti-Kickback antitrust rules, Medicare/Medicaid policies, insurance regulations, HIPAA and privacy constraints, electronic charting requirements, and insurance coding and documentation obligations all combine to bury doctors in additional duties. Because most doctors aren't paid a salary, decreased doctor reimbursement means doctors have to see more patients just to pay overhead, employ a staff, and earn a living. The result is that physicians must see ever-increasing numbers of patients for less and less money, to earn the same income.

C. Examine the Extremes: Physician Suicides

A shocking statistic is the number of physician suicides per year.[7] The United States loses 350 to 400 physicians each year to suicide, due in large part to high stress and tension, burnout or depression and mental illness.[8] That's more or less a doctor a day,[9] a

[6]David W. Hilgers, *Introduction: "Complex Environment—Difficult Choices,"* in ACOs AND OTHER OPTIONS: A "HOW-TO" MANUAL FOR PHYSICIANS NAVIGATING A POSTHEALTH REFORM WORLD (AMERICAN MED. ASS'N 4th ed., 2010-2013).

[7]Dave Chase, *The Story Behind Epidemic Doctor Burnout and Suicide Statistics,* FORBES, Jan. 6, 2016, *available at* http://www.forbes.com/sites/davechase/2016/01/06/the-story-behind-epidemic-doctor-burnout-and-suicide-statistics/#11c3e778570d.

[8]Joan M. Anzia, M.D., *It's Time to Recognize and Prevent the Tragedy of Physician Suicide,* STAT, July 21, 2016, https://www.statnews.com/2016/07/21/suicide-physicians/.

[9]Louise B. Andrew, M.D., J.D., *Physician Suicide,* MEDSCAPE,Oct. 03, 2016, http://emedicine.medscape.com/article/806779-overview.

suicide rate 1.5 to 2.3 times higher than the suicide rate of the general public.[10]

And that appallingly high suicide rate assumes that the number is not significantly under-reported. Most coroners in towns or cities in the United States are physicians (or other medical professionals closely tied to the physician community). So one must wonder whether sympathetic elements influence coroners when it comes to sudden physician deaths. How many cases are determined to be accidental overdoses, rather than suicides? But really, how likely is it that a person trained in prescribing exact dosages of drugs—and having easy access to prescribed drugs—would accidentally fatally overdose?

II. WHY THIS MATTERS TO ATTORNEYS SERVING PHYSICIANS OR ATTORNEYS WORKING WITHIN THE HEALTH CARE SYSTEM

Conflict has costs; dissatisfaction breeds dropouts. Without enough mentally and physically healthy physicians who are able and willing to treat the American population, the health care "delivery train" stops.

This is what we know: On Jan. 1, 2017, according to the U.S. Census Bureau, the U.S. population was 324,310,011,[11] making it the third most populous country in the world, after China and India. Of the entire U.S. population, 14.1 percent (almost 47 million people) are 65 years of age or older.[12] Persons 65 and older are the population requiring the most health care, and they are the population with access to governmental payments through Medicare.

Sick people can't be outsourced to distant providers.

---

[10]*Id.* "Because of their greater knowledge of and better access to lethal means, physicians have a far higher suicide completion rate than the general public. The most reliable estimates of successful completion of suicide range from 1.4-2.3 times the rate achieved in the general population. Although female physicians attempt suicide far less often than their counterparts in the general population, their completion rate equals that of male physicians and, thus, far exceeds that of the general population (2.5-4 times the rate by some estimates)."

[11]U.S. Census Bureau, https://www.census.gov/newsroom/stories/2017/january/new_years_2017.html.

[12]MERRITT HAWKINS, THE AGING PHYSICIAN WORKFORCE: A DEMOGRAPHIC DILEMMA 2, 2015 http://www.merritthawkins.com/uploadedFiles/mhawhitepaper_aging.pdf.

According to the U.S. Census Bureau projections, the number of individuals who are 65 years old and older is expected to almost double to 92 million by 2060.[13]

The Pew Research Center reports that beginning January 1, 2011, every day, 10,000 baby boomers have turned or will turn 65, and will continue to do so for the next 19 years (through January 1, 2030).[14] They will be aging with their generation's high expectations for quality health care, as well as their complicated multiple chronic health problems, such as cancer, heart disease, diabetes, obesity, arthritis, HIV-AIDS, and other health issues.

As millions of baby boomers move into their senior years and large numbers of baby boom generation doctors retire or leave the medical profession, the U.S. will find itself in increasingly dire need of physicians.[15] The doctor shortage has been projected to reach as many as 90,400 physicians by 2025.[16] That 90,400 projection did not fully take into consideration the impact of the 2016 Survey of America's Physicians, in which almost half of the respondents indicated that they intend to voluntarily take themselves out of the work force or reduce their hours by 2020.[17]

And though hospitals and clinics don't like to hear it, paraprofessionals are simply no substitute for physicians, due to the immense

---

[13]U.S. Census Bureau, *U.S. Census Bureau Projections Show a Slower Growing, Older, More Diverse Nation a Half Century from Now*, Dec. 12, 2012, http://www.census.gov/newsroom/releases/archives/population/cb12-243.html.

[14]D'Vera Cohn & Paul Taylor, *Baby Boomers Approach 65—Glumly*, PEW RESEARCH CENTER, Dec. 29, 2010, http://www.pewsocialtrends.org/2010/12/20/baby-boomers-approach-65-glumly.

[15]See MERRITT HAWKINS, THE AGING PHYSICIAN WORKFORCE: A DEMOGRAPHIC DILEMMA 2, 2015 http://www.merritthawkins.com/uploadedFiles/mhawhitepaper_aging.pdf.

[16]ASS'N OF AMERICAN MEDICAL COLLEGES, THE COMPLEXITIES OF PHYSICIAN SUPPLY AND DEMAND: PROJECTIONS FROM 2013 TO 2025, (Mar. 2015). Estimating or forecasting numbers of a particular employment shortage is not an exact science. Forecasters take into consideration many constantly shifting modeling variables (e.g. population growth, the graying of the physician work force, the medical specialty mix and demographics of new entrants to the physician workforce, retirement and mortality patterns of physicians, population mix, how many such new physicians are going into full time clinical medicine as opposed to taking jobs in research, biotechnology, industry, finance, teaching, etc.).

[17]For more information on the physician shortage, see ASS'N OF AMERICAN MEDICAL COLLEGES, THE COMPLEXITIES OF PHYSICIAN SUPPLY AND DEMAND: PROJECTIONS FROM 2013 TO 2025, (Mar. 2015); MERRITT HAWKINS, THE AGING PHYSICIAN WORKFORCE: A DEMOGRAPHIC DILEMMA, (2015) http://www.merritthawkins.com/uploadedFiles/mhawhitepaper_aging.pdf.

difference in education and training. Therefore, the paraprofessionals cannot make up for the physician shortage. Additionally, a new physician who is recently out of training simply does not have skills equal to those of a physician with 30 years of experience.

Since 2010, an estimated 20 to 30 million (or more) previously uninsured Americans have received insurance coverage under various provisions of the Affordable Care Act,[18] but there has not been any corresponding increase in the number of physicians able to care for them. That means more insured patients and a surge in health care demand, but no corresponding surge in the number of doctors available to treat the patients.

What can attorneys representing physicians, hospital systems, insurers, or other healthcare providers do? First, we can understand the physician's perspective, as to why they feel the way they do, so to be better able to negotiate with them or on their behalf.

Second, recognize that the physician shortage is real, and is about to get even more real.

Third, understand that the fair market value of physicians is increasing; physicians have spent 11 to 17 or more years of their lives in higher education, so they resent being treated like a worker on a factory floor. They refuse to suffer the indignity of "take it or leave it" terms in their contracts with insurers, employers or so-called "integration partners."

Attorneys for insurers, hospital systems or other health care providers who recognize the importance of physicians can advise their clients to promote a more tempered and less draconian approach to their treatment of physicians in negotiating contracts. Without healthy and engaged physicians, the entire health care delivery system collapses. Attorneys who understand that will benefit their clients in the short and long run.

Before leaving this chapter and its negative overview, it is important to note that the positive responses which work best often involve collective and cooperative efforts among peer professionals. Some use unions as the optimal professional coalescence. Others

---

[18]Tami Luhby, *Obamacare 2017 Enrollment Hits Record, Despite Trump's Threat to Repeal*, CNN, Dec. 21, 2016, http://money.cnn.com/2016/12/21/news/economy/obamacare-enrollment-record/; 2014, AaronYoung, Humayun J. Chaudhry, Xiaomei Pei, Katie Halbesleben, Donald H. Polk, & Michael Dugan, *A Census of Actively Licensed Physicians in the United States*, 101 J. MED. REG'N 8 (2015), http://www.fsmb.org/media/default/pdf/census/2014census.pdf.

ask for hospital-based professionals to work inside their organization to give more support to the struggles of their colleagues. Some ask for a more active state or federal government role in the balance of power against profit-focused executive managers. As we study the move of professionals into employee roles that had not been encountered in medicine in the past, we hope lawyers and clients will be open to collective support and encouragement. That will help break the downward spiral of concerns, because the profession will align around its members, bolstering them at their time of need. In the next chapter, we'll look at physicians who have left solo practice to join larger groups of employers, and what that means for them, their patients, and counsel representing them.

CHAPTER 2

SETTING THE STAGE FOR CONFLICTS INVOLVING PHYSICIANS

I. UNDERSTANDING THE PHYSICIAN'S PERSPECTIVE

To understand why physicians—particularly experienced physicians—feel as dissatisfied, stressed out, burned out, and pessimistic as they do today, consider how much the practice of medicine has changed. Much of the profession has been taken out of their hands, while at the same time they have significantly increased responsibility and liability. Many feel as if they've been slowly ground up in an industrial medicine machine over which they have little control.

Until fairly recently, physicians were the center of the U.S. health care system, as it related to providing health care to their patients.

They practiced medicine as solo practitioners or in small groups.[1] They enjoyed professional respect, had professional autonomy, cared for their patients in the manner they thought fit, and ordered the prescriptions, tests, and procedures they felt were necessary to best treat their patients. Their professional judgment was deferred to with little interference from insurance companies or federal payors. In fact, even today, physicians' recommendations and decisions still direct as much as 90 percent of all health care spending (although other pressures on spending play a major role and restrict much of physician autonomy).[2] That's why hospitals are still buying medical practices and employing physicians who have a large patient base, are located in coveted geographic neighborhoods, or who perform profitable office clinical procedures.

In prior years, before managed care and other recent changes, if a physician's patient required surgery or hospitalization, the physician admitted the patient to a local hospital where the physician had staff and clinical privileges. In exchange for having medical staff and clinical privileges at the hospital (or several local hospitals), the physician would typically be obliged to provide on-call coverage for the hospital. Rarely was the physician an employee of the hospital. The physician was usually an independent physician who used the hospital's facilities on an independent contractor basis, meaning that the hospital furnished the facilities and equipment without charge to the physician. The physician would treat the patient at the hospital, and the physician billed the patient for the physician's services (or more likely the insurance company or third-party payor). Separately, the hospital billed the patient (or insurance company or third-party payor) for the hospital's services.

For cases that were too complicated for the physician to manage at the local hospital, the physician would refer patients to appropriate

---

[1] See Thomas G. Rundall et al., *A Theory of Physician-Hospital Integration: Contending Institutional and Market Logics in the Health Care Field*, 45 J. HEALTH & SOC. BEHAV. 102, 104 (2004) (noting that for most of the past century, physicians organized themselves into solo practices or small groups).

[2] See John Eisenberg, *Physician Utilization: The State of Research About Physicians' Practice Patterns*, 40 MED. CARE 1016, 1016 (2002) (noting that physician decisions govern as much as 90 percent of how health care dollars are spent); Alan Sager & Deborah Socolar, *Health Costs Absorb One Quarter of Economic Growth 2000-2005*, BOS. UNIV. SCH. OF PUB. HEALTH 29 (Feb. 9, 2005) (stating that physicians' decisions "control fully 87% of the personal health care dollar").

major hospitals or institutions that were staffed and equipped to handle complicated cases.

Before the current changes to the practice of medicine, a physician's hospital medical staff privileges and credentials depended on the physician's education, training, professional qualifications, moral character and level of patient care delivered. It was not reliant upon the physician sending all his or her patients exclusively to that particular hospital, or any other type of "economic credentialing" criteria.[3] Also, the physician could refer patients to whatever specialist the physician thought was best for the patient. The referral of the patient was not done on the basis of employment contract terms or insurance network restrictions.

In the days before managed care, physicians were reimbursed on a fee-for-service basis, meaning they were paid per medical service. So the physician could reasonably predict his or her medical practice income, by the number and nature of medical services provided. Best of all, the physician did not spend an average of 20 hours per week obtaining prior authorization for treatment or prescription drugs for patients, often for routine treatment.[4] Recently, physicians have had to contend with bundled payments, capitated rates, mandated investments in expensive electronic health records systems, and medical coding systems or extra staffing to demonstrate improved quality metrics and improved patient outcomes. These developments have created ever more taxing burdens for physicians merely trying to be paid for medical services provided to patients.

---

[3] The American College of Medical Quality defines economic credentialing as "the use of economic criteria unrelated to quality of care or professional competence in determining a physician's qualifications for initial or continuing hospital medical staff membership or privileges." *Economic Credentialing: Where Is It Going?*, FINDLAW CORPORATE COUNSEL LAW LIBRARY, http://corporate.findlaw.com/law-library/economic-credentialing-where-is-it-going.html#sthash.7sVUsXMl.dpuf. The AMA and a number of its state affiliates have registered strong opposition to economic credentialing.

[4] *See* Ken Terry, Alison Ritchie, Donna Marbury, Lisa Smith & Elaine Pofeldt, *Top 6 Practice Management Challenges Facing Physicians in 2015*, MEDICAL ECON., http://medicaleconomics.modernmedicine.com/medical-economics/news/top-6-practice-management-challenges-facing-physicians-2015?page=full (citing a 2010 AMA survey of the average amount of time physicians spend per week on prior authorization activities).

II. INFLUENCES OF THE ADVENT OF MANAGED CARE

Because health care costs ballooned in the 1980s and 1990s as compared with inflation of other sectors of the economy,[5] intense price consciousness arose, with the direct consequence that insurers, employers, healthcare policy makers, state legislators, and members of Congress all insisted that the healthcare sector become more efficient in delivering healthcare.[6]

Private insurance companies, Medicare, Medicaid, and other government payors responded to this pressure; they changed the means by which they contracted with and reimbursed physicians and other healthcare providers, in an effort to contain costs. Medicare and Medicaid regulations gradually became more complex, particularly the reimbursement methodologies and protocols.[7] Accordingly, individual physicians' administrative burdens and associated costs increased.[8]

Then large employers and private insurers began forcing price competition among physicians, hospitals, and other healthcare providers, by including only a limited number of each provider category onto their approved insurance plans and cutting other competitors out. That in turn led to significant price competition between an area's physicians, hospitals, and other healthcare providers. To be on the approved insurance plan, the physicians, hospitals and other healthcare providers had to agree to accept heavily discounted reimbursement rates, extended payment terms, and other burdensome financial conditions, just to be categorized as "in network" on the insurance plans to which their patients and local employers belonged.

---

[5]*See* Lisa Potetz, et al., *Medicare Spending and Financing: A Primer* 2, THE HENRY J. KAISER FAMILY FOUND. (2011) (showing that from 1985-2009, average annual growth in Medicare spending of 8.5 percent exceeded the annual average consumer price index of 2.9 percent).

[6]*See* Paul Starr, REMEDY AND REACTION 79 (2011) ("From 1987 to 1993, private insurance premiums jumped 90 percent, while wages increased only 28 percent, with the result that fewer Americans could afford health coverage. Despite the limited expansion of Medicaid eligibility, the uninsured population rose to 38.6 million in 1992, an increase of 5.2 million from 1989.").

[7]*See* Carol J. Simon and Patricia H. Born, *Health Tracking: Trends: Physician Earnings In a Changing Managed Care Environment*, 15 HEALTH AFFAIRS 124 (Fall 1996).

[8]*See* Rundall, *supra* note 1, at 103 (discussing changes since the 1980s in the way public and private health plans contract with and compensate health care providers).

III. Consolidations of Solo Practices and Group Practices

A. Lower Reimbursements, Higher Costs, and Heavier Regulatory Burdens

Price sensitivity and the resulting lower insurance reimbursement rates decreased physicians' income, particularly for solo and small group practitioners who typically didn't have much leverage to negotiate with insurance companies, unless they were located in rural or underserved areas. Unfortunately for physicians, the lower income came at a bad time: malpractice insurance premiums, staff salaries, medical equipment costs and other office and clinic overhead expenses continued to rise, leaving private practice physicians caught in an economic squeeze.

On top of these constraints, there were ever-growing regulatory demands of governmental and insurance programs, which meant that physician practice owners were required to spend increasing amounts of time dealing with multiplying administrative and regulatory issues, such as privacy and confidentiality requirements, patient consent, documentation to support billing, fraud and abuse prevention, occupational safety, electronic health records issues, and more—all of which took time away from seeing patients and providing care.

B. Financial Crisis 2007

The financial crisis that began in 2007 cost roughly 7.5 million Americans their jobs, driving the U.S. unemployment rate from 4.4 percent to 10.1 percent.[9] The loss of insurance coverage for workers who otherwise had enjoyed employer-based insurance coverage further harmed the insurance access and medical economics for solo practitioners or physicians who were working in small-group practices. Many solo practitioners and small-group practices found themselves entirely shut out of insurance contract "network coverage," unless they were practicing in rural or underserved areas where there wasn't much competition from major medical groups or universities.

As a result, many medical practitioners faced unpalatable options such as selling their medical practices, merging with or

---

[9] *See* David B. Grusky, The Great Recession 3 (2011).

otherwise joining larger medical groups, becoming employees of hospital systems, working for government agencies or insurance companies, or working for medical staffing companies.

IV. CURRENT TREND: HOSPITAL-EMPLOYED PHYSICIANS

Starting in approximately 2004, hospitals launched—and are continuing—a medical practice "buying spree." Typically, what occurs is that the hospital (or an affiliate of the hospital) purchases one or more physicians' medical practices, and the physicians become employees of the hospital (or a subsidiary of the hospital). Thereafter the physicians refer their patients for medical procedures and medical consults exclusively to the hospital and other co-employed physicians. If this arrangement is structured correctly, there is a "safe harbor" available for bona fide employees, whereby an employed physician can be required to refer patients to his or her employer for services and can enjoy the safe harbor. Such a referral by a physician employee would not violate the Stark Law or the Anti-Kickback Statute.[10] However, an independent solo physician would

---

[10]The Anti-Kickback Statute contains a safe harbor at 42 C.F.R. §1001.952(i) for bona fide employees that states: "As used in Section 1128B of the Act, 'remuneration' does not include any amount paid by an employer to an employee, who has a bona fide employment relationship with the employer, for employment in the furnishing of any item or service for which payment may be made in whole or in part under Medicare, Medicaid or other Federal health care programs." Likewise, the Stark Law provides an exception at 42 U.S.C. §1395nn(e)(2) for employment relationships if the person is a bona fide employee and the following requirements are met:

1. The employment is for "identifiable services";
2. The remuneration paid "is consistent with the fair market value of the services";
3. The remuneration paid isn't tied to the "volume or value of any referrals" made by referring physicians;
4. The compensation paid "would be commercially reasonable even if no referrals are made to the employer"; and
5. The employment "meets such other requirements as the Secretary of Health and Human Services may impose by regulation as needed to protect against program or patient abuse."

Additionally, the Stark Law regulations at 42 C.F.R. 411.354(d)(4) allow employers to use a referral requirement so long as patient preferences are honored, the referral is in the "best medical interests" of the patient, and the requirement is "reasonably necessary to effectuate the legitimate business purpose" of the employment.

risk violating those same laws if he or she were to refer a patient to a facility in which he or she had a financial interest.[11]

Over about the same time period, a confluence of a number of factors resulted in many physicians seeking hospital employment instead of practice ownership.[12] These things included the economic recession, the expense of meeting and maintaining elaborate electronic health records requirements, the implementation of the Affordable Care Act, and the rise of uncertain "pay for performance" reimbursement models. Added to these were significant generational differences, with younger physicians valuing more free time and not wanting the added responsibility of running their own practice.[13] As a result, by 2016, 57.9 percent of physicians responding to the 2016 Survey of American Physicians identified themselves as employees of hospitals or hospital-owned medical groups.[14]

V. HOSPITALS LOSE MONEY ON EMPLOYED PHYSICIANS— SO WHY ARE SO MANY BEING EMPLOYED?

A. Economics of Hospital Employment of Physicians

Hospitals typically lose $150,000 to $250,000 per year over the first three years employing a physician. Somewhat lower financial losses begin in the fourth year of employment, but they are losses nonetheless.[15]

---

[11]Please refer to Chapter 26, *Common Challenges: Stark and Anti-Kickback Compliance*, for a more comprehensive Stark Law and Anti-Kickback Statute discussion. There are ways to manage referrals, but it takes careful analysis and guidance to make sure the referrals fall into a permissible "safe harbor."

[12]See David W. Hilgers, *ACOs and other options: A '"How To"' Manual For Physicians Navigating A Post–Health Reform World*, AMERICAN MED. ASS'N, 2-7, (4th ed. 2014).

[13]Gardiner Harris, *More Physicians Say No to Endless Workdays*, N.Y. TIMES, Apr. 1, 2011, http://www.nytimes.com/2011/04/02/health/02resident.html (reporting the results of a survey where young doctors valued quality of life over finances as the most important consideration in searching for and accepting permanent employment following medical school).

[14]MERRITT HAWKINS, 2016 SURVEY OF AMERICA'S PHYSICIANs: PRACTICE PATTERNS AND PERSPECTIVES 19 (Sept. 21, 2016), http://www.merritthawkins.com/physicians-foundation-survey.aspx.

[15]Robert Kocher, & Nikhil R. Sahni, *The Logic Behind a Money-Losing Proposition*, NEW ENG. J. MED. (May 12, 2011), http://www.nejm.org/doi/full/10.1056/NEJMp1101959#t=article.

Market pressures have pushed hospital compensation and practice expenses for some specialties far above what they actually generate in cash collections. Losses in excess of $200,000 per hospital employed physician are not unusual, according to the Medical Group Management Association. Hospitals make up the cash losses on the practices by placing their employed physicians on RVU-based incentive compensation formulae. (RVUs, or relative value units, are Medicare's billing units for physician services.) These formulae encourage the employed physician to maximize consultative requests for other specialists, as well as to use in-house imaging and laboratory services (which are highly profitable to the hospital). In effect, physician care has become a "loss leader" for the hospital's profitable diagnostic and surgical services.[16]

From the hospitals' perspective, given the impending doctor shortage, they are anxious to have physicians of their choosing on their health care delivery team, instead of that of the competition, making employing them the best choice. Also, they know that satisfied physicians can attract other physicians to work at the hospital, which is one way to help meet the impending physician shortage. (One would think they should know that dissatisfied physicians have the opposite effect as well.)

Additionally, hospitals have found out that physician employment is a good way to ensure that they have a sufficient number of physicians available for emergency department call to meet the hospital's Emergency Medical Treatment and Active Labor Act (EMTALA) requirements, which dictate that hospitals have physicians and appropriate physician specialists on call to treat emergency room patients. Because fewer physicians want to accept "emergency room call" duty due to the bad debt, malpractice exposure, and time and resource interruption of their practices, hospitals have had to employ physicians to obtain the professional services needed for patient care, particularly in rural areas.

The biggest reason for physician hospital employment, however, is so that the hospital can secure a primary care base that provides a reliable source of admissions and patient market share to cover its overhead. The hospital knows that the majority of efforts

---

[16]Jeff Goldsmith, Nathan Kaufman & Lawton Burns, *The Tangled Hospital-Physician Relationship*, HEALTH AFFAIRS BLOG (May 9, 2016), http://healthaffairs.org/blog/2016/05/09/the-tangled-hospital-physician-relationship/.

for modern healthcare reform all point to providing integrated, measurable quality, and cost-effective care across a larger care continuum. This continuum encompasses value-based delivery systems, meaning the hospital or other healthcare entity has to track and report quality measurements to the Centers for Medicare and Medicaid Services ("CMS") to earn quality incentive payments (*i.e.*, more money).[17] Consequently, the hospitals are betting that if they employ physicians they can improve market share, control costs, improve quality, and therefore make money in the long term, in spite of the fact that initially they are losing money.

B. Physician's Counsel Perspective

Any physician or physician's counsel can quickly determine that the hospital's strategy to control costs has to include reducing the physician's income in later renewal contracts because the current physician employment business model is simply not sustainable. How does an employer reduce wages? Simple. Increase the amount of work required of the individual physician, reduce compensation and benefits, and if the physician threatens to end the employment contract, point to the noncompete covenant. Preventing physicians from leaving is the primary reason why the hospital and other health care employers insist on potentially unfair noncompete provisions— the unfairness of which the employers can't acknowledge without risking the covenants being struck down on antitrust grounds. Health care entity employers need to depress physician wages, and one method to accomplish that is by reducing the future professional employment options available to the physician employee (or physician independent contractor) if the employment contract is terminated or expires without being renewed. If the physician can easily move around in the local area and get paid a better wage, receive better

---

[17] Some typical programs are the Merit-Based Incentive Payment System (MIPS, formerly the Physician Quality Reporting System (PQRI or PQRS)), the Readmission Reductions Program (HRRP), and Hospital Value Based Purchasing (HVBP). *See* CTR. FOR MEDICARE & MEDICAID SERVS., PHYSICIAN QUALITY REPORTING SYSTEM, May 2, 2017, https://www.cms.gov/Medicare/Quality-Initiatives-Patient-Assessment-Instruments/PQRS/index.html?redirect=/pqrs/15_measurescodes.asp; READMISSION REDUCTION PROGRAM (HRRP), Apr. 18, 2016, https://www.cms.gov/medicare/medicare-fee-for-service-payment/acuteinpatientpps/readmissions-reduction-program.html; HOSPITAL VALUE-BASED PURCHASE (HVBP), Feb. 15, 2017, https://www.cms.gov/Medicare/Quality-Initiatives-Patient-Assessment-Instruments/hospital-value-based-purchasing/index.html?redirect=/hospital-value-based-purchasing/.

benefits, or enjoy better working conditions, then wages and conditions for the physician and indeed, perhaps all physicians, might rise. That is typically not what hospital or healthcare entity employers want. To make such moves difficult in the local market, hospital and other major healthcare employers typically insist on the broadest noncompete covenants they can negotiate.

CHAPTER 3

HEALTHCARE EMPLOYMENT: STRUCTURE AND STATISTICS

I. UNDERSTANDING THE STRUCTURES OF MEDICAL EMPLOYMENT

A. Statistical Context of Health Care Employment Generally

The Labor Department's Bureau of Labor Statistics (BLS) has many tables on employment; these cumulatively show that in 2016, all U.S. hospitals had about 5.9 million employees, and allied health-care delivery "diagnosing and treating practitioners" were about 2.9 million.[1] Total employment at community hospitals in 2014 was about 4.5 million.[2] The number of physicians in the United States in 2013 was just over one million.[3] These employment figures represent a major increase from those of ten or twenty years ago. In

---

[1] BLS, OCCUPATIONAL EMPLOYMENT STATISTICS, MAY 2016 NATIONAL INDUSTRY-SPECIFIC OCCUPATIONAL EMPLOYMENT & WAGE ESTIMATES, NAICS 622000 – HOSPITALS (2016), https://www.bls.gov/oes/current/naics3_622000.htm#29-0000.

[2] AM. HOSP. ASS'N, CHARTBOOK, CHAPTER 5: WORKFORCE (2016), http://www.aha.org/research/reports/tw/chartbook/2016/chapter5.pdf.

[3] TOTAL NUMBER OF DOCTORS OF MEDICINE IN THE U.S. FROM 1949 TO 2013, STATISTA, http:/www.statista.com/statistics/186260/total-doctors-of-medicine-in-the-us-since-1949.

1990, there were approximately 615,400 physicians,[4] and there were 972,400 physicians nationwide in 2009,[5] an increase of about sixty percent.

The American Hospital Association's Chartbook has a fine layout of data on trends in hospital-related professional employment.[6] One important trend that many inside and outside health care employment fields have analyzed is the aging of the workforce. A large component of health care providers is relatively older. For example, the National Council of State Boards of Nursing reported that more than 50% of nurses were aged 50 and older with 25% over 60.[7] Coupled with the aging of the general population, this trend presents some problems, since older Americans need and receive a lot of health care services, and just as this demand is increasing health care providers are leaving their practices to retire.

In addition to the openings presented by the shortage of providers, the spectrum of opportunities in the healthcare field is wide, far beyond the job prospects in many traditional employment categories like manufacturing. Also, many health care jobs pay relatively well. The BLS has reported that "nurse anesthetists, with an annual mean wage of $160,250; podiatrists ($136,180); and pharmacists ($119,270) were among the highest paying healthcare occupations."[8] Home health care aides, in contrast, were only paid $22,870."[9]

B. Physicians' Employment

Employment arrangements involving physicians typically take one of two forms: the physician either works as an employee or as a self-employed independent contractor. Today, the overwhelming mode is that of physicians as employees. Physicians may be employees of any number of private entities: independent medical groups,

---

[4] *See* U.S. CENSUS BUREAU, STATISTICAL ABSTRACT OF THE UNITED STATES 2012, Table 160 (Census Bureau 131st ed. 2013), https://www.census.gov/library/publications/2011/compendia/statab/131ed/health-nutrition.html.

[5] *Id.*

[6] AM. HOSP. ASS'N, CHARTBOOK, CHAPTER 5: WORKFORCE (2016), http://www.aha.org/research/reports/tw/chartbook/ch5.shtml.

[7] NAT'L COUNCIL OF STATE BDS. OF NURSING, 2015 NATIONAL NURSING WORKFORCE STUDY (Apr. 2016), https://www.ncsbn.org/workforce.htm.

[8] Press Release, BLS, Occupational Employment & Wages 2015 (U.S. Dep't of Labor Mar. 30, 2016), https://www.bls.gov/news.release/archives/ocwage_03302016.pdf.

[9] *Id.*

hospital-controlled medical groups, medical staffing companies, hospitals, clinics, nursing homes, hospices, research firms, insurance companies, health maintenance organizations, or academic centers. Governmental agencies, such as state or local health services, the Veterans Administration, the National Health Service, and more, also employ many physicians. Self-employed independent contractors, on the other hand, are in the minority.

The phenomenon of physicians choosing employee status rather than running a private practice or working as an independent contractor has been called a "movement" and has been documented by many surveys and anecdotal reports.[10] There are several complex reasons for the trend which are discussed in more detail below. But plainly, the landscape of a physician's career has shifted due to the change in employment structure. Physicians are encountering new ethical dilemmas, conflicts over directing patient care, and expectations of performance and productivity that are not realistic.[11] And medical malpractice coverage and terms are presenting challenges in light of these new arrangements.[12]

The move toward employment status for physicians is also affecting the entities and institutions for whom they work. These institutions have experienced significant structural changes of their own, the most significant example of which is the wave of mergers and acquisitions of hospitals and other care providers.[13] Facing the current environment means addressing the political, financial, and regulatory risks of these new employment structures. Some of these are discussed below.

II. Independent Contractor Status for Physicians

According to Black's Law Dictionary, an "independent contractor" is "[s]omeone who is entrusted to undertake a specific

---

[10]Bonnie Darves, *Understanding the Physician Employment "Movement,"* NEJM Career Ctr. (July 23, 2014), http:/nejmcareercenter.org/article/understanding-the-physician-employment-movement.

[11]*Id.*

[12]Herb P. Van der Veer, *Entity-Employed Physicians & Medical Malpractice Coverage Issues*, Parker Smith Feek (Aug. 18, 2011), http:/psfinc.com/articles/entity-employed-physicians-and-medical-malpractice-coverage-issues/.

[13]Jeff Goldsmith, Nathan Kaufman & Lawton Burns, *The Tangled Hospital-Physician Relationship*, Health Affairs Blog (May 5, 2009), http://healthaffairs.org/blog/2016/05/09/the-tangled-hospital-physician-relationship/.

project but who is left free to do the assigned work and to choose the method for accomplishing it."[14] Hiring entities often prefer that physician workers be classified as independent contractors, for cost and liability reasons. If a physician is truly an independent contractor, the hiring entity will not have to pay the physician's malpractice or workers compensation insurance premiums, Social Security, Medicare taxes, or federal and state unemployment insurance costs. Nor would the hiring party have to pay employee benefits. Benefits costs include retirement programs, health and disability insurance, vacation and sick pay, and federally mandated minimum wage and overtime. Avoiding them amounts to a big savings to the employer.

Due to the nature of a physician's work and the need for the hiring party to exercise control over the physician's schedule and work environment, meeting the requirements of true independent contractor status is not easy. Rather, the connection between the physician and the entity usually falls under the category of an employer/ employee relationship, as defined by the Internal Revenue Service (IRS) and other federal and state authorities.

For IRS purposes, determining whether a worker is a true independent contractor is based on seven factors, reduced from a previous twenty. The latest IRS publications, *Topic 762-Independent Contractor vs. Employee* and *Publication 15-A Employer's Supplemental Tax Guide*, have further boiled down the test into three major factors: behavioral control, financial control, and the relationship of the parties.[15]

III. REGULATORY RISKS OF INDEPENDENT CONTRACTOR CLASSIFICATION

In the highly regulated field of healthcare employment, health care hiring entities must be wary of Anti-Kickback Statute and Stark Law violations,[16] and other risks. Such risks are greater when the

---

[14]Bryan A. Garner ed., BLACK'S LAW DICTIONARY (10th ed. 2014).

[15]*See* IRS, TOPIC 762 - INDEPENDENT CONTRACTOR VS. EMPLOYEE (Apr. 14, 2017), https://www.irs.gov/taxtopics/tc762.html, and PUB. 15-A, EMPLOYER'S SUPPLEMENTAL TAX GUIDE (2017), https://www.irs.gov/pub/irs-pdf/p15a.pdf.

[16]Under the Anti-Kickback Statute, it is a felony for anyone to "knowingly and willfully" ask for or receive "any remuneration," of whatever kind, for referrals for services under federal health care programs, or in exchange for purchase, lease, order or arrangement for any "good, facility, service, or item" covered by a federal health care program. 42 U.S.C. § 1320a-7b(b) (2012). Under the Stark Law, if a physician or such

physician is an independent contractor. Treating a physician as an independent contractor may cut off the hiring party and physician from the safe harbors available under the Anti-Kickback Statute[17] and the Stark Law,[18] which further minimize regulatory problems.[19]

Counsel must also convey to a client who is considering engaging an independent contractor physician that, in order to qualify as a true independent contractor, the health care hiring party must give up substantial control over the physician. From a risk standpoint, a health care hiring party ordinarily can ill afford to reduce its control of the physicians serving its patients.

Since misclassification of a physician as an independent contractor when that professional should have been classified as an employee will subject the hiring party to substantial penalties for failing to pay employment taxes and file proper tax returns, counsel might recommend that the parties first obtain a determination from the IRS as to whether a particular physician is a bona fide independent contractor.[20]

Be aware, however, that how a worker is classified and paid by an employer is not the controlling factor in determining whether that worker is an "employee" for purposes of many of the non-IRS federal and state laws discussed here. Regulators do not apply these laws uniformly. Various federal and state agencies and courts use different tests to determine whether a worker is an employee or an independent contractor, and thus that determination depends on which state, agency, or jurisdiction speaks to the question. For example, the U.S. Department of Labor Wage and Hour Division uses a different standard than the IRS.[21] And the National Labor Relations

---

physician's "immediate family member ... has a financial relationship with a [health care] entity ... , then the physician may not make a referral to the entity for the furnishing of designated health services for which payment otherwise may be made under Medicare." 42 U.S.C. § 1395nn (2012). For analysis of these two important health law statutes, see *Common Challenges: Stark & Anti-Kickback, Fraud and Abuse and the Practicing Physician*, Chapter 26, *infra*.

[17] 42 U.S.C. § 1320a-7b.
[18] 42 U.S.C. § 1395nn.
[19] *See* Chapter 26, *infra*.
[20] The parties must submit Form SS-8 to the IRS to receive an official opinion. *See* IRS, DETERMINATION OF WORKER STATUS FOR PURPOSES OF FEDERAL EMPLOYMENT TAXES & INCOME TAX WITHHOLDING (Rev. May 2014), https://www.irs.gov/pub/irs-pdf/fss8.pdf.
[21] A determination of whether a worker is an "employee" for purposes of federal employment law protection turns on a fact-based analysis described further in Chapter 22.

Board (NLRB) has ruled that, notwithstanding other statutory tests, a hospital's interns and residents are employees, not independent contractors, and their rights are protected by the National Labor Relations Act (NLRA).[22]

IV. BENEFITS OF BEING CATEGORIZED AS AN EMPLOYEE

From the physician's standpoint, whether he or she is an employee or independent contractor is important—not only for tax purposes, but also for entitlement to significant employment and labor benefits. As discussed above, employees enjoy employer-provided insurance benefits, paid vacation, disability insurance, and the like, but independent contractors do not. Further, employees may take for granted the protections provided from illegal discrimination under the state and federal employment statutes. True independent contractors are not employees and thus do not enjoy the same privileges. Being an employee instead of an independent contractor affords considerable legal protections under state and federal law, including protection from illegal discrimination in employment based on age,[23] race, color, religion, sex or national origin, by virtue of the protections of Title VII.[24] Employees also enjoy protections afforded by the Equal Pay Act[25] and parallel state laws, among other things. Independent contractors do not have NLRA rights.[26] Moreover, there are valuable reasons for a physician-employee to join along with other employed physicians to collectively bargain with the employer regarding the working terms and conditions of employment. The employee will have the right to join a union to protect his or her professional status and working conditions; these are invaluable rights which employees enjoy, but independent contractors do not.[27]

---

[22]Boston Med. Ctr. Corp. & House Officers Ass'n, 330 N.L.R.B. 30 (1999).
[23]Age Discrimination in Emp't Act of 1967, 29 U.S.C. §§621-634 (2012).
[24]Title VII of the Civil Rights Act of 1964, 42 U.S.C. §§2000e-2000e-17 (2010).
[25]Equal Pay Act of 1963, 29 U.S.C. §206(d) (2012).
[26]BARRY FURROW, THOMAS GREANEY, SANDRA JOHNSON, TIMOTHY STOLTZFUS-JOST & ROBERT SCHWARTZ, HEALTH LAW §10-16.a, at 525 (3d ed. 2015).
[27]"Section 7 of the NLRA gives employees four specific rights: (1) to form, join, or assist labor organizations; (2) to refrain from participating in union activity; (3) to engage in activity for mutual aid and protection, as well as concerted activity unrelated to union organization; and (4) to bargain collectively through representatives of their own choosing. 29 U.S.C. §157." AM. HEALTH LAWYERS ASS'N, REPRESENTING PHYSICIANS HANDBOOK, 759 (4th ed. 2016).

Employees, and not independent contractors, are covered by and afforded the protections of the minimum wage and overtime provisions of the Fair Labor Standards Act (FLSA).[28] Typically, non-exempt employees who work more than forty hours a week are entitled to overtime pay.[29] Unfortunately for most physicians, interns, or residents, Section 13(a)(1) of the FLSA[30] provides an exemption from both minimum wage and overtime protection for "any employee employed in a bona fide executive, administrative, or professional capacity." This has been interpreted by the Department of Labor[31] to include licensed practitioners of medicine, residents, and interns.[32] And the rule also covers teachers, which presumably includes physicians in teaching positions. The result is that physicians, interns or residents generally may be paid on an hourly basis, but are not likely to be eligible for overtime.[33]

---

[28] 29 U.S.C. §§201-219 (2012).

[29] 29 U.S.C. §207(a) (2012).

[30] 29 U.S.C. 213(a)(1) (2012).

[31] Because Congress explicitly delegated to the Secretary of Labor the power to define and delimit the specific terms of the exemptions through notice and comment rulemaking, issued regulations have the binding effect of law. *See* Batterton v. Francis, 432 U.S. 416, 425 n.9 (1977); DEP'T OF LABOR, WAGE & HOUR DIV., 29 C.F.R. pt. 541 (2016).

[32] 29 C.F.R. § 541.304 *Practice of law or medicine*:

(a) The term "employee employed in a bona fide professional capacity" in section 13(a)(1) of the Act [FSLA] also shall mean:

(1) Any employee who is the holder of a valid license or certificate permitting the practice of law or medicine or any of their branches and is actually engaged in the practice thereof; and

(2) Any employee who is the holder of the requisite academic degree for the general practice of medicine and is engaged in an internship or resident program pursuant to the practice of the profession.

(b) In the case of medicine, the exemption applies to physicians and other practitioners licensed and practicing in the field of medical science and healing or any of the medical specialties practiced by physicians or practitioners. The term "physicians" includes medical doctors including general practitioners and specialists, osteopathic physicians (doctors of osteopathy), podiatrists, dentists (doctors of dental medicine), and optometrists (doctors of optometry or bachelors of science in optometry).

(c) Employees engaged in internship or resident programs, whether or not licensed to practice prior to commencement of the program, qualify as exempt professionals if they enter such internship or resident programs after the earning of the appropriate degree required for the general practice of their profession.

(d) The requirements of § 541.300 and subpart G (salary requirements) of this part do not apply to the employees described in this section.

[33] For more information, consult U.S. DEP'T OF LABOR, FACT SHEET #3: PROFESSIONAL OFFICES UNDER THE FAIR LABOR STANDARDS ACT (July 2008), https://www.dol.gov/whd/regs/compliance/whdfs3.pdf.

In the health care world, it can be very difficult to tell who works for whom. For example, often companies that directly employ the physicians that treat a patient (e.g., a staffing company or medical group, "ABC") have contracts with one or more hospitals, clinics, hospices, or other health care entities ("XYZ") to provide physician medical services. ABC-employed physicians ("EMDOCS") show up at XYZ sites to work, perhaps every day and perhaps for years. If procedures are followed correctly, they are technically not employees of XYZ, at least for tax purposes. They are employees of the contractor ABC. What can be even more confusing is that contractor ABC may also hire physicians as independent contractors, rather than as employees ("ICDOCS"), and those ICDOCS may also work at XYZ sites right alongside their EMDOCS counterparts and XYZ employees. In these situations, ABC and XYZ can run into legal problems unless they keep the status of their various workers straight; the hospital should not treat the two persons the same in terms of benefits and other privileges.

Nevertheless, an independent contractor classification may be beneficial to some physicians, depending on whether, for example, the particular situation offers true independence and the other terms of the contract. If the physician's contract offers real autonomy, then that arrangement may be attractive for a physician desiring more flexibility as to whether and how much to work.

Part 2

Physicians' Employment Issues

CHAPTER 4

PHYSICIAN EMPLOYMENT QUALIFICATIONS

I. INTRODUCTION

Licensing requirements for physicians and all other healthcare providers are regulated under the federal and state police power to protect the health, safety, and general welfare of the community, state, and country. These statutes and administrative codes govern the licenses of healthcare professionals and disciplinary actions.[1]

Licensure statutes set minimum requirements and qualifications for a health professional to obtain a license in the state and then privileges at the hospitals. Typical prerequisites for a medical license include graduation from an approved educational institution, passage of a standardized examination, and a review of personal history for character issues.

II. THE PRIVILEGE PROCESS

Simply being licensed as a physician does not guarantee that a doctor will be granted hospital privileges. Hospital privileges are the classifications that allow a healthcare professional to perform certain procedures and surgeries, and even obtain admission of their patients

---

[1] *See, e.g.*, Storrs v. State Med. Bd., 664 P.2d 547 (Alaska 1983), *cert. denied*, 464 U.S. 937 (1984).

to a hospital. Regulatory bodies that license hospitals, such as the national Joint Commission responsible for accreditation of healthcare organizations, provide guidelines for the hospital's privileging process.[2]

The government holds hospitals responsible for appropriately privileging every physician before he or she can practice and provide care at the hospital. The privileging process is necessary to ensure patients are receiving the best care possible, providers are complying with applicable standards of care, and professionals are qualified to admit their patients to the hospital.

Different categories of privileges exist, including admitting privileges, allowing a physician to admit a patient to the hospital; courtesy privileges, allowing a physician to occasionally admit or to visit and treat patients at the facility; and surgical privileges, allowing a physician to perform surgery in the hospital's operating suites or outpatient surgery centers. There are also temporary privileges for a locum tenens physician, who is a physician working in the place of the regular physician when that physician is absent or when a hospital/practice is short-staffed. Limited privileges apply to doctors practicing from a different location by telemedicine. An example is a radiologist, who provides healthcare and interpretations of radiologic films and scans from a distance and even out of the state.

A license is only one part of a much broader arrangement to qualify a physician to practice in a hospital. Hospitals look at certifications by voluntary professional boards and societies and the credentialing system for clinical privileges at the hospitals. The various quality assurance and credential committees, executive boards, and other governing groups have developed their own bylaws, regulations, and policies defining the qualifications that a physician must possess to get permission to treat patients and practice at hospitals, accompanied by an extensive (some might say tedious) application process. The healthcare professional's credentials, education, residences, fellowships, licenses in other states, privileges at other institutions, references, malpractice insurance, and practice experience are reviewed to determine the appropriateness of their training, skills, and competency.

---

[2]THE JOINT COMMISSION, www.jointcommission.org.

III. MEDICAL STAFF PRIVILEGES

Hospital governing bodies typically are required by state laws to adopt a set of standards and procedures for reviewing the medical applicants who seek staff membership or professional privileges. The state requirements and the hospital standards usually are built from accreditation agency norms and from the lessons of state tort law decisions which have held a hospital liable for negligent review of the physician credentials. Injunctive relief is available to individuals harmed by either the hospital's failure to adopt standards and procedures for the consideration of applications or by any discrimination based on the individual's type of license.

For example, in acting upon applications for staff membership or professional privileges, the hospital is prohibited from discriminating against applicants based solely on whether they are licensed as medical doctors rather than as osteopaths. A doctor of osteopathic medicine performs the full scope of a medical practice, but the osteopath emphasizes techniques of hands-on manipulation of the human muscular system. Additionally, a hospital is prohibited from discriminating against osteopaths licensed under a different statute solely because that practitioner was board-certified or eligible under an approved osteopathic certifying board, instead of board-certified or eligible respectively under an approved medical certifying board. Similar requirements apply to podiatrists (a doctor of podiatry treats conditions of the foot and ankle).

The hospital also has the duty of appointing the medical staff. To this end, when granting or renewing staff privileges or when hiring a physician, the hospital must request from the physician:

(1) the name of all hospitals with which the physician has been affiliated;
(2) whether the affiliation was discontinued and why;
(3) whether there are any pending medical malpractice actions or misconduct proceedings against the physician and, if so, the substance of the allegations;
(4) the substance of the findings in the actions or proceedings;
(5) a waiver by the physician for any confidentiality provisions concerning the information requested; and
(6) a verification from the physician that the information provided is accurate and complete.

The hospital must then contact any hospitals with which the physician has been affiliated and obtain information regarding any pending malpractice lawsuits; any judgments, settlements, or disciplinary actions; and any findings of professional misconduct. As another means of helping the governing body to oversee the medical staff, the regulations provide that, before they can become effective, medical staff bylaws and rules must first be approved by the governing body. Pursuant to the regulations, the hospital contributes to a safe and adequate patient care environment through the development of a medical staff structure that assures consistent clinical competence.

The hospital adopts staff bylaws, rules, and regulations that define the medical staff and its organizational structure. These provisions also address qualifications for membership; verification of application data; the appointment and reappointment processes; the length of appointment and reappointment; the process for the granting of delineated clinical privileges; provision for continuous care of patients; assessment of credentialed practitioners' performance; and due process. The regulations also provide that each hospital ensures that criminal history background inquiries are conducted for any employee or healthcare provider who will have unsupervised access to children, vulnerable adults, and developmentally disabled adults.

A physician may admit patients in a specific hospital or institution only if the practitioner has admitting or clinical privileges at the hospital or organization. The Joint Commission provides evaluations and guidelines in order to make the hospital's decisions more objective and continuous.[3] Privileges can be denied if it is determined that the healthcare professional lacks training and cannot demonstrate the necessary skills. Loss of a medical license in another state, exclusion from Medicare or Medicaid, or having been previously found guilty of fraud or abuse are also reasons for denying hospital privileges. The hospital can suspend privileges if a physician does not perform enough of a specified procedure or does not show required competencies.

After verification, a physician's application for admission privileges and supporting material are sent to the applicant's specialty for thorough investigation. Recommendations are made by the Credential Committee, but it is the Medical Executive Board of each

---

[3]THE JOINT COMMISSION, www.jointcommission.org.

hospital that has the final authority to grant privileges, set the scope of practice, and establish the rules and regulations that the healthcare professional must comply with at the hospital.

IV. REGULATION OF MEDICAL STAFF DISCIPLINARY PROCEDURES

The Health Care Quality Improvement Act of 1996 (HCQIA)[4] was intended to offer healthcare institutions, including hospitals, a limited immunity if the institution performs credentialing actions regarding its medical staff in accordance with the minimum due process procedures set forth in HCQIA and its implementing regulations.[5] Each hospital must permit medical staff members an appropriate period of time (30 days) to respond to notices of adverse actions, to obtain the help of an attorney at the privilege termination or disciplinary hearing, and to produce evidence and witnesses. Physicians should always have an attorney represent them throughout grievance proceedings and hospital disciplinary hearings.

An attorney for a physician subject to disciplinary action should get the relevant regulations, policies, and bylaws to review at the beginning of the defense of the physician, along with the factual information. The physician should be advised not to talk about the disciplinary matter within the hospital or with other medical staff. It is very important for the physician to understand that a strong defense is needed to save the doctor's privileges and eventually their license.

Another component of HCQIA was the establishment of the National Practitioner Data Bank (NPDB), with the purpose of affording hospitals and other entities associated with medical practitioners a means to discover healthcare providers' experiences at other institutions. The NPDB is discussed in Chapter 12. The hospital is also required to annually review the listing of individuals who have been sanctioned by the Medicare or Medicaid programs.

---

[4] 42 U.S.C. §11101 et seq.
[5] 45 C.F.R. pt. 60.

V. State Department of Health Disciplinary Actions Against Physicians

Regulations set forth in each state's administrative code or department of health licensing statutes provide details with respect to licensing, limitation of professional fees, specific standards of practice or conduct allowed or prohibited, the scope of practice, and procedures for addressing complaints from patients or others against a physician. To determine the grounds for discipline in any particular healthcare profession, the attorney must examine both the requirements of the disciplinary acts of the states and the specific statutory and regulatory sections under which the professional is licensed.[6]

Each state disciplinary commission or board has a certain number of members who are healthcare professionals in the specialty or discipline that the commission governs, as well as one or two other members. The physician is responsible to determine the criteria for licensure and to meet those criteria. New graduates who seek a license in a particular state and physicians from other states moving to a new state must either qualify for interim permits, where available, or comply with licensing requirements and obtain the license prior to practicing the profession in that state. Those who fail to do so will risk the charge of unauthorized practice of medicine without a license. Also, licensees must be aware of their license renewal date, which is generally the practitioner's date of birth. The state may send one renewal notice by mail. The professional must know and comply with the standards of practice, whether or not they are set forth in statutes or regulations. Departments of health, boards, and commissions uniformly require the level of compliance with generally accepted standards of practice in the community, and some states expect compliance with a national standard.

All healthcare providers must practice within the scope of their license. This is a challenging requirement, given that the scope is often not defined with substantial specificity and the provision of the healthcare services develops and changes over time. The complexity of healthcare, delivered by more team members, increases as healthcare delivery systems develop. Also, practices differ depending on

---

[6]See Note, *Purging Sex Offenders From the Medical Profession: The Impact of New License Revocation Statutes on Medical Board Disciplinary Discretion*, 17 Mich. St. U.J. Med. & L. 57 (2012).

whether practitioners care for patients in large cities or in rural areas. Physicians are required to practice within the scope of accepted standards, even though the disciplining authority may not have specific guidelines.

The U.S. Constitution and the constitutions of most states require due process before the government can revoke a physician's professional license. Under the familiar passage of the Fifth and Fourteenth Amendments to the U.S. Constitution, the state may deprive no person of "life, liberty, or property" without due process of law. Revoking the professional license is a governmental deprivation of "liberty" or "property" interests and so requires due process. Notice to the individual and a hearing before an impartial decision-maker are the two required components of procedural due process. State administrative procedures statutes generally allow the courts to overturn any administrative order that is unconstitutional. But constitutional exceptions such as prosecutorial immunity will apply to the enforcement process.[7]

Most complaints to a state's department of health lead to investigations of varying kinds. Sometimes, there will be a follow-up inquiry or a request for information from the physician. The investigation may last years, and may include the questioning of numerous witnesses as well as obtaining medical records of the patient, and possibly past employment and privilege records of the physician. All letters are subject to review by the state's professional board. The department must notify the doctor when a complaint letter is received unless notification would impede an effective investigation. All letters are subject to review to determine whether an investigation is warranted. Pending the investigation and charges, the letter is not a public record. If closed without an investigation, the matter is not reflected on the practitioner's computerized record as an open or closed complaint, the department does not report the physician to the National Practitioner Data Bank, and the identity of the complainant remains confidential.

VI. DISCIPLINARY PROCESS

Along with notifying the physician of the complaint, investigators are required to advise the practitioner of his or her right to

---

[7]*See* Constantini v. Medical Bd. of Cal., 34 F.3d 1071 (9th Cir. 1994).

an attorney before obtaining a written statement from the physician regarding the issues in the claim. The investigation always results in the compiling of an investigative file. The reviewing member of the disciplinary authority will then read the investigative file and decide whether charges will be filed.

The entire file may be requested by defense counsel during the pre-hearing phase of discovery. However, up until the charging decision is made, disciplinary authorities have generally taken the position they must protect the medical records and other material, along with the identity, of the complainant. The physician will have his or her own medical chart regarding the care of the patient, and usually can review the history with the complainant. The doctor must receive the patient's medical records from the records holder in order to draft her or his narrative statement in defense of that complaint.

Charging decisions are made by one member of the state medical board, commission, or board within the state department of health. The disciplinary authority will generally obtain input from another professional, acting as an outside expert, to review the medical records and to provide the reviewing member and the attorney for the department with their opinions of adequacy of the respondent physician's healthcare. The charged person then is notified by certified mail of the charges; this statement of charges will describe the allegations about the conduct and alleged statutory violations, and will generally allege that license revocation is appropriate. The disciplinary board will immediately request a set of the healthcare provider's medical chart for the patient(s) concerned and a written statement by the physician. If the time period to produce a written statement is a hardship to the physician, the physician may request additional time to respond.

Failure to answer and failure to request a hearing are considered a default, and the disciplinary authority may enter a decision based upon the information collected during the investigation. The department of health may take emergency action against the physician, by ordering summary suspension of the license or restriction of the physician's practice, pending completion of the proceedings by the state disciplinary board, but this does not occur often. The physician can ask for license reinstatement or lifting of limitations by the hearing examiner. If necessary, the physician can apply to the courts for reinstatement before the hearing process commences. These requests are unlikely to succeed in most cases.[8]

Discovery is available to the parties in accordance with the state's administrative procedure statute. This includes the formal request for the medical records and the complete investigative files of the disciplinary authority, made as soon as the charges are filed. Usually, the attorney for the board will remove work product and redact information that the attorney believes is confidential under state procedures. Depositions, interrogatories, and requests for production are formally demanded. The respondent also can subpoena the production of material relevant to the need for defense of the proceedings. Fewer depositions are taken, and material is less frequently requested, than in a similar civil case. If there is litigation pending, both sides can use discovery from that lawsuit during the hearing, once approved by the hearing officer or administrative law judge.

The physician or physician's attorney should notify the respondent's medical malpractice insurance carrier, because the physician's policy should include coverage for defense against the state's charges. However, the amount of coverage for the defense's investigation, discovery, and the hearing is not likely to be large enough to cover all the costs and fees. The physician needs to make a decision to settle with the medical board or department of health or to take the charges to a hearing.

Typically, a medical board hearing will be held before a panel of healthcare providers of the physician's specialty, and sometimes a public member, in front of a healthcare hearing examiner. Hearings are governed by each state's administrative procedure statute. The Rules of Evidence are not necessarily followed at the hearing, based upon the judgment of the hearing examiner. Some states require findings based on clear and convincing evidence, while other states require a preponderance of the evidence. Disciplinary hearings are similar to trials, except they are much shorter and more informal determinations based on criteria under the relevant state statutes.

---

[8]*See, e.g.,* Lundeen v. State Med. Bd. of Ohio, 2012 U.S. App. LEXIS 27112 (6th Cir. Oct. 17, 2012).

As in civil litigation, settlement will be the outcome in the majority of administrative disciplinary matters. Settlement is expected when there is either an obvious violation of the standard of care, or there is enough evidence supporting the position that a violation occurred to warrant some discipline but not revocation of the physician's license. Settlement negotiations always happen before a hearing, sometimes negotiated with the attorney for the relevant board or department, and sometimes with the actual investigating attorney who is prosecuting the matter for the state.

In each case, the department or board must approve the settlement. If settlement is not reached at the first level, the physician may decide to ask for a settlement conference with the reviewing member of the disciplinary authority. The conference should be in person, even though the respondent may be offered a settlement conference via telephone. It is better for counsel to be present. The physician will hear the reviewing member's opinions of the case and their justification for the charges. If the respondent clearly wants a settlement of the matter, a mediation can be arranged with help of a neutral experienced intermediary such as a retired member of the disciplinary board. Settlement is the outcome of most cases brought by the state's department of health or other disciplinary action. Only a few cases are resolved by a formal order by the board after a full hearing.[9]

Revocation of a physician's license might occur after less than a full hearing resulting in a final order. If the final decision of the disciplinary authority is against the physician, and the board finds a violation of the standard of care, the results will be reported to the National Practitioner Data Bank, discussed in Chapter 12. Under federal law and regulations, the contents of NPDB reports remain confidential.[10]

Counsel must pay close attention to state administrative agency requirements. An appeal from an adverse decision of the hearing panel must be filed usually within 30 days. The appeal is filed in the superior court (or equivalent title) of the county where the physician resides or conducts business. The appeal is on the record. It is important that there has been a complete record of facts and

---

[9]Storrs v. State Med. Bd., 664 P.2d 547 (Alaska 1983), *cert. denied*, 464 U.S. 937 (1984).
[10]42 U.S.C. §11101 et seq.; 45 C.F.R. §60.20.

evidence made at the agency level. Findings of fact by the hearing panel and rulings by the healthcare board or agency judge are likely to be upheld, unless clearly erroneous.[11] The burden of proof is with the challenging party to prove that there is no substantial evidence of sufficient quality to persuade a hearing panel. Conclusions of law are reviewed de novo. The judgment of the agency is given great deference, especially in areas involving a professional activity.

Obviously, the system works best—for the public, the state, and the physician—when laws are applied with wisdom and fairness. Just as in civil litigation, disputes are settled most effectively when the lawyers can work together to achieve a solution acceptable to the parties. Neither the licensee's nor the state's financial resources should be wasted on substantive or procedural matters that are not essential. The disciplinary action affects the physician emotionally, physically, and financially. The attorney for the respondent must consider how the physician will deal with an adverse decision, the amount of time that the physician will be worrying about losing his or her medical license, and the personal cost to the physician. All of these ramifications should be discussed with the physician at the beginning of the process and revisited throughout the proceedings.

---

[11]*Storrs*, 664 P.2d 547.

Chapter 5

PRACTICE AFFILIATIONS
AMONG PHYSICIANS

I. Introduction: Affiliation With Whom?

This chapter deals with the reality of physicians who form affiliations. Physicians tend to practice medicine either as equity owners of solo or group practices, or as employees or independent contractors of any number of organizations, including

- solo practices
- medical groups
- hospitals
- clinics
- research firms
- insurance companies
- health maintenance organizations
- government medical programs
- academic centers

- medical staffing companies
- state health services
- the Department of Veterans Affairs
- the Public Health Service
- medical foundations
- medical products companies
- medical charities
- and so on.

The opportunities are endless and changing all the time. Traditionally, however, most physicians worked in solo practice and small group practices.

II. SNAPSHOT OF TODAY'S SHRINKING SOLO PRACTICE

"Solo Practice, once the norm in American medical practice, is disappearing."[1] It used to be that the vast majority of physicians were sole practitioners,[2] but by 2016 only 16.8 percent of physicians remained in solo practice.[3] Interestingly, by medical specialty, psychiatrists are the most likely to be in solo practice, at a rate of 30.4 percent.[4]

A. Positive Features of Solo Practice

According to the American Medical Association (AMA), of the various types of medical practices, a sole practitioner enjoys the highest degree of personal satisfaction and clinical autonomy. The

---

[1]Furrow, Greaney, Johnson, Stoltzfus-Jost, Schwartz, *Physician Duties to be Patient Advocates, in* HEALTH LAW §3-4.d, at 99 (3d ed. 2015).

[2]*See, e.g.,* Stephen L. Isaacs et al., *The Independent Physician Going, Going . . . ,* 360 NEW ENG. J. MED. 655, 657 (2009) (stating that "[t]he percentage of U.S. physicians who own their own practice has been declining at an annual rate of approximately 2% for at least the past 25 years").

[3]The Physicians Foundation, 2016 Survey of America's Physicians: Practice Patterns and Perspectives, http://www.physiciansfoundation.org/uploads/default/ Biennial_Physician_Survey_2016.pdf [hereinafter 2016 Survey of America's Physicians].

[4]Carol K. Kane, Ph.D. & David W. Emmons, Ph.D., American Medical Association, Policy Research Perspectives: New Data On Physician Practice Arrangements: Private Practice Remains Strong Despite Shifts Toward Hospital Employment, at 5, http:// www.nmms.org/sites/default/files/images/2013_9_23_ama_survey_prp-physician-practice-arrangements.pdf.

AMA defines the term "clinical autonomy" as "the physician's ability to make clinical care decisions that they deem in the best interest of the patient, independent of any outside constraints imposed on them by an organization or entity such as a hospital, health system or payer."[5]

B. Negative Features of Solo Practice

Operational risk and financial risk are high for sole practitioners. Due to the financial risk of establishing and maintaining a solo practice, it is a business model recommended as being more suitable for an experienced physician who already knows how to run a medical practice.[6]

A recent final-year medical resident's survey showed that 92 percent of newly trained physicians were not interested in starting their own practice, at least initially. They preferred an employment setting as their first practice situation, further demonstrating the fact that very few young doctors today want to start off in an independent private practice.[7]

That is understandable, considering how much student loan debt many of these young doctors are burdened with after four years of college, four years of medical school, two to three years of residency, and then perhaps additional years spent in internships or fellowships. In 2012 the average student loan debt for physicians was over $166,750, according to a 2014 American Medical Association insurance publication. That is more student loan debt than any prior generation of physicians.[8] Faced with this debt burden, many new physicians may seek the security and compensation offered by a physician employer.

---

[5]See generally American Medical Association, 2015 Practice Options for Physicians, https://www.ama-assn.org/system/files/media-browser/public/ps2/practice-options-for-physicians-updated.pdf.

[6]2016 Survey of America's Physicians, http://www.physiciansfoundation.org/uploads/default/Biennial_Physician_Survey_2016.pdf.

[7]Merritt Hawkins, The 2015 Final Year Medical Residency Survey, https://www.merritthawkins.com/2015-final-year-medical-residency-survey/.

[8]AMA Insurance, Medical School Student Loan Debt, By the Numbers April 08, 2014 | Posted in: Financial Preparedness, https://www.amainsure.com/physicians-in-focus/medical-school-student-loan-debt-by-the-numbers.html ; see also https://www.amainsure.com/physicians-in-focus/medical-school-student-loan-debt-by-the-numbers.html#sthash.3nt3m3qI.dpuf.

III. TRENDS TOWARD GROUP PRACTICE AND LARGE PHYSICIAN GROUP EMPLOYMENT

For the same reasons the number of physicians in solo practice is on the decline, the number of physicians in small group medical practices (2 to 10 persons) is also on the decline.[9] Conversely, the number of physicians practicing in medium and large group practices has increased. Physicians practicing in groups of 11 to 30 increased 1.5 percent from 2012 to 2016,[10] and the number of physicians practicing in groups of 101 doctors or more (20 percent of physicians in 2016) increased 8 percent during the same time period.[11]

A. Structure and Features of Group Practices

In a group practice, the physician partners or shareholders (or members, in the case of a limited liability company (LLC)) make joint decisions regarding management and running of the practice (depending on the extent of their individual voting rights under the organizational documents of the partnership, corporation, or LLC). They generally delegate day-to-day office, scheduling, and administrative functions to an office manager or other administrative staff.

Positive features of a group practice include:

- Shared overhead expenses, spread across a greater number of physicians.
- Shared night and weekend call coverage obligations.
- Shared hospital clinical care obligations.
- Shared administrative and staffing burdens.
- Increased bargaining power with insurers and hospital networks due to increased group size.
- Help with managing insurance and managed care contracts.
- Time for continuing medical education and vacation without disruption of the practice.

---

[9]The number of physicians practicing in groups of 2–5 decreased from 26.2% in 2012 to 21.4% in 2016. The number of physicians practicing in groups of 6–10 decreased from 14.5% in 2012 to 13.5% in 2016. *See* 2016 Survey of America's Physicians, at 11–12.

[10]The number of physicians practicing in groups of 11–30 increased from 14.5% in 2012 to 16.0% in 2016. *See id.*

[11]*Id.*

Negative features of group practice include:

• Less autonomy and flexibility in decisionmaking as group size increases.
• Policy and operational disagreements increase as group size increases.
• Morale sinks and sense of an "assembly-line" atmosphere increases as group size increases.

B. Types of Group Practice —Single-Specialty and Multi-Specialty Groups

Generally, group medical practices fall into one of two basic types: single-specialty medical practices and multi-specialty medical practices.

1. Single-Specialty Group Practice

The defining characteristic of a single-specialty practice is two or more physicians providing patients with the same type of medical professional service (e.g., internal medicine services only, or nephrology only, or neurosurgery only) within one organization.

A major advantage of single-specialty group practice is that daily interaction is normally less complicated in an operational sense among group members who are in the same (or a closely related) medical specialty. The similarity of the group is beneficial when it comes to a wide variety of matters, including call coverage, staffing, equipment and facility purchase needs, clinical issues, and physician hiring needs, because the physicians have a good understanding of each other's work environment. In addition, they generally know the strengths and weaknesses of the group and are focused on their niche in the medical community.

2. Multi-Specialty Group Practice

Multi-specialty group practices offer a combination of medical specialties within one large organization (e.g., internal medicine, gastroenterology, and nephrology).

If structured correctly, multi-specialty group practices are a way to offer and negotiate payment rates for multiple types of physician services to insurance companies, hospitals, and major employers through the use of one organizational umbrella—and without violating federal antitrust laws. Structuring such a practice requires health law attorney advice and counsel, but these are definitely positive features of a multi-specialty group practice.

Multi-specialty group practices also provide the benefit of a built-in consultation referral base from the other specialists in the group, which at least theoretically improves the economics of the medical group. Referred patients' medical records should be already in the practice, which is handy.

The most commonly articulated negative feature of a multi-specialty group practice is that the various specialists within the group may not understand or fully appreciate one another's expertise or needs, particularly when it comes to justifying compensation or equipment and staffing needs. Medical specialists or subspecialists often feel that they should be compensated at a higher rate than internal medicine or family medicine practitioners, which in turn can lead to considerable discord and even breakup of the group.

A medical ethical downside to a multi-specialty group practice is that it may be very uncomfortable for a multi-specialty group physician to refer a patient to someone not aligned with the group, even if that would be the best choice for the patient, since there is internal economic pressure to refer within the group.

IV. WILL SOLO PHYSICIANS MAKE A COMEBACK?

Taking into consideration how discouraged physicians are with lack of professional autonomy, and how they are drowning in endless paperwork and administrative chores, the declining solo practice trend, discussed in Section II, above, may be starting to reverse itself. The number of highly experienced physicians who are now considering concierge practices, and the recent increased popularity of direct primary care practices, are changing the healthcare practice model once again.

In a 2016 survey, 11.2 percent of physicians aged 45 and under stated that they intended to switch their type of practice to a concierge-type medical practice in the next one to three years.[12] So it is quite possible that solo practice, which for experienced physicians lends itself to concierge-type care, may very well pick up again. This

---

[12]2016 Survey of America's Physicians: Practice Patterns and Perspectives, http://www.physiciansfoundation.org/uploads/default/Biennial_Physician_Survey_2016.pdf.

potential increase may occur as initial employment contracts of physicians employed by hospitals and staffing companies come up for renewal, and more and more employed physicians become more and more dissatisfied with the proffered renewal terms.

Scholars studying these trends believe that, for many of the reasons discussed in Chapters 1 and 2 in this book, times are changing. The general dissatisfaction among these highly educated and skilled professionals reflects their dislike for being treated like fungible goods by hospitals, staffing companies, and other healthcare entities. It is foreseeable that there will be a revival of solo and small group practitioners, in the form of direct primary care and concierge care practice models. This prospect is most likely to be observed with internists, pediatricians, and family practitioners. And other types of medical practices will soon follow that path.

Why? One reason is that health insurance deductibles are astronomically high, and many patients are carrying only high deductible health insurance coverage. Routine healthcare is paid for out of pocket by the patient, and casualty-type health insurance is reserved for major medical expenses. It is not unusual for insured patients to have a $3,000 to $6,000 insurance deductible per person. This may arise with an employer contributing to a Health Saving Account (HSA) plan to help defray the deductible. That is a very large per-patient cash payment stream, an attractive feature for a solo or small-practice physician.

Another key factor in this shift is the enormous pool of highly experienced physicians who want to leave the disheartening world of hospital-owned practices and escape the business model of today's hospital manager. One can hear their resentful feelings as they assert that they didn't go to medical school or spend the best years of their lives training to be great physicians, now just to be told what to do and what floor to round on by some 28-year-old MBA office dweller.[13]

The visceral dissent among these talented physicians is harsh: they are tired of having to see 30 patients a day to make enough money to satisfy some corporate employer, who counts their outputs on a traditional discounted reimbursement insurance network plan.

---

[13]Suneel Dhand, M.D., The Time a 28 Year-Old MBA Told a Physician Where to Round First (May 11, 2016), http://www.kevinmd.com/blog/2016/05/the-time-a-28-year-old-mba-told-a-physician-where-to-round-first.html.

Physicians are quickly realizing that they can regain the autonomy and the art and science of practicing medicine by not seeing patients in 8-minute intervals (and charting for 16 minutes) to satisfy some third-party managed-care employer's value units (wRVU) target.

Although the models vary, in the direct primary care and concierge care practices, typically the physician is paid up front by the patient, in annual or monthly dues or other forms of prepayment, for their everyday or routine medical care and lab work. The physician has a contract with the patient that describes exactly the services the physician agrees to provide. The physician accepts a limited number of patients and thus is able to take more time with each patient, emphasizing preventative care. The physician carries malpractice insurance and does not accept or process insurance payments, Medicare, or Medicaid, thus avoiding burdensome federal and state administrative and billing requirements and Stark Act and Anti-Kickback Act liabilities.

Consequently, the physician also does not have the burden or expense of billing or collecting payments, and avoids the very expensive electronic records requirements imposed by the federal Centers for Medicare and Medicaid Services (CMS). The patient contractually accepts the responsibility of submitting any insurance claims to their private insurance provider.

Like any other type of medical practice, a direct primary care or concierge care practice—or indeed any medical practice—must be meticulously structured by an experienced health law attorney to avoid violating any federal or state laws. See Chapter 6, below. However, in terms of a comeback, as stated in the 2016 Survey of America's Physicians: Practice Patterns and Perspectives: "The concierge option is one of the few ways physicians today can maintain a solo or independent practice, and many physicians have reported that this style of medicine enhances the care they are able to provide and hence their professional satisfaction."[14]

---

[14]2016 Survey of America's Physicians, at 31.

CHAPTER 6

STARTING, PURCHASING, OR SEPARATING FROM A MEDICAL PRACTICE

I. INTRODUCTION

This section discusses issues that arise when physicians start, purchase, or separate from a medical practice. A medical practice group can take many forms—professional corporation, S Corporation, C Corporation, limited liability company (LLC), partnership, or some other type of business entity. The decision to establish a medical practice group in one of these forms is a fact- and tax-driven matter that should be discussed with an experienced health law attorney and tax attorney to meet the physician's or group's short-term and long-term needs. That should also include a discussion of basic dissolution or wind-up procedures and costs thereof if things don't work out as expected.

II. THE ROLE OF EXPERT HEALTH LAW COUNSEL

It is critical for physicians starting a medical practice to consult with an experienced health law attorney. Such an attorney will have the most influence in guiding a medical practice in the very beginning of the affiliation decision process, when physicians are initially thinking about forming a medical group. That is the time when an attorney can ensure that the prospective owners get the same information, focus on the same issues, and determine whether their collective interests are actually aligned. If those interests are not aligned, which is often the case, then that is something better flushed out early in the process. That usually happens when discussing the governing agreement, as discussed below.

It also is important, if there are multiple physicians involved in the contemplated transaction, that they understand who counsel represents—and does not represent—and your role as attorney. Each individual physician within the prospective group has his or her own distinct goals; these may conflict with the interests of the prospective entity and with the interests of the other physicians. That's why each physician should be advised to obtain independent counsel to review the documents and offer their comments and suggestions once the initial drafts are available. In the meantime, the prospective "group" needs to try to *think* like a group to see if they can get to a draft agreement.

As a special cautionary warning to the general practice attorney, be aware that transactions that would otherwise be perfectly fine in the non-healthcare business sector are illegal or seriously restricted in the healthcare sector, particularly as they relate to physicians and healthcare providers. There are a number of highly technical regulatory considerations of which attorneys advising physicians and healthcare providers must be aware that are simply not applicable to other industries. If an attorney is not an experienced health law transactions attorney, such attorney is strongly advised to engage a health law transactions attorney as part of the team as early as possible.

For example, there are laws and compliance matters, some with criminal sanctions, which are specific to physicians and healthcare providers.[1] Often these regulations are mind-numbingly complex.[2] Matters such as entering into an office or equipment lease with a hospital or clinic; or how a physician refers, bills, or treats Medicare and Medicaid patients; or how a physician is compensated, obtains vendor services, etc., can trigger federal and state Stark Law anti-referral and anti-financial-relationship laws and Anti-Kickback Statute regulations, some of which have criminal penalties.

As just one example, physicians starting a group practice must consider whether to purchase the practice's site real estate and have the medical practice lease the real estate back to the practice, and whether to invest in or lease office equipment. Real estate and

---

[1] *See* HHS OIG publications at https://oig.hhs.gov/compliance/101/index.asp.

[2] *See, e.g.*, American Health Lawyer Association, *Overview of Regulatory Issues Affecting Physicians*, ch. 2, at 64–201, *in* REPRESENTING PHYSICIANS HANDBOOK (4th ed. 2016) [hereinafter REPRESENTING PHYSICIANS HANDBOOK].

equipment leases between a physician or a physician group and any "designated health service" (DHS)[3] entity (e.g., a hospital) need to be carefully analyzed to avoid inadvertently triggering Stark Law or Anti-Kickback Statute liability, and to make sure a "safe harbor" exception is met.[4] Although basic consideration of these legal matters is provided in Chapter 25 of this text, due to space limitations, detailed advice cannot possibly be presented to provide a non-health-law specialist enough information to provide all-inclusive counsel to his or her physician-client.

There are also Health Insurance Portability and Accountability Act (HIPAA) regulations and other specific health law considerations that physicians need to be advised of—depending on their area of practice—that go far beyond the scope of this employment counseling publication.

Fortunately there are safe harbors that physicians can qualify for, and that is how health law experts can help. Starting and staying in compliance with the health law requirements and available safe harbors is essential, so having an experienced health law professional on the team early, someone who stays current on the latest health law legislation, regulations, and case law, is essential.

III. STARTING A MEDICAL PRACTICE

A. Necessity of a Separate Legal Entity

From a physician's counsel's perspective, the first thing to consider after determining the details of the type of medical practice under consideration by the physician or physicians should be what type of separate legal entity to form. Legal entities commonly

---

[3]The list of designated health services (DHS) includes: (a) clinical laboratory services; (b) physical therapy services; (c) occupational therapy services; (d) radiology services, including magnetic resonance imaging, computerized axial tomography scans, and ultrasound services; (e) radiation therapy services and supplies; (f) durable medical equipment and supplies; (g) parenteral and enteral nutrients, equipment, and supplies; (h) prosthetics, orthotics, and prosthetic devices and supplies; (i) home health services; (j) outpatient prescription drugs; (k) inpatient and outpatient hospital services; and (l) outpatient speech language and pathology services. 42 U.S.C. §1395 nn(h)(6)(A)–(L).

[4]For an outstanding overview and analysis of Stark Law and Anti-Kickback and other regulatory matters affecting physicians please see REPRESENTING PHYSICIANS HANDBOOK, at 64–201.

considered include professional corporations and limited liability companies.

The primary advantages of forming a separate legal entity are to avoid exposing the physician(s) to personal liability for the debts and obligations of the legal entity in case things don't work out as planned; the continuation of the entity's existence after the death or disability of any of its owners; and the fact that ownership of the entity is transferable.[5]

Private corporations are creatures of state statute, and every state has slightly different laws governing the formation of and the rights and obligations of private businesses. Consequently, counsel must consult the corporate and business law of the state where the physicians wish to set up a medical practice for details.

State law issues an attorney should review before choosing an entity for a medical practice include (1) enabling laws regarding the formation and operation of the various professional corporations, general corporations, and limited liability companies; (2) scope-of-practice laws and regulations; (3) agency and vicarious liability laws, particularly as among shareholders or members for acts or negligence of other shareholders or members; (4) duties of loyalty and care imposed upon management or directors; (5) annual filing requirements; (6) what is required to pierce the veil of the entity; and (7) what taxes the state may impose upon the entity.

The mechanics of setting up a medical practice go beyond the scope of this employment counseling publication, although some helpful resource material is referenced in this chapter.[6]

B. Consult Relevant State Statutes on Malpractice Insurance Requirements

Attorneys representing physicians should be aware that many states have professional corporation statutes designed to deal with issues unique to medical professionals, including requirements for malpractice insurance, state medical board licensure requirements, and the limited role of laypersons in the medical legal entity, to name

---

[5]*See generally* HOOPER, LUNDY & BROOKMAN, INC., 1 TREATISE ON HEALTH CARE LAW § 1.01[1][a] *Limited Liability* , at 1-6, pub. 407, rel. 39 (Dec. 2011) [hereinafter TREATISE ON HEALTH CARE LAW].

[6]For highly useful guidance on physician medical entity formation, including tax considerations, see REPRESENTING PHYSICIANS HANDBOOK, chs. 6, 7.

a few peculiar requirements. Those requirements must be researched and complied with.

For example, several states require that all physicians secure a minimum level of professional liability insurance. Examples of these states are Colorado,[7] Connecticut,[8] Kansas,[9] Massachusetts,[10] New Jersey,[11] Rhode Island,[12] and Wisconsin,[13] and there are others, all with their own peculiar requirements.

> **Tip: Corporate Formation Is Not Protection from Malpractice Claims.** Counsel must make it very clear to the physician-client that forming a business entity will not usually (realistically never) protect the physician or physician's group from medical malpractice claims. That's the purpose of professional liability (medical malpractice) insurance.[14] Incorporation or forming a business entity does not change the relationship between the physician and the patient, nor does it relieve the physician from malpractice claims arising from the physician's professional services.

Physician malpractice insurance is discussed in more detail in Section IV, below.

C. Beware of "Corporate Practice of Medicine Doctrine" Prohibitions

Some states observe a legal policy generally known as the "corporate practice of medicine doctrine," which prohibits non-medically-licensed people, corporations, and other business entities from engaging in the practice of medicine or employing physicians (or

---

[7]COLO. REV. STAT. §13-64-301.
[8]CONN. GEN. STAT. §20-11B.
[9]KAN. STAT. ANN. §40-3402.
[10]MASS. GEN. LAWS ch. §112 §2 (malpractice insurance a requirement of licensure).
[11]N.J. STAT. ANN. §45:9-19.17.
[12]R.I. GEN. LAWS §42-14.1-2.
[13]WIS. STAT. §655.23.
[14]See generally 1 TREATISE ON HEALTH CARE LAW §1.01[1][a] Limited Liability, at 1-7.

other types of healthcare providers such as chiropractors or physical therapists).[15]

These restrictions may be imposed by state statute, administrative code, or case law, and they vary from state to state.[16] For example, California, Tennessee, Texas, and Wisconsin have explicit statutes prohibiting or limiting the corporate practice of medicine.[17] Essentially, the doctrine seeks to prohibit nonphysicians from interfering with a physician's professional judgment by prohibiting corporations and other entities not owned or controlled by physicians to employ physicians and then charge and collect for medical services provided by the employed physicians.

The most common reason given for this rule is that a corporation or business entity simply cannot meet the requirements necessary to practice medicine. A corporation or business entity cannot attend or graduate from an accredited medical school, graduate from an accredited residency program, be tested, or possess the requisite moral qualifications, nor can communication or nonverbal skills be tested. Plus, from a public policy standpoint, employment by a non-wholly-physician-owned corporation or business entity may interfere with an employed physician's professional medical judgment by influencing the physician to pursue the profit motives of the non-professional employer, which risks commercial exploitation of the patient.[18]

Consequently, to avoid penalties and unintended disciplinary action and potential loss of medical license for the physician, it is critically important for counsel to know what type of corporate entities are permitted to engage in the practice of medicine in the state

---

[15]FURROW, GREANEY, JOHNSON, STOLTZFUS-JOST, SCHWARTZ, HEALTH LAW §11-7. *The Corporate Practice of Medicine Doctrine*, at 547 (3d ed. 2015) [hereinafter HEALTH LAW]. See also M. Phillips, C. Turner, *Introduction to Healthcare Contracting, Issue Spotting and Regulatory Considerations*, AMERICAN HEALTH LAWYERS ASSOCIATION, FUNDAMENTALS OF HEALTH LAW, at 8 (Nov. 2014).

[16]HEALTH LAW §11-7, at 547.

[17]*See* CAL. BUS. & PROF. CODE §2400; TENN. CODE ANN. §§63.6-201, 63-6-204, 68-11-205; TEX. OCCUP. CODE ANN. §152.004; WIS. STAT. ANN. §448.08. Minnesota has case law prohibiting corporate practice of medicine based on licensure statutes. Isles Wellness, Inc. v. Progressive N. Ins. Co., 703 N.W.2d 513 (Minn. 2005) upholding corporate practice prohibition for physicians and chiropractors on historical and public policy grounds.

[18]*See* HEALTH LAW §11-7, at 547–53. *See generally* 1 TREATISE ON HEALTH CARE LAW §2.01[6][a] *Corporate Practice of Medicine, Background*, at 2-17.

at issue and what type of corporate entities are authorized to and can legally employ physicians and other licensed individuals to practice medicine. The American Health Lawyers Association has published a comprehensive analytical summary and 50-state survey of the corporate practice of medicine that provides attorneys with state-by-state information and guidance with respect to corporate practice of medicine.[19]

Moreover, there are some states that place restrictions on a physician's professional relationship with unlicensed persons or non-professional business entities, and which actually limit the number of offices that a physician may operate, so attorneys need to have a firm understanding of the relevant licensing statutes and case law in the state at issue.[20]

D. Importance of a Comprehensive Governing Agreement

Forming a medical group or buying into an existing group as an equity owner has many pressures, so it is extremely important that the physician go into the relationship with a thorough understanding of what each party expects from the relationship. The governing agreement is the first step in a hopefully long and mutually beneficial legal and professional relationship.

A well-drafted agreement governing a given medical practice could, depending on the business entity chosen, take the form of a shareholder agreement, participation agreement, member operating agreement, or some other type of agreement signed by all the medical group equity owners (the "governing agreement").

Differences among the potential owners usually surface when discussing matters involved in a practice governing agreement. Some highlights for discussion and inclusion in the governing document are set forth below.

Initially, the group should discuss the governing agreement together with their counsel. The individual physicians should also have their own individual attorneys review and offer comments on

---

[19]STUART SILVERMAN ET AL., CORPORATE PRACTICE OF MEDICINE: FIFTY STATE SURVEY, AMERICAN HEALTH LAWYERS ASSOCIATION (2014).

[20]For a discussion of other states, see, e.g., M. Michal, et al., Corporate Practice of Medicine Doctrine, 50 State Survey Summary, published by the Center to Advance Palliative Care, National Hospice and Palliative Care Organization (Sept. 2006). *See also* CORPORATE PRACTICE OF MEDICINE, 50 STATE STATUTORY SURVEYS: HEALTH CARE: HEALTH CARE FACILITIES (Sept. 2015).

the governing agreement, however, including any individual employment agreement connected with the eventual medical group. The prospective owners need to think like prospective owners, not just as co-workers and as friends, and each must determine whether their interests are actually aligned.

Relying on off-the shelf forms and bylaws that are delivered with standard corporate minute books is *not* recommended. In a well-drafted governing contract, the physicians agree upon a wide variety of fundamental decisionmaking, transferability of ownership, employment, financial, and operational matters, such as the following:

- Capital contributions. What form of capital contribution should be accepted? Cash, real estate, personal guarantees, time, expertise, etc.?
- Will there be equal ownership interests for each owner or different classes of owners, so as to allow more senior physicians or the physicians that invested the most money, time, or expertise, to have more votes (control) when it comes to decisionmaking for the group?
- How should minority owners be protected for major decisions (e.g., merger with another group, lease of the group to a hospital, purchase of a building, sale of the practice to a hospital or staffing company, move to another city, borrowing over a certain threshold, participating in an accountable care organization, change to compensation or retirement structure)?
- How and when should owners be compensated or group profits be distributed to owners?
- What provisions should be made for salaries or draws of the owners, the timing of the salaries or draws, and how such payments or withdrawals are to be treated in the annual division of the group's income? What if there is a shortfall?
- Who should have authority to sign checks, contracts, or other obligations on behalf of the group?
- How should decisions on physician and support staff hiring and firing be made?
- What should the on-call coverage obligations for the group be?

- How will other major decisions for the group be made? E.g., what should the process be to negotiate, accept, or reject group insurance plans, payor contracts, capitated fee arrangements, provider contracts, and malpractice insurance coverage contracts?
- How will addition of new owner physicians to the group be approved?
- How will owner equity be valued when a new physician owner is approved or when a physician owner withdraws, is terminated,[21] becomes disabled, or dies? (There are many different owner equity valuation methods that can be considered. Some options include book value, a multiple of corporate earnings, a multiple of compensation, or some other agreed upon formula. Other options include an appraisal or arbitration method. There can also be different agreed upon owner equity valuation methods for different owner termination reasons.)
- What should the policies for sickness or disability be for owners?
- What should owner vacation arrangements be?
- What retirement and health benefit packages should be offered to the owners and staff and how will they be funded?
- What types of general liability and professional liability coverage should be obtained for the individual physicians and for the group?
- How should malpractice premiums be apportioned? What if one or more members of the group have a disproportionate number of claims and malpractice rates for the group increase?
- Who pays for tail end (extended reporting) malpractice coverage for the physician owner when a physician owner dies? Retires? Withdraws? Is terminated for cause? Becomes disabled?
- What should the suspension or termination policy be for physician owners? How many owner votes are required to suspend or terminate an owner?

---

[21]To avoid disharmony in the group, termination of an equity owner is an event that typically requires a supermajority of owner votes.

- What should the restrictions on transferability of ownership interest in the group be?
- Should there be owner restrictive covenants upon leaving the group? If so, what?
- What is the process upon dissolution of the group?
- How will voting deadlocks be resolved?
- What should the method for dispute settlement be for disputes arising under the governing agreement or employment agreements?

These matters should be addressed in the governing agreement while the prospective owners are getting along and can agree on things, while still wearing two hats: working physician and prospective owner. Failing to address these matters up front in the governing agreement means these matters will be handled on an unpredictable ad hoc basis when a situation arises and tempers are flaring. In the absence of an acceptable agreement, matters will be governed by state law and the results (and the size of the attorneys' fees) will be unpredictable. They may lead to totally avoidable and unnecessary stress and expense for the group.

E. Employment Agreements Between Physician Owner and Group Legal Entity

Most often, there is an employment agreement between the legal entity and each of the entity owners, which employment agreement supplements the governing agreement. Certain variable aspects of owner compensation may be addressed in an employment agreement between the group legal entity and the entity owners. Usually the employment agreement between the group legal entity and an equity owner is different (and more favorable) than a typical employment agreement would be as between the group legal entity and an associate physician employee, primarily in terms of compensation and termination provisions. Usually a much higher threshold is required to terminate an equity owner (e.g., no "termination without cause" provisions). In fact, usually the termination provisions in the employment agreement mirror those in the governing agreement or incorporate them by reference. Compensation provisions for equity owner employees and associate employees are different as well, since the equity owners contemplate receiving a share of the profits of the legal entity.

Whether in the governing agreement or in the employment agreement, the parties must also address the matter of who is responsible for obtaining and paying for any "tail end" (extended reporting) malpractice insurance coverage.

> ***Tip: Sample Employment Agreement Provisions.*** The American Medical Association (AMA) has published a helpful guide entitled "Annotated Model Physician—Group Practice Employment Agreement 2014 Edition," an ebook that provides sample annotated contractual provisions specifically for physicians who may be considering employment in a group medical practice.[22] See also Chapter 9 of this text for basic physician employment contract considerations, which apply to all physician employment agreements.

F. Permits and Licenses Commonly Required When Starting a Medical Practice

Counsel for a physician or physician group contemplating opening a medical practice will need to check the statutory and administrative requirements in the relevant state, county and city with respect to the specific licenses, permits and other requirements needed for opening a medical practice. The typical licenses and permits required and websites from which to obtain applications and further information are included in this text at Appendix C, "Common Licenses, Permits and Other Requirements of which to be Aware when Opening a Medical Practice". For local jurisdictional information, the county medical association is often a helpful resource.

G. Observing Corporate Formalities

Undoubtedly, a solo physician or group physician will be asked to sign leases, loans, promissory notes, equipment and service contracts, employment agreements, and contracts. These documents should always be signed in the name of the business entity

---

[22]American Medical Association, Annotated Model Physician—Group Practice Employment Agreement (2014), https://commerce.ama-assn.org/store/catalog/sub CategoryDetail.jsp?category_id=cat1150023&navAction=push.

(including the business designation as a "P.A.," "Inc.," "LLC," etc.) and not signed in the name of the individual physician. That way, any liability will be that of the business entity and not of the individual physician.

Also, attorneys need to counsel the physician owners about the importance of proper capitalization of the business entity name and the observance of basic corporate formalities necessary to avoid giving a local judge an opportunity to "pierce the corporate veil." The last thing the physician shareholders or members want is unexpected personal liability for corporate obligations or torts due to mixing personal assets with corporate assets, or because of failure to observe basic corporate formalities. They need instruction from their legal counsel on the necessity of holding meetings, proper documentation of business transactions, and keeping personal and corporate assets separate.[23]

> ***Tip: Observing the Formalities.*** The biggest favor counsel for a physician or physician group can do is ensure the physician or physician group fully understands the importance of using the business entity name and business entity signature at all times, including on all letterhead, signs, websites, business cards, patient forms, employment agreements, personnel forms, bank checking accounts, and so on. Make it clear to the world that the physicians are doing business as a separate legal entity, not as individuals.

IV. MEDICAL MALPRACTICE INSURANCE CONSIDERATIONS

In addition to possible state law requirements, physicians will undoubtedly face requirements in the workplace to carry, or have carried for them, a certain minimum level of medical professional liability insurance (often known as "medical malpractice insurance"). For instance, most hospitals and clinics dictate insurance minimums for their medical staff. Health insurance plans also require physicians participating in their insurance plans and networks to carry minimum levels of malpractice insurance.

---

[23] *See generally* 1 TREATISE ON HEALTH CARE LAW §1.01[1][a] *Limited Liability,* at 1–7.

A. State Law Requirements

State malpractice laws, statutes of limitations on malpractice claims, damages caps on malpractice claims, and other requirements are relevant when determining how much malpractice insurance coverage to carry, both for the physician and the business entity. If the physician practices medicine in more than one state, that is also a factor to take into consideration, because the laws and malpractice requirements in each state may be different.

It is also essential to obtain advice as to each state's law regarding any physician equity owner's liability for acts committed by another physician equity owner (or a person acting under his or her direct supervision). Such considerations are all determinative as to how much professional liability insurance to carry, both for the individual physician and the business entity. Corporate coverage is important, not only for potential liability for acts committed by another physician, but also because cash flow to all physicians in the group will be affected if a malpractice claimant attaches corporate assets or receivables.

B. Recommended Coverage

Medical malpractice litigators recommend that the physician and the physician's legal entity both need their own professional negligence (malpractice) insurance, because normally the individual physician is named as well as the physician's legal entity in any lawsuit alleging medical negligence.

A minimum of $2,000,000 per claim and $5,000,000 per year per individual physician is believed by medical malpractice litigators to be reasonable to protect the physician's personal assets, because very large malpractice settlements and verdicts are not uncommon today. Realistically, however, it is fully understood that medical malpractice insurance premiums are often the single largest overhead cost in a medical practice, and many practices simply can't afford the medical negligence coverage that they would like.[24]

---

[24]For an outstanding discussion of malpractice insurance considerations and advice for attorneys representing physicians and medical groups, see REPRESENTING PHYSICIANS HANDBOOK, ch. 11, at 493–509.

Tip: Coverage. It is important for the physician and the attorney advising the physician or medical group to understand what is *not* covered in the malpractice insurance policies offered, as well as what *is* covered, since many insurance carriers offer a number of alternative insurance products with different coverage limitations and conditions. Often physicians are surprised to learn that the insurance company has the contractual right in the insurance policy to make the decision as to when to settle a lawsuit without the physician's consent. In other cases, if the insurer must seek the insured's (physician's) consent to settle the case, and if the insured does not consent, the insurance company will cap the insurance company's liability at the amount that the insurance company recommended as an appropriate settlement amount, so that if a verdict goes over the settlement amount recommended by the physician's insurance company, then the physician is responsible for payment of the difference. Even worse, other policies permit the insurer to tender the amount of the rejected settlement and incur no further expense on the case.[25] That is why it is vitally important to understand what *is* and *is not* included in medical malpractice insurance policies before it is too late for your client-physician.

Tip: Professional Licensure Actions. Make sure to find out whether the malpractice policy carried by the physician or physician group includes coverage for defending a professional licensure action by a state medical licensing board arising out of a professional negligence claim. Many professional liability policies offer such coverage as a benefit, and medical licensure actions can be more important in the long run to a physician and be every bit as expensive to defend as a malpractice case.

C. General Types of Medical Malpractice Insurance

Medical professional liability insurance products fall into two general categories: "claims made" and "indemnity" type insurance policies.[26] Indemnity insurance policies cover claims that arise within the term of the insurance policy period regardless of when the claim is filed in court. Claims made insurance policies only cover

---

[25] *Id.* at 500–01.
[26] JAMES O'REILLY, MEDICAL MALPRACTICE (ABA Press 2014).

claims that arise within the term of the insurance policy period and are filed within the insurance policy period. Claims made insurance policies are less expensive policies of insurance.

A physician with a two-year claims made policy beginning January 1, 2017, and effective through December 31, 2018, would be covered *if* (1) the claim arose from an event that occurred during the two-year policy period *and* (2) the claim was filed in court (typically) or the insurance company was otherwise provided written notice of the claim (depending on the insurance contract language) during that two-year policy period. However, if the claim arose from an event occurring before the two-year policy period began (e.g., Oct. 9, 2016), it would not be covered, even if the physician was sued or the insurance company was put on written notice during the two-year policy period. Nor would the physician be covered for an event that arose during the policy period (e.g., Oct. 9, 2018) if the physician was sued or the insurance company was otherwise put on written notice after the policy period expired (e.g., Jan. 30, 2019).

There are other types of insurance policies available, e.g., multiyear claims made policies and indemnity policies. Professional medical liability insurance is a highly specialized area of law and business and the details are beyond the scope of this employment counseling publication. The best advice for counsel representing the physician or medical group is to consult an insurance expert for the nature and extent of insurance coverage reasonably necessary to protect the physician(s) and the medical legal entity, and to find out what is and is not covered by the proffered insurance policies, and guide your client accordingly.[27]

V. BUYING INTO A MEDICAL PRACTICE: DUE DILIGENCE REQUIRED

Counsel for a physician who is considering buying into an existing medical practice will want to perform due diligence on the prospective medical practice and review the prospective group's formation documents, among other things, as described below.

---

[27]For an outstanding discussion of malpractice insurance considerations and advice for attorneys representing physicians and medical groups, see REPRESENTING PHYSICIANS HANDBOOK, ch. 11, at 493–509.

Documents that should be reviewed include all of the relevant governing agreements, whether they are partnership, shareholder, operating, participation, or side agreements (and all amendments, revisions, or updates thereto) among or between the various equity owners. Other important documents requiring review may include, as applicable, bylaws, certificates of incorporation, articles of organization, employment agreements, ancillary surgery center or other real estate leases or agreements, partnership agreements, membership purchase agreements, buy/sell agreements, payor agreements, hospital agreements or arrangements, professional service agreements, facility leases, entity tax returns for the past three years, entity financial statements (including profit and loss statements) for the past three years, entity financing arrangements for the past three years, entity bank letters of credit, current practice policy manuals, and any related party transactions in the group (related party transactions are a major Stark Law red flag), and others. Have a trained medical practice accountant or business adviser review the tax returns and the financial statements to determine if the overall business is increasing or decreasing.

> *Tip: List of Excluded Individuals and Entities.* Counsel must check all of the potential parties in the List of Excluded Individuals and Entities (LEIE) on the website of the Office of Inspector General of the Department of Health and Human Services (OIG)[28] to see if any of the parties have been excluded from any federal healthcare program (such as Medicare or Medicaid). Exclusion is a penalty imposed by the OIG on individuals and entities that have engaged in fraud and abuse or other misconduct related to federal healthcare programs.[29] If any of the parties show up on the list, inform your client immediately and seek health law counsel advice. Counsel will likely advise you and your client to look elsewhere for a practice to join.

---

[28]*Exclusions*, HHS, OIG, http://oig.hhs.gov/exclusions/.

[29]See the OIG Special Advisory Bulletin on the Effect of Exclusion from Participation in Federal Health Care Programs (May 8, 2013), at http://oig.hhs.gov/exclusions/files/sab-05092013.pdf.

VI. TERMINATION OR RESIGNATION OF EQUITY OWNERS OR DISSOLUTION OF A PRACTICE

There are times when a physician equity owner dies, moves, retires, becomes disabled, or simply wants to leave the group. At other times disputes or conflicts arise that make it best for one or more owners to leave, or for the medical group to reconfigure or entirely dissolve.

> ***Tip: Avoid Attorney Conflict of Interest.*** If you are counsel to the medical group, it is advisable to decline the opportunity to represent any party to a practice breakup or physician departure transaction, even in the case of a deceased physician's estate, since all the physicians in the group will likely view you as having a built-in conflict of interest.[30] No matter how amicable the parties claim the termination, breakup, or dissolution is going to be, it is invariably a stressful situation that leads to misunderstanding and often to contentious litigation. Avoid getting disciplinary charges brought to the state bar association, and advise all the parties to get separate counsel, because you may end up being a witness.

A. Overview

In a private professional organization such as a medical practice, the process of resignation or termination of a physician equity owner is typically covered in the governing agreement, which should describe, among other things, (1) the method to establish the value of the departing physician owner's equity interest in the practice; (2) when a departing physician owner's equity ownership share of the liabilities of the practice will cease; (3) when and how the departing physician owner will be paid for his or her equity share of the practice, including (a) any accounts receivable earned by the departing owner prior to resignation or termination, (b) any pro-rata share in year-end bonuses, (c) any pro rata share in the practices' contribution to the departing owner's retirement plan, and (d) any capital contributions to which the departing owner is entitled; and (4) who is responsible for obtaining and paying the costs associated

---

[30]ABA MODEL RULES OF PROFESSIONAL CONDUCT (2002), Rule 1.7 (and Comment).

with obtaining medical malpractice "tail end" (extended reporting) coverage insurance for the departing physician, and what happens if the responsible party fails to do so.

This book on employment counseling focuses on employment issues relating to resignation or termination of one or two physicians. Although the considerations are largely the same, in the case of an actual practice dissolution, the considerations may require the sale of all the practice assets and payment of all practice liabilities. These situations may require bankruptcy or other corporate wind-up actions, and these considerations go beyond the scope of this publication. However, helpful reference material for such situations is provided below.[31]

B. Initial Steps

If a physician departure or practice breakup is on the horizon, then the parties need to carefully review the governing agreement and any relevant compensation or employment agreements (including any recruitment agreements with the local hospital, if applicable), medical directorship agreements, professional services agreements, exclusive contract agreements, etc., that may be applicable. For example, it is important to identify and observe the relevant notice period(s) before resignation or termination of employment so as to avoid any easy breach of contract claims.

Other documents that need to be reviewed include those on which the departing physician may have been a signatory to or otherwise have liability for in some capacity. These include, without limitation, personal guarantees (particularly for office lease space); bank loans; security agreements; real estate and equipment purchase or lease agreements (including any loan documentation and security agreements related thereto); ambulatory surgery center agreements (if applicable); office sharing arrangement agreements; lines of credit; company credit cards; current and historical financial statements; indemnity agreements; joint venture agreements; participation agreements; and any other business arrangements with other physicians, hospitals, medical groups, or other healthcare entities.

---

[31]For a comprehensive discussion on medical practice breakups, personal guarantees for debts of the practice, and negotiation strategies, including practical advice, helpful checklists, and sample separation and other agreements, consult REPRESENTING PHYSICIANS HANDBOOK, ch. 8, at 350–83.

Counsel will need to determine whether liability for any of those obligations has been previously allocated in the governing agreement.

Other important documents, from the physician's standpoint, that need review include accounts receivable relating to the departing physician for all payors; billing and collection statements and reports for the departing physician; employee manuals, retirement plan information, life, health, paid time off, reimbursement of business expenses, and disability insurance plan manuals, to see if the departing physician is entitled to an extension of benefits; and malpractice insurance plans and umbrella liability policies, to determine what coverage is available in terms of any extensions on malpractice coverage. Since extended coverage often depends on how long the underlying malpractice policy has been in place, it will be essential to know how long the physician has been covered under the underlying policy; whether the departing physician is retiring or going somewhere else to practice next; and whether the next position is covered by the same insurance provider.

> *Tip: Separation Agreement.* If at all possible, obtain an exit or separation agreement from the departing physician to avoid future lawsuits between the departing physician and the practice. Agree to let the departing physician owner or the departing physician owner's accountant or bookkeeper have reasonable access to the financial data and information necessary to review and verify the calculation of post-termination payments and valuations of equity interest and liabilities. Something as simple as agreeing to let the departing physician keep his or her cell phone number, as long as the physician pays for it, will go a long way in making the transition smoother.

C. Lingering Liabilities

In the exit or separation agreement, in addition to the issues described in the paragraphs above and below, other typical matters that must be addressed include lingering liabilities such as future IRS claims, potential malpractice claims, or potential CMS audits, all arising from the departing physician's activities at the practice. These concerns, however remote, should be fairly addressed in the separation agreement.

D. Other Terms of Separation Agreements

Smaller and more daily items should also be covered in the separate agreement, such as permission to open mail addressed to the departing physician but delivered to the practice. How should the parties determine its importance and whether it contains payment, information, or communications that should stay with the practice, and if not, where and how to send the information or communications to the departing physician?

Furthermore, several other steps are recommended, as discussed in Section F, below on notices required when leaving practice or changing employment. The separation agreement should address the content of written notices to be sent to patients and referring physicians, when such notices will be sent out, who will pay the cost of mailing such notices, and how the parties will "manage" the message to patients.

Also determine how access to patient records will be provided, whether any proprietary software licenses may be assigned to the departing physician to access such medical records, and who will need access to the software and data. Unfortunately, often the electronic medical record systems don't "talk" to each other, so software licensing can be a significant issue. Other issues that must be addressed are who will physically keep (particularly if patients are minors), secure, and update the patient's records.

The separation agreement should also address what indemnifications (if any) will be provided in favor of the departing physician for any guarantees given by the departing physician for the practice debts, what mutual liability releases will be provided and when, and any agreement on nondisparagement provisions.

It is important to avoid ugly and costly surprises that invariably lead to litigation, so the separation agreement should include requirements for written notification about changes in malpractice insurance coverage; notification of any malpractice claims brought against the parties that affect the practice or the departing physician; and notification of any settlements reached with third parties that may affect the practice or the departing physician. It is absolutely essential that the parties document their resolution of these issues by means of a written separation agreement to avoid future lawsuits between the parties.[32]

E. Obtaining "Tail End" Medical Liability (Malpractice) Insurance Coverage is Critical

"Tail end" (extended reporting) medical liability insurance is something that any medical group and any departing physician must consider, since both have continuing liability for the professional care provided by the departing physician while working in the practice.

"Who pays for it?" is often contentious because it may be expensive, depending on any number of factors, such as the type of malpractice coverage the group already carries, how long the group has had such coverage, how long the departing physician has had coverage with the carrier, the departing physician's prior claims history, the type of medical practice, whether the departing physician can obtain "nose coverage" in the next employment setting, etc. The group's malpractice insurance carrier should be consulted immediately. Who pays for tail end (extended reporting) medical liability insurance is one of those important issues that *should have been covered* in a good governing agreement among the owners, before a nasty termination happens and tempers run high.

F. Notices Required When Leaving a Medical Practice or Changing Employment

Depending on the jurisdiction, there are many people, companies, providers, and organizations that are required, by law or contract, to be notified of a change in a physician's employment or practice status. Be advised that the following includes only the "core" persons to consider notifying, and is not exhaustive. Counsel should review the relevant state statutes, administrative codes, state medical licensing board requirements, and contracts relevant to the client. Important notification requirements are discussed below.

---

[32]This is a brief overview of basic matters for counsel to consider. For a more thorough discussion, including practical advice, helpful checklists, sample separation and other agreements, consult REPRESENTING PHYSICIANS HANDBOOK, ch. 8, at 350–83.

1. Notification of Patients

Some states, e.g., Ohio,[33] have statutes that require the health-care entity to provide written notice to the departing physicians' patients upon termination of a physician's employment for any reason. The lesson here is that counsel for any departing physician or the medical practice needs to be aware of the existence of these types of notice requirements to patients and check for similar statutes or administrative regulations in the physician's or medical practice's jurisdictional state to make sure that compliance doesn't become an unwelcome issue.

Furthermore, the American Medical Association Code of Medical Ethics, Opinion 8.115, states: "Physicians have an obligation to support continuity of care for their patients. While physicians have the option of withdrawing from a case, they cannot do so without giving notice to the patient, the relatives, or responsible friends sufficiently long in advance of withdrawal to permit another medical attendant to be secured."

Separately, the American Medical Association Code of Medical Ethics, Opinion 7.03, Records of Physicians Upon Retirement or Departure from a Group, specifies that when a physician leaves a practice, "patients should be notified and urged to find a new physician and be informed that upon authorization, records will be sent to the new physician." When the physician is leaving a group, the patient "should also be notified of the physician's new address and offered the opportunity to have their medical records forwarded to the departing physician at his or her new practice."

When a practice is being sold, American Medical Association Code of Medical Ethics, Opinion 7.04, "Sale of a Medical Practice," recommends that patients should be notified and their records should

---

[33] See OHIO REV. CODE §4731.228, which provides that notice must be sent within 30 days after the healthcare entity has actual knowledge of the termination or resignation of the physician to any person who received the departing physician's services in the two-year period immediately preceding the date of employment termination. The notice must include, among other things, the departing physician's contact information, contact information for an alternative physician at the healthcare entity, and contact information that enables the patient to obtain information on the patient's medical records. The legislation exempts physicians providing episodic or emergency services, medical students, hospice medical directors and physicians working in community mental health agencies or a federally qualified health center.

be transferred to another physician who will, upon written request, send copies to a physician of the patient's choice.

Counsel for the departing physician needs to be aware that the AMA Code of Ethics is often incorporated by reference into physician employment and independent contractor agreements. Thus, a breach of the AMA Code of Ethics could wind up being a breach of the employment contract.

2. Malpractice Carriers

Medical professional liability insurance policies normally have provisions requiring immediate notification of any change in physician employment status.

3. Managed Care Plans, Insurance Networks, Licensing Boards, Medicare and Medicaid, Hospital Privileging Boards

Medicare and Medicaid and other federal- or state-funded payment programs need to be advised of the physician's new contact information and employment details as soon as possible, for billing purposes. Other organizations that may require notification, depending on the circumstances, are managed care plans, insurance networks, and medical licensing boards.

Be advised that many hospitals have included what is known as a "clean sweep" provision in their exclusive contracts with medical groups, which often require that any physician who is part of the exclusive contract medical group and who later departs the medical group for any reason must also resign his or her privileges at the hospital. Counsel can determine that easily by reviewing the contract between the group and the hospital.

G. Physician Covenants Not to Compete in Connection With a Partnership Agreement or the Purchase or Sale of a Medical Practice

There may be restrictive covenants in the governing agreement or employment agreement that contractually limit the right of the departing (or selling) physician-owner to engage in certain medical practice activities within a certain geographic area for a certain period of time after leaving the medical practice. These types of restrictions are ripe for litigation.

Theoretically, the purpose of such restrictive covenants is to protect the medical group from disruption by one (or more) of the physician-owners leaving the group and taking away patients, staff, and referral sources, and thereby exploiting the contacts made while being a part of the medical group. While covenants not to compete involving physicians are not favored in the courts when litigated, they tend to be tolerated when ancillary to the sale of a physician-owner's share of the medical practice; *provided always* that the restrictions are reasonable in terms of time, geographic area, and scope of activity restricted.[34]

Counsel should be aware that laws pertaining to covenants not to compete, particularly those involving physicians, are changing very rapidly. For a comprehensive discussion of physician covenants not to compete in general, please refer to Chapter 9 of this text.

---

[34]For a discussion of this topic and recent cases from all jurisdictions, see Validity and Construction of Contractual Restrictions on Right of Medical Practitioner to Practice, Incident to Partnership Agreement, 62 A.L.R.3d 970.

CHAPTER 7

PHYSICIANS' RELATIONS WITH HOSPITALS: "IT'S COMPLICATED"

I. TENSIONS

Relations between physicians and hospitals have always included a certain amount of tension and distrust. Today, however, as hospitals and hospital systems become more competitive with each other, the tension and distrust among physicians and medical groups on the one hand and hospitals and other healthcare entities on the other is exponentially increasing. Medical groups, hospitals, and other healthcare providers are all reacting to the intense pressure being placed on them by government payors, insurance companies, and other third-party payors. Reimbursements for professional medical services and healthcare are being slashed, and payors insist on improved clinical outcomes, so payors are forcing healthcare providers to "align'" with one another. In some cases, providers are forced to align exclusively within the network that the payor is creating.

The tension between individual and institution relates primarily to control. The tension is due, from the physician's perspective, to the hospital's interference with both the physician's livelihood and the physician's practice of medicine. This interference is perceived to include the hospital's disrespect of the doctor's vast educational and clinical knowledge, and disrespect of the thousands of personal relationships developed by the physician over the best years of his or her life with patients and their extended families. So it is an understatement to say there is tension and distrust between physicians and hospitals, and physician groups and hospitals. Physicians are not widgets, and neither are patients.

Consequently, before counsel can successfully solve any legal or business issues among physicians, physicians groups, and hospitals or hospital networks, counsel must appreciate the layers of tension and distrust there. Such an understanding is essential to representing any party effectively, whether it is an individual physician, a medical group, or a hospital.

II. "ALIGNMENT" AND RELATED DIFFICULTIES

For many years, and particularly since the implementation of the 2010 Patient Protection and Affordable Care Act,[1] physicians, hospitals, and other mega healthcare providers have been encouraged to "align" to find ways to deliver more affordable healthcare to the American population. However, tensions arise from the "hammer on hammer" way in which hospitals and other large healthcare systems are achieving this "alignment."

---

[1]Patient Protection and Affordable Care Act, Pub. L. No. 11-148, 124 Stat. 119 (2010).

Some of the ways in which hospitals and other healthcare entities have been seeking "alignment" with physicians and medical groups appear disturbing and high-handed to those physicians and groups. These methods include refusing staff privileges for "economic" or "conflicts" reasons, as explained below.

- **Economic Credentialing.** Hospitals are denying or refusing to renew medical staff and clinical privileges to physicians who do not refer enough patients to the hospital. This is referred to as "economic credentialing" and is discussed in Section V, below. Physicians find this grossly unfair because patients may prefer to go to a different hospital for treatment for any number of valid reasons, including geographical location, personal or family matters, religious affiliation, and insurance reasons. The physician has no control over such decisions, and she or he can't guarantee a particular hospital a certain volume of incoming patients.[2]

- **Conflicts Credentialing.** Hospitals are denying medical staff and clinical privileges or refusing to renew medical staff and clinical privileges to physicians because they aren't "loyal" enough. This may mean that the physician refers patients to a competing hospital, or that he or she (or another member of the same medical group, or even his or her spouse, if the spouse is a physician) is a medical staff member of a competing hospital or has a financial interest in a competing ambulatory surgical center, or that some other apparent conflict exists to which the hospital objects. This is referred to as "conflicts credentialing" and is discussed in Section V, below.

- **Exclusive Contracting.** Hospitals are entering into exclusive contracts only with certain physicians, thus preventing physicians who are not members of the selected contracting group from exercising their medical staff and clinical privileges at the hospital. In other words, the nonselected physicians have

---

[2]For an informative law review article on the subject of exclusive contracting between hospitals and physicians and the use of economic credentialing, see David J. Behifar, *Exclusive Contracting Between Hospitals and Physicians and the Use of Economic Credentialing*, 1 DEPAUL J. HEALTH CARE L. 71 (1996).

medical staff and clinical privileges at the hospital, but those
privileges are useless.[3]

- **Closing the Medical Staff.** Hospitals are closing their medical staffs by entering into exclusive contracts with certain
physicians (under terms and conditions favorable to the hospital and unfavorable to the physicians), and then not renewing medical staff or clinical privileges of already admitted
physicians and not accepting new member physicians.

- **Use of Unreasonable Restrictive Covenants and "Clean
Sweeps" Provisions in Contracts.** When entering into employment contracts with physician employees or physician
independent contractors, hospitals are requiring what are
commonly referred to as "clean sweeps" provisions, which
require both the physician and the medical group to which
the physician belongs to resign all medical staff privileges
when the agreement with the hospital ends. Such an agreement waives the benefit of any medical staff pre-termination
hearing, to which the physician may otherwise have a right by
virtue of the medical staff bylaws, prior to revocation or termination of hospital privileges. Furthermore, such employment
contracts typically impose covenants not to compete that try
to restrict the physician from working in the surrounding geographical area or working for a competing healthcare delivery
system for a period of time. The contracts also may try to
impose other restrictions on the physician after his or her employment with the hospital ends. Such a clause puts the physician in a highly unfavorable bargaining position when the
employment contract or independent contractor agreement is
up for renewal.[4] From the physician's viewpoint, that is the
main purpose of a noncompete clause—to make the physician feel compelled to stay in the present job for lower pay or
suboptimal working conditions because of restrictions placed

---

[3]For a more detailed discussion of exclusive contracting and legal challenges
raised thereto on the basis of antitrust and medical staff bylaw issues, see AMERICAN
HEALTH LAWYERS ASSOCIATION, REPRESENTING PHYSICIANS HANDBOOK §10.3.2
Exclusive Contracting, at 454-56, and §14.4 *The Exclusive Nature of the Exclusive
Contract—Relevant Laws* at 616–68 (4th ed. 2016) [hereinafter REPRESENTING
PHYSICIANS HANDBOOK]. *See also* Behifar, *Exclusive Contracting Between Hospitals
and Physicians and the Use of Economic Credentialing.*

[4]See Chapter 10 of this text for a more complete discussion of covenants not to
compete in physician employment contracts.

on the physician's future employment opportunities by the present employer.

• **Direct Employment of Physicians That Excludes Independent Physicians for "Business Reasons."** Hospitals are directly employing physicians and not granting medical staff or clinical privileges to nonemployee physicians who have sick patients that need to be admitted. The result is that independent physicians are forced to use the services of hospital employee physicians (e.g., hospitalists) or independent contractors of the hospital to care for their sick patients at such hospital.

III. SETTING THE STAGE

A physician's right to practice medicine at a hospital is granted upon approval of the physician's application to be part of the hospital's medical staff, known as "medical staff membership," and the grant of "clinical privileges" to the physician to perform certain medical services that he or she is qualified to perform. Hospital privileges are essential to most practicing physicians. A physician cannot admit or treat sick patients in a hospital unless the physician has admitting and clinical privileges. Imagine if there is only one hospital in the area. The impact on a local physician of not being granted staff and clinical privileges at the local hospital would be devastating.

Even though courts have consistently found that physicians have no absolute right to medical staff membership and clinical privileges,[5] physicians can invoke judicial review of negative credentialing decisions under a variety of laws, including constitutional and common law theories and federal and state statutes. The latter include antitrust statutes,[6] antidiscrimination statutes (prohibiting discrimination on the basis of, e.g., gender, race, age, national origin, religion, and disability), and whistleblower statutes.[7]

---

[5]Taylor v. Horn, 189 So. 2d 198 (Fla. Dist. Ct. App. 1966) (explained by Hull v. Bd. of Comm'rs of Halifax Hosp., 453 So. 2d 519 (Fla. Dist. Ct. App. 1984)); Hughes v. Good Samaritan Hosp., 158 S.W.2d 159 (Ky. 1942).

[6]*See* Furrow, Greaney, Johnson, Stoltzfus-Jost & Schwartz, HEALTH LAW §§13-14 to 13-21, at 718–43 (3d ed. 2015) [hereinafter HEALTH LAW].

[7]*See id.* §10-2.A, at 503–16.

IV. WHAT ARE PHYSICIAN HOSPITAL PRIVILEGES?

The Joint Commission and the National Committee on Quality Assurance are two of the leading organizations involved in accreditation of healthcare entities, including hospitals.[8] The Joint Commission defines physician clinical privileges as "[p]ermission to provide medical or other patient care services in the granting institution, within well-defined limits, based on the individual's professional license and his/her experience, competence, ability and judgment."[9]

The Joint Commission requires that hospitals have an actual physician credentialing process to review a physician's performance in several areas of competency before approving membership on the medical staff, and that there be a separate standardized process to continuously evaluate and "flag" practitioners when there are competency concerns.[10] Specifically, the credentialing process is expected to assess the physician's competency as to patient care, medical knowledge, interpersonal and communication skills, and professionalism.[11]

V. ECONOMIC CREDENTIALING AND CONFLICTS CREDENTIALING

A. What Is "Economic Credentialing"?

"Economic credentialing" is a type of hospital medical staff privileging consideration or requirement that has nothing to do with a physician's qualifications or quality of patient care. It has to do with the economics and business of the hospital. The American Medical Association (AMA) defines economic credentialing as "the use of economic criteria, unrelated to quality of care or professional competence, in determining a physician's qualifications for initial or

---

[8]See id. §2-20, at 65–66.

[9]See id. §10-2, at 503 (citing JOINT COMMISSION, 2013 ACCREDITATION MANUAL FOR HOSPITALS, MS 1.1.2).

[10]See id. (citing JOINT COMMISSION, 2013 ACCREDITATION MANUAL FOR HOSPITALS, MS 4.00, 4.10, 4.15, 4.30, 4.40).

[11]See id. §10-8.a., at 513.

continuing hospital medical staff membership or privileges."[12] The AMA strongly opposes the practice of economic credentialing.[13]

Perhaps the best way to recognize economic credentialing is by using the following guidelines:

Economic credentialing tends to come in three forms:

1) hospitals entering into *exclusive contract arrangements* with specialty providers (thereby *excluding other providers*) or *closing their staff to new providers*;
2) *physician profiling* (hospitals using *utilization patterns* such as costs, utilization, and reimbursement to make credentialing decisions); and
3) *conflict credentialing* or *loyalty provisions*, requiring physicians to agree not to possess an investment interest or even have a relationship with an alternative facility that might compete with the hospital.[14]

B. What Is "Conflicts Credentialing"?

"Conflicts credentialing" is another type of hospital medical staff credentialing that has nothing to do with quality of patient care. It denies appointment or renewal to, or terminates medical staff privileges of, physicians who own or use competing medical facilities. Conflicts credentialing "is a term often used to describe privileges decisions concerning a physician who practices within or owns an entity that competes directly with the hospital and who wants to hold staff privileges at the hospital as well."[15]

Conflicts credentialing happens to physicians when they are seeking medical staff and clinical privileges at a hospital (either initial or renewed privileges). Or it can happen at any time during the medical staff membership. The physicians are asked information about the nature and extent of their relationships with other hospitals, imaging centers, laboratories, ambulatory surgical centers, or

---

[12]American Medical Association Policy H-230.975, https://www.ama-assn.org/about-us/policyfinder.

[13]*See* AMERICAN MEDICAL ASSOCIATION, POLICY COMPENDIUM 230.975, at 197 (1993); Thorn Wilder, *AMA Calls Exclusive Credentialing By Hospitals a Fraud Violation*, 9 HEALTH L. REP. (BNA) 344 (Mar. 9, 2000); *see also* Economic Credentialing: Where Is it Going?, http://corporate.findlaw.com/law-library/economic-credentialing-where-is-it-going.html.

[14]Leigh Walton, et. al., *Hospitals Employing Physicians: A Practical Guide to Buying Physician Practices and Compensating Employed Doctors*, 22 HEALTH LAW. 1, 17 (Dec. 2009) (emphasis added).

[15]*See* HEALTH LAW §10-8.d, at 515.

other (usually competing) healthcare entities. This includes detailed information such as privileges in other hospitals, board positions held, income received, referral patterns, extent of any financial investment or interests, memberships in or relationship with any other healthcare entities, etc. Often the same questions extend to the physician's associates and even the physician's spouse (if the spouse is a physician).

C. Hospitals' Position on Economic Credentialing and Conflicts Credentialing

Hospitals justify exclusive contracting and economic credentialing on the need to use their hospital resources effectively, citing the need to use their "business judgment" to reduce inefficiency, control costs, and reduce the number of doctors and other professionals to whom they grant permission to use their facilities, so as to be better able to measure quality and control other aspects of hospital operation.

With respect to conflict credentialing, hospitals defend the policy on the basis of fear that physicians might obtain strategic information by being a member of the medical staff, particularly if a particular physician would become an officer or otherwise occupy a position of leadership. The argument is that such physician might use inside information against the hospital and to the advantage of the competing entity.[16]

The other argument hospitals use is that they don't want a physician to have privileges at their hospital (Hospital A) and at a competing hospital (or ambulatory surgery center) because the physician might direct lesser-paying patients to Hospital A and admit the better-paying patients to the competing hospital (or ambulatory surgery center) where the physician also refers patients (or may have a financial interest). For the record, the AMA has a policy that expressly prohibits a physician from doing exactly that.[17] However, those are the two main arguments that the hospitals put forth in favor of conflict credentialing.

As the authors of a legal hornbook state in their chapter on "Staff Privileges":

---

[16]See id.
[17]The AMA has issued Opinion 8.03 stating that "[U]nder no circumstances may physicians place their own financial interests above the welfare of their patients."

the central concern in the incidents of conflicts credentialing may have more to do with the hospital's desire or need to depress competition in its more profitable operations. Excluding competing physicians from access to hospital facilities provides the hospital significant leverage against the competing organization.[18]

D. Court Decisions on Conflict Credentialing Are Split

At this time, there are only a few reported cases. Among those, there is a split of authority as to whether conflicts credentialing is a legitimate basis for denying or terminating a physician's hospital privileges. At least one court has permitted it.[19] Others have not.[20]

E. Cases and State Statutes Addressing Economic Credentialing

There are few reported cases that have directly addressed the broader subject of "economic credentialing" (as opposed to just "conflicts credentialing") as a basis for denying or terminating a physician's hospital privileges. The majority of those cases considering the matter have upheld the hospital governing body's decision to deny privileges or close the hospital staff to otherwise qualified

---

[18]See HEALTH LAW §10-8.d, at 515.

[19]E.g. Mahan v. Avera St. Luke's, 621 N.W.2d 150 (S.D. 2001). The court in *Mahan* held that a not for profit, religiously affiliated, rural hospital's newly closed staff policy could be justified solely by economic concerns, when the hospital closed its staff in direct response to a new surgery center being built by certain orthopedic surgeons who were medical staff members at Avera St. Luke's, while at the same time the hospital was trying to recruit two new orthopedic surgeons for its medical staff. Thereafter, an orthopedic surgeon hired by the orthopedic surgeon group that formed the competing ambulatory surgery center applied for medical privileges at the hospital and was refused on the grounds that the hospital had closed its orthopedic surgical staff except for the physicians that were being recruited by the hospital. The Court stated the medical staff closure was "necessary to insure the continued economic viability of the hospital. The board must be allowed to make such reasonable, independent decisions if it is to continue to provide comprehensive medical services." *Id.*, 621 N.W.2d at 160. *See also* Balaklaw v. Lovell, 14 F.3d 793, 795 (2d Cir. 1994).

[20]E.g. Baptist Health v. Murphy, 373 S.W.3d 269 (2010) (exclusion of physicians violated state deceptive trade practices statute); Pacific Radiation Oncology, LLC v. Queen's Med. Ctr., 861 F. Supp. 2d 1170 (D. Hawaii 2012), *aff'd* 2014 WL 689748 (9th Cir. 2014), granting preliminary injunction to require hospital to afford competing physician limited privileges for services that could only be performed at the hospital. Cases and text cited from footnote 118 of HEALTH LAW §10-8.d at 515. *See also* Medical Staff of Comm'y Mem. Hosp. of San Buenaventura v. Community Mem. Hosp. of San Buenaventura, CIV 219107 (Ventura Cty., Cal. Super. Ct. Aug. 7, 2003).

physicians, for the hospital's stated economic or business reasons.[21] There are also some states that have permitted by statute certain forms of economic considerations to be considered in physician medical privileging decisions.[22]

Other courts and state legislatures have taken a contrary view.[23] For example, Montana Code Ann. §50-5-117 generally prohibits "economic credentialing"—which is defined by Montana statute— by hospitals or outpatient centers that require a physician to agree to make referrals to the hospital or outpatient center or any other facility related to the hospital or outpatient center, or refuse to grant staff or medical staff privileges or limit any staff participation because the physician or any partner, associate, or employee of the physician has an ownership interest or occupies a leadership position on the medical staff of a different hospital, hospital system, or healthcare facility, or participates or doesn't participate in a particular health plan, or hospital, hospital system, or healthcare facility. (There are exceptions whereby physicians with competing interests may be required to be recused from board of director membership or being the president of the medical staff of the hospital or outpatient center or from sensitive financial decision-making or information if there is a conflict of interest relevant to certain decisions or information.)

F. Are There Anti-Kickback Statute Implications for Medical Staff Credentialing?

Is the federal Anti-Kickback Statute[24] implicated when hospitals insist on an independent physician sending a certain number of patients to their hospital or otherwise denying medical staff privileges?

Yes. The federal Health and Human Services (HHS) Office of the Inspector General (OIG) has stated that medical staff

---

[21]Jefferson Parish Hospital District No. 2 v. Hyde, 466 U.S. 2 (1984); Balaklaw v. Lovell, 14 F.3d 793, 795 (2d Cir. 1994); Hassan v. Independent Practice Assocs., 698 F. Supp. 679 (E.D. Mich. 1988); Mahan v. Avera St. Luke's, 621 N.W.2d 150 (S.D. 2001).

[22]See, e.g., FLA. STAT. ANN. §395.0191; GA. CODE ANN. §31-7-7; IND. CODE ANN. §16-21-2-5; IOWA CODE §135B.7; KAN. STAT. ANN. §65-431; MD. CODE ANN., HEALTH—GENERAL §19-319; N.Y. PUB. HEALTH §2801-b; N.C. GEN. STAT. §131E-85.

[23]E.g., CAL. WELF. & INST. CODE §14087.28; COLO. REV. STAT. §25-3-103.7; D.C. CODE ANN. §44-507; IDAHO CODE §41-3920; 210 ILL. COMP. STAT. 85/2(b); LA. REV. STAT. ANN. §37-1301; MASS. ANN. LAWS ch. 111, §51C; MONTANA CODE ANN §50-5-117; R.I. GEN. LAWS §23.17-52; TENN. CODE ANN. §§68-11-205, 68-11-207; TEX. HEALTH & SAFETY CODE ANN. §241.1015; VA. CODE ANN. §32.1-134.1.

[24]42 U.S.C. §§1320a-7b(b)(1)(B).

credentialing practices may implicate the Anti-Kickback Statute. The OIG stated: "For example, conditioning privileges on a particular number of referrals or requiring the performance of a particular number of procedures beyond volumes necessary to ensure clinical proficiency potentially raises substantial risks under the Anti-Kickback statute."[25]

G. Are There Joint Commission Standards or Medicare Considerations Promoting Economic or Conflict Credentialing?

Do Joint Commission standards or Medicare considerations encourage or legitimize economic credentialing or conflict credentialing?

No. On the contrary, the Joint Commission hospital standards emphasize objective, evidence-based processes when determining a physician's professional competence and clinical ability for purposes of granting, denying, or renewing clinical privileges. There is no mention of criteria approving of a minimum number of physician referrals of patients to a particular hospital, or excluding physicians with a relationship with a competing hospital as a basis for medical staff privileging or deprivileging. The same is true for CMS.[26]

---

[25] 69 Fed. Reg. 32,022 (June 8, 2004). *See* REPRESENTING PHYSICIANS HANDBOOK, at 427.

[26] In a well-researched article on the subject by the America Health Lawyers Association, it was pointed out in the REPRESENTING PHYSICIANS HANDBOOK that with respect to the Joint Commission standards and medical staff privileging decisions:

Any decisions on appointment, reappointment, and privileges (i.e., renewal, revision, or limitation) must necessarily consider and comply with Joint Commission standards, and specifically MS.06.01.05 *["MS" stands for Medical Standard]* and 06.01.07. MS.06.01.05 requires that hospitals have an objective, evidenced-based process for granting, denying, or renewing clinical privileges. MS.06.01.07 requires the organized medical staff to review and analyze all relevant information regarding each requesting practitioner's current licensure status, training, experience, current competence, and ability to perform the requested privilege. MS.06.01.07 has nine EPs, *[EPs are "elements of performance"]* and numbers 6 and 7 are directly on point:

(6) Decisions on membership and granting of privileges include consider[ed] criteria that are directly related to the quality of health care, treatment and services.

(7) If privileging criteria are used that are unrelated to quality of care, treatment and services or professional competence, evidence exists that the impact of resulting decisions on the quality of care, treatment and services is evaluated.

These elements of performance suggest that economic criteria should not be used or must, at least, be only incidental to the clinical factors." *[Italics and brackets are supplied by the authors.]*

Of course, physicians participating on the governance board of a hospital or hospital medical staff would be expected to comply with the hospital policy on conflicts of interest (e.g., being subject to the terms of a nondisclosure agreement or being disqualified from certain executive officer positions or having to recuse oneself from those parts of a meeting where sensitive financial information is discussed, etc.). But that is distinguishable from the situation where an otherwise fully capable physician is disqualified from having medical staff privileges and being able to admit and treat sick patients at a particular hospital on the basis that he or she happens to have one or more relationships with other hospitals or medical institutions.

> ***Suggestion:*** What hospitals could consider to alleviate some of the ill will that physicians are feeling toward them is for the hospital administration to be more flexible when making unilateral business decisions that will affect physician staff and clinical privileges. Administration could (1) simply carve out already credentialed physicians from the exclusive provider arrangement, (2) invite credentialed physicians to join the exclusive provider group, or (3) have the professional courtesy to wait for the periodic expiration of the clinical privileges of the already credentialed physicians before implementing exclusive contracting decisions that affect already credentialed physicians.

VI. The Wildebeest Migration: Hospitals and Physicians Aligning Through Hospital Purchase of Physician Practices, and Employee Status Thereafter

Hospitals have been on a buying spree, purchasing physicians' medical practices on a massive scale as a way to increase market share. In response, medical groups have been selling (or sometimes leasing) their practices to hospitals (or hospital subsidiaries) as a

---

Representing Physicians Handbook, ch. 10 at 427. Similarly, the Medicare Conditions of Participation provide that the governing body "must ensure the criteria for selection are individual character, competence, training, experience and judgment. No mention is made of economic criteria. In fact, all criteria listed point toward quality of care concerns." *Id.* at 427–28 (citations omitted).

way to ride out an unpredictable future in the healthcare delivery world.

A former executive of the American College of Cardiology likened the shift of physicians selling their practices to hospitals and becoming employees of hospital systems to "a migration of wildebeests."[27] The imagery is apt.

The benefits to physicians in selling their practices include avoiding investment in expensive EHR systems and IT support, avoiding having to compete directly with the hospital, better alignment with larger healthcare delivery systems, assistance in billing and collection, assistance in human resource and administrative activities, and more time to focus on providing professional medical services. The downside is loss of professional autonomy and being treated as a "worker bee," while suffering more stress. See Chapters 1 and 2 of this text.

The mechanics of selling a medical practice to a hospital are often accomplished by the hospital (or a subsidiary thereof) purchasing (at fair market value) the medical group's practice, generally through the use of an asset purchase agreement, coupled with a physician employment agreement with an initial term averaging five years.[28]

Recommendations for evaluating physician employment agreements, particularly provisions regarding termination with and without cause, nonrenewal provisions, post-employment noncompete restrictions, tail end (extended reporting) malpractice insurance requirements, indemnification requirements, "clean sweeps" provisions, and much more may be found in Chapter 9 of this text.

---

[27]*See* Margo Sanger-Katz, *When Hospitals Buy Doctors' Offices, and Patient Fees Soar*, N.Y. TIMES, Feb. 8, 2015.

[28]Details of how and why to structure the purchase and sale of a medical practice to a hospital (or third-party staffing company) are fact-dependent and go well beyond the scope of this employment counseling publication. However, helpful practical information as to the mechanics and health law regulatory considerations, tax, liability, and other considerations relating to the purchase and sale of medical practices may be found in Leigh Walton, et. al., *Hospitals Employing Physicians: A Practical Guide to Buying Physician Practices and Compensating Employed Doctors*, 22 HEALTH LAW. 1, 16–39 (Dec. 2009), and REPRESENTING PHYSICIANS HANDBOOK, ch. 13, at 584–612.

VII. EMPLOYMENT RELATIONSHIPS BENEFIT HOSPITALS

Hospitals have a clear advantage over solo physicians and small group practitioners due to the fact that there are statutory exceptions and safe harbors for employment arrangements[29] under the federal Anti-Kickback Statute,[30] and also exceptions for bona fide employment relationships[31] under the Stark Law (the federal physician self-referral prohibition).[32] Employment arrangements are a way for hospitals to obtain the physician coverage and professional services they need, as well as to impose all sorts of additional contractual requirements—and restrictions—on the physician, including post-employment restrictive covenants.

> Direct employment also gives hospitals the freedom to impose additional requirements on the physician, such as requiring employed physicians to refer to the hospital's service lines instead of to other entities (again, provided certain regulatory conditions are met). A hospital's freedom to require a provider to use and refer to that hospital insulates the hospital's market share and guarantees use of the facility by physicians who are responsible for patients. ... The fraud and abuse protections available for bona fide employment allow for a referral and compensation structure that could not be attempted, or at least would be much riskier, outside an employment setting.[33]

For example, in the absence of state legislation prohibiting the same,[34] hospitals can require physicians to refer patients to the

---

[29]See 42 C.F.R. §1001.952(i).

[30]42 U.S.C. §§1320a-7b(b)(1)(B).

[31]See 42 C.F.R. §411.357(c).

[32]42 U.S.C. §1395nn(a)(1).

[33]Leigh Walton, et. al., *Hospitals Employing Physicians: A Practical Guide to Buying Physician Practices and Compensating Employed Doctors*, 22 HEALTH LAW. 1, 8 (Dec. 2009).

[34]For example, in Colorado, a hospital statutorily may not "limit or otherwise exercise control over the physician's independent professional judgment concerning the practice of medicine or diagnosis or treatment or ... require physicians to refer exclusively to the health care facility or to the health care facility's employed physicians." COLO. REV. STAT. §25-3-103.7(3). Other states impose similar statutory conditions on hospital employment of physicians. *See, e.g.*, 210 ILL. COMP. STAT. 85/10.8(a)(3); N.D. CENT. CODE §43-17-42; S.D. CODIFIED LAWS §36-4-8.1(1); TENN. CODE ANN. §63-6-204(f)(1)(A); WIS. STAT. §448.08(5)(a)(1). Violation of this prohibition may subject the hospital to regulatory penalties or any resulting liability to patients or the physician. COLO. REV. STAT. §25-3-103.7(3); *see also, e.g.*, 210 ILL. COMP. STAT. 85/10.8(c)–(d) (containing similar provisions).

hospital by use of a written employment agreement, *provided* that the agreement meets certain contractual requirements and contains some federally mandated (e.g., Stark Law) carve-outs. Those contractual requirements and carve-outs are described in Chapter 25 of this text.

CHAPTER 8

NONEMPLOYEE CONTRACT ROLES FOR PHYSICIANS

I. INTRODUCTION: WHAT CAN INDEPENDENT PHYSICIANS DO?

Individual and group physicians who wish to remain independent but be associated on a business level with hospitals are seeking new opportunities to do so in today's complex healthcare environment. They are entering into contractual arrangements under which the physician or medical group provides defined services (including professional, administrative, or supervisory services) to various health delivery parties on a contractual basis, while remaining independent.

For convenience in this chapter, we use the term "hospital" to refer to all types of healthcare entities, including without limitation hospitals, clinics, urgent care centers, ambulatory surgery centers, and nursing homes.

II. TYPICAL NONEMPLOYEE CONTRACT RELATIONSHIPS

Contractual business relationships being explored today are as numerous as there are needs for professional services and imaginative attorneys. How intimately linked the parties are with one another will depend on the terms of the agreement. Some examples of agreements include:

• professional services agreements
• medical directorship agreements
• management services agreements

- on-call coverage agreements
- medical consulting services agreements
- equity and nonequity joint venture agreements
- ambulatory surgical center joint venture agreements
- exclusive and nonexclusive contracting agreements
- hospital service line co-management agreements
- private or public accountable care organization agreements, and
- other types of contractual arrangements in which hospitals and other healthcare entities outsource services to physicians or medical groups.

The name of the agreement is not what is important or controls the relationship. The terms of the agreement are what control, and these types of agreements can satisfy the professional healthcare needs of the hospital and also be satisfying for the physician, if structured properly by a capable health law attorney, and provided that the physician has his or her own capable health law attorney representing the physician's interests.

III. INITIAL CONSIDERATIONS

Whenever physicians and hospitals are seriously considering entering into any type of healthcare business relationship, counsel should be conscious of three things:

- Ensure your client does not feel pressured to sign a "form agreement" because "everyone else does" or "because they trust the hospital."
- Have your own physician health law "sharpshooter."
- Determine who your client is.

Each of these points is discussed further below.

A. Avoid Form Agreements

Never rely on the hospital to look out for or protect the physician's interest—or anyone else's interest *other than the hospital's*. Sadly, this is often front page news to many physicians working on a contract basis, particularly if the physician thinks he or she is going to be "working on the same team" as the hospital hiring entity, and particularly if the physician is being asked to sign a "form" agreement that "everyone else signs." A new physician may not be familiar with the view of the world held by both hospital administrators and lawyers, which is to promise as little as possible and to protect the hospital as much as possible, by shifting as much liability as legally and contractually possible to any available third party (e.g., to the physician independent contractor, no matter how small).

If the physician is your client, explain that there is no such thing as a "form" business contract involving physicians, and that it needs to be reviewed and commented on by an experienced health law transactions attorney.

B. Have Your Own Physician Health Law "Sharpshooter"

Experienced health law transactions advice is needed early in any contract discussions, and definitely before any documents are signed, to ensure the parties are in compliance with, among other things, federal and state laws and health law regulations. Some laws and regulations, particularly the antitrust laws, carry criminal penalties. Physician service agreements must be meticulously structured—or at a minimum carefully reviewed and commented on—by experienced and capable health law transactions counsel.

In addition to the federal Stark Law and Anti-Kickback Statute, discussed in Chapter 25 of this text, other laws to be aware of include the state versions of the Stark Law and Anti-Kickback Statute, the federal False Claims Act,[1] the Civil Monetary Penalties Law,[2] IRS 501(c)(3) tax exemption laws, Medicare Anti-Markup Rules,[3] state corporate practice of medicine prohibitions, fee splitting laws, state insurance regulations, and so forth. Additionally, the physician or physician group requires an experienced health law transactions attorney to advise the physician or the group on the appropriateness of the overall structure, and whether the payment, billing, collection, audit, assignment, indemnification, noncompete, and confidentiality

---

[1] 31 U.S.C. §3729-33.
[2] 42 U.S.C. §1320a-7a.
[3] Section 1842(n)(1) of the Social Security Act requires CMS to impose a payment limitation on certain diagnostic tests where the physician performing or supervising the test does not share a practice with the billing physician or other supplier.

requirements (to name just a few matters) are appropriate under the circumstances, or whether the arrangement needs revising.[4]

For a general practice attorney, developing a professional relationship with an experienced healthcare transaction attorney early, and having the ability to make a quick phone call for reassurance and advice on how best to navigate the healthcare law regulatory waters, will save major headaches down the road.

C. Conflicts of Interest: Who is My Client?

If counsel is representing more than one physician, counsel must determine "who is my client?" Is it the youngest member of the group practice, who might want a long relationship with the hospital? Is it the oldest member of the group practice, nearing retirement, who couldn't care less about a long-term relationship with the hospital? Is it the CEO of the group? There are as many interests as there are physicians in the group!

As a practical matter, in some cases, depending on the complexity and length of the proposed transaction and the various ages of the physicians, stages in their professional career, and risk appetite, each of the physicians may require his or her own attorney to advise as to their particular situation and how best to manage their risk.

IV. Walk-Through of a Nonemployment Business Arrangement Between a Physician and a Hospital or Other Healthcare Entity

A. Professional Services Agreement Mechanics

At a high level, a professional services agreement (PSA) is a written contract between the hospital and a physician, or group of physicians, to provide professional medical services at a location (or several locations) operated by the hospital, on an independent contractor basis. Some PSAs may be exclusive arrangements, whereby the physician or physician group is the only party providing a particular professional service to the hospital, in which case that exclusive arrangement should be made very clear in the body of the PSA.

---

[4]For an overview of fundamental physician fraud and abuse considerations, see Chapters 6 and 25 of this text.

B. Exclusive PSAs

Exclusive PSAs are most often used for emergency room physicians, anesthesiologists, hospitalists, radiologists, pathologists, intensive care unit (ICU) intensivists, and neonatologists.[5] The common feature of these types of physician workers is that the work they do and the procedures they perform are usually performed at the hospital, and the patients are typically hospital inpatients and outpatients.

> *Tip:* With respect to any exclusive medical service agreement, counsel must check the medical staff bylaws and hospital corporate bylaws to see whether exclusive contracts have been addressed, whether they are permitted at the hospital, and what rights (if any) existing members of the hospital medical staff have in terms of challenging or working around any proposed exclusive contract. Counsel must also check the statutes and case law in the particular state to see if exclusive contracting is expressly permitted, expressly prohibited, or has not been decided. This will impact the indemnity provisions that counsel for the physician should require from the hospital, in favor of the contracting physicians, if the exclusive contract is challenged by any members of the medical staff.

C. Other Considerations

Other considerations for counsel to address in any exclusive PSA would be restrictions on the hospital's ability to hire new physicians, advanced practice nurses, or physician's assistants (except through the group) who would be practicing in the physician's area of specialty, and also whether the physicians should have a right of first opportunity or first offer to be the exclusive provider, if the hospital *were* to acquire any other entities during the term of the PSA.

---

[5] For a useful guide to exclusive physician and hospital agreements with suggested clauses and sample agreements, please see AMERICAN HEALTH LAWYERS ASS'N, REPRESENTING PHYSICIANS HANDBOOK §14.4, at 616–68.

D. Nonexclusive PSAs

Although some PSAs may be exclusive, many PSAs are not. That means other physicians, physician groups, or medical staff physicians may provide some or all of the same professional services that are the subject of the PSA, which of course affects the physician's revenue-producing opportunities and eventual bottom line.

E. PSA Arrangement Benefits

PSA-type arrangements are reportedly a good way for physicians and medical groups who are flirting with the idea of integrating with a hospital to find out whether the working relationship is workable, while at the same time not becoming an actual employee of the hospital. Another benefit of PSAs is that they provide certainty in income, while the physician or group still maintains ultimate control over the operation of their medical practice.

From the hospital's perspective, having a PSA makes economic sense if the hospital is looking for a specific type of clinical service and can obtain it without the upfront costs of having to purchase the assets of a physician's practice or medical group's practice to obtain such service.

F. Typical Assigned Billing and Collection Arrangements, Compensation

In a traditional PSA, the hospital requires the physician or the medical group to assign to the hospital the right to bill and collect for the physician's professional medical services, and the physician or physicians are (typically) paid on a wRVU basis,[6] along with some quality-based incentives incorporated into the compensation structure.[7] Naturally, the compensation structure depends on the particular professional service provided by the physicians and the type of practice. It is recommended that the physician consult a qualified independent healthcare valuation firm, one with experience in valuing physician compensation with hospitals, to obtain the latest information as to the fair market value of the physician's services

---

[6]Work relative value units (wRVUs) are Medicare's billing units for physician services.

[7]Neatly qualifying for an Anti-Kickback Statute safe harbor can be an issue when using wRVU as the basis for compensation.

in question, just to make sure the physician isn't getting low-balled when it comes to compensation.

However, it is not uncommon that in *exclusive* PSAs involving certain types of hospital-based medical groups (radiologists, pathologists, emergency room physicians, and anesthesiologists in particular), the exclusive contract terms are structured so as to permit such groups to separately negotiate their professional service fees with networks and third-party insurers, and to separately bill and collect for the medical services rather than the hospital doing so. Generally in such cases, the hospital charges, bills, and collects for everything *other than* the actual professional medical service personally provided by the physician.

> *Practice Tip:* Even though the hospital typically requires the independent contractor (and employee) physician to expressly assign the physician's right to bill and collect payment for medical professional services to the hospital, the physician will still be liable for, at a minimum, any CMS overpayments. So counsel for the physician must insist that the agreement require, at a minimum, that the physician have the right to inspect and audit any billing and collections performed in the name of the physician, and that the hospital defend and indemnify and hold harmless the physician for any costs and expenses suffered by the physician in defending any such audits or claims or paying any fines or judgments related to errors caused by the hospital's or hospital agent's action in billing or collection activities not caused by the physician.

Sample Clause [A]:

Physician assigns to Hospital or its delegate, and Hospital hereby assumes responsibility for, preparing, billing, submitting, obtaining, transacting, and collecting all amounts owed for Services provided by Physician pursuant to this Agreement. Such services shall be performed on a timely basis and in an accurate manner, and in accordance with applicable policies and procedures of the Hospital, and in accordance with all applicable Medicare, Medicaid and any other governmental reimbursement program accreditation standards and other applicable private payor requirements, and all laws relating to the preparation, billing, submission, obtaining, transacting, and collection of amounts for Physician's Services. Physician shall have the right to review any and all codes assigned or bills submitted for Physician's Services and demand correction of errors in such codes, including a refund to payors if necessary.

Sample Clause [B]: Indemnification of Physician For Hospital's Billing or Collection Errors Clause:

Hospital agrees to defend, indemnify and hold harmless Physician from any claim, loss, damage, cost, expense, liability, judgment, cause of action, or expense (including reasonable attorney's fees and disbursements) arising out of or related to Hospital's or its respective officers, directors, administrators, employees, representatives, independent contractors, agents or designees, record keeping services, establishment of medical fees and Professional Service charges, Professional Service documentation, billing activities, Professional Service documentation and record completion requirements, third party reimbursement, and collection activities, when such claim, loss, damage, cost, expense, liability, judgment, cause of action, or expense is not directly due to Physician error.

Tip: Because the physician may very well encounter a situation where a patient's records are needed quickly for any number of legal reasons, both during and after the end of the employment relationship, *always* include a provision permitting access to such records. See Chapter 9 of this text.

G. Physician Office Staff Arrangements Vary

There are various models of PSAs. The hospital may or may not employ the physician's or group's office staff. If not, the nonclinical staff will normally be required to operate under an agreed-upon budget, which is reimbursed by the hospital up to the budgeted amount. If there is not such a budget, then the hospital typically requires approval of the practice's expenditures, which can be an unwelcome layer of management bureaucracy for the medical practice.

H. Malpractice and Other Insurance and Benefits Arrangements

In a typical PSA scenario, the contracting physician or group furnishes professional medical services on an independent contractor basis, and is responsible for providing malpractice insurance coverage for such professional services. Depending on the type of malpractice insurance obtained during the term of the PSA, that would include any "tail end" (extended reporting) malpractice insurance required after the term of the PSA for events occurring during the term of the PSA but reported afterwards.

Assuming the hospital has employed the medical group's *non-clinical / non-PSA billing* office staff, then the contracting individual physician or contracting medical group is normally responsible for providing the salaries and other benefits for the physicians and other clinical employees (physician's assistants and nurse practitioners) who are or will be providing billable professional services under the PSA.

Therefore, when determining the wRVU rate or other compensation rate, it is essential to determine whether the physician or group has a clear understanding of what the salaries, professional liability insurance premiums, fringe benefits, continuing medical education expenses, retirement plan contributions, health and disability insurance benefits, mileage reimbursement, and all other benefits that are offered by the practice to the physicians and other medical staff (e.g., nurse practitioners and physician's assistants) *actually cost,* so the practice knows if what they are being offered in terms of wRVU rates (or other compensation rates) are acceptable. Does the physician or group practice have a firm grip on their costs to know whether this is a profitable arrangement? These are all things for a physician and medical practice to consider when thinking about entering into any type of arrangement with a hospital or other healthcare system.

It is imperative that the advice and counsel of the physician's or the medical group's financial manager and accountant is incorporated in the negotiation planning, to ensure that the negotiated compensation for the medical services is sufficient to cover the actual costs and overhead of providing such services, including the costs of all malpractice insurance and all the other benefits provided to the physicians and other workers who will be providing services under the PSA, plus a reasonable profit.

V. GET INSURANCE CARRIER ADVICE AND COUNSEL ON INSURANCE AND INDEMNIFICATION MATTERS

Before entering into a PSA (or any other agreement) where there are any insurance requirements or contractual indemnification requirements, including any hold-harmless provisions, counsel is strongly advised to consult with the client's professional liability (i.e., malpractice) and general liability insurance carriers' legal or senior business representatives for advice and counsel, for the reasons described in Section IV., above.

Experienced insurance professionals are (typically) very knowledgeable and can put into plain English what is and what is not acceptable in the draft PSA language from an insurance standpoint. They can often suggest how to make the contract language acceptable, in the framework of your client's particular malpractice and general liability insurance coverage, and importantly, where the physician client risks having exposure to some noninsured liability.

> *Tip:* In the healthcare world, it is often the same insurance carrier that represents one or more (if not all) the parties to the PSA. Sometimes, the insurance carrier can suggest acceptable language that can accomplish what the hospital and the various parties want—or at least explain the moving parts—so that the parties can understand the risks and perhaps work out an acceptable solution.

VI. BEWARE OF CONTRACTUAL INDEMNIFICATION OBLIGATIONS

Hospitals often include indemnification and hold-harmless provisions in agreements with physicians who perform professional services for the hospital or at the hospital's care sites. Counsel needs to be very careful that the physician or medical group does not agree to contractually assume indemnification or hold-harmless obligations, since these "contractual" liabilities are typically excluded from the scope of the physician's or physician group's professional liability (malpractice) insurance coverage. That means that the physician's or the medical group's assets will be at risk, and may be insufficient to cover the contractually assumed liabilities.

Tip: Counsel should ensure that the physician or group *specifically excludes* responsibility or liability for acts or omissions of any hospital employees, hospital staff members, or hospital independent contractors (other than the client physician or the client physician group), even if your client is performing administrative, supervisory, or management functions for the hospital. For that matter, counsel should specifically exclude responsibility or liability for acts or omissions of *anyone other than* the client-physician or the client-physician group's employees or independent contractors.

Hospitals commonly have excess insurance coverage available to them, so their losses above that which is available from the physician's insurance proceeds are likely covered by such excess insurance. If counsel must agree to some sort of indemnification provision, make sure it is a minimal dollar cap; otherwise the physician or physician's group risks bankruptcy.[8]

How much sense does it make to require a physician or a physician group to risk bankruptcy or have to charge the hospital more in professional fees to obtain insurance coverage for events for which the hospital is already covered? That is not to say that the physician or the physician group should not have adequate insurance to compensate for their own negligence. This comment has to do with the mindless use of sweeping indemnification provisions by hospitals, which apparently don't understand that contractual indemnification provisions and hold-harmless clauses in PSAs and other agreements can easily eliminate the very insurance coverage the physician otherwise would have available, and which that physician was relying on to take care of any potential claims with the hospital.

VII. CONSIDER PLACING A NONSOLICITATION-OF-EMPLOYEE PROVISION IN THE PSA

To preserve the medical group structure, consider including a nonsolicitation clause in the PSA, so as to prevent the hiring hospital from soliciting or hiring the medical group's physicians (or perhaps other key staff personnel, if the hospital is directly employing the

---

[8]For a thoughtful discussion of indemnification and insurance requirements, see REPRESENTING PHYSICIANS HANDBOOK, ch. 11.2.10, at 525, and ch. 14.5.12, at 638–40.

same as part of the PSA) for a term of a few years after the agreement ends. Such a provision may keep medical group physicians from "jumping ship" to join the hospital, if that is a concern.

VIII. BUSINESS QUESTIONS NEEDING ANSWERS FOR THE PHYSICIAN OR PRACTICE

Some basic questions for the physician or the medical group to get answered before getting involved with a hospital on any long-term basis are discussed below.

Patient Assignment: How are the hospital's patients assigned to the physician? Are the patients "cherry picked" in terms of being less complicated to treat, having better insurance coverage, etc., before being assigned to the physician?

Market Position: Has the physician or group thoroughly evaluated the hospital's true position in the marketplace? How good is the support staff that the physician will need to rely on? How vulnerable is the hospital to competition from surrounding healthcare providers? Realistically, what are the hospital's short- and long-term financial prospects, particularly considering all the terms and conditions the hospital may want to impose on the physician or the group in terms of covenants not to compete? Does the physician or group risk struggling to get paid for amounts due, or having the hospital cut their client's pay when things don't work out as planned?

Hospital Administration: Has the hospital administration locked the hospital into unprofitable insurance contracts or health maintenance organization (HMO) agreements that will invariably trickle down to the physician or medical group? How does the hospital treat the physicians generally? Is the hospital run by physicians who have actually been in practice, or is it run by business management executives? Do other physicians have faith in the business administration of the hospital?

Compensation Arrangement: Is the physician's compensation based on billable services or amounts collected?[9] (Think about how much of today's payments for health services come from patients in the form of high deductibles and copayments, and how that might affect the physician's pocketbook if compensation were based on the actual amount of current collections.) What is the collection

---

[9]See Chapter 9 of this text. This is a critical compensation concept to understand.

success of the hospital compared to the group's success at collection? What is the population base supporting the service area in terms of long-term viability and economic health? What is the payor mix? How many patients are self-pay vs. private insurance vs. government payor? How much charitable work is expected? How does the amount of charitable work affect compensation?

Legal Due Diligence: Does the hospital pay its bills on time? How many lawsuits has the hospital been involved in, and what is the nature of the lawsuits? How many malpractice suits have been filed against the hospital? How does the hospital treat the physicians in those malpractice suits?

Technical Assistance: How much down time will there be in the transition from the practice's electronic health records (EHR) system to the hospital's EHR system? What type of and how much onsite information technology (IT) support will be provided at no charge? Who maintains the IT system?

Travel Time: How long will it take the physicians to travel from healthcare site to satellite healthcare site? How much physician productivity will be lost in drive time? What are the on-call coverage requirements, and how far away are the remote sites?

Credentialing Assistance: How long will it take for the physicians to be credentialed at each of the hospitals or clinics where they will be required to work? Will the hospital or clinic facilitate the credentialing process, since credentialing is often a political process as well as an administrative process?

Non-Revenue-Producing Administrative Work: How much time will be spent on administrative work, staff meetings, and the like, as opposed to revenue-producing patient care? How will the physician be credited for attending to the administrative and other non-revenue-producing work?

Payment Terms: How and when will the group be paid for its professional services and overhead reimbursement? Is it to be paid in advance each month based on estimated wRVUs or some other methodology? Paid in arrears? Obviously, being paid in arrears puts the group at a cash flow disadvantage.

Other Services: Will the practice manage or supervise a medical service line of the hospital and be paid a management fee? If so, of what will the management or supervision services consist, exactly? How will completion of the services be measured? What documentation will be required? And how and when will the practice get paid for such services?

Income Assurances: What assurances do hospital-affiliated physicians have that the hospital will not agree to short- or long-term contracts with payors that have a strong possibility of losing money, just to stay competitive, or agree to contracts that are "front loaded discount contracts" in the hopes of making up early losses on later volume? What assurances do the physician or group have that the hospital will not agree to contracts that affect the physician disproportionately as compared to the hospital? By analogy, how will the physician look when the hospital agrees to take a financial haircut amounting to a one quarter inch trim, while the physician must take a full buzz cut? How does that haircut option sound to your client when it is thought about in that way? It could happen, unless there is a protective measure included in the agreement to the effect that the physician either (1) will not suffer disproportionately as compared to the hospital or any other physician, or (2) is not required to participate in that particular contract at such discounted rate, or (3) can walk away from the PSA and not trigger any of the restrictive covenants. The same is true for "bundled" or "discounted fee" agreements where physicians are expected to accept a bundled or discounted fee rate that may be proportionately greater than the rate that the hospital agrees to take, and where the physician cannot afford to perform the service or accept the liability for the service for the rate negotiated by the hospital.

The Solution: Knowledgeable physicians who actually perform the procedures and have experience with complicated patients and procedures must be at the table when the hospital is negotiating compensation agreements with the public and with private insurance companies. Something is very wrong with a system when business managers who know little or nothing about what actually happens in the operating room or the practice environment make financial and business decisions without knowledgeable physician involvement.

IX. OTHER CONTRACT CONSIDERATIONS

Consider a clause in the PSA that requires the hospital to use its best commercial efforts to ensure that the physician or group is immediately included in all the managed care network panels or contracts with which the hospital participates, since managed care companies may limit or close their panels to physician participants.[10] It doesn't do any good for the physician to have a PSA with the hospital, but not be included in all of the hospital's managed care arrangements, insurance panels, and other networks. Some networks are limited, so it is important to get your physician clients included into the network "pool" by the hospital as soon as possible.

X. INITIAL TERM

Because of the length of time needed to negotiate a PSA, the initial terms of PSAs vary considerably, averaging approximately five years for more complicated business arrangements. Every situation is different, depending on the immediate need of the hospital, the size of the medical group, and whether an exclusive arrangement is being contemplated. Small medical groups (fewer than five physicians) with nonexclusive arrangements tend to have shorter initial terms (two to three years) with shorter renewal periods. Larger groups (more than 25 physicians) with exclusive arrangements tend to have longer initial terms and longer renewal periods, and particularly so when groups have 100 or more physicians. The length of the initial contract period varies depending on the service contracted for; the size, location, and market value of the hospital; the specific need of the hospital; the size, reputation, and strategic importance of the medical group; whether the medical group is a specialty group or a subspecialty or multispecialty group; where the hospital or other healthcare entity is located; whether the hospital is located in a rural or urban community or an underserved area; and so forth.

XI. TERMINATION PROVISIONS

Probably the hardest thing for counsel to do is to get their physician clients to focus on employment termination scenarios, such as what will happen if things don't work out as planned during the term of the PSA. Like most clients, physicians think they are special and an exception to the rule—until they're not—and then they will be back in your office complaining about how they didn't understand

---

[10]See Chapter 9 of this text.

the ramifications of the contract. Your job is to make it clear what will happen in the event of a nonrenewal, an early termination, or a material breach of the PSA.

There is too much rapid change occurring in healthcare delivery organizations for anyone to be so naive as to think hospitals (and physicians) are not going to rely on their contracts to get out of unprofitable agreements. They are. The client may not want to believe the PSA won't be renewed, or that the hospital would terminate the PSA "without cause" or invoke the noncompete clauses. But if the client physicians talked candidly to their physician counterparts, they would find out that this is exactly what is happening, as hospitals try to reduce costs and hurt their competition.

Hospitals are being bought and sold frequently.[11] In the event of a merger or acquisition, the PSA physician could become a "surplus" physician in no time. Counsel needs to thoroughly explain to the physician client the various ways the PSA could be terminated, and what the effect of that termination would be to the physician.[12]

XII. IMPORTANCE OF NONASSIGNMENT AND CHANGE-OF-CONTROL CLAUSES

When considering the hundreds of mergers and acquisitions of healthcare entities occurring annually, which are largely kept "secret" until concluded or called off, physicians may unhappily find themselves in the awkward situation of having their PSA contract assigned to or acquired by a competing hospital system—where a competing physician group is already fully ensconced, and which certainly does not have your client's best interest at heart. This is exactly why counsel for the physician *must* insist upon a nonassignment clause (prohibiting assignment of the PSA without the physician's express written consent) and a change-of-control clause in any PSA.

Why? Because these events changing control are happening all the time, and the impact is twofold. One, if the hospital is acquired by an entity in the geographic area that is the same size or larger than the hospital with which the PSA physician has contracted, then

---

[11]*Modern Healthcare* magazine carries stories each week about the latest acquisitions.

[12]See also Chapter 9 of this text.

the amount of business the PSA physician had counted on when entering into the PSA (and accepted the compensation rate based thereon) will likely be reduced, because the cost savings expected by the newly combined entities will undoubtedly include eliminating the PSA physician(s). Two, the larger entity normally has its own favorite physician group employed by (and threatened by) the presence of the competing PSA physician group.

Also, seriously consider including a termination clause that permits the physician(s) to terminate the PSA in the event of any merger, consolidation, or change of control of the hospital. (See sample clause below for ideas.) At the end of the day, if a change of control occurs, the party with which the physicians initially contracted has changed, and the new party may or may not be acceptable to the physicians. Whether or not to continue performing the contract with that new party should be the physicians' choice, since the physicians are the professionals performing the professional services for whomever that new party happens to be. The termination provisions should include negotiated payment provisions through the date of termination or PSA date expiration, whichever is later (and any attendant collection period of revenues for the professional medical services, if collections are any part of the basis of physician's compensation formula).

Merger and acquisitions in healthcare are occurring so very often that physicians must recognize that this type of situation can turn financial assumptions upside down. That is not the scenario that the physicians bargained for when going into the business relationship with the hiring entity. Counsel needs to help the physician client(s) think carefully about that situation, because it is not a farfetched scenario. *Also make sure to add a provision that any covenants not to compete shall not apply in this situation, since the change of control occurrence was through no fault of the physician.*

> ***Sample Clause:*** Change of Control / No Application of Restrictive Covenants Provision.
> The Physician/Group may terminate this Agreement upon occurrence of a Change of Control of Hospital. "Change of Control" means the sale or transfer of all or substantially all the assets of Hospital, however accomplished, including, without limitation, by merger, consolidation, or acquisition of Hospital, with, by or into another corporation, entity or person, or any

change in the ownership of more than fifty percent (50%) of the voting capital stock of Hospital or any of its parent companies in one or more related transactions. Upon the Change of Control, Physician shall have the right to terminate the Agreement upon 30 calendar days written notice, and upon such notice of termination physician shall be entitled to full compensation through the date of termination and shall be entitled to receive an additional sum equal to [___ % of the monthly base salary that Physician would have received for the remainder of the term of the Agreement had Physician continued employment for the full term of the Agreement or ___ times the last ___months compensation]. This additional sum shall be paid to Physician in a lump sum. These amounts shall be paid within 30 days of Physician's termination notice provided under this paragraph ___.

Furthermore the restrictive covenants described in Paragraphs ____ shall not apply in the event Physician/Group exercises his/her right to terminate the Agreement by reason of a Change of Control.

XIII. RENEWAL TERMS

Renewal terms for PSAs are normally two to five years, depending on the initial term of the base agreement, and depending largely on the physician's contract performance, negotiation leverage, and the hospital's administration turnover. During renewal term discussions, the hospital will focus largely on reducing the physician's compensation, which is why it is critically important for counsel for the physician or medical group to have fixed the compensation terms in the initial contract for as long a period as possible, and also *to include a "walk away" provision* as described in the next section.

XIV. REVIEW OF COMPENSATION PROVISION / NO COVENANT NOT TO COMPETE TRIGGERS

It is essential for counsel for the physician or the medical group to include a provision in the initial PSA or any renewal PSA that provides that if the parties are unable to agree to an acceptable compensation formula at the time of renewal, or any time during the contract when compensation is reviewed, and particularly if the hospital is suggesting a decrease in compensation from the initial (or latest renewal) term, the physician has the right to walk away and terminate the agreement, *and any covenant not to compete shall not apply.* That is critical.

> ***Sample Clause:*** Review of Compensation Provision/Walk Away Rights.
> The compensation hereunder may be reviewed by the parties on an [annual / 24-month] basis and, based upon such review; either party may propose an adjustment to such compensation. If, after sixty (60) calendar days of good-faith negotiations, the parties are not able to agree upon an adjusted compensation amount, either party may terminate the Agreement by giving the other party sixty (60) calendar days prior written notice. If the parties agree to such adjustment, the parties shall either amend this Agreement or terminate this Agreement and enter into a new agreement, as allowed by applicable law, with such amendment or new agreement to reflect the necessary adjustments to the compensation and other terms and conditions as agreed upon in writing by the parties. In any event, if the parties are unable to reach agreement on compensation after the above described 60 calendar days, then the agreement shall terminate, *however the restrictive covenants set forth in [Paragraph(s) __ Identify all relevant provisions___] shall not apply.*

Initially, the hospital will be reluctant to agree to such provisions, as they will argue they have to pay fair market value (FMV) as required by the Centers for Medicare and Medicaid Services (CMS), and if CMS or the insurance companies are reducing reimbursements, then the hospital also has to reduce compensation to physicians, and the physicians will just have to live with it, etc. Counsel must remind the hospital that the physician client is not the one making the (poor) hospital services arrangements with the insurance networks. Actually the physician is the one on the receiving end of those poor arrangements. The physician is the one delivering healthcare to the sick patients and their families day in and day out, and answering their endless questions and educating and consoling them. The executives are not doing so. Furthermore, the physician is not getting paid the hospital executive salaries, nor does the physician enjoy the hospital executive work hours or other executive perks. This applies particularly to hospital CEOs, who, incidentally, approve the (poor) reimbursement deals. CEOs have an average turnover rate of 20 percent per year[13] and, in many cases, are paid handsomely to leave.

It is the role of counsel for the physician to remind the hospital that there is a physician shortage, and physicians are a vital, highly skilled and sought after resource that deserves consideration and respect. They are the ones who need to be paid fairly, which does not include pay cuts. When no one else knows what to do, it is the physician who is called at 2:00 a.m. to admit patients, answer questions about patients, or go into the hospital to take care of sick patients. And then she or he will be expected to start another full day at 6:00 a.m., on little sleep, and to be "friendly" and "engaged" so as to score a perfect "patient satisfaction score," so as to get their "quality metrics" boxes checked.

Without physicians, healthcare delivery stops. And, since there is a physician shortage,[14] the fair market value of physician professional services, if anything, should go up, not down. That is where advice of an experienced health law transactions attorney is key. FMV depends on the region of the country, the specialty, and the efficiency of the physicians you represent, among many other factors. A professional who knows whom to contact to find the right economic information and data to counter the hospital's *"fair"* market value compensation point of view with respect to your client's professional services is fundamental. FMV information is available through sources such as the Medical Group Management Association, and there are other resources as well.[15]

XV. REJECT ANY COVENANT NOT TO COMPETE; INSTEAD, OFFER COMPROMISE TERMS

Counsel for the physician must use his or her best efforts to reject the inclusion of a "covenant not to compete" clause, regardless of the time period of the restriction, to avoid harming the client's future employment opportunities. In a quickly increasing number

---

[13]Paul H. Keckley, Ph.D., Navigant Healthcare (July 27, 2015), http://www.paulkeckley.com.

[14]See discussion in Chapters 1 and 2 of this text.

[15]MEDICAL GROUP MANAGEMENT ASSOCIATION, http://www.mgma.com/industry-data/mgma-surveys-reports.

of states, contracts containing covenants not to compete involving physicians are unlawful and unenforceable except in limited circumstances (e.g., the sale of the physician's medical practice). See Chapter 10 of this text for a more extensive discussion and see the Appendix for relevant state statutes and case citations.

Interestingly, restrictive covenants may also jeopardize the hospital's tax treatment of independent contractors' 1099 relationships (for both IRS and Labor Department purposes). Restrictive covenants show "employer like" control, as opposed to "independent contractor like" relationships, because they dictate the physician's or the medical group's future employment opportunities. Conceptually, an independent contractor should be independent. An independent contractor should be free to do business with multiple hospitals. Noncompete agreements specifically restrain the ability for independent contractors to do business with other parties, and that is completely contrary to the identity of an independent contractor compared to that of an employee.

Counsel should be sure to carve out any application of a covenant not to compete in an instance where the PSA is terminated due to the hospital's material breach of the agreement or if the hospital terminates the physician "without cause." Such language should be rejected on the grounds that it is just plain unfair (and in many states, unenforceable as a matter of public policy), especially in cases where the physician's compensation is sought to be reduced or in the event of an unacceptable change of control of the hospital. These are events that penalize the physician for events over which the physician has no control.

As alternatives to a noncompete clause, counsel should suggest signing a reasonable nondisclosure agreement, as well as an agreement for nonsolicitation of hospital employees, patients, or referral sources (in states where they are lawful).

As a last resort, counsel might consider, in lieu of a noncompete clause, a "most favored customer" clause, whereby the physician agrees to refrain from providing the *exact* same medical services (in the *exact* same quantities and under the *exact* same terms and conditions) at a *lesser rate* to nonaligned (i.e., competitor) hospitals located within a very tightly defined geographical area, for a very limited time period, but with no ability of the hospital to see or verify the terms of the future agreement with the future competitor hospital.[16] The former hospital can ask for some type of certification from the physician, but it can't obtain or verify the documents from the so-called competitors (i.e., future physician customers). This is not a recommended option because it can "open up a can of worms." But if it is limited as to time and geographic scope, having such a clause is better than having a noncompete clause, from the physician's standpoint, because at least the physician can do business with nonaligned hospitals.

XVI. PHYSICIAN "FOR CAUSE" TERMINATION TRIGGERS

Termination provisions found in most PSAs are long on termination provisions favoring the hospital and short on termination provisions favoring the physician or medical group. Here are some physician- or physician group–side termination "for cause" triggers to be considered. If the PSA is with a hospital subsidiary, all triggers must extend to the parent hospital.

Sample Clauses:
Termination with Cause. Physician shall have the right to terminate this Agreement with cause if the Hospital defaults on or breaches any of the terms of this Agreement and fails to cure such default or breach within ten (10) calendar days of the giving of written notice by the Physician specifying such default or breach. This paragraph only relates to independent causes of default or breach and is not intended to provide for a cure period for any of the rest of the causes described below.

---

[16]For counsel unfamiliar with antitrust law, it would be advisable to have any such provision reviewed by antitrust counsel, so as to make sure such a clause is styled as a "most favored nations/most favored customer" contract provision. Make sure the provision relates to the totality of all the services the physician would be providing the other hospitals, including the time period, so that the clause would only be triggered if the physician was providing another "customer" the *exact* same services, the exact same quantities of services, under the same terms and conditions, including the same quality parameters, same payment terms, same billing and collection arrangements, same nature and scope of liabilities and indemnities, same malpractice insurance requirements, same contract term, same termination provisions, all as previously provided by the physician to the original hospital, etc. All of these comparative details are impossible to match, which is why these clauses are hard to trigger unless the contracts are public contracts. For obvious reasons, the hospital cannot be granted any right to examine the proprietary contract your client may obtain with the future customer or competitor hospital, or otherwise verify the terms of any contract the physician may enter into.

Immediate Termination. Physician may terminate this Agreement immediately upon the occurrence of any of the following:
- Hospital licensure, certification or accreditation is revoked, terminated, limited, conditioned, suspended, not renewed, or restricted in any way
- Hospital's exclusion, revocation, termination, suspension, or other ineligibility from participation in Medicare, Medicaid, or any other federal or state governmental program providing compensation for medical services rendered to patients
- Failure of physician to be included in Hospital's payor networks, Hospital HMO plans, or other third-party group plans for physician professional services through no fault of Physician
- Hospital's or any Hospital parent company's bankruptcy, receivership, or reorganization
- Hospital undergoes a Change of Control [See Section XII of this chapter, above.]
- Hospital's assignment of the PSA without Physician's written consent
- The parties' inability to agree on acceptable compensation when compensation is reviewed under the terms of paragraph [insert appropriate contract provision] hereof. See Section XIV of this chapter, above.]
  [or]
- Negative change in compensation or reimbursement rate for any of the professional services covered by the PSA.

XVII. UNWIND PROVISIONS

At some point the PSA will come to an end, whether by termination or expiration. Therefore, counsel for the physician or group contemplating a PSA arrangement should make sure that there are thoughtfully considered "unwind" provisions in the PSA, to permit the physician or group to be in a position to resume or restructure their private practice without unnecessary downtime.

Unwind provisions should permit the physician or group to re-acquire any practice assets that they sold or leased to the hospital (including phone numbers, office space, office staff, patient records, and office equipment that still meets the needs of the practice) or, to the extent new equipment has been purchased by the hospital and now is used by the group at the practice site, to purchase such equipment at fair market value. Hopefully, the group has been able to keep up its practice entity's taxpayer identification number by processing a minimum number of claims for Medicare, Medicaid, and private payors, so that the physicians don't lose their CMS provider credentialing through the practice entity. If not, then the physicians will have to check and most likely go through the credentialing process again with CMS and all the insurers, and that could take months. With CMS there are ways that an experienced office administrator can work around the problem and get things expedited, so the physicians don't suffer a cash flow issue due to not being able to properly bill and receive payment for their services immediately upon unwind.

> *Tip:* If the hospital has purchased an expensive electronic health records (EHR) system, the physician or group might or might not want to purchase or lease that system from the hospital upon PSA termination. Therefore, counsel should consider making reacquisition of that type of system optional.

XVIII. LOOKING FORWARD

These are exciting times in the healthcare delivery world. There are creative opportunities for physicians and hospitals to work together without having an employer–employee relationship, unless that's what they want. Moreover, the relationship does not have to be an oppressive or punishing one for the physician in terms of pay, liability, or post-contract restrictive covenants. There are creative ways that contracts can be tailored to fairly suit the needs of the physician and the hospital.

Prudent counsel will be aware of the coming collision of two key demographic trends: the ballooning "baby boomer" generation's healthcare requirements, versus the decreasing number of physicians who are available and prepared to treat them and all the rest of the patient population.

Our best suggestion is for the general practice attorney to seek out experienced health law transactions attorneys to make sure both physician and hospital parties to contracts start and stay on the right track, given the number of federal and state rules and regulations related to antitrust, healthcare, and insurance that may (or may not, depending on the factual circumstances) apply to the arrangement being considered. Some contractual arrangements are simple and may appear to require little review by an experienced healthcare attorney (e.g., the physician group limited to on-call weekend coverage arrangements). However, because of federal laws discussed in Chapter 25 of this text, even limited on-call weekend coverage arrangements have brought a number of hospitals and physicians into serious legal trouble.[17] Other contractual arrangements are quite sophisticated (e.g., multi-year, multi-hospital exclusive provider arrangements with multiple renewal options). These obviously may require more detailed and expert advice and guidance, depending on the number of similar transactions the particular attorney or firm has handled in the past.

More generally, the reader who is a generalist in the field of healthcare law should recognize the "minefield" problem of drafting the very detailed set of contractual terms that will meet your physician client's needs. A friendly, positive, long-term relationship with a specialist healthcare transactional lawyer will be very helpful to your client's long-term protection. The ability to call informally and ask the "what if" and "what works" questions is enormously valuable to the generalist attorney. Consider it money well spent so that none of the "mines" in this legal minefield explode under your client's feet as the client performs life-saving surgeries or prevention-based counseling. Your legal malpractice insurance carrier and all of those who depend on your counsel expect that you will know when to get specialist advice for these specialized and difficult topics. Consider this book a starting point for these very crucial professional challenges.

---

[17]On-call agreements and medical-director agreements may create a financial relationship for purposes of the Stark Law or Anti-Kickback Statute because hospitals typically enter into such agreements with physicians who are a referral source. See Chapter 25 of this text for further discussion of these laws. For example, if a physician has a contract to be a paid on-call physician or a paid medical director for a hospital, that creates a financial relationship between the physician and the hospital for the purposes of the Stark Law. And from an Anti-Kickback Statute perspective, it can easily look like a way to provide additional money to a physician to induce the physician to refer Medicare business to the hospital. There are three Office of Inspector General (OIG) advisory opinions that are instructive and provide guidance as to how to structure such contracts. OIG Adv. Op. No. 07-10 (Sept. 20, 2007); OIG Adv. Op. No. 09-05 (May 14, 2009); OIG Adv. Op. No. 12-15 (Oct. 23, 2012).

XIX. TELEMEDICINE

The introduction of telemedicine has invited new scrutiny of the definitions of the practice of medicine and healthcare. Telemedicine is the use of technology to undertake activity constituting the practice of medicine when the healthcare provider and patient are not in the same physical location. There is no single definition of telemedicine. Indeed, a 2007 World Health Organization study had found 107 definitions in peer-reviewed publications.[18] In this growing field, the definitions are changing alongside the rapid evolution of technology.

The American Telemedicine Association uses a definition that is as broad as the information network at the physician's disposal, including email, telephone, and fax: *"[T]he use of medical information exchanged from one site to another via electronic communications to improve a patient's clinical health status. Telemedicine includes a growing variety of applications and services using two-way video, email, smart phones, wireless tools and other forms of telecommunications technology."*[19]

The legal definition of telemedicine in the U.S. varies based on the location of the act and the governmental agencies that have authority to regulate the act. The definitions are crucial for legal counsel in advising physicians because they describe, specifically and by implication, what a physician can and cannot do across state lines without having a license to practice medicine in that jurisdiction.[20] For example, CMS defines telemedicine to include two-way, real-time interactive communication between the patient and distant-site physician,[21] but not communication via telephone, email, or fax.[22]

Many state laws follow CMS's lead in this definition of telemedicine for the purposes of state Medicaid participation, but other state law definitions of telemedicine include telephone calls, emails,

---

[18]WORLD HEALTH ORG., TELEMEDICINE: OPPORTUNITIES AND DEVELOPMENTS IN MEMBER STATES: REPORT ON THE SECOND GLOBAL SURVEY ON EHEALTH 8 (2010).

[19]American Telemedicine Ass'n, www.americantelemed.org.

[20]A very useful comparative chart compiled by state licensure agencies can be found on the website of the Federation of State Medical Boards (FSMB) at http://www.fsmb.org/Media/Default/PDF/FSMB/Advocacy/Agency%20Jurisdiction%20Chart--Internet.pdf.

[21]CMS, Telehealth Services (Nov. 2016), https://www.cms.gov/Outreach-and-Education/Medicare-Learning-Network-MLN/MLNProducts/downloads/TelehealthSrvcsfctsht.pdf.

[22]CMS, Next Generation ACO Model Telehealth Waiver (May 2017), https://innovation.cms.gov/Files/x/nextgenaco-telehealthwaiver.pdf.

or faxes. The definition of telemedicine can even vary within a given state, depending on the regulatory authority or purpose of the particular law in question, such as medical licensure, pharmaceuticals, private health insurance, or rural utilities services. To further complicate the issue, telemedicine laws and regulations do not always explicitly refer to "telemedicine" and may use other words, such as "telehealth," "practicing medicine across state lines," or "practicing medicine by electronic means," to name a few.[23]

Any physician or medical group interested in a telemedicine practice should be aware of their "duty of care"[24] under state healthcare practitioner licensing statutes or regulations, which may create heightened licensing or practice requirements for each jurisdiction that the physician seeks to reach through telemedicine.[25] Physicians should be aware of not only any additional permits or licenses that may be required by a given state, but also the additional practice requirements that may be imposed on any physician who uses telemedicine within the state or reaches into the state through telemedicine. Physicians should also be aware of any additional licensing or practice requirements on those healthcare practitioners whom they supervise in relation to a telemedicine activity.

States have developed their medical licensing laws independently of one another, and the lack of state consistency in regulating the practice of medicine presents a significant barrier to any multistate telemedicine program.[26] One of the initial questions when thinking about a telemedicine practice is whether a license to practice medicine is required in each state. Some states explicitly address telemedicine in their state medical licensing laws and define the practice of telemedicine to include telemedicine that reaches into their state. Some states indirectly address telemedicine by including the act of diagnosing or recommending treatment through any "electronic" means in the practice of medicine in their state. Other states use broader language such as "by any means or instrumentality" to implicitly subject out-of-state telemedicine physicians to their medical licensing laws. Still other states do not address telemedicine, directly or indirectly, in their state physician licensing statutes or regulations. Even for those states that do not directly or

[23]FSMB.org.
[24]*See* White v. Harris, 190 Vt. 647, 36 A.3d 203 (2011).
[25]FSMB.org.
[26]*Id.*

indirectly address telemedicine in their medical licensing laws or define the location of the practice of medicine, it is generally assumed that any act of diagnosing or recommending treatment constitutes the practice of medicine in the state where the patient is located for the purpose of medical licensing and falls within the state's interest in protecting public health. The Federation of State Medical Boards has the best current charts of legal obligations on its website.[27]

All state physician licensing boards explicitly require a license granted by the board to practice medicine in their state. In the absence of licensure exceptions for telemedicine, each state medical board would likely require a physician to obtain a license to practice medicine in their state before allowing the physician to provide telemedicine services to a patient physically located in their state. Physicians should reconsider their medical licensing law coverages even when they only seek to provide telemedicine services within their licensed state. This is because many states have special telemedicine licensing or permitting requirements for currently-licensed physicians seeking to commence telemedicine activities within the state.

It is important to review the statutes and administrative codes for each state where your client may want to practice electronically. Obtaining valid licenses to practice medicine can be expensive, time consuming, and burdensome. The healthcare provider will be subject to multiple state medical boards, statutes, and regulations whenever they participate in out-of-state licensing processes or exceptions.[28]

Another alternative to obtaining licenses in multiple states is the common exception for out-of-state doctors. Some states follow Alaska, where medical licensing boards offer a consultation exception for those physicians who are licensed in another state.

Telemedicine activities often are intertwined with technologies providing pharmaceutical prescribing and dispensing. Many state and federal regulations and enforcement efforts have been aimed at telepharmacies, and each year more laws are passed. The regulations relate to informed consent, medical records, credentialing and regulating telemedicine licenses, standard of care, transmitting orders for medicines, and contractual arrangements. The federal government has enacted requirements concerning the reimbursement to

---

[27]FSMB.org.
[28]*See generally* FSMB.org.

the distant site practitioner if the services are provided to a Medicare patient at an acceptable site.[29]

Minimum requirements will apply for physicians who use physician practice websites, Internet advertising, or email for patient communications. For example, physicians who use email for patient communications must have periodically evaluated policies for email management, processing, responses, privacy, archiving, and hours of operation. Physician-practice websites must include numerous disclosures, such as website ownership, in-office contact information, licensure and qualifications of affiliated physicians and healthcare professionals, complaint and feedback processes, and disclosure of any financial interest the physicians may have in any products or services discussed or advertised on the website.

Existing state malpractice case law, tort law, and civil procedure govern telemedicine malpractice issues not directly addressed by a specific telemedicine statute or case.[30] The standard of care to which the physician's actions is compared to determine negligence is not always clear, even in traditional medical encounters. Some courts prefer using a local or community standard of care, while others use a national standard of care.

In addition to pre-existing standards of care based on the type of physician or disorder being treated, states and private organizations have taken proactive steps to create standards of care specific to telemedicine encounters. For example, some states have created telemedicine-specific informed consent standards, privacy standards, and general telemedicine standards of care. This may create an additional, heightened standard of care to which the physician's actions might be compared in a telemedicine malpractice case.[31] Controlled substances prescribing rules apply under Drug Enforcement Administration (DEA) requirements.[32] Finally, professional healthcare and technology organizations and the U.S. Food and Drug Administration (FDA) have published standards and

---

[29]CMS, Telehealth Services (Nov. 2016), https://www.cms.gov/Outreach-and-Education/Medicare-Learning-Network-MLN/MLNProducts/downloads/TelehealthSrvcsfctsht.pdf.

[30]*See* JAMES O'REILLY & MICHELLE YOUNG, MEDICAL MALPRACTICE, ch.7 (ABA Press 2014).

[31]*Medical Malpractice and Liability*, TELEHEALTH RESOURCE CENTERS, http://www.telehealthresourcecenter.org/toolbox-module/medical-malpractice-and-liability.

[32]21 C.F.R. §1300.04.

guidelines for various aspects of telemedicine that are good reference material to review on the standard of care for telemedicine.

Of course, traditional rules on joint and several liability will apply to telemedicine encounters in which more than one physician is involved and is found to be responsible for an indivisible injury to a patient during a single encounter.[33] However, it would be better for the physicians involved in the telemedicine encounter to communicate their respective responsibilities at the outset rather than waiting for something to go unattended and result in a jury's determination of who was responsible. In addition to negligence, once the relationship is established, physicians can be held liable for patient abandonment if the physician unilaterally severs the relationship with the patient without reasonable notice or without providing adequate alternative medical care at a time when there is a necessity of continuing medical attention. Telemedicine encounters are often one-time encounters for a specific purpose. Failed communication between the consulting or referring physician's role in the ongoing care of the patient could result in an unintentional patient abandonment case, in which both physicians assumed that the other was responsible for the ongoing care of the patient.

Again, communication at the outset could prevent these unnecessary risks that arise in telemedicine. Thus, counsel should identify the range of risks presented by the particular telemedicine activity and preempt these issues by developing processes to ensure continuity of care, coordination of care, creation and termination of the physician-patient relationship, and ultimate responsibility over the patient among multiple healthcare providers and facilities.[34]

Telemedicine is challenging the tradition of independent state control over medical malpractice.[35] States have significant variances in statutory and common law authority governing the elements of medical malpractice, including standards of care, statutes of limitations, informed consent requirements, arbitration requirements, burden of proof, joint and comparative liability, immunity, and

---

[33]See MEDICAL MALPRACTICE, ch. 7.

[34]Tara Kepler & Charlene L. McGinty, *Telemedicine: How to Assess Your Risks and Develop a Program That Works*, PHYSICIANS & JUDICIAL ORGS. L. INST., AM. HEALTH LAW. ASS'N (Feb. 2009),

[35]See AMERICAN TELEMEDICINE ASS'N, http://www.americantelemed.org.

damage caps. The Federation of State Medical Boards has a useful compilation.[36]

Another issue to consider is whether the physician's malpractice insurance covers multi-state telemedicine encounters. Insurance policies vary from state to state, and some policies may only cover malpractice claims in the state in which the physician is licensed to practice, even though the physician may qualify for an exception to practice medicine in the state without a license. Malpractice insurance policies should be examined to determine if multi-state telemedicine encounters are directly addressed, or if additional coverage is necessary. Counsel should first identify the possible states where the specific telemedicine is practiced, and then review the similarities and differences in medical malpractice law for the identified states. These variances allow for increased attention to potential telemedicine claims and the need for heightened risk management.[37]

The intensity of regulatory control for telemedicine practices within a state and throughout different states is increasing daily.[38] CMS reimbursement issues are also evolving rapidly.[39] Besides considering licensure requirements for each state in which the physician is involved, there are ethical guidelines applicable to the physician's activities. There are many new areas of regulation, conflicts, and legal principles about which attorneys must become knowledgeable and advise their clients. These issues go beyond conventional employment counseling and require counsel to be continuing learners.

---

[36]See the FSMB website at http://www.fsmb.org/Media/Default/PDF/FSMB/Advocacy/Agency%20Jurisdiction%20Chart--Internet.pdf.

[37]See generally MEDICAL MALPRACTICE.

[38]See AMERICAN TELEMEDICINE ASS'N, http://www.americantelemed.org.

[39]CMS, Telehealth Services (Nov. 2016), https://www.cms.gov/Outreach-and-Education/Medicare-Learning-Network-MLN/MLNProducts/downloads/TelehealthSrvcsfctsht.pdf.

CHAPTER 9

PHYSICIAN EMPLOYMENT CONTRACTS

I. Introduction

The proper time to think about protecting your physician client's future is *before* the draft employment agreement ever lands in your inbox. Without question, the employment agreement is the most important document defining the relationship between the physician and the employer, and it will definitely impact how the physician is treated by the employer during the period of employment. The employment agreement is not something to be taken lightly. That message of urgency, and importance of attention to each detail of the agreement, must be clearly communicated to your physician client.

We urge you to use this chapter as the starting point, from which further inquiry will be required, to gain a greater understanding of the legal issues that physician clients face when negotiating employment contracts, and to be ready to provide guidance and support as they face professional challenges and opportunities from day to day.

II. WHO DO YOU REPRESENT?

Counsel must make clear who it is that counsel represents such as in the case of a medical group practice sale, where the group is then entering into an employment agreement with the acquiring hospital or staffing company or medical group. There are inherent conflicts of interest among the group physicians for the simple reason that their various ages, economic vulnerabilities, and risk appetites vary from individual to individual, and each of the physicians' goals are different when it comes to employment. The best advice is that each physician obtain his or her own experienced physician employment attorney. The need for specialized advising arises because there will most likely be "buy back" provisions of the practice at the end of the employment agreement term, if the group doesn't renew the employment agreement, as well as other issues such as termination provisions, restrictive covenants, exclusive arrangements, etc., that affect each of the physicians differently, depending on the physician's personal circumstances.

III. NECESSITY OF OBTAINING PHYSICIAN EMPLOYMENT CONTRACT ADVICE

Physician employment contracts are not like other high-end professional employment contracts. There are health law regulations that don't arise in other types of employment contracts. The message of experience is clear: there is a very high return on investment for each acquired physician in a group, and each should have their employment contract separately reviewed by and receiving advice from a health law attorney who is experienced in physician employment contracts. It is critical to the success of the physician's employment experience. If a physician retains a general practice attorney, or any attorney who does not practice specifically in the area of representing physicians in employment contract matters, the physician is not consulting the best qualified professional for the issues presented. Counsel should be certain to consult such an attorney for guidance.

IV. DUE DILIGENCE ON THE EMPLOYER IS AN ABSOLUTE MUST

To avoid a potential professional dead end—or an unhappy professional detour—the physician should do serious due diligence regarding the potential employer before entering into any type of employment agreement.

As this text has discussed, there is a physician shortage. According to a recent Merritt Hawkins survey, 46 percent of 2015 final-year medical residents received *over* 100 contacts from recruiters during their residency training, while another 17 percent received 50–100 contacts from recruiters during the same time period.[1] So, we can safely say that U.S. residency trained physicians are in demand. And how much more so will be those physicians with valuable experience?

Since it's the physician's professional life under consideration, he or she needs to get his or her professional practice setting right, and not be afraid to ask reasonable questions to be able to sort through the list of potential employers quickly.

Some basic due diligence questions that physicians might initially ask of potential employers and then follow up on can be found in Chapter 8 of this text, in the context of an independent contractor–hospital relationship, but it is really the same type of questioning when it comes to any type of physician-employment relationship. A business attorney would find such preliminary questions second nature. However, the reality is that physicians are trained in the sciences of healing, and are not trained in business or law, so they don't know what questions to ask, and they ultimately end up paying the price.

Fortunately there are outstanding guides available on the American Medical Association's website, where a physician can easily access exceptionally instructive information at a reduced rate for AMA members. Another valuable resource is an experienced health law physician employment attorney who are plugged into the

---

[1] Merritt Hawkins, 2015 Survey of Final Year Medical Residents, www.merritthawkins.com.

local physician healthcare market, in the geographic area where the physician is interested in practicing or has received an offer. These local experts can also provide invaluable information on local hospital and university employers and major medical groups.

V. BEWARE "GOTCHA" CLAUSES IN EMPLOYMENT CONTRACTS

Before compensation matters are finally agreed upon, urge your client to explore the specifics of what the clauses in their employment contract will mean. Beware a common mistake by the eager doctor who likes the site and likes the people during their visit. *Counsel must warn the physician repeatedly not to sign any type of agreement with the following types of "gotcha" clauses—or in any way to indicate that such a clause "sounds OK" or "sounds reasonable"*:

- Termination of employment "without cause"
- Post-employment restrictive covenants (the worst being covenants not to compete)
- "Clean sweeps" provisions , where the physician automatically loses hospital privileges when employment ends, even when employment ends "without cause"
- Compensation methods that require repayment of compensation by the physician
- Compensation methods based on amounts collected instead of billable services
- Termination clauses that require the physician to pay for malpractice tail insurance
- Unspecified on-call obligations
- Unspecified or unlimited administrative and "quality" chores
- One-way indemnity and hold harmless provisions, only in the employer's favor
- Unspecified medical records access after end of employment

These "gotcha" clauses are usually sprung on the physician at the last minute, in the form of a draft employment contract, after the physician has lost most of his or her negotiating leverage. Flush out these "gotcha" clauses early, before any verbal acceptance, letter of intent, or draft contract is issued. Explain the significance of the "gotcha" clauses to the physician *before* the physician loses his or her bargaining power. Emphasize that accepting one of the "gotcha clauses" will have bad long-term consequences for the physician. Tell the physician to simply note down the information or get it in email form, say "that's a concern for me" or "that's an issue," and move on with the rest of the visit. *But do not finally negotiate compensation—even in a letter of intent—until the "gotcha" clauses are closed out!*

- **Covenants not to compete.** Get the specifics as to how long they last, how wide a geographic area they cover, and exactly what scope of medical practice they prohibit. Your client needs exact specifics, not human resource fluffy answers. The answers from the employer may very well be a nonstarter on any number of fronts, in which case the physician should move on to the next employment opportunity. Virtually every employer will say "don't worry, we never enforce these clauses" or "we only put these clauses in to make the doctors think twice." Don't believe it. Make sure any exceptions the employer promises to such clauses are made in writing.

  To begin with, a covenant not to compete is not enforceable in many states although it is found in physician employment agreements anyway (see Chapter 10). Second, in any event, make sure there is a carve out in the event of a layoff, or a merger with another healthcare entity, or if the physician terminates the agreement for that employer's material breach (e.g., the employer doesn't pay its bills on time (not uncommon)), or if the physician is terminated without cause, or the situation does not work out through no fault of the physician, or the physician and the employer are unable to come to an acceptable renewal contract at the end of the contract period (which happens more and more frequently, since more employers are trying to reduce employee salaries to reduce healthcare costs). The physician must have all those situations carved out of any such proposed covenant not to compete. Get all these exceptions in writing, along with the other "gotcha" clause modifications, before the physician agrees on any compensation or agrees on any draft letter of intent.

  With respect to covenants not to compete, see the extended discussion in Chapter 10 of this text. The client physician may agree that she or he would consider signing a reasonable nondisclosure agreement and a nonsolicitation of coworkers and referral sources agreement, but not a noncompete agreement, except in the situation where the physician voluntarily resigned. That would be the only case for which you would consider a covenant not to compete. There is a physician shortage, and for all the reasons set forth in Chapter 10, you, as counsel for the physician, are not going to advise your client to agree to limit his or her future employment opportunities in the geographic area just to be employed by that employer.

• **"Without Cause" Termination**. Is there a termination "without cause" clause where the employer can terminate the physician for no reason upon X number of days written notice? If so, that turns the physician's years-long employment contract into an "X number of days rolling employment" contract. The physician may find that unacceptable, particularly in the case of a relocating physician, unless the employer agrees not to invoke the termination "without cause" provision for the first 24 to 36 months, or otherwise to negotiate some other acceptable clause. Acceptable clauses would include "no physician repayment of paid moving expenses," "no physician reimbursement of any paid hiring bonuses," "no physician reimbursement of paid student loan benefits," etc., if the employer terminates without cause or in the event of a layoff, etc. In such a situation, however, counsel should be careful of overly broad and subjective termination "for cause" provisions, since that is how an employer usually compensates for the removal of a "without cause" termination clause.

• **Malpractice Insurance Coverage/Tail End Extended Reporting Coverage.** Define exactly who is responsible for obtaining and paying for the physician's malpractice insurance (1) during the period of employment and (2) after the period of employment (i.e., upon expiration or termination of employment). Normally it is the employer. However, in some circumstances employers try to shift this to the physician. If so, find out under exactly what circumstances this might happen and be sure it is taken into consideration when determining the physician's compensation, since malpractice insurance, particularly tail end (extended reporting) coverage insurance can be expensive if the physician has to obtain it.

- **"Clean Sweeps."** If the potential employer is a hospital, medical group, or staffing company, have the physician ask the potential employer whether the physician will be contractually required to resign his or her hospital staff privileges and hospital clinical privileges when the physician's employment with the employer ends. Some employers require physicians who are no longer employed to resign their privileges, while others do not. That could be an issue for the physician (along with any covenants not to compete) if the physician is interested in keeping privileges at the hospital, or staying in the area, in the event the employment situation didn't work out as planned.

Definitely the physician or counsel for the physician should determine the precise answers to these types of information very early. Get the answers (and any waivers) in writing, and definitely get them before a letter of intent is signed.

> ***Warning:*** More often than not, the potential employer will have the employer's management physician, "Dr. Business Person," call the client physician directly. Then, in the midst of talking "business issues" or clinical duties, that business person will implore the physician to disregard counsel's advice and agree to the "gotcha" provisions. That is because it's all "lawyer stuff anyway," and the employer "never" enforces it, and "even he, Dr. Business Person, had to agree to all that stuff in his contract." Furthermore, the physician has the word of Dr. Business Person (who will be gone in a few years) word that the "gotcha" provisions "will never be a problem for an outstanding physician such as yourself." Even though Dr. Business Person may sincerely believe all that, it is terrible advice. As all attorneys know, if it's not in writing it didn't happen—so please coach the physician client to always get promises in writing.

VI. EMPLOYMENT CONTRACTS ARE INTENDED TO BE NEGOTIATED

Contrary to what employers would like physicians to believe, an employment agreement is not a "form document" or a "standard agreement" that "every physician signs with no changes." True, it may be a "form document," and true, at the end of the form, or variation thereof, it has a signature page, but rest assured, it is a "form document" in name only. These forms are routinely negotiated and changes are made to the document, whether directly on the face or through appendixes, schedules, or amendments, so that the employer can keep claiming that they use the same "form document" "with no changes" for everyone.

Both sides need a fair and respectful relationship for a professional relationship to work. Physicians are not ordinary people. Counsel for both parties need to thoroughly appreciate the fact that a physician has invested 11 to 17 years *or more* of his or her life in an intensely competitive environment of higher education and training, and invested a personal fortune obtaining that education and training. Along with that incredibly intense training environment is the emotional sacrifice the physician made, such as missing birthdays, weddings, graduations, baptisms, funerals, vacations, postponing having serious relationships, postponing having a family, and simply missing the joyfulness that other people experience in their 20s and 30s, to instead study and work 80 hours and more a week to become a well-trained physician. They have sacrificed the best years of their lives to obtain life-saving skills and knowledge and should be treated with utmost respect, not as some fungible good that deserves little or no voice or consideration when it comes to the terms of their employment. **So the physician and his or her counsel should not be shy about negotiating hard to protect the physician and the physician's future, both during and after the employment relationship.**

> *Negotiating Tip:* Counsel for the physician can tell a lot about the employer during the negotiation of the employment contract, both good and bad. Obviously pick your battles, but if the agreement is one-sided, and the other side is uncooperative and

unreasonable or won't address the physician's concerns in the employment agreement, then the best alternative might be for the physician to try another employer.

Commonly negotiated terms for any physician in an employment agreement are the term of the agreement, compensation and benefits, termination provisions, post termination restrictions, tail end malpractice insurance provisions, and exit provisions. The attorney has to constantly think about the many ways that the relationship can change for the worse and lead to an early end. In such a case, how does your physician client exit the relationship, and are those exit terms acceptable to your client?

VII. THE EMPLOYMENT AGREEMENT: MAJOR PROVISIONS

There is no standard physician employment agreement. There are as many different employment agreements as there are physicians and physician specialties. Often employment agreements have been reused and modified over time and the terms are inconsistent and confusing.

Certain basic provisions should be incorporated into such employment agreements. This section reviews a number of these important provisions. Sections VIII and IX, below, discuss provisions related to compensation and termination, respectively.

Look to the future! If counsel has a question or thinks something is unclear today, then a future arbitrator or judge will feel the same way. So raise any such concerns with the potential employer, and be a persistent advocate until the terms are clarified and made consistent.

A. Introductory Paragraph and Recitals in Text

The introductory paragraph and recitals explain the general background and reason for the agreement to the reader. They explain who the parties are, where the parties are located, and what their relationship is to one another. It is a best practice to have the introductory paragraph and recitals incorporated by reference into the body of the agreement to make sure they have legal affect.

B. Parties

Sometimes, a physician is employed in a hospital but is also required to teach at an affiliated medical college or perhaps work at a clinic. Consequently there could be several legal entities with different duties and obligations owed to the physician. They all need to be named as parties and sign the employment agreement, and their various obligations owed to the physician need to be made clear, particularly with respect to any payment or performance guarantee obligations.

Make sure to include the precise legal names and addresses of all the parties to be bound with respect to all of the various obligations; that they are in good standing; and that the agreement is signed by authorized representatives of all the parties who are to be bound. That requires checking with the Secretary of State for the relevant state where the employing corporate entity and other signing business entity parties were formed. This checking can often be done on line.[2]

> **Due Diligence Tip:** If any of the parties rely on any type of federal healthcare program (such as Medicare or Medicaid) for reimbursement, make sure that none of the individual parties to the agreement have been excluded from participation in such programs. Check them in the List of Excluded Individuals and Entities (LEIE) on the website of the Department of Human Services Office of Inspector General (OIG) website.[3] Exclusion is a penalty imposed by the OIG on individuals and entities that have engaged in fraud and abuse or other misconduct related to federal healthcare programs.[4] No physician wants to work at a place that has been excluded from receiving federal healthcare dollars.

From the group or hospital employer perspective, if a healthcare provider employs or contracts (even as an independent contractor) with an individual physician that the healthcare provider

---

[2]*See* STATE & LOCAL GOVERNMENT ON THE NET, www.statelocalgov.net/50 states-secretary-state.cfm.

[3]*Exclusions Program*, HHS OIG, http://oig.hhs.gov/exclusions/.

[4]*See* OIG Special Advisory Bulletin, Effect of Exclusion from Participation in Federal Health Care Programs (May 8, 2013), http://oig.hhs.gov/exclusions/files/sab-05092013.pdf.

knows or should have known has been excluded from a federal healthcare program (such as Medicare or Medicaid), then the OIG may fine that provider and likewise exclude such provider from future federal healthcare programs.

C. Beware Corporate Practice of Medicine Prohibitions

Some states observe a legal policy generally known as the "corporate practice of medicine doctrine," which prohibits unlicensed business corporations and other business entities from engaging in the practice of medicine, which often includes employing physicians. To avoid serious penalties and unintended disciplinary actions, it is important to determine whether the particular employer (e.g., a nursing home) can legally employ the physician.[5] Check the current state law to be safe.[6] Please see Chapter 6 of this text and the guidance referenced therein for further discussion on corporate practice of medicine issues.

D. Key Definitions

"Effective Date," "Starting Date," "Commencement Date." Terms such as "effective date," "starting date," and "commencement date" confuse physicians (and their attorneys) and are often left completely blank in the agreement, or otherwise not clearly defined. The difference in dates can have unintended consequences, particularly when it comes time for the parties to provide notice of renewal (or notice of nonrenewal or termination) of the employment agreement, or when it is time to end medical malpractice coverage at a previous employment venue or to begin malpractice coverage at a new employment venue. It can also make a very large financial difference when calculating compensation, e.g., accounts receivables that will be due to a physician upon termination of employment.

Make it clear to your physician-client that there is a difference between the "effective date" of the employment agreement, the "commencement date" of the agreement and the "starting date" of

---

[5]The American Health Lawyers Association (AHLA) has published a helpful 50-state survey and analysis detailing the corporate practice of medicine practice restriction for the entire U.S. *See* STUART SILVERMAN ET AL, CORPORATE PRACTICE OF MEDICINE: FIFTY STATE SURVEY (AHLA 2014) (available through American Health Lawyers Association website, http://www.healthlawyers.org).

[6]*Id.*

employment. All of these affect the term of the contract. The "effective date" is generally the date on which the agreement—and the obligations stated in the agreement—become binding, as between or among the parties. That may or may not be the same date the parties signed the agreement. The "starting date" is the date the physician is actually supposed to show up and begin work.

The "commencement date" might be a totally different date, because of certain conditions subsequent, e.g., the physician's need to obtain a particular state medical license, or to obtain provisional or attending hospital credentials at specific hospitals, or an asset purchase agreement that has to be signed in the case of a medical group purchase, etc. And so if those events do not happen by a specified date—and usually there is a "drop dead" date in the agreement—the employer may terminate the agreement, or the employment agreement becomes null, void, and of no force and effect.

These terms are often used interchangeably. That leads to misunderstandings when giving notice and calculating compensation and benefits, among other things. So be careful that the terms are used correctly and the dates are clearly identified in terms of calendar dates. This confusion occurs more often than it ever should. The confusion can be resolved by clear drafting and including an appendix clearly showing the exact "Commencement Date" or "Effective Date" or "Starting Date"—whatever the relevant dates are that are used in the employment agreement—and having the doctor initial that appendix.

"Physician." When reviewing and negotiating a physician employment agreement for a medical specialist, such as a gastroenterologist, pathologist, radiologist, neurologist, surgeon, etc., specifically tailor the definition of "Physician" to that particular specialty or subspecialty or license, because that role will play out in a number of ways throughout the employment agreement.

"Services." Restrict terms such as "Services," "Professional Services," "Professional Medical Services," or "Medical Services," or whatever term is used to describe what it is that the physician is employed to provide the employer, limiting them to services only in the physician's particular specialty or subspecialty license. Otherwise, the physician may find him or herself required to perform much more general medical and administrative chores than those for which he or she was trained. That will lead to immense employee dissatisfaction. Make sure the agreement is limited to professional medical services "in the specialty of X" or "in the subspecialty of Y" if your physician is a specialist or subspecialist.

"Special Procedures." If the physician performs special procedures, such as invasive procedures (e.g., if a gastroenterologist performs unique invasive procedures that can also be performed by surgeons), the employment agreement should describe such special medical procedures as part of the "**Services**" to be performed by the physician. The same goes for radiologists and cardiologists who perform overlapping procedures. This can be important if and when hospital departments start competing for patient service work, particularly if the employer enters into an exclusive contract with another group, whose work then includes procedures performed by your client.

E. Agreement to Employ

This section of the employment agreement typically sets forth the basic agreement of the parties to enter into an employment relationship. The relationship usually is described as full time or part time, and describes whether it is an exclusive relationship or whether other activities are allowed (i.e., moonlighting), and if so, what type of outside activities are permitted. With physicians coming out of medical school drowning in debt, moonlighting opportunities could be important. Often the employee is allowed to keep the revenue; but sometimes, depending on the circumstances and what kind of time commitment is required, the employer may want part of the remuneration. Moonlighting opportunities include outside patient care, outside ER call, teaching, research, expert witness consultation, medical directorships, writing, speaking, etc.

F. Necessary Qualifications of the Physician

This section of the employment agreement describes the qualifications the physician needs to possess to qualify for employment, such as what licenses and malpractice insurances are required in the relevant state, etc. These qualifications have to be worded artfully so as to avoid being too one sided in favor of the employer. They include the relevant state medical license, obtaining provisional or staff hospital privileges at specified hospitals (if applicable to the employment setting), ability to qualify for medical malpractice insurance (and not at some discounted group policy rate over which the physician has no control), medical board certification (if a requirement of employment), and necessary narcotics and controlled substances numbers and licenses (if a requirement of employment). See Article 2 of Appendix B (*Sample Physician Employment Agreement*) for some well-drafted examples.

G. Physician Representations and Warranties

Employers commonly ask employees to make written representations and warranties about certain matters. If the representations and warranties are not true, or no longer remain true, the employer can later fire the employee "for cause" under the termination provisions of the employment contract. Normally there is also a provision requiring the physician to report any adverse event about licensure, credentialing, or so forth.

The following are some standard physician representations and warranties. Notice the italicized text that may need to be added, in the event there has been some event about which there is some restriction or an event that needs to be disclosed to the employer, in order to make the representation true. Since the physician can get fired for these representations and warranties being untrue, the statements must be modified so that each statement is true before the physician signs the employment agreement.

Sample: Physician hereby represents and warrants that Physician meets all of the following requirements and covenants and that Physician shall continue to satisfy all of the following requirements throughout the term of this Agreement:

a. Physician has a valid, unrestricted license to practice medicine in the State of _____, and *except as previously disclosed in writing to the Employer* has never had a professional license revoked, limited, suspended, or denied, either voluntarily or involuntarily, and has never been subject to any formal action or disciplinary proceeding before any governmental or administrative body or board.

b. Physician is a member in good standing of the Medical/ Dental Staff of [identify by name of all appropriate hospitals] Hospitals with clinical privileges appropriate to Physician's practice.

c. Physician is board certified in [if applicable] and shall remain certified consistent with Hospital staff by-laws.

d. Physician has all necessary narcotics and controlled substances numbers and licenses to provide the Professional Services necessary under this Agreement.

e. *Except as previously disclosed in writing to the Employer,* Physician has not been denied membership or reappointment on the medical staff on any hospital due to quality of care issues or professional misconduct, has never had [his/her] hospital medical staff membership or clinical privileges suspended, curtailed, or revoked **due to quality of care issues or professional misconduct,** and has never resigned under threat of such denial, suspension, curtailment, or revocation.[7]

f. Physician has never had a professional license revoked, limited, suspended, or denied, either voluntarily or involuntarily *except as previously disclosed in writing to the Employer.*

g. Physician has never been (i) convicted of healthcare fraud; (ii) convicted of a healthcare-related crime; (iii) suspended, sanctioned, restricted, or excluded from participating in any private, federal, or state health insurance program; (iv) convicted of theft or embezzlement relating to a healthcare program; (v) convicted of making a false statement relating to a healthcare entity; (vi) convicted of obstructing a criminal healthcare investigation; or (vii) convicted of laundering money that came from the commission of a federal healthcare offense.

h. Physician has no direct or indirect ownership or controlling interest of 5% or more of a "sanctioned entity" that has been convicted of any offense under the Code of Federal Regulations, or that has been terminated or excluded from participation in Medicare or a Medicaid program, nor has

---

[7]If representing a physician, never agree to a representation or warranty or contract termination provision tied to a statement such as "Physician has never been denied membership or reappointment on the medical staff of any hospital or clinic" without limiting it further to *"due to quality of patient care issues or professional misconduct."* Because "economic credentialing" has recently become common as hospitals and clinics align more and more with only certain physicians or medical groups, many non-aligned physicians are losing their privileges. In their cases, the act of being denied privileges or not having hospital privileges renewed may have been for reasons having nothing to do with their competence as physicians. See Chapter 7 of this text.

Physician been an officer or managing employee of such an entity.

i. Physician is in good standing as a participating provider under the Medicare and Medicaid programs.

j. Notice. If any of the foregoing statements are not true or accurate on the Commencement Date, then notwithstanding anything to the contrary herein, Physician's employment shall not commence and this Agreement shall be deemed null and void for all purposes. Physician shall promptly notify Employer if any of the foregoing statements no longer remain true or accurate during the term of this Agreement.

H. Term of the Agreement (Duration of the Contract)

One of the most challenging matters to negotiate is the term of the physician's employment agreement. If counsel were to ask a physician how long his or her contract of employment was, the physician is bound to say "two years" or "five years." Except that isn't true, particularly if there is a "without cause" or "without fault" or "termination with notice" type termination clause slipped into the agreement. In such case, all the physician has is a rolling 30-day employment contract, or however long a notice period the attorney for the physician was able to negotiate. A skilled specialist has written:

> Regardless of the length of the term, most employment agreements allow for early termination under certain conditions. Termination provisions generally fall into three broad categories: (1) termination with or without cause upon a specified number of days' prior written notice, e.g., 30 to 90 days; (2) termination for a material breach of the agreement subject to an opportunity to "cure" or correct the breach; and (3) immediate termination for certain very serious problems.[8]

These nasty early termination provisions are discussed in more detail in Section IX, below.

Employment contracts may be for any length of time. However, in independent contractor arrangements, to comply with applicable Stark and Anti-Kickback Statute (AKS) safe harbors, compensation-related terms may not change within one year from the original date of the contract. (See Chapter 25 for more information on Stark

---

[8]Jeremy N. Miller, *Employment Agreements and Other Working Relationship, in* AMERICAN HEALTH LAWYERS ASSOCIATION, REPRESENTING PHYSICIANS HANDBOOK 235 (4th ed. 2016).

Law and AKS contract details.) Although the contract may be for less than one year; if it terminates within a 12-month period, the parties may not execute a new agreement for substantially the same services with different compensation. Within independent contractor arrangements, it is typically a good idea to provide for automatic renewal to avoid the unintentional lapse of a written agreement and corresponding Stark or AKS liability. The Stark law does permit a 6-month hold-over grace period, but it is safer to simply allow for automatic renewal.

I.   How is the Employment Agreement Renewed?

One of the biggest favors counsel for the physician can do is make sure your physician client fully understands *how* the employment agreement renews. Does it renew automatically? Is there an "evergreen" clause? Or is there some affirmative action on the physician's or the hospital's or group's part that is necessary to renew the agreement before it expires? Otherwise the physician could be in a delicate posture going into the second contract negotiation if there is a timing issue as to renewal.

If there is an "evergreen clause," be aware that the parties would be bound by the same provisions of the existing contract for such extended period of time, unless the parties agreed otherwise in writing. Therefore, if the parties want to renegotiate some of the terms (e.g., compensation, benefits), the parties may wish to renegotiate those terms prior to expiration of the initial term, for application to the new contract.

> *Tip:* Make sure the renewal notice is reciprocal, and have identical renewal dates so that one side does not have a built in time advantage or disadvantage. Be certain your client knows whether the employer or the employee has the contractual obligation to give the other party notice if they do not intend to renew the employment agreement. Take a careful look at any proposed restrictive covenants, because they will have an impact on the physician's future employment prospects. See also Chapter 10 for a discussion of states that do not permit covenants not to compete in cases of nonrenewal or termination without cause.

In today's environment, the best advice is to begin contract renewal discussions as early as possible, prior to expiration of the employment contract, to give the physician a long lead time to look for another position, in the event the employer does not intend to rehire the physician, or if it becomes apparent that the parties cannot reach agreement on terms for renewal. For example, if the underlying employment agreement was for 5 years, then a minimum of 180 days is needed to begin contract change discussions. And hopefully if the employment agreement was part of a group acquisition, there is a clause in the employment agreement (or the asset purchase agreement) that allowed for the group to vote and leave as a group and reorganize if the majority of physicians want to leave the employer and in such case the restrictive covenants would not apply). That is a common feature of medical group acquisitions.

> *Practice Tip:* In drafting or reviewing or negotiating employer/ employee agreements, make sure that all the notice periods for termination coincide with other ancillary agreements that the physician may have with any associated employer entities (e.g., office leases, medical directorship agreements, department chair agreements, etc.), so that the physician's notice of ter- mination of employment is synchronized between the various ancillary agreements, and so there is no uncomfortable lag time as among the various agreements.

J. Standards of Conduct in Physician Performance: Avoid All Superlatives

The employment agreement should be carefully worded so that it does not obligate the physician to a standard of care that is higher than that required by the law in the state where he or she will be practicing. Otherwise, the employer may unwittingly be expos- ing both the employer and the physician to unnecessary liability by holding the physician to a standard of care that is higher than that imposed by state law in a medical malpractice action.

Strike all subjective and superlative terms in an employment contract, such as any requirement for the physician to use his or her "highest professional skills, knowledge, and experience in the performance of the medical services." What does any of that mean? How is that measured? Or "best medical skills"? "Highest medical skills"? What do any of those superlatives actually add to the contract?

The same is true of "faithfully and honestly and diligently perform the physician's obligations." What does that language imply? That otherwise the physician is unfaithful, dishonest, and lazy? Strike such language as subjective and offensive and just bad drafting. A medical malpractice attorney will often subpoena employment records in malpractice cases just to look for such superlatives in the physician's employment agreement, to be able to argue to the jury that the physician breached the employment contract and therefore imply that the physician also committed malpractice.

Instead, try something such as: "Physician shall conduct Physician's (Specialty) medical practice and professional duties in accordance with the current medical standards in the community [*or insert whatever else is the appropriate legal standard is in the relevant state of practice*], and shall act in a manner consistent with the applicable ethical standards and professional standards of conduct and practice as may from time to time be required by the American Medical Association or American Osteopathic Association, as applicable."

K. Physician's "Best Efforts"—An Essential Qualifier

Typically, an employer-drafted employment contract will include several sweeping "catch all" clauses requiring something to the effect of "the Physician shall perform his or her obligations under this Agreement in accordance with all applicable federal, state, and local laws, rules, and regulations in effect from time to time, including all applicable standards of public and private payors." As counsel for the physician, do *not* agree to such a sweeping clause.

First, no one, including counsel for the employer, can identify, much less furnish the physician with copies of, all the laws, rules, and regulations, etc. to which they refer. As an attorney representing the physician, always make sure such sweeping clauses are limited to the physician's "best efforts" to comply with those hundreds of thousands of laws, rules, regulations, etc., so as not to set your client up for an easy breach of contract.

Second, limit any laws, rules, and regulations to only those involving the practice of medicine, and particularly in the physician's specialty (or subspecialty).

Third, relate the laws, rules, and regulations to only those medical services to be provided pursuant to the employment agreement. Nothing more. Don't get swept up into agreeing to an ocean of other laws and regulations that have nothing to do with the medical services or actual obligations your client is providing to the employer under the specific employment agreement.

If counsel for the employer won't agree to the physician's "best efforts," then insist that counsel for the employer provide a copy of every single law, every single regulation, every single rule, and every single administrative code with which the physician must comply. That is not humanly possible. Alternatively, counsel could require the employer to agree to a reciprocal covenant to comply with every single law, regulation, and administrative code that may be in any way applicable to the employer. That won't happen either. In the meantime, counsel should only agree that the physician will use his or her "best efforts" to comply with all such obligations.

> **Sample Clause:** Physician shall use Physician's *best efforts* to perform Physician's obligations under this Agreement in accordance with all applicable federal, state, and local laws, and applicable rules and regulations relating to the licensure and regulation of physicians in Physician's specialty that are necessary for the performance of the Professional Services and obligations to be provided by Physician under this Agreement.

L. "Will Cooperate and Participate" vs. "Will be Bound By"

Often, employers want employees to provide medical services to patients under agreements with third-party public or private payors. That makes sense because the employer wants to be paid for the physician's professional services by the third parties (usually insurance companies). Yet it is unfair to make an infraction or breach of a term of a third-party payor contract by a physician also a breach of the physician's employment contract, particularly when the physician is not a party to the third-party contract and has no notice of what the terms of that were. Worse yet is when the physician's employment contract tries to bind the physician to terms of future employer payor contracts of which the physician has no knowledge, and makes failure to be accepted by those future employer networks or future employer payor plans a breach of the physicians employment contract.

So rather than setting your client up for a breach of contract by agreeing to unknown terms and conditions, state that your client will agree to "cooperate and participate" with the employer in providing professional medical services to third parties when the physician has specific notice of the specific requirements. But not agree that if such performance does not comply with some standard, rule, or other term and condition contained in the third-party public or private payor's contract that the employer has signed, that does not constitute a breach of the physician's employment contract.

> *Sample Clause:* The Physician shall cooperate with and participate in the provision of professional medical Services that are within the Physician's reasonable control as the Employer may be required to perform in connection with agreements for public and private payors, insurance companies, self-insured employer groups, medical service agreements, etc., which are entered into by the Employer and of which Employer has furnished Physician notice and details of such agreements.

M. Incorporation of Corporate Policies and Bylaws

If the standards of conduct in the physician's draft contract incorporate policies of the employer or hospital medical staff bylaws, make sure you obtain a copy of the same as part of the due diligence so that the physician is aware of the policies and bylaws. The employer can and will use the language in such policies and bylaws to bind the physician to all sorts of unknown obligations that may not be acceptable to your client and could very well affect what he or she should ask for in terms of compensation or other terms of employment.

At the very least, counsel for the physician should fix a date of the policies to which the physician has been provided notice and is obligated to abide prior to signing the employment agreement, so that the employer doesn't have the equivalent of a "blank check" to unilaterally change the policies to the physician's detriment while the physician is employed without the physician's knowledge or agreement. The same is true with any other language in the agreement stating anything to the effect of "as may be changed or amended from time to time."

N. Physician's Duties

For the individual physician, the part of the employment agreement that describes the actual medical duties and administrative services to be performed by the physician is absolutely key. The attorney representing the physician must ensure that this section is as objectively and clearly stated as possible. Unfortunately, poorly drafted physician employment agreements often have the physician's obligations scattered in various places throughout the agreement and are often inconsistently worded. Be on the lookout for such inconsistencies. In well-drafted agreements, the physician's duties are primarily contained in one or two sections and use consistent standards and consistent phrasing throughout the agreement so as to avoid ambiguity. Make sure the contract reflects a clear understanding of what both parties expect the physician's day-to-day duties to consist of. According to physician surveys, the number one cause of unhappiness and extreme dissatisfaction of employed physicians was the "disconnect" in expectations as between their duties (as described in their employment contracts) and reality. Wherever possible, you as counsel for the physician should try to limit the number of hours per week that the physician is required to spend in meetings or performing administrative chores, because those kind of chores can take up literally hundreds of hours per year that could otherwise be devoted to revenue-producing patient care, charting, or spending time with family.

Beware of any language such as: "Physician and the Employer shall mutually agree on the Physician's clinical and hospital duties." *That is a recipe for disaster.* Itemize and narrow these duties as much as possible, e.g., eliminating chores to be performed at far-flung hospitals or clinics or care sites that require time-consuming travel, have low revenue-producing patient bases, or have ill-trained support staff or outdated equipment. Also reject terms that let the employer pawn off on the physician client low-value administrative chores that no one else wants to do.

Be as specific and objective as possible with respect to what the physician's clinical and hospital duties will be and where those clinical and hospital duties and hospital procedures will be performed. This is particularly important for specialists and subspecialists.

O. Work Schedule

Avoid "Physician and the Employer shall mutually agree on the Physician's work schedule."

Make sure to include in the agreement the days the physician is expected to work, whether the work is full time or part time, the number of days per week, the minimum number of days per week if it is a part-time position, average hours per day, minimum hours per day, whether weekend hours are required, and if so when and how many, what vacation and holiday benefits there are, what paid time off there is, etc., and get that information set forth in the agreement or in a schedule to the agreement. Otherwise, the physician could be working every weekend and every holiday. Many contracts will specify a minimum number of required of hours per week but fail to include a maximum. Also, if the physician needs, or is required, to have protected time for administrative tasks, traveling, teaching, or research time, this should be included in the contract.

> ***Sample:*** Physician shall work to provide Professional Services to Employer on a [full-time] [exclusive] basis of [28 average] scheduled clinic patient hours per week with each work shift generally not to exceed 8 hours per day. Physician is expected to be available to provide Professional Services amounting to an average of [___] assigned patients per working day. Physician is expected to perform Professional Services between Monday through Friday (excluding major holidays or vacation days, illness, and attendance at seminars and meetings) unless performing on-call services [as described below] and also to participate in the administrative duties described below. Physician is expected to complete whatever charting requirements are necessary to accurately bill and collect for the Professional Services and [if applicable] perform necessary hospital rounds on patients. [Modify if Physician shall perform Professional Services on a part time basis or perform Professional Services on the weekend or perform on some other schedule.]

Find out how many patients the physician employee will be expected to be seen in an average day. Also, find out how the employer assigns patients to its physician employees? That is important when it comes to compensation if compensation is based on revenue production, particularly if the physician is not assigned well insured patients.

P. Work Location(s), Importance of Defining for Restrictive Covenants

Be sure to include in the agreement where the physician shall work. Location of performance will be critical for two reasons. First, as a new physician, it is not good to be sent to the worst places or the places with the worst payor mix, particularly if the physician's compensation depends in any way on revenue production.

Second, location is important when it comes to the restrictive covenants, if the employment arrangement does not end well for the physician. If the hospital or medical group develops a larger footprint or merges with another healthcare provider, then the area of the restriction may become much larger during the period of employment and thereafter. And as a new or young physician, he or she could be particularly vulnerable to layoff or termination in any merger or acquisition of a hospital or practice. Limit the geographic area of any restrictive covenant to the particular geographic area which the physician knows about *at the time of signing the initial agreement*, not years thereafter. See Chapter 10 of this text on restrictive covenants.

Will the physician employee be expected to cover satellite locations? If yes, how often? That needs to be put in the employment agreement, and if traveling to and from satellite locations is time consuming, then thought has to be given to compensation credit for the amount of travel time lost from other revenue production opportunities.

Sample Location Clause: Physician shall perform Professional Services for the Employer pursuant to this Agreement primarily at the medical office space located at [Street Address, City, State, Zip] ("Medical Office") and at the hospital located at [Street Address, City, State, Zip] "Hospital," or another location mutually agreed upon in writing by Employer and Physician.

Drafting Tip: Try to get assurances in writing that the employer won't reassign the Physician without his or her written consent (not to be unreasonably denied). Also, get written assurances that the employer won't reassign the Physician to an area with a less desirable payor mix or charitable case mix, or a significantly longer commute, etc., particularly if the physician is being compensated or otherwise measured on a productivity compensation model (such as wRVUs)[9] or if the support staffing ratio or quality of support staff is worse at the new location, at least without the physician being given some consideration in terms of credit for such disadvantage. A physician, particularly one who does invasive procedures, who has to travel all over town and rely on unpredictable support staff of varying skill mix throughout the day cannot possibly be as productive as one who remains at one location with a known and steady support staff.

Q. On-Call Coverage

Beware of any employment contract language such as "Physician shall participate in Employer's after-hours call schedule as required by Employer." The physician employee loses bargaining power as soon as he or she signs the letter of intent or employment agreement, so get the call schedule at least sketched out in writing beforehand and put in the employment agreement. One of the biggest reasons physicians leave private practice and become employees of hospitals and large groups is to have help with call coverage so as not to be having call obligations every night and every weekend and every holiday. Make sure the oral assurances are in the contract about there being other physicians in the specialty that will also be taking call along with your physician.

Sample On-Call Coverage Clause: Physician shall provide on-call service coverage as scheduled by the [employer] from time to time for physicians in the Specialty on the same equitable basis as required of the other physicians in the Specialty, but such on-call service coverage shall generally not exceed every [e.g., 5th] weeknight / [e.g., one calendar week per fifth calendar week] or every [e.g., fifth] weekend or every [e.g., fifth] holiday. Holiday assignments are to be rotated equally between Physician and other physicians in the Specialty. [Note:

---

[9]See Section VIII.B, below.

obviously, all of these distribution formulas depend on the number of physicians in the Specialty.]

R. Physician's Obligations With Respect to Medical Patient Care Decisions

The House of Delegates of the American Medical Association (AMA), at its 2012 Interim Meeting, adopted the AMA Principles for Physician Employment[10] (the "AMA Principles") in an effort to "identify and address some of the unique challenges to professionalism and the practice of medicine arising in the face of physician employment. The AMA Principles recognize that an employed physician has a duty of loyalty to the hospital employer. That duty, however, cannot outweigh the physician's "paramount responsibility" to patients. Typically, a physician employment agreement might document that the physician must exercise his or her independent professional judgment on behalf of the patient, and that the hospital employer will not interfere with the exercise of that judgment.

The AMA wisely suggests that there be clear language contained in the employment agreement regarding the physician's ability to have exclusive responsibility to make medical care judgments for patients. Such clauses are commonly found in physician employment agreements. Hospitals also like to put this clause in there for reasons of corporate practice of medicine.

Suggested AMA Clause: Notwithstanding anything to the contrary contained herein, the Physician shall have the sole and exclusive responsibility for making medical care judgments and determinations on behalf of patients to whom the Physician delivers professional medical services. Under no circumstances will the Employer or any parent, subsidiary, or related companies of Employer exercise any control over or interfere with the independent professional judgment or determination of the appropriate healthcare to be delivered by the Physician to the patients receiving the professional medical services provided by Physician. Nothing in this Agreement shall interfere with the independent relationship between the Physician and the

---

[10]AMA, Principles for Physician Employment (2013), http://www.ncmedsoc.org/wp-content/uploads/2013/09/ama-principles-for-physician-employment.pdf.

patients to whom the Physician provides professional medical services hereunder.

S. Limit the Physician's Administrative Duties

Most physicians say the most attractive feature of leaving private practice for hospital or large group employment was the elimination of administrative and billing and collection duties. That is also one of the biggest selling points the hospital uses when offering to purchase the physician's practice. So, when reviewing and negotiating a physician's employment agreement avoid language, particularly vague and open-ended language, obligating the physician to perform administrative duties.

If the employer insists that the physician perform administrative duties, the parties should detail the exact scope and amount of such duties, estimate in writing the expected time involved in such duties, and determine when or if additional compensation is warranted. This is definitely not a minor issue. Administrative duties can suck up hundreds of hours. Since this type of activity takes time away from seeing patients, which is a revenue-producing activity and for which the physician is also measured, it is not fair to saddle the physician with unpaid administrative chores for which he or she is not provided compensation credit.

Sample Physician's Administrative Duties Clause: The Physician shall participate in a reasonable amount of administrative, supervisory, medical education, staff meeting, and quality improvement initiatives directly relating to the Services on substantially the same basis and on the same terms as other Employer physicians in the Specialty; such duties shall be assigned on an equitable basis and be no more burdensome than those required of the other Employer physicians in the Specialty; and such duties shall generally not exceed more than [X] hours cumulative per week.

T. Charitable Cases and Outreach Services

If the employer is a tax-exempt employer, the physician is likely required to engage in charitable cases and outreach services. If so, find out what percentage of cases is required, who assigns such cases and how are they assigned, and how the physician is given credit for the time spent on those cases, particularly if the physician is paid on a production or wRVU methodology. Also double check to make sure (in the case of outreach clinics) if such cases are covered by the employer's malpractice insurance, and if not what malpractice coverage is applicable.

U. Educational Activities and Resident Oversight

Is the physician expected to lecture or promote the hospital or group? If so, what amount of time is this expected to take and how much credit will the physician be given in terms of revenue production? This type of activity takes time away from the practice of medicine, and that time could otherwise be spent finishing endless charting requirements, seeing patients, etc.

V. Hospital Privileges

For some types of physicians, working in the hospital and having hospital privileges is a necessity. Since obtaining hospital staff and clinical privileges is as much a political exercise as an administrative exercise, physicians and their counsel should always ask for the employer's assistance in obtaining such medical staff and clinical privileges at the hospitals where physician will be required to work. Since the employer is local or, in many cases, is the hospital itself, it can provide valuable assistance in expediting the process and ensuring that such hospital privileges are obtained. Obviously, the physician has to furnish the necessary educational, letters of recommendation, and background records, but the employer can get the necessary forms and have the privileging committee meeting expedited.

Sample Clause Hospital Privileges: With reasonable assistance from Employer in initially obtaining the same, Physician shall obtain and maintain active membership on the medical staff of the [identify exactly which hospitals by name] "Hospitals," and shall provide patient care according to the Hospital bylaws relating to the medical Services to be provided by Physician under this Agreement.

W. Supervisory Responsibility

If any of the physician's duties require supervision of nonphysician personnel, it is in the physician's best interest to have considerable input regarding the hiring, firing, evaluating, promoting, relocating and disciplining of such nonphysician personnel. That authority needs to be noted in the employment agreement, particularly when the physician has to depend on co-workers (e.g., nurses, physician's assistants, X-ray technicians, etc.) for the team to run smoothly. Usually the employer wants to retain the final administrative authority, which is understandable for liability reasons, but it is more than reasonable for the supervising physician to be provided considerable input, especially if the supervised co-employee is a critical team member whose performance affects the physician's or the team's ability to efficiently and capably carry out the duties the physician was hired to perform on behalf of the employer.

X. Training or Other Considerations

If advanced training with a particularly gifted or named physician is a material reason your client physician chose employment at the hospital or medical group, then make sure the training with that particular physician is memorialized in the employment contract and provide an outline of what and how much of such personalized training is to occur. That way there is a chance that it will actually occur when practice gets busy, or at least there will be a risk of a breach of contract claim if the training does not occur.

Y. Coding, Billing, and Collection

Normally the employer will, *at a minimum*, want the right to (1) set the physician's professional fee, (2) bill for the professional service, and (3) collect for the service, and will require the physician to assign those rights to the employer. Why? Because the employer wants to control the money that the physician earns through providing the professional medical services.

To avoid both breach of contract and compliance issues, the physician must timely complete and submit accurate patient records to, among other things, support the coding and billing for the professional services performed by the physician. There is typically a provision in the employment agreement that makes it a material breach of the employment agreement—and worse—if the physician fails to timely and accurately provide medical record support for coding patient services. The employee has to select a code for each of his or her professional services with respect to the patient—*and there are presently at least 10,000 different codes.*[11]

Compliance issues are also implicated. One only has to open the newspaper to see that healthcare fraud and abuse claims under the False Claims Act are on the rise. One 2017 case involving Florida long term care facilities resulted in a judgment exceeding $300 million[12] for submitting claims for services that were not medically necessary. So the physician has to understand that if the patient's medical records do not properly support the need for the care or the medical services for which reimbursement is sought (i.e., coded and billed), then that could result in significant liability. The care or services must be medically necessary and the chart has to support that determination. Then the reimbursement claim for a patient's care or services is supported.

Every employer has its own unique system of medical record keeping, chart documentation, transmitting data, etc., all of which have their electronic problems and defects that are constantly being adjusted and worked out. Counsel for the employer knows, and counsel for the physician must recognize, that for the physician to provide timely and accurate information to support an accurate code and therefore an accurate billing, the physician more often than not must rely on the timeliness and accuracy of records and information in the possession of and provided by the employer (e.g., lab work, pathology reports, imaging reports, past patient records). The physician's ability to timely and accurately chart, diagnose, code, and support the billing is not accomplished in a vacuum.

> ***Important Tip:*** It is imperative that the responsibility for chart documentation, coding, billing, collection, allocation of professional fees to the physician, and record retention of the medical

---

[11]HCPCS–General Information, CMS, https://www.cms.gov/Medicare/Coding/MedHCPCSGenInfo/index.html?redirect=/medhcpcsgeninfo.

[12]United States v. Sea Crest Health Care Management LLC, Case 8:11-cv-01303-SDM-TBM (M.D. Fla. 2017).

records and all the supporting documentation for the billing be clearly allocated in the employment agreement, and that the physician have the right to audit and make sure that the employer is accurately coding and billing for the physician's services, particularly to government payors.

Moreover, in the employment agreement, since invariably the employer requires the physician to timely and accurately complete and code for all professional services or face termination, counsel for the physician should insert an affirmative obligation that the hospital will timely provide the physician all the requisite supporting information necessary to enable the physician to timely and accurately diagnose and code and that physician shall be able to rely on the accuracy of such information. Suggested language is provided below.

Suggested Clause: Employer shall provide Physician, or shall cause the provision to the Physician of, all the requisite patient records and documentation and supporting information reasonably necessary for the Physician to be able to timely and accurately provide coding and billing information, and Physician shall be able to rely on the accuracy of such information in performing such coding and billing obligations.

From the physician's viewpoint, there is no way for the physician to provide information without relying on the accuracy of information provided by the employer or another third party—including the patient's past medical records, accurate and up to date lab reports, pathology reports, imaging reports, and all the other clinical supporting information that is relevant to help the physician furnish services in a timely manner (i.e., "ASAP!"), and to correctly code and support the medical billing, and even to respond to a government or insurance audit (which might take place years in the future). But more importantly, what the physician is worried about on a day-to-day basis is: Can the physician rely on the information provided by the employer to provide the correct diagnosis and treatment plan for his or her sick patient? The physician doesn't operate in a vacuum, and the employer needs to recognize that very real fact in the employment agreement. Cost cutting by the employer is the elephant in the room that can't be ignored, and which definitely impacts the ability of the physician to perform.

Z. Right of Access to Medical Records for Legal Proceedings

The physician needs access to the medical records of his or her patients in the event of legal proceedings involving he physician (e.g., claims, disputes, lawsuits, audits, etc.), both during the period of employment and after the employment relationship ends. Counsel for the physician is advised to check the laws in the state(s) where the physician will be practicing to confirm how long the physician should require access to such records. State Medicaid investigations, for example, may have a longer statute of limitations than federal Medicare investigations, sometimes as long as 10 years. And, without question, if the physician client treats minors or is involved in a neonatal medical practice, keep in mind that lawsuits with respect to minors are another matter altogether. Both the age of majority and the statute of limitations for medical malpractice in the relevant state may affect the time frame applicable to the physician's need for records access.

The physician client will need access to and full copies of all relevant medical records for a pending investigation—and not in the employer's time frame, either. If the physician's medical license is under investigation or review by the state licensing board or the Centers for Medicare and Medicaid Services (CMS), or your client is the subject of a lawsuit, the documents that the third parties will demand must be provided quickly or your client may be subject to sanctions. Awaiting access during a stressful conflict concerning the facts that the documents would reveal may feel like an eternity for your client.

So a mere representation in the physician's employment agreement that the employer will get the records to the physician employee in "due course" or when the employer gets around to it, hoping your client will go away, or after the employer's outside counsel screens the documents, just won't work, and is unacceptable. A licensing board or a judge will simply not accept that kind of provision as an excuse. Counsel negotiating the terms must put in a 10 business day limit, as a reasonable time frame for producing the records, so the parties will get serious. See the example below.

> ***Sample Medical Records Clause:*** In the event that there is an audit, review, claim, dispute, lawsuit, inquiry, governmental investigation, governmental agency inquiry, medical licensing board inquiry, or issue regarding the physician's medical license, which involves the care of a patient, then Physician may

release the patient records and discuss the patient's healthcare as allowed by law, and if requested in writing, the Employer shall ensure that a complete copy of the entire record of the relevant patient shall be promptly provided to Physician or his or her legal representative in no more than 10 business days after such written request has been received. This obligation to provide medical records shall extend beyond any expiration or termination of this Agreement.

VIII. PHYSICIAN COMPENSATION AND BENEFITS

It is critical for an attorney representing a physician to question and fully understand the various elements that make up the physician's compensation, how such compensation is calculated, and whether there is any repayment obligation in case there is not a rosy outcome. Something as supposedly simple as a "guaranteed" base salary can get complicated, so pay attention to all aspects of the compensation arrangement. (A "guaranteed" base salary can be clawed back by the employer if counsel and the physician-client are not watchful.)

A. Overview

Physician employment agreements normally contain one of the following compensation methodologies: a fixed salary; a base salary with productivity bonus; or compensation based solely on productivity. There could be some bonus opportunity based on "quality" incentives sprinkled in, but those types of incentives are usually so fuzzy and ill-defined that they must be nailed down precisely as to what and how they will be measured, and when they will be paid, in order to be meaningful. If such incentives are based on patient satisfaction scores, then you should have the actual patient satisfaction surveys attached to the agreement, so the physician knows what incentives the employer is emphasizing so as to be able to meet them.

Typically, hospitals and large groups deal with physicians just out of residency and relocating physicians by offering a guaranteed base salary for one or two years, and then weaning them off a guaranteed salary and onto either a combination of a guaranteed base salary and a productivity compensation model or a straight productivity model. Those productivity models will be discussed below.

Beware of any compensation model that allows for the employer to claw back compensation already paid. Beware any compensation methodology based on collections, instead of billable services, for the reasons described below. Also, no matter how great the guaranteed salary is in the first few years, the physician must find out what happens after the guaranteed salary stops. Then what happens?

Beyond a base salary, it is critical to understand how the rest of the compensation is measured, and how and when compensation will be paid. Particularly when compensation amounts are a blend of productivity-based incentives and quality-based bonus amounts, this information is crucial. And the physician should learn whether any of the productivity or bonus amounts are prorated and paid through the year. This is important, so that in the event your client either doesn't start at the beginning of the calculation period or is terminated before the end of the calculation period, he or she is eligible to be paid for earned productivity or bonus amounts. That is critical because that "earned" amount can be a substantial sum.

Most hospitals and most practices compensate their physicians using a wRVU model, which compensates physicians based on the nature and level of work performed rather than the number of patients seen, since the level of work required varies from patient to patient. This model is discussed in the next section.

B. What Is a wRVU?

The "wRVU" is a "work relative value unit." It is the basis of a "pay for performance type" compensation that takes into consideration the physician's training, his or her skill set, and the time and intensity expended by the physician to provide a given service when establishing the physician's compensation for that service. The focus is on the level of care provided to patients and not on the volume of patients. It is the method by which Medicare sets reimbursement rates for each physician encounter. Medicare establishes base reimbursement levels for over 10,000 physician services (as of October 2016) by assigning each a relative value unit (RVU).[13]

---

[13]Each component of the relative value unit assigned to each CPT Code (i.e., work, practice expense, and professional liability) is then multiplied by the Geographic Practice Cost Index (GPCI) for each Medicare locality, which takes the cost of delivery of healthcare services based on locale into account, and which is further adjusted by a conversion factor that is set by CMS on an annual basis. The Medicare Conversion

Today, wRVUs are frequently used by employers to determine physician compensation because they are thought to be the best available model to take into consideration the varying levels of the physician's work (and stress) when treating all the different types of patients the physician sees throughout the day. Some patients are very complicated to treat, with multiple chronic diseases, and some patients are not. Some benefits of wRVUs are that they don't penalize the physician for charity care provided on behalf of the hospital or for other financial matters outside of the physician's control, or for employer negotiated rates, capitated fees, patients' insurance coverage issues, reductions in reimbursement rates, or failure or delays in collections.[14] Whatever services the physician performs count toward the wRVU production total.

Note that wRVUs are not a panacea. WRVUs have no direct correlation with quality or results, which is not where value-based healthcare is going on a national level. WRVUs reward the faster physician and don't reward the more methodical physician who may achieve higher patient satisfaction scores or better results. And wRVU compensation encourages "cherry picking" of the highest value procedures since those procedures are rewarded at the highest compensation per procedure level. Also counsel needs to be aware that a physician client that works nights or in far flung clinics is not going to have the same opportunity to obtain the same number or high value wRVU procedures, so if his or her compensation is based on a certain target number of wRVUs being achieved during a certain time period that fact has to be taken into consideration in determining whether the target is realistic.[15] It is important for counsel for the physician to understand the function of wRVUs in qualifying physician "productivity" and "opportunity to achieve productivity," which in turn impact the physician's compensation.[16]

Factor (CF) is a national value that converts the total RVUs into the dollar amounts paid by Medicare to physicians for the services they provide. That is the amount the physician in that locality is paid by CMS. *See* CMS, Overview of Medicare Physician Fee Schedule, https://www.cms.gov/apps/physician-fee-schedule/overview.aspx. RVUs are published in the Federal Register each November. *See also* CMS, Medicare Physician Fee Schedule (Feb. 2017), https://www.cms.gov/Outreach-and-Education/Medicare-Learning-Network-MLN/MLNProducts/downloads/MedcrephysFeeSchedfctsht.pdf.

[14]*See* Ruskin Moscou Faltischek P.C., What Is an RVU? (Mar. 8, 2012), http://www.rmfpc.com/what-is-an-rvu/.

[15]*See id.*

[16]For an easy-to-read white paper on understanding exactly how wRVUs are used in compensation formulas in various types of physician employment contracts, please refer to Merritt Hawkins, RVU FAQ Understanding RVU

C. Compensation Tied to Quality Metrics

Because wRVUs measure "productivity" and not quality, many employers are also tying some element of compensation to "quality" metrics. The problem is that the metrics are not well defined and change throughout the performance period. If there are specific quality metrics, get those in writing. For example, if the quality bonus is based on achieving a certain score on a particular physician satisfaction survey, refer to the exact physician satisfaction survey in the employment agreement. If the physician is going to be measured on things he or she knows about and can control, that's fine. If the physician's compensation is going to depend on something he or she cannot control, such as diminished compensation because of a patient being readmitted 12 days after discharge because the patient developed an infection through no fault of the physician, then that is a different matter. The physician is a highly trained professional and has to know the exact metrics or benchmarks the employer is going to use to measure him or her when it comes to performance, which in turn affects the physician's paycheck.

D. Compensation Based on Billable vs. Billed or "Billed and Collected" Amounts

An employed physician can only control what goes on in his or her office, laboratory, examination room, or operating room. No physician wants his or her mortgage payment, child's day care, or tuition payment hinging on the effectiveness of a billing and collection department over which the physician has no control, and which may be located in another building, city, state, or country. Therefore, an attorney advising a physician employee must understand whether there is any possibility of the physician having a repayment obligation, whether the physician's compensation is based on any of the following amounts, and why it matters.

Billable Services. This is the best case for the employed physician. It only requires the physician to properly chart and code the services that the physician performs. The employer is responsible

Compensation in Physician Employment Agreements (2014), https://www.merrit thawkins.com/uploadedFiles/MerrittHawkins/Pdf/RVU_FAQ-%20Understanding_ RVU%20Compensation_Physician_Employment_Agreements.pdf.

for the billing and collection. So if the employer writes off the bill, loses the bill, accepts a discount or negotiated rate, fails to bill, or is unable to collect, the physician still receives compensation from the employer.

Billed Services. This requires the physician to properly chart and code the services the physician performs, but also requires the services to be properly billed and sent out by the employer. Unfortunately, an employed physician generally has no control over the employer's billing department and whether they write off the bill, lose the bill, accept a discount or negotiated rate, do not properly bill, or the billing person takes a vacation or quits. In these cases, the physician's compensation might suffer if it is based on a formula that includes *billed* services instead of *billable* services.

Billed and Collected Services. This is the absolute worst case for the employed physician. Even if the physician properly charts and codes for the services the physician performs, the physician's compensation depends on the employer's billing and collections efforts (and success), over which the physician has no control. On top of all the risk described in the preceding paragraph under "billed services," the physician is expected to take collection risk too! Counsel for the physician must also take into consideration the delay between billing and collection, particularly at the beginning of the employment relationship and definitely at the end of the employment relationship. Again, it doesn't take too much imagination to figure out how the physician's compensation might suffer if it is based on a formula that includes *billed and collected* services instead of *billable* services.

Insert something to the effect of the following into the physician's employment agreement:

> ***Sample Clause:*** The parties agree that, for purposes of determining compensation, a wRVU shall include those services and procedures that may be lawfully or contractually billed to and collected from a payor, whether such payor be an individual, governmental payor, insurance company, employer, managed care company, or any other third party payor. Physician shall receive wRVU credit for all such services or procedures, regardless of whether or not Employer bills or collects for such services or procedures.

E. Think About Compensation Due to the Physician Upon Termination Now, Not When Termination Occurs

How will the physician collect payment for the physician's professional services after the hospital relationship ends, particularly if any of the amounts are related to or dependent upon outstanding collections or accounts receivable? There could easily end up being hundreds of thousands of dollars in outstanding accounts receivable that the physician-client may have a right to, so this is definitely not a minor issue.

Make sure that productivity or bonus amounts are prorated through the year, so that in the event your client either doesn't start at the beginning of the calculation period, or is terminated before the end of the calculation period, he or she is eligible to be paid for the earned productivity or bonus amount upon termination.

> *Practice Tip:* The AMA has an excellent publication for physicians and their advisors entitled *ACOs and Other Options: A "How-To" Manual for Physicians Navigating a Post-Health Reform World.*[17] In Chapter 7, the authors discuss hospital physician employment agreements and provide a concise description and discussion of physician compensation models and issues to watch out for that is definitely worth consulting.[18]

F. Right to Audit for Purposes of Verifying Compensation

The following is a clause suggested in an extremely helpful guide published by the American Medical Association.

> *Sample Provision:* **Employee Right to Access Books and Records**. Upon reasonable written request, Employee and his or her accountant or attorney shall have the right, at a time during ordinary business hours as reasonably determined by Employer, to inspect and copy records relevant to the calculation of Employee's compensation hereunder. Employer may impose a reasonable charge for the expenses, including labor, associated

---

[17] AMERICAN MEDICAL ASS'N (AMA), ACOS AND OTHER OPTIONS: A "HOW-TO" MANUAL FOR PHYSICIANS NAVIGATING A POST-HEALTH REFORM WORLD (4th ed. 2013).

[18] Wilson Hayman, Steven Mansfield Shaber & Kimberly Licata, *Hospital Physician Employment Agreements, in* AMA, ACOS AND OTHER OPTIONS: A "HOW-TO" MANUAL FOR PHYSICIANS NAVIGATING A POST-HEALTH REFORM WORLD, ch. 7.

with providing such inspection and copying. The right to inspect shall survive the termination of this Agreement, and the legal representative of Employee if deceased or under a legal disability shall have the same rights as Employee to access to Employer's books and records for proper purposes to the extent they pertain to the period during which Employee was entitled to formula compensation. Employee may not copy or take demographic data on Employer's patients, which shall remain Employer's confidential proprietary information as provided below under Confidential Information.[19]

G. Other Typical Employer-Paid Benefits

Other typical employer-paid benefits include the following. These should be described in the employment agreement:

- Health, dental and vision insurance for Physician and family
- Disability insurance for Physician, long term and short term
- Life insurance for Physician
- Retirement benefits for Physician
- Malpractice insurance coverage
- Malpractice tail insurance coverage
- Hospital medical staff dues payments
- Licensure payments
- Professional membership dues payments
- Subscriptions and professional book payments
- Continuing medical education expense budget
- Paid time off for vacation and holidays
- Paid time off for sick leave
- Paid time off for continuing medical education
- Moving or relocation expense reimbursement
- Cell phone and monthly service fee and phone insurance
- Home or mobile computer
- Home Internet

---

[19]N. Jeddeloh & T. Conley, AMA ANNOTATED MODEL PHYSICIAN-GROUP PRACTICE EMPLOYMENT AGREEMENT, ch. 1.11 *Audit Rights*, at 31 (2014).

- If Physician is expected to serve on any administrative boards, or act in an executive capacity, then directors and officers (D and O) insurance is essential and not expensive to obtain, and the employer should obtain it and pay for it.
- Sometimes: signing bonus to help with expenses
- Sometimes: help with student loan repayment

H. Helpful Resources for Compensation Information

When assisting the physician client, counsel must clearly understand and get in writing exactly what the compensation productivity and quality metrics are. Make sure the physician has a realistic opportunity to meet the baselines, and get some examples of the compensation formula placed into the agreement, so that everything is clear as people change jobs and memories fade.

The AMA Office of General Counsel and AMA Organized Medical Staff Section have published two outstanding annotated guides for physicians and their advisors with informative explanations, negotiation tips, and sample model clauses. These guides explain, among other things, various types of physician compensation arrangements that counsel or the physician may be presented with and how wording can affect the compensation arrangements.[20]

IX. EARLY TERMINATION PROVISIONS

The early termination provisions are the most important provisions in the employment agreement to negotiate vigorously. All the opportunity and great expectations invested in the employment relationship by both sides come to a crashing halt when the early termination provisions (and associated "gotcha" provisions) are invoked.

When representing the physician, it is essential to define the contractual termination provisions as narrowly and objectively as possible. Avoid any subjective and reputational type phrasing. Remember, physicians are highly trained professionals that are in short supply today. Avoid all the subjective "in employer's sole

---

[20]*See id.* (includes a compensation section with a discussion on deferred compensation that is well worth the reasonable investment); *see also* AMA, ANNOTATED MODEL PHYSICIAN-HOSPITAL EMPLOYMENT AGREEMENT (2011, updated March 2012), *available at* ebooks.ama-assn.org.

discretion" and even the "in the employer's reasonable discretion" clauses. Objective standards that are directly related to employment licensure and insurance qualifications and physical and mental ability to perform the medical services make sense. Subjective reputational, vague, or ambiguous infractions don't.

A. The "Gotcha" Clauses

Counsel for the physician has the task of sorting out how the termination provisions in the employment agreement connect to other provisions that will negatively impact the client. "Usual suspect" items to check include:

- post-employment restrictive covenants;
- loss of hospital privileges upon termination of employment;
- requirements regarding payment of "tail" (extended reporting) malpractice insurance coverage;
- nonspecific rights for access to patients' medical records after termination;
- loss of compensation benefits otherwise payable for earned compensation;
- repayment of relocation and signing bonuses;
- overly broad nondisclosure prohibitions;
- overly broad confidentiality and proprietary information prohibitions (styled as "trade secret" protections);[21]
- and others.

B. Termination Without Cause Upon Written Notice

Regardless of the stated length of term, most employment agreements allow for early termination, either "for cause" or "without cause." If there is a "without cause"-type termination clause slipped into the agreement, the physician actually only has a rolling contract for 30, 60, 90, or 180 days (or whatever other length of stated notice period you, as counsel for the physician, can negotiate into the contract).

Under ordinary circumstances, it is easier to terminate an employee who has a "without cause" termination provision in his or

---

[21]See Chapter 10 of this text.

her employment contract than it is to terminate an employee with only "for cause" termination provisions. But be advised that it is not unusual for employers to try to enforce covenants not to compete even when the employed physician was let go "without cause": "Doctor, you're fired for no reason. And don't forget your restrictive covenants!" Fortunately, there are states (e.g., Connecticut) where enforcing covenants not to compete in such situations is not permitted.[22]

Anecdotally, in spite of the fact that there is a physician shortage, what is happening is that hospitals and staffing companies are using "without cause" termination clauses as the "go to" tool to weed out and terminate, or threaten to weed out and terminate, physicians who are not producing enough revenue for the employer. Not that the employed physician necessarily has any control over who sits down in the employer's waiting room or clinic, or how sick the patient is, or how good the patient's insurance is; screening patients for insurance and collecting payment for medical services are the duties that the employer assumes, not the employee physician. Not surprisingly, the other physicians being terminated "without cause" are those who protest or complain about the patient care provided by the employer.

However, the employer can be sued for a "without cause" termination if the employee can show that the termination was based on unlawful reasons, since the employee has all the protections available under state and federal employment laws, including whistle-blower protections.[23] And those laws often extend to independent contractors as well.

The key issues with termination "without cause" provisions are (1) the time frame (i.e., the "notice period"), (2) the effective date of the termination, and (3) the nonapplication of restrictive covenants and other "fault"-based termination provisions.

The longer the notice period, the better, so that the physician has time to relocate to another position. Use of 120 to 180 days is standard in three- to five-year initial term employment agreements.

---

[22]Under Connecticut Public Act No. 16-95, effective July 1, 2016, physician non-competes are unenforceable if the employer terminates the physician without cause, or the contractual relationship terminates without cause, or if the employment contract or agreement expires or is not renewed. The statute also limits the allowable duration and geographic scope of any new, amended, or renewed physician noncompete agreements. Also please refer generally to Chapter 10 of this text.

[23]Please refer to Chapter 25 of this text.

Use of 60 to 90 days is average in shorter (one- to two-year) initial term employment agreements.

Employers don't like longer notice periods because the employer will either have to allow the employee to keep working and earning, or the employer will have to pay the employee the value of future salary and benefits in exchange for having the employee leave sooner than the contract requires. Commonly, there is a contract provision that allows for the employer to remove the employed physician from the premises but provides that the employer will continue to pay the physician compensation and benefits throughout the notice period.

If the employer insists on a "without cause" termination provision, make sure it is mutual, not one way in the employer's favor only. That is a common employer tactic of which to be aware. It is vitally important that notice periods be identical and mutual for both parties. It must be made mutual so that if the physician decides to quit there will be no breach of contract claim as long as the physician provides the appropriate notice. Never let the employer have a shorter or longer notice or performance period than that required of the employee.

"Without cause" termination provisions are particularly unfair for physicians who have agreed to relocate to the area to take the proffered position with the employer. Ensure that carve outs letting an employer terminate a physician "without cause" render inapplicable any covenant not to compete, repayment of relocation expenses, repayment of signing bonuses, and procurement of tail end malpractice insurance obligations on the part of the physician. These are common carve outs in physician employment contracts because they are fair and promote physician trust in the employer, as well as support from other physicians in the community.

Also make sure that the compensation provisions upon termination are clear so that the physician is paid all amounts that the physician earned, on a pro rata basis, while the physician was employed. Otherwise, unless the physician is paid purely on a straight salary, the physician may not be compensated fairly due to the fact that the physician may have earned credit for compensation based on productivity, account receivables, or other metrics, but not be paid for them at the time of termination. There could be outstanding accounts receivables in the amount of hundreds of thousands of dollars that need to be accounted for.

Word to the Wise: If counsel for the physician is unable to remove the "without cause" termination provision and ends up with a mutual termination without cause provision in the employment agreement and it is the *physician* who ends up voluntarily terminating the employment agreement, that could trigger noncompete clauses and other restrictive covenants that may be contained in the employment agreement (or in the practice purchase agreement if the hospital purchased the physician's practice) and might also trigger an obligation to purchase professional liability (tail end) insurance coverage. Such a possibility needs to be thought through with the physician-client because sometimes the employer ties the applicability of the restrictive covenants (if any) or requirement to obtain and pay for professional liability (tail end) insurance to the reason for termination of the employment relationship. In other words, if the employer terminated the physician without cause, then the employer would not enforce the restrictive covenants and the employer would pay for the tail end insurance coverage. That is not necessarily so if the employee voluntarily terminated the employment agreement without cause.

Another Tip: in reviewing physician employment agreements, make sure that all the notice periods for termination coincide with other ancillary agreements the physician may have with the employer (e.g., lease agreements, medical directorship agreements, department chair agreements, etc.) so that the physician's notice of termination of employment is synchronized among the various agreements.

Another Suggestion: If your client wants a contract for a fixed term, then work to remove the "without cause" termination provision altogether and have any termination be "for cause." Or work to have the "without cause" provision nonapplicable for the first 12 months or whatever the client desires (or whatever can be negotiated). On the other hand, the physician may also negotiate that after a certain period of time (e.g., 24 months) there cannot be a termination of the physician "without cause" because any type of probationary "let's get to know you" period is long past.

C. Termination For Cause—Two Types

There are two basic "termination for cause" provisions. One provides for immediate termination of the contract, and one allows the other party an opportunity to cure an alleged breach before the contract is finally terminated.

1. Immediate Termination For Cause Provisions

In a well-drafted physician employment agreement, there is typically a section identifying specific major events that the parties agree from the outset permit a party to end the employment relationship immediately upon the occurrence of such event. These provisions work for the benefit of both the employer and the employee; because there are circumstances where the employee may also want to terminate the employment relationship immediately.

Unfortunately, trouble arises when poorly drafted employment agreements include subjective and reputational type events as reasons for immediate termination. Such subjective wording needs to be removed, or at least modified so as to not be subjective or not be grounds for immediate termination.

Common Immediate Termination Provisions for Physician Employment Contracts—Employer's Perspective. Common immediate termination events found in the employment agreement that allow for automatic termination of the employment agreement from the employer's perspective include the following major events. These are considered reasonable because the employer requires the physician's professional services, and without the physician being able to perform those professional services, the employment relationship simply doesn't work.

> *Tip:* Limit any termination "for cause" only to laws, licenses, privileges, insurances or approvals in states, territories, jurisdictions, hospitals, clinics, etc., that have a *direct* connection to the *specific* location and the *specific* medical services to be provided by the *specific* physician under the *specific* employment contract for the *specific* employer in question. Not some other more universal description.

- Physician's death or permanent disability. (***Note:*** any reference to "disability" must specifically take into consideration

applicable federal and state laws, such as the Americans with
Disabilities Act, to which the employer is subject, and should
also be defined with regard to any applicable disability insurance policy for which the physician may become eligible.)
- Physician's voluntary surrender of medical license, or the
  suspension of physician's medical license for more than [30]
  days, or termination of Physician's medical license, in each
  case following a hearing.[24]
- Physician's loss of Drug Enforcement Agency (DEA) or
  parallel state license privileges that permit Physician to legally
  prescribe and administer controlled substances in the relevant
  state of employment (and only if Physician is employed in
  a capacity that requires the prescription or administration of
  controlled substances).
- Physician's exclusion, debarment, or sanction by a relevant federal or state sponsored healthcare program, such as
  Medicare or Medicaid (following a hearing and any pursued
  appeal, unless Physician does not dispute the allegation(s)).
- Employer's inability to obtain and maintain malpractice
  insurance coverage for or on behalf of Physician after
  employer's good-faith efforts to obtain the same, or Physician
  becomes ineligible for such insurance.[25]
- Physician's loss of board certification (but only if board certification is a necessary job requirement or required by major

---

[24]But only the physician's license in the relevant state where the physician is to
perform medical services under the employment agreement, not a different state where
the physician may happen to hold a license.

[25]Be careful about malpractice insurance requirements. Some employer-sided contracts include as a basis for a physician-employee's *immediate termination* a clause to
the effect that the physician must be insurable under the employer's medical malpractice insurance policy *at a rate no higher than the group discounted rate* provided by
the employer's malpractice carrier. Remove any such provision from the employment
agreement. It's one thing to require that a physician be insurable and remain insurable
during the term of an employment agreement. It's entirely another thing to require in-
surability at a *particular rate* under a *particular policy*. The employed physician has no
control over what insurance company the employer selects, no control over the other
physicians in the group or hospital who also contribute to the group rate determination,
no control over what insurance coverage terms or increased deductibles the employer
might agree to, no control over medical malpractice legislation in the state of practice
(which in turn affects insurance rates), no control over any number of other factors that
impact insurance rates for the employer—much less *discounted* insurance rates for the
employer. That should not be held against the physician as a basis for his or her immediate firing. Alternately, counsel should negotiate a more reasonable cap of 3 times the
standard malpractice coverage rate for the specialty.

insurance providers), unless such failure is excused, in writing, by Employer.

* Termination of Physician's essential medical hospital or clinic staff membership or essential hospital or clinical privileges *due to Physician's clinical competence or patient quality of care issues* and after completion of all steps provided in the medical staff fair hearing plan.[26]

* Physician's conviction *(not arrest or indictment, but conviction)* of an offense punishable as a felony or a crime involving fraud, theft, embezzlement, or similar crime of dishonesty or a crime of moral turpitude or immoral conduct such as nonconsensual sexual behavior, use or distribution of illegal substances, or a plea of no contest to such charges.

* Physician's alcohol use affecting work or substance abuse affecting work if such is established after all steps provided in the medical staff fair hearing plan or by the applicable Medical Board.[27]

Warning About Recent Contract Developments: This field is evolving. Provisions that were recently found in some physician employment agreements under the "immediate termination for cause with no opportunity to cure" category are to the effect of: "If *any* insurance company, HMO, or prepaid plan, private or government payor, provider networks, managed care programs, or other third-party payor arrangements in which Physician is required by Employer to participate etc. refuses to credential

---

[26]Counsel should be careful regarding any termination provision relating to denial, qualification, termination or nonrenewal of the physician's hospital medical staff or hospital clinical privileges. Experienced counsel will always get these termination provisions qualified as being denied, qualified, terminated, or nonrenewed for "quality of patient care issues" or "professional clinical competency," because it becoming all too common for physicians (and other medical professionals such as dentists) to be denied privileges or have reappointments denied or have medical staff membership closed for "economic credentialing" reasons for the convenience of the employer which have nothing to do with patient care or professional competency. Also it is very easy to get privileges suspended for administrative things such as failing to sign a medical record on time, which can be fixed by simply signing the medical record. See Chapter 7 of this text on economic and conflicts credentialing.

[27]WILSON HAYMAN, STEVEN MANSFIELD SHABER & KIMBERLY LICATA, ACOs AND OTHER OPTIONS: A "HOW-TO" MANUAL FOR PHYSICIANS NAVIGATING A POST-HEALTH REFORM WORLD ch. 7 *Hospital Physician Employment Agreements*, at 7-A2 (4th ed. 2013), https://www.acponline.org/system/files/documents/running_practice/delivery_and_payment_models/aco/physician_howto_manual.pdf.

or contract with Physician or if Physician's contract with any of the foregoing expire or are terminated, suspended, or materially restricted, then Employer can immediately terminate Physician."

As counsel for the physician, don't agree to anything so malignant—particularly as an immediate termination event for the physician. Also don't agree to any termination event for the physician unless the refusal to credential or contract with the physician is exclusively due to repeated physician quality of care issues that have been vetted by the hospital Medical Staff, not just the employer.

First, there is no link to the physician's status with the health maintenance organization (HMO) HMO or other payor as being within the physician's ability to control. Or that the employer has even provided the physician with *notice* of the credential or contract issue in question. Or whether the physician's status with the HMO or other payor is capable of being cured, and if so, how? And why shouldn't the physician be provided an opportunity to cure any alleged defect before being terminated, particularly if there is no connection to physician's being on or off a particular HMO or payor panel for reasons of quality of patient care? If it is due to a physician number limitation on a panel, there is nothing the individual physician can do, but there is often something the employer can do, given the greater bargaining power of the employer with the HMO or payor panel.

Second, the employer is responsible for getting the physician on the various third-party payor and HMO plans, particularly in the case of HMOs, since the number of physicians included on such panels is limited. The physician relies on the hospital employer or medical group employer to get the physician included on the panels and plans with which the employer contracts.

Third, there is no qualification that the "arrangement" for which physician's status is in issue is a *material* arrangement. The employer seeks to fire the physician if he or she can't participate in "any" payor arrangement, even if it is a minor one or one set to expire soon.

Fourth, the physician's failure to maintain participation in major federal programs such as Medicare and Medicaid (following a hearing and any pursued appeal, unless the physician does not dispute the allegation(s)) has already been covered in a separate termination provision and is redundant here.

If the physician were being removed from panels due to patient quality of care issues, that would be a different issue and would be addressed under a hospital quality review program or other quality metric, with the physician being provided an opportunity to cure.

> *Tip:* Refuse to include any contract language that includes employment termination for "threatened" events or "possible claims" or "notification of possible claims or suspension incidents," or a matter that "is under investigation" or other events involving staff privileges, medical licenses, lawsuits, crimes, etc., which may be reinstated by signing of medical records, cured by payment of dues, or that are only "alleged" or "under investigation"—that is, for matters that haven't been finally proven or can be appealed, etc. Anyone can make an accusation. It's another thing to prove an accusation or a crime to be true.

Immediate Termination Provisions—Employee Physician's Perspective. It is important that the physician have the right to end the employment relationship immediately for serious employer events too. Typically, there is no cure period permitted for these types of termination events because of the severity of their nature. Such events include:

- Employer or any of Employer's parent companies or any of the Hospitals are suspended, terminated, debarred, or excluded from participation in Medicare, Medicaid, or any other federal or state healthcare program.
- Employer's or any of Employer's parent companies' or any of the Hospitals' accreditation, licensure, or certification expires or is suspended, conditioned, revoked, terminated, or restricted in any way or not renewed.
- The sale, transfer, or assignment of all or substantially all of the assets of [Employer or any of Employer's parent companies]; the commencement by [Employer or any of Employer's parent companies] of a voluntary case under any applicable bankruptcy, insolvency, reorganization, or other similar law

now or hereafter in effect; or the entry of a decree or order for relief in respect of [Employer or any of Employer's parent companies] in a case under any such law, or appointing a receiver, liquidator, assignee, custodian, or trustee (or other similar official) of [Employer or any of Employer's parent companies] or for any substantial part of [Employer's or any of Employer's parent companies'] property, or ordering the wind-up or liquidation of [Employer's or any of Employer's parent companies'] affairs; or the filing and pendency for thirty (30) days without dismissal of a petition initiating an involuntary case under any such bankruptcy, insolvency, or similar law; or the making by [Employer or any of Employer's parent companies] of any general assignment for the benefit of creditors or the failure of [Employer or any of Employer's parent companies] generally to pay [Employer's or any of Employer's parent companies'] debts as such debts become due; or the taking of action by [Employer or any of Employer's parent companies] in furtherance of any of the foregoing.

- If Employer enters into any arrangement that restricts, limits, or materially interferes with Physician's continued ability to provide professional medical services under this Agreement.
- In the event of a Change of Control. See Chapter 8 of this text. [This is something the physician should seriously consider in this age of mergers in the event the hospital or group is purchased by a competitor that the physician doesn't want to work for or has had issues with in the past.]

2. Termination For Cause—Material Breach Subject to Cure

Separate from the reasons for termination for which the parties have agreed there is no opportunity for cure, there is a common law remedy that is available in contract law for early termination of the contract on the basis of material breach, permitting a party to terminate the agreement due to the other party's breach of a material term of the agreement. Normally there is a provision in the agreement that permits the other party to be given written notice of the alleged breach and be provided a specified time to correct or "cure" the alleged breach before the agreement terminates. Note however, if the terminating party is wrong about the material breach and wrongfully terminates the agreement early, he or she could be liable for damages. Parties often argue over the amount of time permitted to cure the alleged breach, but not about whether there is an opportunity to cure the alleged breach.

> *Sample:* **Termination With Cause.** Either party shall have the right to terminate this Agreement with cause if the other party breaches a material provision of this Agreement and fails to cure such breach within ten (10) calendar days of the giving of written notice by the nonbreaching party specifying such breach, which cause has not been cured (assuming such cure is possible) within ten (10) days after receipt of such written notice. [Optional: If it is not reasonably possible to complete the cure within 10 days, then so long as the breaching party has taken reasonable steps to begin the cure, and so long as the breaching party is continuing those steps and other reasonable steps that may become necessary, then the breaching party will have the additional time reasonably needed to complete the cure.]
>
> This paragraph only relates to independent causes of breach and is not intended to provide for a cure period for any of the causes of breach described in Paragraph ___ (*Immediate Termination*) above.

D. Avoid Ambiguous, Reputational, or Subjective Grounds for Termination

Counsel for the physician must avoid agreeing to the multitude of subjective and reputational "causes" that may be included in employment agreements and that are intended to give the employer the right to fire the physician "for cause." Most of these are incredibly ambiguous, vague, and impossible to interpret, and we could devote an entire attorney bar exam question to them.

"Nonharmonious behavior with others" or "failing to work harmoniously with others"—what *exactly* does that mean? Does the "nonharmonious behavior" affect patient care in any way? Does it affect patient or employee safety? Does it mean failure to attend the office Christmas party? Is behavior nonharmonious because the physician happens to be from a foreign country and has an accent that others may not understand? Is it nonharmonious if the physician is loud by nature? Or the physician is fussy about procedures in the operating room? Is that nonharmonious behavior, or is that being a good doctor? Or if the doctor raises concerns about having to work with untrained nurses or untrained technicians in the operating room during delicate procedures on complicated patients—is that "non-harmonious" behavior for which counsel for the physician should allow the physician to be fired "for cause"?

The same concern applies to being able to fire the physician "for cause" if the "physician engages in unprofessional conduct" or "physician engages in conduct injurious to the reputation of the employer" or "physician fails to maintain a good reputation or character." So, if the physician is in a rock band on the weekends, would that be unprofessional conduct suitable for firing? But if he's in a church band, that is OK?

Obviously, the above kind of vague "for cause" grounds for firing can be abused and pulled out whenever it is convenient for the employer. Such firing will have many undesirable repercussions for the physician. The employer's argument can be summed up as: "Well, we can't describe every situation, so we use broad, sweeping language." First, that is untrue. The employer has been down this road before. The goal is to separate serious instances of bad conduct from minor "nonharmonious" or "reputational type" instances or conduct, so the physician doesn't get fired at the employer's whim, particularly if the physician is otherwise interested in being employed by the employer.

All of these "causes" must be teased out, limited, defined, and tied to some objective written policy or written examples in the employment agreement to which the physician can refer, and the termination "causes" must always relate back to the professional duties the physician has agreed to provide under the employment contract. Furthermore, the physician must have actual notice of the occurrence of any of the "for cause" matters, and have the opportunity to cure the deficiency, particularly in the case of "nonharmonious" conduct (whatever that is). In a "nonharmonious conduct" case, the actual termination event should be conditioned on repeated material instances of behavior of which the physician was provided written notice, and that relate directly to patient care or patient safety.

On a separate note, subjective and reputational type termination "causes" need to be removed from the employment agreement, or at least limited to events that objectively relate directly to the professional services to be provided by the physician, because it is exactly such types of subjective clauses that come back to haunt the employer. It is impossible to apply them evenly among employees, and they leave the employer open to lawsuits based on unlawful discrimination.

E. Effect of Termination: Beware of "Clean Sweep" Provisions

A "clean sweep" clause requires that if the employment contract expires, is terminated for any reason, with or without cause, or is not renewed, then the physician's hospital privileges are automatically terminated. Such termination occurs without the benefit of any hearing to which the physician would normally be entitled under state and federal law, or under the hospital's medical staff bylaws, before losing his or her hospital medical staff or hospital clinical privileges. The reason for this is simple and economic. The hospital doesn't want a former (presumably disgruntled) employee in the hospital, and doesn't want to take the time and money to go through a Health Care Quality Improvement Act (HCQIA) hearing—or any state law equivalent type hearing—before depriving the physician of hospital medical staff or clinical credentials. From the employer's perspective, it wants to terminate and replace the physician as soon as possible. The problem is that the physician will have to explain the loss of hospital privileges for the rest of his or her professional life, because every malpractice insurance application and every employment application asks whether the physician has ever involuntarily lost his or her privileges. This is a serious career threat.

To avoid these "clean sweeps," the AMA Annotated Model Physician–Hospital Employment Agreement publication suggests insertion of the following language:

> Upon termination of this Agreement Physician shall retain full Medical Staff membership and clinical privileges as he or she held during the term of this Agreement and nothing herein shall adversely affect Physician's Medical Staff membership or clinical privileges or require Physician to resign the same, unless an independent action by the Medical Staff has called for the same, and Physician has been afforded full due process under the Medical Staff Bylaws.[28]

However, be aware that if the physician is a member of a medical group or staffing company that provides exclusive services to

---

[28]N. Jeddeloh & T. Conley, AMA ANNOTATED MODEL PHYSICIAN-GROUP PRACTICE EMPLOYMENT AGREEMENT §9.6 *Effect of Termination*, at 81 (2014).

a hospital, such a carve out may not be possible, depending on the terms of prime contract between the medical group or staffing company and the hospital. The prime contract might insist that all the physicians in the group or staffing company resign their privileges if the employment relationship ends for any reason. That is largely situational.

In reality, in most physician employment contracts with hospitals, it is not uncommon to include a provision to the effect of:

> Termination of this Employment Agreement shall not, in and of itself, be deemed to adversely affect Physician's medical staff appointment or clinical privileges or membership status in the [insert name of] Hospital.

That is because it is financially beneficial to the hospital that, even if the employment agreement ends, the physician can still direct and admit patients to and perform procedures in the hospital (unless the privileges were terminated for reasons of patient care or professional conduct).

> *Tip for Hospital Counsel.* It would be very helpful in hospital employment draft contracts, and in hospital bylaws, if there were specific definitions of what the hospital means by "medical staff privileges" and "hospital clinical privileges." Definitions would be particularly useful on the issue of whether the physician has the right to use those privileges in the hospital, and exactly for what and for how long, because many times the parties (and when it comes down to it, attorneys and judges) are making assumptions when it comes to the terms "staff privileges" or "clinical privileges," and are talking past each other when it comes to those very essential points. From a hospital employer standpoint, drafting clear physician contracts with termination provisions that are completely consistent with the hospital bylaws regarding hospital credentialing and termination of privileges will go a long way to avoid termination disputes.

F. Noncompete Covenants

For all the reasons set forth in Chapters 8 and 10 of this text on restrictive covenants it is essential for counsel for the physician to **resist any covenant not to compete**. If that is impossible, then make sure there is a carve out (1) for any employer termination of the physician "without cause; (2) for any employee termination of the employment agreement "for cause" due to the *employer's* breach; or (3) if the parties are unable to agree to an acceptable compensation formula at the time of renewal, or any time during the contract when compensation is reviewed, and particularly if the hospital is suggesting a decrease in compensation from the initial (or latest renewal) term.

G. Obligation to Provide Tail End Malpractice Insurance

Since there is exposure for both parties after the employment relationship ends, it is essential for both parties to be protected for professional negligence claims for events arising during the physician's employment, but reported after the employment relationship ends. Although employers generally pay for tail end malpractice insurance for their employees, there are some employers, usually smaller employers, who may allocate the cost to procure tail end malpractice insurance to their employed physicians upon termination of the employment relationship. The physician must be fully aware of any such requirement. This requirement can often be negotiated away or negotiated such that if the employee is terminated "without cause" or the employee terminates the employment relationship "for cause" due to employer's breach, the employer pays for all the cost of the tail end malpractice premium.

Some malpractice insurance policies contain a special endorsement, such as no additional cost for tail end malpractice coverage, if the physician has had the malpractice policy for a certain number of years. Some employers make an allocation based on how long the physician remains employed. The important thing is that the physician must avoid any lapse of professional liability coverage between the coverage at the old employer and any new employer. It is often possible to obtain "nose" coverage at the new employer, but that is something that requires consultation with a knowledgeable medical malpractice insurance expert to avoid any gaps in coverage. In any event, the obligation to provide tail end (extended reporting) malpractice insurance and who pays for it must be clearly documented in the employment agreement. Please see the attached sample physician employment contracts in the Appendices for suggested clauses.

H. Indemnification Provisions Relating to Setting, Billing, and Collection of Professional Fees by Employer

Next to termination "for cause" provisions, indemnification provisions are frequently the most overused, poorly drafted, and disputed portions of the employment agreement.

First, consult the relevant state common law with respect to indemnification rights, which varies by state.[29] Also, please see Chapter 8 of this text on insurance and indemnification matters for practical advice before tackling any indemnification or hold harmless provisions.

There are some times when particular indemnification provisions are appropriate. For example, these provisions are appropriate in the situation where the employed physician has been required to assign to the employer the right(s) to establish the charges for the physician's professional services, the right to finally code and bill for such professional services, the right to collect for such professional services, or the right to disburse the compensation received for such professional services. The physician has little or no control over what happens in such situation, and it is fair for the physician to require the employer to defend, indemnify, and hold the physician harmless from any liability that arises from the employer's failure to perform those duties properly—particularly since doing so improperly could result in criminal and civil liability for the physician. It is a particularly fair request because, among other reasons, the employer normally has insurance to cover this type of liability.

> ***Suggested Clause:*** **Indemnification of Physician.** The Employer agrees to defend, indemnify, and hold harmless Physician from any claim, loss, damage, cost, expense, liability, cause of action, or judgment, including reasonable attorney's fees and disbursements, arising out of or related to any of the following actions by Employer or its respective officers, directors, administrators, employees, physicians, representatives, staff, independent contractors, agents, or designees: (i)

---

[29] *See Statement on Legal Opinions Regarding Indemnification and Exculpation Provisions under Texas Law*, 41 TEX. J. BUS. L. 271 (2006) (summarizing legal opinion reports from various state business law sections relating to enforceability of indemnification provisions, including Florida, Maryland, Michigan, and North Carolina).

failure to comply with applicable state, local, or federal laws, rules, and regulations in connection with performance of their obligations hereunder, with respect to filing and medical record keeping services, establishment of medical fees and charges for Physician's Professional Services activities, or third party-reimbursement and collection activities, or (ii) errors or defects in coding, billing, or collection related to Physician's Professional Services, in each case not due to Physician error.

Tip: If the employer requests any indemnity provisions from the physician employee, attempt to make it only for willful or intentional violations by the physician employee, and only to the extent that such claim, loss, damage, or liability is not otherwise covered by insurance held by the employer. Also, be careful that the indemnification provision is not so broad that it could be interpreted as one party indemnifying the other in instances of a simple breach of contract, which is typically not intended by the parties entering into a contract, unless that *is* what the parties actually intend.

Great care must be taken when it comes to any indemnification or hold harmless provision, and there is no question that the client's professional insurance carrier should be consulted. Otherwise, both parties could end up with no insurance coverage because of their assumed contractual indemnification obligations. See also Chapter 8 of this text.

I.   Overbroad Confidentiality and Nondisclosure Provisions

Because the physician will have access to medical records which are protected by Health Insurance Portability and Accountability Act (HIPAA) and parallel state laws, it is appropriate that the physician agree to keep such records private in accordance with applicable state and federal law.

However, that doesn't mean that the physician will not need access to such medical records, which access must be assured by counsel. See Section VII.Z, above.

What is common to find, however, are thoroughly overbroad provisions in physician employment contracts under the guise of "trade secret" or proprietary information agreements or nondisclosure agreements, which are vague, ambiguous, and can be misconstrued and create the risk of inadvertent disclosure. Even showing the employment agreement to one's counsel could trigger a proprietary information agreement prohibition, so that is why counsel has to pay attention, and should insist on carving out large categories of information that is not truly proprietary or protected "trade secret" information.

> *Sample:* **Exceptions to Confidentiality**. Notwithstanding anything to the contrary contained herein, information, technology, or data shall *not* be considered to be secret or confidential or proprietary, and Physician shall not be liable for the use and disclosure thereof if such information, technology, or data (i) was in the public domain at the time of disclosure or thereafter comes into the public domain through no fault of the Physician, (ii) is otherwise available to the receiving party without restrictions on use or disclosure, (iii) was known to the receiving party at or before the receipt thereof from the Physician, (iv) is independently developed by the receiving party, (v) is disclosed after Physician's receipt of a governmental, medical board, or healthcare agency request or investigative demand, (vi) is required to be disclosed to a court, governmental or regulatory authority of competent jurisdiction, or by deposition, interrogatory, document production request, subpoena, or other similar legal demand, or (vii) anything in a patient's records or other thing for which Physician is entitled to provide copies upon a specific request in writing from a patient or patient's representative.

> Additionally, Physician may disclose this Agreement (a) in confidence to Physician's attorneys, accountants, auditors, tax preparers, and financial advisors; (b) upon request from any government entity or court of law; and (c) insofar as such disclosure may be necessary to enforce its terms or as otherwise required by law.

J. Beware of Assignment Provisions

An employment agreement for the professional medical services of a physician is a personal services agreement. Do not permit the physician's employment to agreement to be assigned without the physician's consent, even to a parent or affiliated company of the employer. Even with guaranteed payment and performance obligations, the physician could still wind up working for a company he or she does not want to work for. The physician needs to look at the situation when it's happening, and not agree to it beforehand. The physician can agree to not unreasonably withhold consent, but that's it. There is too much consolidation in the industry right now for a physician to wind up working for an entirely different employer without their consent. Physicians are professionals and need to be treated as such.

X. EMPLOYER'S DUTIES

What are the employer's duties or responsibilities to the physician? Typically, in one-sided employer agreements, the list of the employer's duties to the physician is very short and skimpy. Other than paying the physician and providing benefits, it typically consists of something as noncommittal as "Employer shall provide Physician with 'adequate' facilities, equipment, supplies, and staff as necessary to perform his or her duties hereunder." What does that mean? And who pays for it? And is it some third-party supply or staffing company that does the supplying or staffing? How much control or input does the physician have, if any? Often what the employer will say is "oh well, that is just assumed." Get it in writing anyway.

A. Facilities, Equipment, Supplies, Medicine, and Support Staff

Make sure that the employment agreement specifies as much as possible what the employer needs to supply, or arrange to be supplied, *at employer's expense* and on a continuing and timely basis to support the physician's activities. The hospital administration knows very well that facilities, equipment, supplies, and support staff are expensive. And staffing and equipment purchases are one of the first things a hospital or clinic eliminates to reduce overhead.

So before the physician signs the employment agreement, while the physician still has negotiating leverage, make sure that these matters are specified in the agreement (particularly if the employer has not employed a physician in that specialty before or the employer is not totally familiar with the needs of the physician). Important items to put in the agreement include, e.g., a furnished office (specify lo-cation and whether a cubicle is OK or not) and examining room(s) (specify location and number); medical supplies, dressings, gloves, masks, medicines, computers, and medical equipment; services of physician's assistants, nurses, technicians, and—as necessary—administrative personnel and scheduling, billing, and collection clerks; and other items, things, and services in such amounts as may reasonably necessary for the physician to efficiently and compe-tently carry out all the professional medical duties required to be performed under the employment agreement. The agreement should also provide that they will continue to be furnished throughout the term of the agreement.

Remember, the physician is being employed to provide profes-sional medical services and to make money for the employer—and the physician can't do that without proper facilities, equipment, and supplies, trained clinical staff, and other scheduling, coding, billing, and technical and security personnel to help the physician deliver quality healthcare in a timely fashion.

The employer will resist specificity because the employer doesn't want their failure to provide the space, equipment, trained personnel, etc., to be raised as a defense when it's time to lower the physician's salary, typically for failure to meet unrealistically high productivity targets, or if they want to terminate the physician with or without cause and enforce the covenants not to compete, etc., since the employer's breach can be used to void restrictive covenants. See Chapter 10. But specificity is imperative from the physician's standpoint because staffing, equipment, and facilities are always an issue, particularly in renewal contract negotiations after the physician has learned the hard way what "lean performance" is all about. It is well known that hospitals are losing over $200,000 per employed physician per year (see Chapter 2), so make sure that the nature and extent of the facilities, equipment, and support staff your physician needs are recorded in your physician's contract, if nothing else as a defensive measure.

Anecdotally, it is often reported that physicians are not able to make their minimum yearly wRVUs because the hospital does not have enough trained X-ray technicians or operating room nurses, because the hospitals have cut trained support staff, so the surgeons and other physicians who do invasive procedures are often left wait-ing hours upon hours for adequately staffed operating or procedure rooms. That wastes time that would otherwise be billable. Now that nurses and physicians are all "coworkers," there doesn't seem to be the same urgency on the part of other "coworkers" to please the physicians, since they are all employees of the hospital.

> ***Sample Provision:* Operational Support, Facilities, and Equipment.** Employer shall provide and maintain, or shall cause to have provided and maintained, at Employer's expense, facilities including a furnished office and work space and [number] examination rooms, located at [describe location], for use by Physician to efficiently and effectively perform his or her obligations under this Agreement in the Physician's specialty. Such facilities shall be and remain equipped with such furniture, lighting, [identify specialty] medical equipment, medicines, supplies, and other items normally required for the performance of the Professional Services. Physician shall notify Employer of any perceived deficiency in any equipment, technology, or supplies in the office or clinical space.
>
> Employer, at its expense, shall engage the services of [insert number] [such] clinical nursing support staff, [insert number] physician assistants, [insert number] x-ray technicians (if applicable), medical assistants and other professional technicians, administrative clerical and scheduling and billing and collection support staff services, and other technology staff services as necessary for Physician to efficiently and effectively perform Physician's medical Services in Physician's specialty and other duties required under this Agreement.

B. Professional Liability Insurance

Professional liability insurance must be included in the employment contract, and the employer normally pays for it in the case of a nonindependent contractor relationship, including any "tail" (extended reporting) liability insurance. But some employers still try to shift the responsibility to the employee physician.

There are two general types of malpractice insurance: (1) "occurrence-based," which covers a physician indefinitely for acts that occurred during the coverage period no matter when the lawsuit is filed; and (2) "claims made," which is limited and only covers for claims filed while the policy is in effect for occurrences during the life of the policy. The latter is much cheaper and requires a "tail" policy to cover lawsuits filed after a physician leaves the practice, in case a patient later sues for something that occurred during the time period when the physician was previously employed. Who pays for the tail policy? That must be defined in the employment contract. Most employers pay for malpractice insurance including tail insurance.[30] Please see Chapter 6 for a brief overview on the types of malpractice insurance for which a physician should ask, including the type that covers the defense of professional licensure actions, since that coverage is an available and commonly offered feature of many professional liability policies. Also, if the physician is asked to be on the board of directors or act as an officer of the employer or perform executive work on behalf of the employer, then it is fair to ask the employer to provide the physician with Directors and Officers liability insurance coverage as well.

> ***Important Practice Tip:*** The responsibility of obtaining and paying for tail end (extended reporting) malpractice insurance is an absolute *must* to document before signing a letter of intent or any employment agreement. It can be expensive to obtain if the physician has to obtain it individually, and that is why this matter needs to be finally settled before determining the physician's final compensation.

> ***Suggested Clauses:***

> ***Sample #1:*** **Professional Liability Coverage Clause** Employer shall provide professional liability insurance through a licensed reputable insurance carrier in the minimum amount of [Two] Million Dollars per occurrence and [Five] Million Dollars in the aggregate (the "Minimum Amount") and Employer shall be responsible for payment of all insurance deductibles. Upon expiration or termination of employment for any reason, Employer shall provide extended reporting endorsement

---

[30]American Academy of Family Physicians (AAFP), Contract Negotiations: Five Elements to Consider, at 3, http://www.aafp.org/practice-management/payment/contracts.html.

coverage (tail end coverage) in the Minimum Amount for Physician for claims that arise during the time Physician was employed by Employer. Such extended reporting (tail end coverage) shall be of unlimited duration and shall name Physician as Named Insured and Employer shall provide or shall cause its insurer to provide Physician evidence of such tail coverage upon request.

Employer shall provide the maximum available coverage for Physician for legal defense in administrative and disciplinary proceedings for medical staff or licensure proceedings, CMS audits, etc., to the extent it is available by purchase of medical malpractice insurance coverage.

Sample #2: **Professional Liability Coverage Clause.** For all activities performed pursuant to this Agreement, Employer shall, at its sole cost, procure and provide Physician professional liability insurance during the term of this Agreement in the amount of [Two] Million ([$2,000,000]) per occurrence and [Five] Million ([$5,000,000]) in the aggregate (the "Minimum Coverage Limits"), and Employer shall be responsible for payment of all insurance deductibles. Upon the expiration or termination of this Agreement, whether voluntary or involuntary, with or without cause or reason or by Employer or Physician, Employer shall pay the cost of "tail" coverage (extended reporting) with respect to Physician's employment under this Agreement (which "tail" coverage shall have the Minimum Coverage Limits, shall be for an unlimited duration, and shall name Employer and Physician as named insureds), and Employer shall provide evidence of such "tail" coverage upon request.

Employer shall not provide liability insurance coverage for any occurrences, acts, activities, or services engaged in by Physician that (i) are not within the scope of Physician's duties under this Agreement or (ii) occurred prior to Physician's employment with Employer under this Agreement. Employer shall provide the maximum available coverage for Physician for legal defense in administrative and disciplinary proceedings for medical staff or licensure proceedings, CMS audits, etc. to the extent it is available by purchase of medical malpractice insurance coverage.

C. Commitment for Employer to Use Best Commercial Efforts to Obtain Membership for Physician on Employer Panels and HMOs

The AMA Annotated Model Physician-Hospital Employment Agreement wisely recommends that it is important for physicians who are considering hospital employment to find out about all the managed care contracts, preferred provider organizations (PPOs), health maintenance organizations (HMOs), physician-hospital organizations (PHOs), independent practice associations (IPAs), accountable care organizations (ACOs), and any other self-insured employer plan or third-party payor plan in which the hospital is currently involved or intends to become involved in the future. Find out the patient mix and reimbursement terms of the managed care contracts, because those contract terms will definitely impact the employed physician. If the employer wants the physician to sign a nondisclosure agreement, then sign it. But find out what the deal is before the physician "hitches his or her wagon" to the employer.

Also, since managed care companies limit their panels to participants, the AMA rightly recommends that a clause be included in the physician's employment agreement that the hospital (employer) be obligated to obtain membership for the physician on the above-described managed care panels, so the physician can participate in all the managed care contracts.[31] What good does it do for the physician to be employed when the physician is not included—or is actually excluded—from the panels, for reasons that have nothing to do with the physician's professional qualifications? Much of this issue of panel participation is political, and the employer has more bargaining power than an individual physician.

Suggested Clause from AMA: [Employer] "shall use its best commercial efforts to ensure that Physician is eligible to participate in all managed care contracts, accountable care organizations, health maintenance organizations,

---

[31]American Medical Association (AMA), Annotated Model Physician-Hospital Employment Agreement §3.6 *Managed Care Contracts, Discounted Fees and Bundled Payment,* at 41 (2011).

physician-hospital organizations, independent practice associations, and any other managed care organizations with which [Employer] participates so that Physician may fulfill his or her obligations under this Agreement."[32]

Caution: Be aware that one-sided employer termination clauses often contain provisions that permit the employer to fire the physician "for cause" if the physician fails to qualify for such type of managed care contracts, HMOs, etc. That is why this clause is vitally important to protect your client physician.

D. Other Employer Duties to Require in Writing

Make sure the employer has the obligation to notify your client physician if there is any claim made or threatened against your client. After all, this provision is what the employer requires of the physician in the representations and warranties. Better to know than to be surprised later.

Sample Notice Clause: Employer shall immediately notify Physician of any professional liability or any other claim received by Employer made or threatened against the Physician related to the Physician's rendering of Professional Services under this Agreement, and Employer shall furnish copies of any writings reflecting or discussing the same.

---

[32] *Id.*

CHAPTER 10

RESTRICTIVE COVENANTS IN PHYSICIAN EMPLOYMENT CONTRACTS

I. WHAT IS A COVENANT NOT TO COMPETE?

A covenant not to compete in an employment agreement is a contractual provision designed to control the activities of a former employee after the employment relationship ends. It is often referred to as a restrictive covenant.[1] It limits an employee's ability to lawfully compete against the employee's former employer and is designed to have the employee give up rights that the employee would otherwise have in the absence of such a contractual provision.[2]

Subcategories of covenants not to compete include post-employment nondisclosure agreements and post-employment covenants not to solicit coworkers or customers of the former employer.[3]

II. SUMMARY

Attorneys have probably never encountered a post-employment covenant not to compete. Thanks to strong protections provided by all fifty state supreme courts through adoption of Codes of Professional Responsibility, a strong American Bar Association, and other safeguards, no lawyer or law student is faced with an employment contract that would require them to sign away the right to move, say, from one law firm to another. Or a contract that would bar

---

[1] *See* BLACK'S LAW DICTIONARY (10th ed. 2014). A noncompetition covenant is "[a] promise, usu[ally] in a sale-of-business, partnership, or employment contract, not to engage in the same type of business for a stated time in the same market as the buyer, partner, or employer. Noncompetition covenants are valid to protect business goodwill in the sale of a company. In employment contexts, requiring the employee, after leaving the employment, not to do a particular type of work, they are disfavored as restraints of trade. Courts generally enforce them for the duration of the relationship, but provisions that extend beyond that relationship must be reasonable in scope, time, and territory.— Also termed *noncompetition agreement; noncompete covenant; noncompetition covenant; restrictive covenant; covenant in restraint of trade; promise not to compete; contract not to compete.*"

[2] *See* RESTATEMENT OF EMPLOYMENT LAW §8.05 *Competition by Former Employee with Former Employer* (2d ed. 2015).

[3] *See* Bishara, Martin & Thomas, *An Empirical Analysis of Noncompetition Clauses and Other Restrictive Postemployment Covenants,* VANDERBILT L. REV., vol. 68 (Jan. 2015).

them from practicing law in the same city, or in the same building, as their current firm. Yet physicians are routinely subject to post-employment covenants not to compete. Furthermore, they must accept these restrictions just to be initially hired!

A covenant not to compete is required by virtually all major physician employers, with few exceptions, because the employers have closed ranks. The covenants not to compete add enormously to the daily professional, financial, and emotional burdens that the physician bears in an already stressful work environment. For example, if another suitable job becomes available locally, it is barred to the physician, because of the covenant not to compete. Unlike attorneys, physicians must uproot themselves and their families and relocate outside the scope of the contract just to earn a living in a particular field.

Physicians consider the covenants not to compete as one of the most abused, over-reaching, and vile employment practices imaginable. Covenants not to compete for ordinary physicians have one principal purpose: to prevent a former employee from lawfully practicing medicine in the same community as the former employer. The covenants have little to do with trade secrets or other proprietary information, which could be protected by a suitable proprietary information or nondisclosure agreement. Solicitation of clients or patients could be handled by a suitable nonsolicitation of patients or referral sources agreement. Physicians (and many attorneys) agree that any true trade secrets already enjoy the protection of existing Uniform Trade Secrets Act laws. Thus, covenants not to compete for most ordinary physicians are simply unduly harsh restrictions that cannot be justified, especially during a time of physician shortages.

Today, legislation at the state level is advancing far faster than case law. Legislation restricting use of covenants not to compete has either been passed or been introduced in many states, mostly due to the recognized need by state legislatures to respond to abuses by businesses and employers. Most of the state legislation seeks to curb practices that are having a negative impact on the labor force and economy in the healthcare, informational technology, and banking sectors, among others.

When there is a legal challenge to a covenant not to compete in a jurisdiction where such covenants are legal or enforced, counsel seeking to uphold the covenant needs to anticipate that the true purpose of the covenant and the overall contract language will be highly scrutinized.[4] If the employer can pass the first level of scrutiny and show a legitimate, protectable business interest, then any such restriction must be narrowly tailored in the scope of activities restricted, the time period for which such activities are restricted, and the geographic area in which such activities are restricted. Counsel must check the latest state law, including any proposed or pending legislation, because many states have introduced legislation, or modifications to existing legislation, to limit covenants not to compete, due to their adverse impact on the economy. The public policy reasons for limiting or eliminating such covenants are a serious topic in state legislatures across the country, as discussed below.

III. BACKGROUND AND POLICY OF NONCOMPETES

For centuries, covenants not to compete were viewed as restraints of trade and were simply invalid at common law.[5] Over time, even though disfavored, some types of restraints became more acceptable, such as when ancillary to a sale of a business or a partnership agreement. The restraints were accepted on the basis that such types of transactions involved property and goodwill interests, and the parties presumably had equal bargaining position and could negotiate the terms of the transaction and decide whether or not to sell the business or enter into the partnership.[6]

Unfortunately, covenants not to compete began appearing in employment contracts, where their use became more problematic and subject to employer abuse. Today they are particularly controversial for many reasons, as the U.S. Department of the Treasury, the U.S. Department of Labor, the White House, and numerous state

---

[4] See Valley Med. Specialists v. Farber, 194 Ariz. 363, 982 P.2d 1277, 1283 (1999); Sammarco v. Anthem Ins. Cos., 723 N.E.2d 128, 132 (Ohio Ct. App. 1998), *overruled on other grounds*, 839 N.E.2d 49, 54 (Ohio Ct. App. 2005) ("[R]estrictive covenants that purport to limit a physician's ability to practice medicine in a geographic area are scrutinized more carefully than similar covenants restricting other types of employment.")

[5] See *Valley Medical*, 194 Ariz. 363, 982 P.2d 1277; Ohio Urology, Inc. v. Poll, 72 Ohio App. 3d 446, 594 N.E.2d 1027, 1031 (1991). See generally Harlan M. Blake, *Employee Agreements not to Compete*, 73 HARV. L. REV. 625 (1960); Serena L. Kafker, *Golden Handcuffs: Enforceability of Noncompetition Clauses in Professional Partnership Agreements of Accountants, Physicians, and Attorneys*, 31 AM. BUS. L.J. 31, 33 (1993).

[6] See generally RESTATEMENT 2D OF CONTRACTS §188 *Ancillary Restraints on Competition*, cmts. b, f (Oct. 2016 Update).

courts, policy makers and legislatures have observed. It is unfortunate because in employment situations, covenants not to compete are largely the product of unequal bargaining power and they have the effect of, among other things:

- depressing wages (because the employer knows the employee is contractually prohibited from changing jobs to work with a competing company in the locality);
- preventing workers from finding new employment with their existing skill set, even after being forced to leave the job involuntarily, such as when "down-sized," terminated without cause, or an employment contract is not renewed;
- reducing competition by routinely requiring covenants not to compete from nonexecutive workers who are unlikely to ever possess any meaningful trade secrets in the first place;[7]
- requiring existing workers to sign covenants not to compete after they've been on the job for years, or requiring new workers who have accepted the employer's offer of employment (and turned down other job offers) to sign a "surprise" noncompete agreement as part of the stack of hiring papers (and not being in a position to refuse to sign the agreement);[8]
- having a detrimental effect on the health and well-being of the public by restricting the labor pool and consumer choice, particularly in the area of healthcare workers; and

---

[7]Famously, Jimmy Johns, a national chain, required its thousands of sandwich makers and drivers to sign a two-year noncompete buried in the fine print of its job application form. The noncompete was justified on the grounds of protecting "trade secrets." It prohibited former employees from working in "any business which derives more than 10% of its revenue from selling submarine, hero-type, deli-style, pita and/or wrapped or rolled sandwiches located with three miles of either [the Jimmy John's location in question] or any such other Jimmy John's Sandwich Shop" for two years after the workers employment ceased at Jimmy John's. http://www.forbes.com/sites/clareoconnor/2014/10/15/does-jimmy-johns-non-compete-clause-for-sandwich-makers-have-legal-legs/#771063402740.

[8]There is a split of authority as to whether continued employment of an at-will employee is sufficient consideration to support the validity or enforceability of a restrictive covenant such as a covenant not to compete. See RESTATEMENT OF EMPLOYMENT LAW §8.06 *Enforcement of Restrictive Covenants in Employment Agreements*, cmt. e, and the cases cited therein. There are also state statutes governing what consideration is necessary and what notices have to be provided to a potential job applicant if a covenant not to compete is contemplated. *E.g.*, N.H. REV. STAT. ANN §275.70 (non-compete must be disclosed and provided to employee prior to the employees acceptance of an offer of employment).

- employers habitually inserting overbroad and unenforceable covenants not to compete and other restrictive covenants in employment agreements and relying on the courts to bring the contracts in line with the state law, gambling on the fact that the employee is unlikely to know the law or have the re sources to challenge the employer in court.[9]

To date there is no U.S. federal standard governing enforcement of noncompete agreements. That leaves enforcement of covenants not to compete or other restrictive covenants in employment agreements, partnership agreements, and other agreements to be governed by state law. Consequently, enforcement results differ from state to state.

State law, particularly state legislation regarding covenants not to compete is extremely dynamic. The reader is strongly advised to check the very latest legislation in the relevant state, including any introduced legislation that might be in a legislative committee, to find out what to expect in terms of future legislation.[10] State statutes pertaining to physician noncompete agreements is discussed in Section V, below.

IV. TYPES OF RESTRICTIVE COVENANTS RELEVANT TO PHYSICIAN EMPLOYMENT AGREEMENTS

For physician employment agreements, there are three main types of post-employment termination restrictive covenants: (1) a covenant not to compete, which sets forth a time period and a geographic area in which a former employee cannot practice close to

---

[9]See generally The White House, Non-Compete Agreements: Analysis of the Usage, Potential Issues, and State Responses (May 16, 2016), for an overview of the misuse of noncompetes and the effect on the national economy and samplings of various state legislative and court solutions to curb such abuse. *See also* Non-Compete Contracts: Economic Effects and Policy Implications, https://www.treasury.gov/resource-center/economic-policy/Documents/UST%20Non-competes%20Report.pdf (providing overview of research on non-competes' prevalence, enforcement, and effects on economy).

[10]An outstanding analysis of relevant state authority for all 50 states and the District of Columbia can be found in an American Bar Association (ABA) publication by Brian Malsberger, *Covenants Not to Compete—A State by State Survey* (10th ed. 2016), which is supplemented annually. It provides a concise analysis of cases, statues, treatises and more relating to covenants not to compete and is an essential resource for the healthcare employment legal practitioner.

the former employees former place of employment; (2) a patient and physician referral source nonsolicitation covenant, which sets forth rules about soliciting patients or referral sources from the former practice to go to the new practice; and (3) an employee nonsolicitation covenant, which sets forth rules about employing former employees when the physician departs from the former place of employment.[11]

V. Covenants Not to Compete in Physician Employment Contracts Are Strongly Disfavored and Banned or Restricted by Statue in Many States

Covenants not to compete in employment contracts have always been controversial and are disfavored by the courts, legislatures, and the public in general.[12] But they are even more disfavored in contracts involving physicians and thus require a higher level of scrutiny than the already high level of scrutiny generally applied to covenants not to compete in commercial relationships.[13]

---

[11]*See generally* Ferdinand S. Tinio, Annotation, *Validity and Construction of Contractual Restrictions on Right of Medical Practitioner to Practice, Incident to Employment Agreement*, 62 A.L.R.3d 1014 (1975).

[12]"Many courts are more suspect of restraints accompanying employment contracts than they are of restraints accompanying the sale of business and so these courts apply a stricter scrutiny to covenants accompanying employment agreements." CORBIN ON CONTRACTS §80.15 (2013).

[13]*See* Valley Med. Specialists v. Farber, 194 Ariz. 363, 982 P.2d 1277 (1999); Intermountain Eye & Laser Ctrs., v. Miller, 142 Idaho 218, 127 P.3d 121, 127 (2005) ("Covenants not to compete in employment contracts are 'disfavored' and 'strictly construed against the employer.' Non-compete provisions must be reasonable, which is to say they must not be more restrictive than necessary to protect a legitimate business interest, must not be unduly harsh and oppressive to the employee, and must not be injurious to the public." (quoting Freiburger v. J-U-B Engs., Inc., 141 Idaho 415, 419–20, 111 P.3d 100, 104–05 (2005), and Stipp v. Wallace Plating, Inc., 96 Idaho 5, 6, 523 P.2d 822, 823 (1974)); Ohio Urology, Inc. v. Poll, 72 Ohio App. 3d 446, 594 N.E.2d 1027 (1991); Sammarco v. Anthem Ins. Cos., 723 N.E.2d 128, 132 (Ohio Ct. App. 1998), *overruled on other grounds*, 839 N.E.2d 49, 54 (Ohio Ct. App. 2005) ("[R]estrictive covenants that purport to limit a physician's ability to practice medicine in a geographic area are scrutinized more carefully than similar covenants restricting other types of employment."). *But see* Medical Specialists Inc. v. Sleweon, 652 N.E.2d 517, 527 (Ind. Ct. App. 1995) ("Covenants ... which restrict the provision of medical services ... are not per se against public policy.").

While California and North Dakota have banned covenants not to compete in employment agreements for all employees,[14] others have either banned them for some employees such as physicians and other healthcare workers or limited covenants not to compete in general. This has been accomplished by statute and by case law.

Since this chapter focuses on physicians, we will focus on the statutes and case law banning or restricting covenants not to compete and other restrictive covenants in employment agreements involving physicians. The importance of being aware of the latest developments in terms of state legislation and state case law on the subject of covenants not to compete cannot be overstated.

A brief overview of some of the state statutes involving physicians are provided below. See Appendix A for a more complete list of statutory text. Case law is discussed in Section VI, below. Appendix A also lists a selection of relevant physician-specific and other case law particular to the identified state.

In addition to California and North Dakota (referenced above) presently the following states have statutes relating specifically to physicians:

- **Colorado:** Provides that any covenant not to compete in employment, partnership, or corporate agreements between physicians that restrict the right of a physician to practice medicine upon termination of such agreement is void. However, the statute itself leaves open the question of whether hospitals, which are corporations and not "physicians" and which are permitted to employ physicians, are also banned from using noncompetes in their employment contracts with physicians.[15]

- **Connecticut:** While Connecticut does not outright prohibit physician noncompetes, it does limit the duration to one year and geographic scope to no more than 15 miles from the primary site where such physician practices. Any such noncompete is *unenforceable* if the physician's employment or contractual relationship is terminated without cause or if

---

[14]CAL. BUS. & PROF. CODE §16600 prohibits all employee noncompete agreements. (Note that in California, limited noncompetes are permitted in connection with the sale of a business.) N.D. CENT. CODE §9-08-06 (permits limited covenant not to compete exceptions involving the sale of a business or in the case of a partnership dissolution).

[15]COLO. REV. STAT. §8-2-113(3) (1982).

the employment contract or agreement expires or is not re-newed.[16]

- **Delaware:** Provides that covenants not to compete are void in any employment agreement, partnership, or corporate agreement between and/or among physicians that restricts the right of a physician to practice medicine in a particular locale and/or for a defined period of time.[17]

- **Massachusetts:** Provides that a contract or agreement that includes a restriction of the right of a physician to practice medicine in any geographic area for *any* period of time after the termination of a partnership, employment, or professional relationship shall be void and unenforceable.[18]

- **New Hampshire:** Provides that any contract or agreement which includes any restriction on the right of the physician to practice medicine in any geographic area for *any* period of time after the termination of such partnership, employment, or professional relationship shall be void and unenforceable with respect to such restriction.[19]

- **New Mexico:** Makes noncompetition covenants unenforceable against employee healthcare practitioners, defined to include dentists, osteopathic physicians, physicians, podiatrists, and certified registered nurse anesthetists, but allows the employer to recover relocation expenses and signing bonuses, authorizes the enforcement of nonsolicitation provisions, and allows the recovery of reasonable liquidated damages if certain conditions are met. The New Mexico statute does not apply to healthcare practitioners who are shareholders, owners, partners, or directors of a healthcare practice.[20]

- **Rhode Island:** Declares void and unenforceable "[a]ny contract or agreement that creates the terms of a partnership, employment, or other form of professional relationship with a physician licensed to practice medicine pursuant to [chapter 37 of title 5 of the Rhode Island General Laws] that includes any restriction on the right to practice medicine." It also voids

---

[16]Pub. Act No. 16-95 (effective July 1, 2016).
[17]6 DEL. CODE ANN. §2707.
[18]MASS. GEN. LAWS, c 112, §12X (effective Nov. 23, 1977).
[19]N.H. Rev. Stat., tlt. XXX, ch. 329, §329:31-a (effective Aug. 5, 2016).
[20]N.M. STAT. ANN. §§ 24-1I-1 through 24-1I-5 (effective July 1, 2015).

any contract that seeks to prevent a physician from soliciting patients of the physician's former employer. There is an exception for the purchase and sale of a physician's practice if the restrictive covenant is for less than five years.[21]

- **Tennessee:** Provides that covenants to compete are not applicable to physicians specializing in emergency medicine. However, other employed or contracted healthcare workers may be subject to covenants not to compete after termination or conclusion of the employment or contractual relationship, provided that certain statutory requirements are met. See Appendix A attached hereto for more details.[22]

- **Texas:** Specifies the requirements for enforceable covenants not to compete with respect to a physician. A covenant not to compete against a physician is enforceable provided certain statutory requirements are met. See Appendix A attached hereto for more details.[23]

Some states do not completely ban covenants not to compete, but only allow them in limited circumstances, such as in the sale of a business or in an employment situation only if they meet certain statutory requirements (e.g., if they do not exceed a certain length of time,[24] if they describe the precise geographic region,[25] etc.). Other states have passed legislation setting forth other types of minimum requirements as to the use of covenants not to compete and other restrictive covenants in employment contracts. Such requirements must be complied with or the covenants will be void or otherwise enforceable.

---

[21] R.I. GEN. LAWS §5-37-33.
[22] TENN. CODE ANN. §63-1-148(d).
[23] TEX. BUS. & COM. Code §§15.50–.52.
[24] *E.g.*, UTAH CODE §§34-51-101. Utah 34-51-101.34-51-101. restricts any employer–employee noncompete to no more than one year from termination, applicable to all employment agreements that go into effect beginning May 10, 2016. *See also* OR. REV. STAT. §653.295(2) (for agreements executed after January 1, 2016, the covenant may not exceed 18 months after the date of termination and is voidable for any time period thereafter).
[25] *E.g.*, LA. REV. STAT. ANN. §23:921. The parties have to specify the parish or parishes, municipality or municipalities, or parts thereof where the employer is actually doing "like business" for the noncompete to be enforceable, and the noncompete cannot exceed two years.

Essential Resource Tip: For information on covenants not to compete, the best compilation and analysis of relevant state authority for all 50 states and the District of Columbia is found in Brian Malsberger's *Covenants Not to Compete—A State by State Survey* (10th edition), published in 2016 and supplemented annually. It is well organized and easy to navigate. It provides the relevant state statutes, a concise analysis of the relevant case law interpreting the statutes, and an analysis of the significance of any legislative change. Among many other things, this publication identifies protected classes of worker (such as physicians, attorneys, newscasters, information technology (IT) workers, low-income workers, and other workers who may be entitled to special protections). It also includes thoughtful information on obtaining injunctions, burden of proof, "blue-penciling," assignability, and other information with respect to relevant business, litigation, and intellectual property issues related to this important topic, as interpreted in the relevant state.

VI. STATE COMMON LAW RULES APPLICABLE TO PHYSICIAN NONCOMPETE AGREEMENTS

A. Synopsis of the Common Law

Because most states do not have specific statutes banning covenants not to compete, the courts have to apply the common law as it exists in that particular state or as it is modified by statute. The *Restatement of Employment Law* §§8.05–8.07, set forth in Section V.C, below, recognizes the majority rule, which in summary provides that unless the employer and employee have an enforceable agreement stating otherwise, after the employment relationship ends, the employee is free to make a living and compete in the marketplace, including competing with the former employer and soliciting former clients and employees of the former employer.

That said, the *Restatement of Employment Law* also recognizes that fair competition does not include the use of the former employer's specifically identifiable trade secrets. Such trade secrets must be protectable trade secrets or other confidential information that the employer made reasonable efforts to keep secret. Trade secrets do not include the employee's knowledge or skills that the employee obtained prior to coming to the job, or training, experience, or skills the employee developed during the ordinary course of the employee's employment.

B. Common-Law Rule of Reason Test

A typical common-law rule of reason test was set forth by the U.S. Court of Appeals for the Fourth Circuit in *Deutsche Post Global Mail, Ltd. v. Conrad*, applying Maryland law and declining to enforce an overbroad restriction.[26] All of the following must apply for any type of covenant not to compete to be enforceable:

(1) The employer must have a legally protected interest;
(2) The restrictive covenant must be no wider in scope and duration than is reasonably necessary to protect the employer's interest;
(3) The covenant cannot impose an undue hardship on the employee; and
(4) The covenant cannot violate public policy.[27]

C. Analysis Based on the Restatement of Employment Law

Because covenants not to compete are such a highly contested area of employment law today, particularly with respect to healthcare workers, an examination of the relevant common law is necessary. Even in states that ban physician covenants not to compete, there are other types of restrictive covenants involved in a physician employment agreement, such as patient nonsolicitation covenants or referral nonsolicitation covenants, which may require a similar common

---

[26]116 F. App'x 435, 438–39 (4th Cir. 2004).

[27]*See e.g.*, Omniplex World Servs. Corp. v. U.S. Investigations Servs., Inc., 618 S.E.2d 340 (Va. 2005) ("[p]rotection of the employer, not punishment of the employee, is the essence of the law"; noncompetition agreement between employer and employee enforced if contract is narrowly drawn to protect employer's legitimate business interest, is not unduly burdensome on employee's ability to earn a living, and is not against public policy); Healthcare Services of the Ozarks, Inc. v. Copeland, 198 S.W.3d 604 (Mo. 2006) ("Enforcing non-compete agreements involves delicate balance of practical business considerations. While the former employee is free to compete, the former employer is entitled to utilize non-compete agreements to protect itself from unfair competition by misuse of its trade secrets or misuse of the employee's customers contacts developed at its expense. Protection of the employer, not punishment of the employee, is the essence of the law." (internal quotation marks omitted)).

law-analysis. The following information is provided to help counsel think through whatever employment situation may be presented.

The *Restatement of Employment Law*, Sections 8.05 through 8.07, address noncompete agreements.[28]

§8.05 Competition by Former Employee with Former Employer

A former employee may compete with, or work for, a competitor of the former employer, including by soliciting customers or recruiting employees, unless:

(a) the former employee is bound by an agreement not to compete (or not to solicit or recruit) enforceable under §§8.06 and 8.07; or

(b) in doing so the former employee discloses, uses, or by words or conduct threatens to disclose or use, specifically identifiable trade secrets of the former employer in violation of §8.03.

§8.06 Enforcement of Restrictive Covenants in Employment Agreements

Except as otherwise provided by other law or applicable professional rules, a covenant in an agreement between an employer and a former employee restricting the former employee's working activities is enforceable only if it is reasonably tailored in scope, geography, and time to further a protectable interest of the employer, as defined in § 8.07, unless:

(a) the employer discharges the employee on a basis that makes enforcement of the covenant inequitable;

(b) the employer acted in bad faith in requiring or invoking the covenant;

(c) the employer materially breached the underlying employment agreement; or

(d) in the geographic region covered by the restriction, a great public need for the special skills and services of the former employee outweighs any legitimate interest of the employer in enforcing the covenant.

---

[28]RESTATEMENT OF EMPLOYMENT LAW §§8.05–8.07.

Comment (b) to Section 8.06 is particularly instructive:

A court will enforce a restrictive covenant only if it is reasonably tailored to the protection of a legitimate interest of the employer as set forth in § 8.07. To be reasonably tailored, the covenant should be no more restrictive in duration, scope of activities, or geography than necessary to protect the legitimate interest at stake.

§8.07 Protectable Interests for Restrictive Covenants

(a) A restrictive covenant is enforceable only if the employer can demonstrate that the covenant furthers a legitimate interest of the employer.

(b) An employer has a legitimate interest in protecting, by means of a reasonably tailored restrictive covenant with its employee, the employer's:

(1) trade secrets, as defined in § 8.02,[29] and other protectable confidential information that does not meet the definition of trade secret;

(2) customer relationships;

(3) investment in the employee's reputation in the market; or

(4) purchase of a business owned by the employee.

D. Applying the Rule of Reason in Case Law

In the absence of controlling legislation requiring otherwise, state courts apply the common law in deciding whether to uphold post-employment restrictive covenants. That requires closely scrutinizing the purpose of the restrictive covenant, the specific language of the restrictive covenant, and the specific facts of the case at hand to determine whether the employer has established a legally protectable business interest sufficient to justify the restrictive covenant. (Simply wanting to avoid competition from a former employee is

---

[29] See §8.02 Definition of Employer's Trade Secret: "An employer's information is a trade secret under this Chapter if: (a) it derives independent economic value from being kept secret; (b) the employer has taken reasonable measures to keep it secret; and (c) the information is not (1) generally known to the public or in the employer's industry; (2) readily obtainable by others through proper means; or (3) acquired by employees through their general experience, knowledge, training, or skills during the ordinary course of their employment."

not a legally protectable interest.)[30] If a legally protectable business interest is established, the court must consider whether the imposed limitation as to time, geographical area, and type of employment restricted is reasonable under the circumstances, considering the potential harm to the employee and the public. Each stage of the analysis is intensely fact dependent, regardless whether the contract provision at issue is a covenant not to compete or a nonsolicitation covenant.

The Arizona Supreme Court rendered a thoughtful and in-depth analysis of the physician-patient relationship and its effect on restrictive covenants between doctors in *Valley Medical Specialists v. Farber*,[31] a case between a pulmonologist and his former pulmonology group. It is worthwhile to understand the rationale involved in this case because it is this type of analysis that courts apply in cases involving physician covenants not to compete.

Dr. Farber was a shareholder and employee of a pulmonary group known as Valley Medical Specialists (VMS). The noncompete in question prevented him from practicing medicine for a period of three years following termination of employment (for any reason) within a five-mile radius from any pulmonology facility owned or used by VMS. The agreement included a patient nonsolicitation provision restricting him from practicing medicine or treating any former patients, and included a liquidated damages clause in the event of breach. It also included a provision where he expressly acknowledged and agreed that the various covenants not to compete contained therein were reasonable in scope and necessary to protect the legitimate interest of VMS and its goodwill.

Dr. Farber left VMS and subsequently practiced medicine within the restricted area, treating patients who were former patients of VMS. VMS filed a complaint against Dr. Farber seeking (1) preliminary and permanent injunctions enjoining Dr. Farber from violating the restrictive covenant, (2) liquidated damages for breach of the employment agreement, and (3) damages for breach of fiduciary duty, conversion of patient files and confidential information, and intentional interference with contractual and/or business relations.

---

[30]Ohio Urology, Inc. v. Poll, 72 Ohio App. 3d 446, 594 N.E.2d 1027 (1991); Valley Med. Specialists v. Farber, 194 Ariz. 363, 982 P.2d 1277 (1999).
[31]194 Ariz. 363, 982 P.2d 1277 (1999).

After testimony, the trial court denied the preliminary injunction, finding that the restrictive covenant was unenforceable because it violated public policy or, alternatively, that it was unenforceable because it was too broad. Specifically, the trial court found that (1) any covenant over six months was unreasonable; and (2) the five-mile radius from each of the three VMS offices was unreasonable because it covered a total of 235 square miles, it did not provide an exception for emergency medical aid, and was not limited to pulmonology. On appeal, the appellate court reversed, saying the non-compete provisions could be made reasonable if modified by the trial court. Thereafter the case was appealed to the Arizona Supreme Court.

In relevant part, the Supreme Court stated:

> By restricting a physician's practice of medicine, this covenant involves strong public policy implications and must be closely scrutinized. *See Peairs*, 164 Ariz. at 60, 790 P.2d at 758; *Ohio Urology, Inc.*, 594 N.E.2d at 1032 (restrictive covenant in medical context "strictly construed in favor of professional mobility and access to medical care and facilities"). Although stopping short of banning restrictive covenants between physicians, the American Medical Association ("AMA") "discourages" such covenants, finding they are not in the public interest. ... In addition, the AMA recognizes that free choice of doctors is the right of every patient, and free competition among physicians is a prerequisite of optimal care and ethical practice. *See* AMA Opinions, Section 9.06; *Ohio Urology, Inc.*, 594 N.E. 2d at 1030. For similar reasons, restrictive covenants are prohibited between attorneys. ...
>
> We therefore conclude that the doctor-patient relationship is special and entitled to unique protection. It cannot be easily or accurately compared to relationships in the commercial context. In light of the great public policy interest involved in covenants not to compete between physicians, each agreement will be strictly construed for reasonableness.[32]

The court examined whether the employer had a legitimate interest to protect:

> To be enforced, the restriction must do more than simply prohibit fair competition by the employee. In other words, a covenant not to compete is invalid unless it protects some legitimate interest beyond the employer's desire to protect itself from competition. The legitimate purpose of post-employment restraints is "to prevent competitive use, for a time, of information or relationships which pertain peculiarly to

---

[32]*Id.* at 368–69, 982 P.2d at 1282–83 (citations and footnote omitted).

the employer and which the employee acquired in the course of the employment. Despite the freedom to contract, the law does not favor restrictive covenants. *Ohio Urology, Inc. v. Poll*, 594 N.E. 2nd 1027 (1991), at 1031. This disfavor is particularly strong concerning such covenants among physicians because the practice of medicine affects the public to a much greater extent. Id. In fact, "[f]or the past 60 years, the American Medical Association (AMA) has consistently taken the position that noncompetition agreements between physicians impact negatively on patient care." Paula Berg, Judicial Enforcement of Covenants not to Compete Between Physicians: Protecting Doctors' Interests at Patients' Expense, 45 RUTGERS L. REV. 1, 6 (1992).[33]

On the nature of reasonableness, the court said that

> [r]easonableness is a fact-intensive inquiry that depends on the totality of the circumstances. A restriction is unreasonable and thus will not be enforced: (1) if the restraint is greater than necessary to protect the employer's legitimate interest; or (2) if that interest is outweighed by the hardship to the employee and the likely injury to the public. ... Balancing these competing interests is no easy task and no exact formula can be used.[34]

VMS first claimed it had a legitimate protectable interest in its patient base (i.e., its customer base) and should be allowed to restrict Dr. Farber from seeing its patients. The Arizona Supreme Court disagreed, distinguishing a doctor-patient relationship from a commercial situation:

> In the medical context, however, the personal relationship between doctor and patient, as well as the patient's freedom to see a particular doctor, affects the extent of the employer's interest. *See Ohio Urology Inc.*, 594 N.E.2d at 1031–32. "The practice of a physician is a thing so purely personal, depending so absolutely on the confidence reposed in his personal skill and ability, that when he ceases to exist it necessarily ceases also ... ." *Mandeville* [*v. Harman*, 42 N.J. Eq. 185, 7 A. 377 A. 37, 40–41 (1886)] (holding medical practice's patient base is not a protectable interest); [*see also Mandeville*, 7 A. at 38–39 *Karlin v. Weinberg*, 77 N.J. 408, 390 A.2d 1161, 1165 (1978)]; *see also* Berg, *supra*, 45 RUTGERS L. REV. at 17. ...
>
> Dr. Farber was a pulmonologist. He did not learn his skills from VMS. Restrictive covenants are designed to protect an employer's customer base by preventing "a skilled employee from leaving an employer and, based on his skill acquired from that employment, luring away the employer's clients or business while the employer is vulnerable—that is—before the employer has had a chance to replace the

---

[33]*Id.* at 367, 982 P.2d at 1281 (citations omitted).
[34]*Id.* at 369, 982 P.2d at 1283 (citations omitted).

employee with someone qualified to do the job." *Bryceland*, 160 Ariz. at 217, 772 P.2d at 40. These facts support the trial judge's conclusion that VMS's interest in protecting its patient base was outweighed by other factors.[35]

After the court disposed of the first argument, it considered VMS's second argument, which was that VMS had a legitimate interest in protecting its referral sources. The court agreed, and once determining that the initial threshold of establishing a legitimate protectable interest (i.e., protecting its physician referral source) was met, the court moved on to the next step of the analysis, which was to look at the unique facts of the case at hand and determine whether the scope of restrictive covenants with respect to time and geography and other restrictions was limited enough to protect the employer, the employee, and the public.

After determining that the employer had a protectable interest in protecting its physician referral source, the court applied the "rule of reason" balancing test recognized in Arizona and most other states, scrutinizing every argument that VMS raised to justify the noncompete clause to see whether the noncompete restriction was reasonable and should be enforced.

The court determined that the covenant not to compete was unreasonable and therefore unenforceable for public policy reasons and because the restrictive covenant was overbroad. Specifically, (1) three years was too long a time restriction and therefore unreasonable, since the trial court had determined that six months would be a reasonable time period based on the nature of the pulmonology practice; (2) the geographic restriction of a five-mile radius from the former employer's three office locations was too broad; and (3) in Dr. Farber's case, he was a pulmonologist and internist but the covenant not to compete prohibited him from engaging with any competitor "in the practice of medicine." This restriction was entirely too broad and excluded Dr. Farber from practicing emergency medicine, brachytherapy treatment, or HIV-positive and AIDS patient care, all of which medical services he was capable of performing.

The Arizona Supreme Court determined that patients should be able to see the doctor of their choice, and that right was entitled to

---

[35]*Id.* at 370, 982 P.2d at 1284.

substantial protection, and in that regard VMS's protectable interests were comparatively minimal.

> Valley Medical Specialists' interest in enforcing the restriction is outweighed by the likely injury to patients and the public in general. ... The public policy implications here are enough to invalidate this particular agreement. We stop short of holding that restrictive covenants between physicians will never be enforced, but caution that such restrictions will be strictly construed. The burden is on the party wishing to enforce the covenant to demonstrate that the restraint is no greater than necessary to protect the employer's legitimate interest, and that such interest is not outweighed by the hardship to the employee and the likely injury to the public. Here VMS has not met that burden. The restriction fails because its public policy implications outweigh the legitimate interests of VMS.[36]

If a noncompete restriction is not reasonable under the circumstances, it is not enforceable. Courts can, however, use their equitable powers to consider whether the restrictive covenant should be modified or entirely rejected, depending on the jurisdiction and the judge hearing the request. Some courts may address unenforceable or overly broad covenants not to compete by "equitable reformation" to bring the offending provisions in line with state law. Some courts will "blue pencil" the offending provisions if striking the offensive language renders the remaining language enforceable under the state's law,[37] but other courts "red pencil" the provisions, that is, void the entire noncompete for any unenforceable provision. The reader is advised to check the relevant state to find out how a court in the relevant jurisdiction will likely treat an overbroad noncompete provision.[38]

---

[36]*Id.* at 372, 982 P.2d at 1286. For other interesting cases, see *Board of Regents v. Warren*, 2008 Iowa App. LEXIS 1192 (Iowa Ct. App. 2008) (unpublished) (finding a noncompete agreement overbroad because it prohibited a physician from practicing any medicine, not just oncology, and also finding that enforcement would be inappropriate because the physician's practice was in an area suffering from a shortage of oncologists, and thus enforcement would detrimentally affect the public interest); *Dick v. Geist*, 693 P.2d 1133 (Idaho App. 1985); *Iredell Digestive Disease Clinic, P.A. v. Petrozza*, 373 S.E.2d 449 (N.C. App. 1988).

[37]See *Valley Medical Specialists*, 194 Ariz. 363, 982 P.2d 1277.

[38]*See* White House Briefing, Non-Compete Agreements: Analysis of the Usage, Potential Issues, and State Responses, at 11 (May 2016).

VII. COMPETING PERSPECTIVES

In reviewing the relevant provisions of the *Restatement of Employment Law* §§8.05–8.07, the common-law rule of reason test, and the *Farber* case, discussed in Section VI.D, above, keep in mind that in cases involving physicians, except in jurisdictions where states have outright banned physician noncompetes, courts will end up balancing competing perspectives. Here are the most often cited perspectives from the employee/physician versus the employer that each side will need to be prepared to address to a judge or other finder of fact.

A. Physician's Perspective

From the perspective of the physician-employee and physician's counsel, covenants not to compete are unnecessary and unduly burdensome because of the following considerations:

- Physician employment contracts are essentially contracts of adhesion due to the consolidation of the healthcare delivery system.[39] Today hospitals, large medical groups, staffing companies, and other major healthcare provider employers present employment contracts that include covenants not to compete to physicians on a take-it-or-leave-it basis in an effort to protect themselves against competing healthcare systems, and have essentially "closed ranks" with respect to

  (1) insisting on overbroad noncompete provisions which the employer is gambling won't be challenged by the Physician in court;

  (2) insisting on termination of employment without cause provisions (with written notice);

  (3) insisting on vague, subjective or reputational termination "for cause" provisions;

  (4) insisting on noncompete provisions even in cases of termination without cause or nonrenewal of Physician's employment contract; and

---

[39] Allison E. McClure, *The Professional Presumption: Do Professional Employees Really Have Equal Bargaining Power When They Enter Into Employment-Related Adhesion Contracts?*, 74 U. CIN. L. REV. 1497, 1518–19 (2005–2006).

(5)   requiring that the physician automatically lose or resign the physician's hospital privileges along with the loss of their employment status (known as "clean sweeps provisions").

All of these provisions typically trigger the overbroad noncompete and nonsolicitation clauses.

• Employers are simply trying to avoid normal competition by making it unworkable for physicians to change jobs and stay in the area. Requiring physicians to interrupt their career, drive long distances, suffer moving expenses, take their children out of school, and restart in a new community, and so on, are simply tactics to keep physicians from leaving their employer even if they are unhappy, overworked, underpaid, or otherwise being mistreated. Employers are making it harder than it needs to be on physicians in what is becoming a more and more closed system. Most covenants not to compete in employment contracts have zero to do with protecting trade secrets or proprietary information, but everything to do with protecting employers from any perceived competition, no matter how remote.

• Physicians come to the job already highly trained, with many years of graduate medical school education and residency, and in many cases, specialized internship, board certification, and other advanced training, all of which was hard earned by the physician, not the employer. A covenant not to compete that impacts a physician's future employment and economic opportunities for months or years after the end of the employment relationship cannot be justified on the basis of employer-provided human capital training. In fact, often the reverse is true—the physician ends up training other employees.

• Physicians are in high demand and should have the freedom to practice medicine in a community of their choosing, without being controlled by a former employer. Why should a physician have to relocate his or her family to earn a living after leaving—or having to leave—an employer instead of joining another medical practice or hospital in the same area?

• The physician earns referrals through his or her hard work and largely through other patient referrals. Referrals come to the physician who has been in practice for years and has earned those referrals based on the individual physician's clinical knowledge, affability, availability, and ability to attract and retain referring physicians' trust and patients' trust.

- Covenants not to compete have utterly no legitimacy for emergency room (ER) or urgent care physicians, radiologists, anesthesiologists, or pathologists, who have no patient base or referral base to take to another employer. Their so-called "patients" don't come to see them in particular. ER physicians don't control the patients they treat. They see patients that end up in the ER. Any concept of a "referral source" is a joke. What legitimate, protectable patient base will that physician walk away with when the physician leaves that would harm the former employer to such an extent as to justify a covenant not to compete restricting a highly trained and publically needed physician from future employment opportunities in the immediate area?[40] How likely is it that a patient is going to show up in the ER only to see a particular ER doctor? Or get an X-ray performed and read by a particular radiologist who just happened to be reading X-rays at the time in question? Or come to a particular hospital to get their lab sample read by a particular pathologist?

- The employer needed the physician's medical services or the employer wouldn't have hired the physician. The employer received the benefit of the physician's professional services and presumably charged patients for the physician's professional services, at the rate set by the employer, not the physician. The employer received the benefit of any employment bargain and should not later be able to limit the physician's future employment opportunities after the employee has fully performed for the employer.

- A typical physician does not have access to nonpublic, executive-type "trade secret" proprietary technology or confidential

---

[40]Larry D. Weiss, MD, JD, FAAEM, AAEM, *White Paper on Restrictive Covenants: A Policy Paper of the American Academy of Emergency Medicine*, J. OF EMERG. MED. 30:473–75 (2006), http://www.aaem.org/em-resources/position-statements/practice-rights/restrictive-covenants. Dr. Weiss is Professor of Emergency Medicine at the University of Maryland School of Medicine. The white paper was approved with revisions by the American Academy of Emergency Medicine Board of Directors at its July 16, 2007, meeting.

information of an employer. Unlike CEOs of major businesses, most physicians are not in positions where they direct or have access to any material aspect of a healthcare business or its strategic decisions or direction. So the thought of the physician having confidential information that could sink the former employer is disingenuous.[41]

- An employer's trade secrets can be protected by a nondisclosure agreement or by existing Uniform Trade Secrets Act laws instead of resorting to a covenant not to compete that serves no purpose other than the hidden purpose of preventing a former employee from lawfully practicing medicine in the same community as the former employer.

- State medical boards often place obligations on physicians regarding continuing care of patients. Physicians have to avoid what is referred to as patient abandonment. Noncompete provisions and patient nonsolicitation covenants interfere with those obligations.[42]

- It is the individual physician, not the employer, who takes responsibility for making the patient better and satisfying the patient and the patient's family. If a patient has faith and trust in a particular physician and the patient wishes to continue to see that particular physician, then the patient should have the free choice to continue to see who that patient thinks is the best physician for his or her needs. The patient does not suspect that the employer can interfere in the doctor-patient relationship due to a covenant not to compete.

---

[41] Such information could include the employer's financial statements, proprietary formulas, breakthrough technologies, patent applications, cost and pricing information, payor negotiations, payroll details, tax strategies, benefit strategies, supplier agreements, financial plans, product development plans, long term strategic plans, restricted company technology, etc.,

[42] Once the physician-patient relationship has been created, physicians are subject to an obligation of continuous treatment once the relationship or treatment has started. As stated in *Ricks v. Budge*, 91 Utah 307, 64 P.2d 208 (1937), "the obligation of continuing attention can be terminated only by the cessation of the necessity which gave rise to the relationship or by the discharge of the physician by the patient, or by the withdrawal from the case by the physician after giving the patient reasonable notice so as to enable the patient to secure other medical attention." As succinctly stated by expert health law professor, Barry Furrow, "[r]efusal to continue to treat a patient is abandonment, and it may also be malpractice." Furrow, Greaney, Johnson-Jost & Schwartz, HEALTH LAW §3-1.a, at 72–73 and cases cited therein (3d ed. 2015).

B. Employer's Perspective

From the perspective of the employer and employer's counsel, covenants not to compete are necessary because of the following considerations:

- The employer should protect its good will, trade secrets,[43] and confidential information from unfair use by the former employee. Reasonably restricting where and how the former employee may practice medicine in the future is an acceptable means to accomplish that purpose.

- The employer won't be able to confidently share confidential information with employees if the employer has to worry about an employee using that information in competition with the employer later, so restricting the employees employment opportunities for a reasonable time as to competitors is a reasonable way to protect that confidential information.

- The employer may have invested in staff and equipment to support the employed physician beyond what the employer received as payment from the physician's medical services. It would be unfair for the physician to voluntarily leave and open a new practice or work for a competing practice in the area before the employer can hire a replacement.

- Where the employer has invested in the physician employee by furnishing medical facilities or patients (or buying the practice of a physician and then employing the physician), the employer should be able to protect that investment and can do so by obtaining assurances from the physician that upon his or her departure, the physician won't set up or work for a competing medical firm nearby or solicit patients and referral sources until some reasonable time period has passed.

---

[43]Trade secrets are generally defined as "technical or nontechnical data, a formula, pattern, compilation, program, device, method, technique, or process that derives independent economic value, actual or potential, from not being generally known to, and not being readily ascertainable by proper means by other persons who can derive economic value from its disclosure or use." Conseco Fin. Serv. v. North Am. Mortg. Co., 381 F.3d 811, 818–19 (8th Cir. 2004). Practice note: this could be defined by statute in your jurisdiction. Be aware that the employer must have taken reasonable steps to protect the information from disclosure.

VIII. NONSOLICITATION OF EMPLOYEE CLAUSES

Nonsolicitation of employee clauses are a different type of restrictive covenant that prohibit the recruitment of co-workers in an effort to get them to work for or with an employee after that employee quits or otherwise leaves the employer. The employer's business interest in this type of covenant is to preserve its talent pool and avoid as much as possible the threat of that talent pool being raided by—or going to work for—a potential competitor (such as the former employee). On the other hand, co-employees have a right to job mobility and opportunity to improve their work circumstances. They may very well have only stayed on with the employer to work with the employee that left.

Since nonsolicitation-of-employee clauses are restrictive covenants, the analysis described in Section VI, above, applies.[44]

> ***Practice Tip:*** When drafting or commenting on a nonsolicitation contract provision, define nonsolicitation as "purposeful" and "direct" contact with an employee in an attempt to convince the employee to leave the employer's employment and join the departing physician. Also limit the provision as to a time period starting from the date the departing physician left the employment of the employer and ending at a time certain (e.g., "twelve months following the date of physician's termination").

"Solicitation" has been defined as "asking; enticing; urgent request."[45] Therefore, make sure it is clear in the contract that if other employees contact the former employee or leave the employer voluntarily and the former employee did not contact them or ask them to leave, the nonsolicitation clause is not triggered. The clause should be limited to current employees of the employer (i.e., employees who are employed at the time of the former employee's departure), not past or future employees. This avoids triggering the nonsolicitation covenant for past or future employees and does not disqualify workers who happen to be past or future employees from responding to an employment advertisement.

---

[44]*See* RESTATEMENT OF EMPLOYMENT LAW §8.06 *Enforcement of Restrictive Covenants in Employment Agreements*, cmt. a.

[45]BLACK'S LAW DICTIONARY (4th ed. 1968).

Practice Tip: It may be wise for members of a medical group being acquired by a hospital or healthcare system to exclude their former group's employees from application of this restrictive covenant if the members of the former group have retained the right to terminate their employment as a group or reestablish themselves as their former practice.

IX. NONSOLICITATION OF PATIENTS OR REFERRAL SOURCES (CUSTOMER) CLAUSES

Another form of restrictive covenant is a customer nonsolicitation clause, which in the context of physicians means nonsolicitation of patients or referral sources. This type of restriction attempts to limit when, how, and under what circumstances a departing physician may contact or provide notice to the physician's patients or referral sources, and in some cases, the general public, about the physician's new location and availability for practice.

As is the case for any covenant not to compete, the same strict judicial examination should be applied to this form of restrictive covenant.[46] Depending on the relevant state statutes and case law, if permitted at all, the covenant's validity and enforceability will turn on the purpose of the covenant, the exact language of the covenant, the competing public policy interests, the hardship to the physician and the public, the unique facts of case, and how tailored the proposed covenant is in terms of time, geography, and type of contact.

Be aware that some states have statutes or case law prohibiting such nonsolicitation agreements as a violation of public policy. Counsel should check the relevant state statutes and any introduced legislation to determine what the requirements are with respect to, among other things, patient notification requirements and patient nonsolicitation covenants. Some states (e.g., Ohio) require healthcare entities to either promptly send a notice to patients after a physician's employment has terminated (for any reason) or provide the physician with the names and contact information of patients so that the physician can directly contact his or her former patients.[47]

---

[46]*See* RESTATEMENT OF EMPLOYMENT LAW §8.06 *Enforcement of Restrictive Covenants in Employment Agreements*, cmt. a.

[47]OHIO REV. CODE §4731.228 provides that notice must be sent within 30 days after the healthcare entity has actual knowledge of the termination or resignation of the physician to any person who received the departing physician's services in the two-year

Tip: Define solicitation as something to the effect of "purposeful or active contact with patients or referral sources in an attempt to convince them to use the physician's new practice." Then, if a patient or referral source voluntarily contacts the physician, it is not solicitation by the physician. Exclude general mailings to zip codes or other general advertisement and marketing activities as limiting such activities would be overbroad and unenforceable.

Tip: Be very specific as to the definition of "solicitation" when it comes to nonsolicitation of patient or referral source (customer) covenants, and be careful not to confuse the concept of not treating a patient with not soliciting a patient. A patient always has the right to seek out a physician of the patient's own choosing and obtain treatment from that physician. A physician who has not solicited a former patient should not be stopped from providing treatment to that patient. And always make an exception in any nonsolicitation covenant for an event of emergency, so that if a former patient shows up in urgent care or emergency room and the physician is attending, such an occurrence isn't a breach of the nonsolicitation clause.

Tip: Restrict application of any nonsolicitation of patient covenant or nonsolicitation of referral source covenant only to patients that the physician actually treated or to referral sources that referred to the physician while the physician was working at the former practice or employer within the last 12 months (or some other reasonable period depending on the type of practice). Do not have the covenant include "all patients" or "all referral sources" of the former practice or employer. That is entirely too broad a restriction, and the physician wouldn't know or remember who all those patients of the former practice or employer were anyway.

---

period immediately preceding the date of employment termination. The notice must include, among other things, the departing physician's contact information, contact information for an alternative physician at the healthcare entity, and contact information that enables the patient to obtain information on the patient's medical records. The legislation exempts physicians providing episodic or emergency services, medical students, hospice medical directors, and physicians working in community mental health agencies or a federally qualified health center.

Suggested Negotiated Solution: Avoid a general noncompete clause entirely and instead settle on a narrowly tailored (as in time and geography) nonsolicitation of patient or narrowly tailored (as in time and geography) nonsolicitation of referral source provision if the employer's legitimate business interest is protecting its patient base or referring doctor base. Make this for a period not to exceed six months (or some other reasonable period) after the last day of physician's work at the former practice and only for the physician's patients that the physician was actively treating in the past (e.g.,12 months of practice). For one thing, covering other patients of the employer is impossible to enforce because the physician wouldn't know who those other patients were unless the employer wanted to release that information to the physician, which would be highly problematic on any number of levels. Also there must be an exception for emergency care of former patients.

X. BEWARE OF AMA ETHICAL OPINIONS THAT CAN TRIGGER DISCIPLINARY SANCTIONS

Be aware that American Medical Association Ethical Opinion 7.03 provides in relevant part:

> The patients of a physician who leaves a group practice should be notified that the physician is leaving the group. Patients of the physician should also be informed of the physician's new address and offered the opportunity to have their medical records forwarded to the departing physician at his or her new practice location. It is unethical to withhold such information upon the request of a patient.[48]

A former employer's (or former Physician employee's) violation of ethical rules such as AMA Opinion 7.03 could trigger disciplinary sanctions under the applicable state's board of medicine rules and regulations.

---

[48]American Medical Association, Ethical Opinion 7.03.

XI. Covenants Not to Compete May be Avoided in Situations of Involuntary Termination or Material Breach by Employer or for Other Equitable Reasons

In addition to the reasons discussed above with respect to the basic public policy reasons that various state legislatures and courts have used to prohibit covenants not to compete, a growing number of jurisdictions, either by statute or case law, may permit covenants not to compete but make them unenforceable in certain situations, such as those involving layoffs or termination without cause. Connecticut[49] and New York[50] are two such states. Again this is determined by state law and principles of equity. See Appendix A for guidance with respect to state statutes relating to physicians. Also refer to *Restatement of Employment Law* §8.06, *Enforcement of Restrictive Covenants in Employment Agreements*, whose annotated comment section includes cases from numerous jurisdictions that have considered the question of enforcement of covenants not to compete in cases of involuntary termination of employment. Courts in these cases generally consider the circumstances surrounding the employee's termination to be an important, if not decisive, factor in determining whether the restrictive covenant should be enforced.[51]

---

[49]*See* Conn. Pub. Act No. 16-95 (effective July 1, 2016).

[50]See, although not a physician case, *Buchanan Capital Markets, LLC v. DeLucca*, 41 N.Y.S.3d 229 (1st Dept. 2016).

[51]See Restatement of Employment Law §8.06 cmt. f for numerous cases supporting the majority rule: "Most courts will not enforce an otherwise reasonable restrictive covenant against an employee who is discharged without cause, who quits for cause attributable to the employer (a form of 'constructive discharge'), or who is let go because of a downturn in business." *See also* Bailey v. King, 398 S.W.2d 906, 908 (Ark. 1966) (reasoning in dicta that "[o]f course, if an employer obtained an agreement of this nature from an employee, and then, without reasonable cause, fired him, the agreement would not be binding"); Bishop v. Lakeland Animal Hosp., PC, 644 N.E.2d 33, 36 (Ill. App. Ct. 1994) ("We agree with the [S]eventh [C]ircuit's reasoning and find that the implied promise of good faith inherent in every contract precludes the enforcement of a non-competition clause when the employee is dismissed without cause."); Ma & Pa, Inc. v. Kelly, 342 N.W.2d 500, 502 (Iowa 1984) ("[D]ischarge by the employer is a factor opposing the grant of an injunction, to be placed in the scales in reaching the decision as to whether the employee should be enjoined."); Orion Broad., Inc. v. Forsythe, 477 F. Supp. 198, 201 (W.D. Ky. 1979) (applying Kentucky law; "had [the employee] voluntarily severed her relationship with plaintiff, the Court has no doubt that the non-competition covenant would have been enforceable against her. To hold that [the employee], at the whim of [her former employer], could be deprived of her livelihood in a highly competitive market, seems to the Court to be an example of industrial peonage which has no place in today's society" (citations omitted)).

Likewise, the employer's material breach of the employment agreement (or partnership agreement, or other related agreement to which the covenant not to compete or other restrictive covenant is ancillary) is also recognized as making a covenant not to compete unenforceable on equitable and basic contract principles, for the basic reason that a material breach by one party generally excuses the nonbreaching party from having to perform its contractual obligations.[52]

Other recognized grounds for not enforcing a covenant not to compete include the employer's bad faith in requiring or invoking the covenant not to compete, a great public need for the employee's special skills, and other equitable reasons.[53]

XII. Injunctions and Other Considerations With Respect to Restrictive Covenants in General

Beware all contractual stipulations supporting reasonableness of covenants not to compete!

Buried in physician employment agreements in the restrictive covenant section, there are often a number of unnecessary one-sided stipulations acknowledging how the physician agrees that the covenant not to compete restrictions are fair and reasonable, that consideration was given to the physician in exchange for the restrictions, that the physician agrees that the employer has legitimate business interests to protect to justify all the restrictions, and so forth. These stipulations are not essential to the employment contract and are intentionally designed to put the physician in an unfavorable position and make it easier for the employer to threaten to obtain or actually obtain a preliminary injunction, get a restraining order, or sue the physician if he or she later leaves the employer and goes into practice somewhere the employer doesn't approve of. As a practical matter the employer knows it makes it more difficult or embarrassing for an employee to later argue that a covenant not to compete is unreasonable or unfair when the employee has previously agreed in writing that it was reasonable and fair when the contract was signed. Most importantly, it makes it more difficult for a judge to invalidate

---

[52]*See* Comment g to RESTATEMENT OF EMPLOYMENT LAW §8.06 *Enforcement of Restrictive Covenants in Employment Agreements*, cmt. g, and cases cited therein.

[53]See RESTATEMENT OF EMPLOYMENT LAW §8.06 and cases cited therein.

the covenant when a presumably smart professional agreed to it and later challenges it, even though the challenge might come years later after circumstances have changed.

From the physician employee's counsel's perspective, avoid stipulating to any such language and particularly any agreement to waive the employer's obligation to post a bond when seeking injunctive relief to enforce the restrictive covenant against the physician. These issues can be determined by a judge on a case by case basis at the time in question, not the physician potentially years before the covenant may become operational. And for obvious reasons, do not contractually agree up front to pay the employer's legal fees. If the parties have to go that far, let a judge be the one to award attorneys' fees or make the attorney's fees clause applicable to the prevailing party. The vast majority of these matters never go to court and employers have in-house counsel to handle these matters.

XIII. WHAT IF THE EMPLOYER CHANGES? SUCCESSORS, ASSIGNS, AND THIRD-PARTY BENEFICIARIES

After first determining whether a restrictive covenant is enforceable in the first place—based on legitimate business interests, supported by consideration, reasonable under all the circumstances and so forth—the question is who can enforce it? Many states do not permit the assignment of employment agreements or noncompete agreements in the event of an employer change, unless the employee explicitly agreed to an assignability provision in the employment agreement. Again, it is vitally important for counsel to consult state law.

For example, the Ohio Court of Appeals has stated that "the employment relationship is a personal matter between an employee and the company who hired him and for whom he chose to work. Unless an employee explicitly agreed to an assignability provision, an employer may not treat him as some chattel to be conveyed like a filing cabinet, to a successor firm."[54]

---

[54]Cary Corp. v. Linder, 2002 WL 31667316 (Ohio Ct. App. Nov. 27, 2002); *see also* Reynolds & Reynolds v. Hardee, 932 F. Supp. 149 (E.D. Va. July 11, 1996) (employment agreement is based on mutual trust and confidence; noncompete is not assignable). *See generally* Adam Schneid, *Assignability of Covenants Not to Compete: When Can a Successor Firm Enforce A Noncompete Agreement*, 27 CARDOZO L. REV. 1485 (2006).

On the other hand, Florida has a statute requiring courts to enforce restrictive covenants against third-party beneficiaries, assignees, and successors; however the restrictive covenant must expressly authorize enforcement by assignors or successors.[55]

Ultimately counsel representing the physician has to make sure the physician understands the significance of agreeing upfront to any assignment provision in the employment agreement. The best advice from the physician's counsel's perspective is to not agree to any assignment of such a personal contract (i.e. employment contract) without the physician's written consent because the employment environment for the physician may dramatically change as a result of the assignment. That should be something the physician has the opportunity to evaluate at the relevant time not before the physician has the necessary facts.

XIV. CONCLUSION

As the American Medical Association[56] and many court decisions and state legislatures have recognized, there are professional liability and medical ethics issues involved in the doctor-patient relationship that are unique, as well as state medical licensing board issues. All of these issues are highly relevant when determining the reasonableness and enforceability of any contractual restrictions on the right of a physician to practice medicine.[57]

---

[55]FLA. STAT. §542.335(1)(f).

[56]American Medical Association, Code of Medical Ethics, §E-9.02. *Restrictive Covenants and the Practice of Medicine*: "Covenants not to compete restrict competition, disrupt continuity of care, and potentially deprive the public of medical services. The Council on Ethical and Judicial Affairs discourages any agreement which restricts the right of a physician to practice medicine for a specified period of time or in a specified area upon termination of an employment, a partnership, or a corporate agreement. Restrictive covenants are unethical if they are excessive in geographic scope or in the circumstances presented, or if they fail to make reasonable accommodation of patients' choice of physician." For concisely summarized physician noncompete cases referencing AMA §9.02, see http://academicdepartments.musc.edu/faculty_senate/pdfs/CodeofMedicalEthicsAMA%20Sec%209.02.pdf. The case summaries are instructive and include cases from many jurisdictions.

[57]For further discussion and cases from across the United States, see Ferdinand S. Tinio, Annotation, *Validity and Construction of Contractual Restrictions on Right of Medical Practitioner to Practice Incident to Employment Agreement*, 62 A.L.R.3rd 1014 (1975).

Consequently, this area of law is in a state of flux, but this much is clear: The employer has the burden of proof to establish that the purpose of any covenant not to compete is to protect a legitimate business interest; that the covenant not to compete is reasonably tailored as to time, geographic area, and type of employment activity; and that these elements are restricted so as to be fair to the employer, the physician, and the public.

Each case should be examined on its own facts when negotiating an employment agreement, and the latest case law and legislation should be consulted. An experienced physician employment attorney should be consulted when negotiating or reviewing a physician employment contract. If the employment contract has been signed and the physician is concerned about its application to a particular situation, an experienced litigator should be consulted when determining how best to challenge or defend a covenant not to compete. A litigator understands how to quickly navigate the court system and obtain evidence, affidavits, etc., if necessary, whereas the transactional attorney who negotiated the agreement may not have that expert knowledge and may also need to be called as a witness.

Fortunately, when it comes to covenants not to compete, the recent legislative currents are turning in favor of employees, and even more so in terms of protecting professional healthcare workers. Also, as a practical matter there is usually some claim, breach, or grounds for whistle blowing that the physician can assert that can make enforcing the covenant not to compete a negotiable matter. This is particularly true if the employer has been selective about enforcing noncompetes in the past, or if the covenant is vulnerable to attack as being unnecessarily overbroad.

Another effective claim is to show that the covenant is based on protecting information in the public domain or that the physician knew or possessed through his or her own education or training, or during the ordinary course of the physician's employment, none of which is protectable as a "trade secret," and all of which could be protected by less draconian measures such as the use of nondisclosure or proprietary information agreements instead of restricting the physicians future employment opportunities through covenants not to compete.

The AMA is right. Covenants not to compete with respect to physicians restrict competition, disrupt continuity of care of patients, and potentially deprive the public of needed medical services.

Attorneys, like physicians, are trusted professionals and have a protected relationship with clients. As attorneys enjoy legal protection from post-employment covenants not to compete, so too should physicians. Particularly deserving and vulnerable are physicians who are employees (as opposed to physician owners of a medical practice, who can sell their ownership share). But all physicians must be shielded from these oppressive covenants not to compete, especially now that the need for qualified physicians has never been greater.

CHAPTER 11

PHYSICIANS AND COLLECTIVE BARGAINING

I. UNION-RELATED EMPLOYMENT RIGHTS OF PHYSICIANS

Physicians who are "employees" can exercise their rights under section 7 of the National Labor Relations Act (NLRA) to collectively bargain and can strike.[1] But doing so is controversial,[2] and counter-intuitive for many independent-minded doctors. Unions have found that gathering sufficient support among physicians for walking away from patient care duties has historically been difficult, so there have been few strikes by physicians in the United States, compared to the labor conflicts of doctors in the health systems of other nations.[3]

A wave of academic commentary about physician labor organizing and the theoretical potential for strikes reached in legal periodicals around the year 2000,[4] but the topic appears less conceptual

---

[1] 29 U.S.C. § 157 (2012); 29 C.F.R. pt. 103 (2015).

[2] Guy O. Farmer, II and & John H. Douglas, *Physician "Unionization": A Primer & Prescription*, 75 FLA. BAR J. 37 (2001); Larry W. Bridgesmith & John E. Gerth, *The Summer of Union Discontent Portends a Season of Employer Discomfort*, 39 HOSP. L.W. 117 (2006).

[3] Solveig A. Cunningham, Kristina Mitchell, K.M. Venkat Narayan & Salim Yusuf, *Doctors' Strikes & Mortality*, 67 SOC. SCI & MED. 1784 (2008).

[4] *See* Thomas H. Segars, *Bad Medicine: The Anticompetitive Side-Effects of Physician Unionization*, 76 CHICAGO-KENT L. REV. 1303 (2000); Dionne K. Fine, *Exploitation of the Elite*, 45 ST. LOUIS UNIV. L.J. 207 (2001); Monique A. Anawis, *The Ethics of Physician Unionization: What Will Happen If Your Doctor Becomes a Teamster?*, 6 DEPAUL J. HEALTH CARE L. 83 (2002); E. Douglas Baldridge, *Physicians Versus Managed Care: Is It Time For Physician Unions?*, 28 N..KY. L. REV. 65 (2001); Elizabeth M.Devine, *Physician Unionization: A Prescription for Modern Managed*

for scholars today, as more structured employment relationships have removed the novelty of unions representing employed doctors. The medical profession sat up and took notice of the cultural and legal implications of this shift.[5]

Today, the cutting edge of conflict is between the hospital and the union. In the early days of the unionization movement, one hospital network reportedly spent $150,000 to oppose unionization of physicians.[6] Hospitals also argued that doctors were "supervisors," and therefore not able to organize under the NLRA.[7] The AMA also came out against physicians' right to strike.[8] Although more recently the rights of doctors to organize and strike is becoming accepted, there are still debates about the ethics of permitting them to do so.[9]

II. PREDICTING FUTURE EXPERIENCES WITH STRIKES[10]

Large cohorts of physician employees would seem to be ripe for an aggressive union mobilization leading to a strike, as occurred in Britain in 2016.[11] As of mid-2017, however, U.S. physicians have not gone on strike in significant numbers.[12] But given that the U.S. physician community is now more than one-quarter foreign born, it seems likely that physicians will lose their reticence to strike in the future, as these non-native doctors bring their familiarity with collective action and strikes to this country. Simultaneously, the financially driven mergers of the current U.S. healthcare industry are

---

Care, 4 QUINNIPIAC HEALTH L.J. 39 (2000); William S. Brewbaker, III, *Physician Unions and the Future of Competition in the Health Care Sector*, 33 U.C. DAVIS L.REV. 545 (2000); and Ellen L. Luepke, *White Coat, Blue Collar: Physician Unionization and Managed Care*, 8 ANNALS HEALTH L. 275 (1999).

[5]David J. Leffell, *The Doctor's Office as Union Shop*, WALL ST. J. (Jan. 29, 2013).

[6]*When Physicians Try to Unionize Against HMOs*, N.Y.L.J. (Oct 30, 1998).

[7]*Id.*

[8]*Id.*

[9]*See* David S. Kemp, *Can Health Care Providers Ethically Go on Strike?*, VERDICT, Jan.14,2013,https://verdict.justia.com/2013/01/14/can-health-care-providers-ethically-go-on-strike.

[10]Strikes by physicians have been studied in numerous articles as a part of the discussion of collective bargaining powers. *See, e.g.*, Brian Carroll, *Getting Your Docs in a Row*, 9 J. HEALTH & BIOMED. L. 117 (2013).

[11]Stephen Castle, *Junior Doctors' Strike in England Disrupts Care for Thousands*, N.Y. TIMES (Jan. 12, 2016).

[12]*See* Roy Poses, *Time to "Look for the Union Label?" First US Doctors' Strike in Decades*, NAKED CAPITALISM, Feb. 2, 2015, http://www.nakedcapitalism.com/2015/02/time-to-look-for-the-union-label-first-us-doctors-strike-in-decades.html.

concentrating physicians, who were previously independent or in small practice groups, into a set of corporate employees who follow common protocols for action and who receive compensation set through a central administration. This sets the "fuel for conflict over physicians' unionization rights in place and ready for sparks to set off a conflagration. Union employees in the healthcare industry are now raising the typical complaints of workers in other fields. As an example, a unit of the nationwide AFSCME union, the "Union of American Physicians & Dentists," features photos on its website of white-coated doctors, some of them holding a picket sign: "TOO MANY EXECUTIVES, TOO FEW DOCTORS."[13]

III. GLIMPSING THE FUTURE

When hospitals replace their employed physicians with a third-party staffing company as an outsourcing "cost savings initiative," the alarmed physician employees will complain, and may decide to form a union as a defensive tactic.[14] In the present cost-cutting health care environment, expect more movement toward unionization as hospitals and other employer entities attempt to improve their books at the expense of doctor employment and compensation.

Another aspect of these trends is the push for expanding the roles of advanced practice nurses, a trend that perhaps somewhat limits the organizing leverage of physicians. Will doctors be replaced by advanced practice nurses (APRNs) in more institutions, as they have been in retail store clinics?[15] And will a similar substitution occur in emergency care settings? The levels of patient satisfaction suggest wide acceptance of the implementation of the doctor-free emergency care concept.[16] Advocacy for the nursing profession asserts that APRNs can play a greater part in providing care:

---

[13]UNION OF AM. PHYSICIANS & DENTISTS, https://www.UAPD.com (last visited May 22, 2017).

[14]David Barkholz, *Ore. Hospitalist Union Plans Picket in Quest for Contract*, MODERN HEALTHCARE (June 23, 2016), http://www.modernhealthcare.com/article/20160611/MAGAZINE/306119948.

[15]Weinick, R. M., Burns, R. M., & Mehrotra, A., Many Emergency Department Visits Could Be Managed At Urgent Care Centers And Retail Clinics, 29 Health Affairs 1630 (2010)

[16]Jamesetta Newland, *Retail-Based Clinics a Viable Resource for Primary Care*, 33 Nurse Practitioner 6 (2008).

Decades of research has shown that APRNs provide care that is as high in quality and patient satisfaction as that provided by physicians. As of 2008, an estimated 251,000 RNs report they are prepared as an APRN in one or more specialties or fields; an increase of just over 4% since 2004. Each year Americans are unable to acquire timely healthcare services either because of an inability to access physician care or because the provider no longer accepts the patients' insurance coverage (such as Medicare). APRNs play a critical role in fulfilling this unmet need.[17]

The National Association of Nurse Practitioners has enrolled more than 75,000 members, and their policy statements assert their basis for receiving statutory freedom to prescribe drugs fully in their area of practice.[18] But countering this trend, at least partially, is the ever-growing shortage of nurses.[19]

IV. CONCLUSION

As more doctors become employees,[20] labor organizing activity rises. The factors that are impacting the changing dynamics of physician unionization are many. They include: fiscal pressures on Medicaid, which continues to cut provider payments; more foreign-born healthcare immigrants; and the demographic pressures of an aging population, which uses more care services as well as more drugs and devices. Healthcare roles will divide further as the roles of APRNs and "community paramedics" for non-emergency care expand and cross boundaries between doctors, nurses, and other individual care providers.[21]

---

[17] AMERICAN NURSES ASS'N, *Imagine a World Without Registered Nurses* (2012), http://nursingworld.org/MainMenuCategories/Policy-Advocacy/AdvocacyResources Tools/WorldWithoutNursesBrochure.pdf.

[18] *See, e.g.,* AM. ASS'N OF NURSE PRACTITIONERS, *Nurse Practitioner Prescriptive Privilege* (2015), https://www.aanp.org/images/documents/publications/prescriptive privilege.pdf.

[19] *See* Rebecca Grant, *The U.S. is Running Out of Nurses,* ATLANTIC (Feb. 12, 2016), https://www.theatlantic.com/health/archive/2016/02/nursing-shortage/459741/.

[20] *See* Chapter 3, text accompanying nn. 10-13.

[21] *See* Mattie Quinn, *A New Kind of Paramedic for Less Urgent 911 Calls,* MODERN HEALTHCAREGOVERNING: THE STATES AND LOCALITIES (Sept. 2016), http://www. governing.com/topics/health-human-services/gov-community-paramedicine-emer gency-care.html.

CHAPTER 12

EFFECTS OF THE NATIONAL PRACTITIONER DATA BANK REPORTS

I. NATIONAL PRACTITIONER DATA BANK

The Health Care Quality Improvement Act of 1986[1] established the National Practitioner Data Bank (NPDB) to improve the availability between the states and among healthcare institutions of information concerning doctors with records of disciplinary actions, staff privileges actions, and malpractice judgments. The Act imposes affirmative duties on healthcare institutions to report malpractice payments and disciplinary actions to the Data Bank in exchange for statutory immunity.[2]

The Data Bank is operated by the Department of Health and Human Services and became operational in 1990. Its operations since that time have been updated in an attempt to improve the utility of the data as part of the improvements in the "people side" of healthcare quality. Prior to May 6, 2013, the Data Bank comprised the National Practitioner Data Bank and the Healthcare Integrity and

---

[1] 42 U.S.C. §§11101–11152 (2012); 45 C.F.R. pt. 60 (2016) [hereinafter the Act, or HCQIA].

[2] 42 U.S.C. § 11111(a)(D) (2012). "[A]ny person who participates with or assists the body with respect to the action, shall not be liable in damages under any law of the United States or of any State (or political subdivision thereof) with respect to the action."

Protection Data Bank. Section 6403 of the Affordable Care Act of 2010 consolidated the two.[3]

State medical and other health care professionals licensing boards and commissions are required to report to the Data Bank certain disciplinary actions relating to the professional competence or conduct of licensed professionals covered by the Data Bank.[4] In addition, medical and other health professional societies and associations must report certain adverse actions taken against their members to the state licensure boards and commissions, which must send a copy of the report to the Data Bank.[5] Hospitals must query the Data Bank at least every two years for each member of their medical staff. State licensure boards are not required to make an inquiry, but most states do.[6]

II. CONTENTS OF THE BANK

The Data Bank collects information on a broad group of adverse actions taken against licensed health care practitioners, including:

- Medical malpractice payments[7]
- Any adverse licensure actions or loss of license[8]
- Adverse clinical privileging actions[9]
- Adverse professional society membership actions[10]
- Any negative action or finding by a State licensing or certification authority[11]
- Private accreditation organization negative actions or findings against a health care practitioner or entity[12]

---

[3]42 U.S.C. § 1320a-7e (2012).
[4]42 U.S.C. § 11132 (2012). A wide variety of healthcare practitioners are potentially subject to Data Bank reporting, from accountants to x-ray technicians. See U.S. DEP'T OF HEALTH & HUMAN SERVS., NATIONAL PRACTITIONER DATA BANK, REPORTING COMPLIANCE STATUS BY PROFESSION, https://www.npdb.hrsa.gov/servlet/ComplianceStatusByProfessionServlet?selectedTab=Status.
[5]42 U.S.C. § 11133 (2012).
[6]42 U.S.C. §§ 11135 (a), 11137(a) (2012). See U.S. DEP'T OF HEALTH & HUMAN SERVS., NATIONAL PRACTITIONER DATA BANK, 2010 ANNUAL REPORT 37 (Mar. 2012).
[7]42 U.S.C. § 11131 (2012); 45 C.F.R. § 60.7 (2016).
[8]42 U.S.C. § 11132 (2012); 45 C.F.R. § 60.8 (2016).
[9]42 U.S.C. § 11133 (2012); 45 C.F.R. § 60.12 (2016).
[10]42 U.S.C. § 11133 (2012); 45 C.F.R. § 60.11 (2016).
[11]42 U.S.C. § 11132 (2012); 45 C.F.R. § 60.9 (2016).
[12]42 U.S.C. § 1396r-2 (2012); 45 C.F.R. § 60.11 (2016).

- Any negative action or finding by a Federal or State licensing and certification agency if it is publicly available information[13]
- Civil judgments or criminal convictions that are healthcare-related[14]
- Exclusions from Federal or State healthcare programs.[15]
- Other adjudicated actions or decisions (formal or official actions, involving a due process mechanism and based on acts or omissions that affect or could affect the payment, provision, or delivery of a health care item or service)[16]

Congress created the Data Bank to ensure healthcare quality through national identification of physicians and other healthcare practitioners that have been disciplined or suffered one of the other adverse actions described above, thus foreclosing the possibility that such practitioners could simply move to another state and escape their disciplinary record. Despite its purpose, the existence of the National Practitioner Data Bank and its reporting requirements have become a source of significant tension among physicians and hospitals in disciplinary cases and have led to some results that are arguably not in the interests of patients. For example, physicians facing the possibility of an NPDB report due to a malpractice payment have little incentive to settle cases, even meritorious ones; rather, most physicians will defend such cases to the bitter end.[17] One study of the effects of the NPDB found that the chances that a patient with a malpractice claim would receive a payment "fell to 59% of pre-NPDB levels."[18]

---

[13]42 U.S.C. § 11133 (2012); 45 C.F.R. §§ 60.09, 60.10 (2016).
[14]42 U.S.C. § 1396r-2 (2012); 45 C.F.R. § 60.14 (2016).
[15]42 U.S.C. § 1396r-2 (2012); 45 C.F.R. § 60.15 (2016).
[16]42 U.S.C. § 1396r-2 (2012); 45 C.F.R. § 60.16 (2016).
[17]See Darryl S. Welman, *The National Practitioner Data Bank*, HUFFINGTON POST (Nov. 23, 2016), http://www.huffingtonpost.com/darryl-s-weiman-md-jd/the-national-practitioner_b_13173046.html.; Haavi Morreim, *Moral Hazard: The Pros and Cons of Avoiding Data Bank Reports*, 4 DREXEL L. REV. 265 (2011).
[18]Teresa M. Waters et al., *Impact of the National Practitioner Data Bank on Resolution of Malpractice Claims*, 40 INQUIRY 283, 290 (2003).

III. CHECKING AND CONTESTING DATA ENTRIES

Individual practitioners may request their own records from the Data Bank, and are to receive a copy from the Data Bank of each confidential report at the time that it is filed.[19] Physicians who are reported to the Data Bank may dispute any report made against them, but the basis for the dispute is limited to "the factual accuracy of the report," and whether the report was filed within the requirements of the Act.[20] Healthcare professionals may not contest the merits of the malpractice claim, settlement, or the basis for the adverse action against the practitioners' clinical privileges or license.[21] Under the NPDB regulations, the Secretary of the Department of Health and Human Services has the authority "to review, at the request of the subject of a report, the accuracy of NPDB reports."[22] This authority has been delegated by the Secretary to the Division of Practitioner Data Bank (DPDB) of the Health Resources and Services Administration.[23]

Only state licensure boards, healthcare entities mandated to query the Data Bank, individual healthcare providers, and researchers using non-identifiable information are permitted access to the Date Bank.[24] The general public and patients do not have access to the information in the Data Bank, even though consumer groups and attorneys continue to lobby for access to the material.[25]

Malpractice insurers and third-party payors are required to submit reports to the Data Bank, but they are not permitted access to the Data Bank.[26] They may, however, ask the practitioner to turn over their own records, which the practitioner obtains from the Data Bank, before granting the practitioner coverage or reimbursement. Controversies regarding the scope of the mandated reporting to the

---

[19]See U.S. DEP'T OF HEALTH & HUMAN SERVS., NPDB GUIDEBOOK C-9 (Apr. 2015) [hereinafter Guidebook].

[20]See 45 C.F.R. § 60.21 (2016); Guidebook at F-3.

[21]Guidebook at F-5.

[22]Id. at F-4.

[23]U.S. DEP'T OF HEALTH & HUMAN SERVS., NATIONAL PRACTITIONER DATA BANK 2012 ANNUAL REPORT 77 (Feb. 2014) (giving examples of outcomes of dispute resolution adverse action and medical malpractice payment reports).

[24]See id. at 8.

[25]See, e.g., Laura A. Chernitsky, Constitutional Arguments in Favor of Modifying the HCQIA to Allow the Dissemination of Physician Information to Health Care Consumers, 63 WASH. & LEE L. REV. 737 (2006).

[26]See Guidebook at B-7.

Data Bank have occurred in connection with reports from healthcare institutions about privileges actions,[27] and from malpractice insurers concerning malpractice payments and settlements.[28] Some federal hospitals are required to file NPDB reports, though they may disagree with the requirements.[29]

State licensing boards, hospitals, or healthcare entities that take an adverse action regarding clinical privileges, malpractice insurers, professional associations, and boards of medical examiners must report revocations, censure, reprimand, suspension, probation, payments for malpractice claims, and surrender of a license, along with reporting revisions to an adverse outcome and the reinstatement of a license.[30] State licensing boards are not required to report denial of initial applications due to, for example, failure to meet education requirements or to pass a required examination.[31] State licensing boards are also not required to report certain fines or monetary penalties that are not connected to healthcare services delivery or to adverse certification or licensure actions.[32]

Individual healthcare professionals are not required to report to the National Practitioner Data Bank. But under certain state laws, the licensed professional may have a duty to report to the state licensing board information relating to unprofessional conduct of that professional.[33]

---

[27] *See, e.g.*, A.Y. Mahajan, D.H. Stacey & V. Rao, *The National Practitioner Data Bank: Issues in Plastic Surgery*, NCBI (Dec. 2010), https://www.ncbi.nlm.nih.gov/pubmed/20697316.

[28] Gabriel H. Teninbaum, *Reforming the National Practitioner Data Bank to Promote Fair Med-Mal Outcomes*, 5 William & Mary Policy Rev. 83 (2013).

[29] Indian Health Service, National Practitioner Data Bank Reporting, https://www.ihs.gov/riskmanagement/resources/processing/npdbr/.

[30] *See supra* text accompanying notes 4–5.

[31] *See* Health Resources & Servs. Admin., Reporting State Licensure & Certification Actions, https://www.npdb.hrsa.gov/guidebook/EStateLicensureActions.jsp.

[32] *See id.*

[33] *See, e.g.*, Guide to the Laws Governing the Practice of Medicine by Physicians & Surgeons 21, Medical Board of Cal. (7th ed. 2013); Important Information for Physicians Regarding the MCARE Act (Act 13 of Mar. 20, 2002), http://www.dos.pa.gov/ProfessionalLicensing/BoardsCommissions/Medicine/Documents/Board%20Documents/MedM%20-%20MCare%20Information%20and%20Reporting.pdf.

IV. CONFIDENTIALITY

Information submitted to the National Practitioner Data Bank is considered confidential, and generally may not be disclosed.[34] Any person or entity that violates the confidentiality of the information is theoretically subject to civil monetary penalties.[35] In practice, however, this penalty has rarely been imposed.[36]

Ironically, the National Practitioner Data Bank itself has been implicated in divulging confidential NPDB information. The issue arose in connection with the Data Bank's disclosure of "de-identified" information. The "HCQIA ... provides for public disclosure of information, provided that the data are in a form that would not permit identification of a specific physician/practitioner. ... Such de-identified data are considered non-confidential: 'Information reported under this sub-chapter that is in a form that does not permit the identification of any particular health care entity, physician, other health care practitioner, or patient shall not be considered confidential.'"[37] Pursuant to the de-identification provision of the Act, the NPDB maintains a "public use file," which "contains selected variables from National Practitioner Data Bank Reports."[38]

In 2011, the Health Resources and Services Administration temporarily removed the public use file from its website in the wake of reporters using the information to name individual doctors with

---

[34]42 U.S.C. § 11137 (2012); 45 C.F.R. § 60.20 (2016).

[35]*Id.*

[36]*See* Gabriel H. Teninbaum, *Reforming the National Practitioner Data Bank to Promote Fair Med-Mal Outcomes*, 5 WILLIAM & MARY POLICY REV. 83, 90 (2013) (in response to Freedom of Information Act request, HRSA responded that it had never, "in the entire history of the NPDB, levied a single fine against any person or entity for failure to report a malpractice claim."); Lawrence R. Huntoon, *The Debacle of the National Practitioner Data Bank*, 16 J. OF AM. PHYSICIANS & SURGEONS, 100 (Winter 2011), http://www.jpands.org/vol16no4/huntoon.pdf; *First Civil Monetary Penalty Case Settled Over Databank Confidentiality Violations*, 18 REP. ON MEDICARE COMPLIANCE, Mar. 2, 2009, no. 7, at 1. https://aishealth.com/sites/all/files/latest-issue-pdf/August_17_2010/rmc030209.pdf.

[37]Lawrence R. Huntoon, *The Debacle of the National Practitioner Data Bank*, 16 J. OF AM. PHYSICIANS & SURGEONS, 99 (Winter 2011), http://www.jpands.org/vol16no4/huntoon.pdf (quoting 42 U.S.C. § 11137(b)(1)).

[38]U.S. HEALTH RES. & SERVS. ADMIN., NATIONAL PRACTITIONER DATA BANK PUBLIC USE DATA FILE, https://www.npdb.hrsa.gov/resources/reports/PublicUseDataFile-POR-Format.pdf.

NPDB records.[39] In an additional twist, a former NPDB official was involved in giving portions of the file to a newspaper reporter, and an HRSA official apparently inadvertently disclosed the name of the physician in her letter to the newspaper protesting the story.[40]

V. LITIGATION USE OF NPDB RECORDS

Reports from the National Practitioner Data Bank formed the basis for a defamation case brought against an affected physician, *Swafford v. Memphis Individual Practice Assoc.*[41] Entities that a plaintiff physician had been associated with (a health maintenance organization and an organization responsible for supervising physicians who treat policyholders in Tennessee) had reported to the National Practitioner Data Bank that the plaintiff's clinical privileges had been revoked due to violations of quality care standards. At least three entities had retrieved information about the plaintiff from the Data Bank. *Swafford* held that each dissemination of information from the Data Bank, in response to an affirmative request by a certified hospital or other healthcare entity, gave rise to a separate cause of action for defamation.[42] Defamation claims can in some cases yield a significant jury award.[43]

Absence of a Data Bank entry for a physician has been claimed as a partial basis for belief in the quality of the physician's work.[44] And discovery requests against a physician may be attempted for those documents which she or he had submitted in response to Data Bank requirements. In general, though, the Bank's confidentiality will be preserved.[45] While some government-filed reports to the Data

---

[39] ASSOC. OF HEALTH CARE JOURNALISTS, NATIONAL PRACTITIONER DATA BANK PUBLIC USE FILE (2017), http://healthjournalism.org/resources-data-details. php?id=10#.WSCgYhPyui4.

[40] Lawrence R. Huntoon, *The Debacle of the National Practitioner Data Bank*, 16 J. OF AM. PHYSICIANS & SURGEONS 99–100 (WINTER 2011).

[41] Swafford v. Memphis Individual Practice Ass'n, 1998 WL 281935 (Tenn. Ct. App. June 2, 1998).

[42] *Id.*

[43] Brown v. Presbyterian Healthcare Servs.,101 F.3d 1324 (10th Cir. 1996).

[44] El-Roeiy v. Bd. of Medical Licensure and Discipline, 2014 WL 7150035 (Del. Super. Ct. 2014).

[45] Huntsman v. Aultman Hosp., 2008 WL 2572598, 2572603 (Ohio App. 5th Dist. 2008)

Bank are contested, a reporting entity or official may enjoy qualified immunity for, among other things, a report to the NPDB.[46]

VI. CONCLUSION

While the policies behind the Data Bank are laudable, there are a number of significant issues related to Data Bank reporting, including the limits on the ability of an affected practitioner to oppose a potentially flawed report, the unintended consequences arising in malpractice situations, the pressures on the part of consumer groups and others for broader public access, and serious issues around confidentiality. Many stakeholders on all sides have advocated for various reforms of the Data Bank. Currently, NPDB reforms are being debated in the context of broader medical liability reform proposals.[47]

---

[46]Randall v. U.S., 430 F.3d 518 (4th Cir. 1994).
[47]See, e.g., American College of Surgeons 2017 Statement on Health Care Reform, BULLETIN OF THE AM. COLLEGE OF SURGEONS (May 1, 2017).

CHAPTER 13

REGULATORY OVERSIGHT OF PRACTITIONERS' EMPLOYMENT[1]

I. STATE LICENSING BOARDS

State medical and nursing boards have an oversight role in the careers of physicians, nurses, and other medical professionals. These bodies set and enforce standards of practice. State legislatures have delegated to them the powers to suspend licenses and to end careers. This delegation of power is usually made through statutory language that has been influenced by the testimony and lobbying efforts of state associations representing doctors and nurses.

Protection of the interests of licensed professionals is an underlying theme in many of these state licensing laws. Anti-competitive effects of these controls are sometimes reviewed in the federal antitrust context, to the extent that they inhibit competition.[1]

Enforcement of disciplinary rules has economic consequences[2] as well as legal consequences. Litigation against state discipline is usually unsuccessful.[3]

Termination of a state license to practice is not easily accomplished, except in the most egregious behavioral, drug abuse, or

---

[1] North Carolina State Bd. of Dental Examiners v. FTC, 135 S. Ct. 1101 (2015).

[2] Shirley Svorny, *Licensing Doctors: Do Economists Agree?*, ECON. J. WATCH; FAIRFAX 1.2, at 279 (Aug. 2004).

[3] *See, e.g.*, Read v. Haley, 650 F. App'x 409 (9th Cir. 2016); Mitchell v. McGovern, 609 F. App'x 553 (10th Cir. 2015); Ahmad v. Beck, 480 SW3d 166 (Ark. 2016).

criminal cases. That is because the state's judiciary will generally insist that the license revocation or suspension be managed with due regard for administrative due process. The licensee must cooperate in the process.[4] Once the procedures are adequate, the courts tend to avoid getting into the content of the witness testimony against the nurse or doctor.[5]

Employees who expect due process should bring their own legal counsel into the matter very early. Due process has its limits. Neutral hearing officers, adequate notice, lists of witnesses, pre-hearing exchange of exhibits, and other methods of avoiding surprise at the hearing are essential, yet they elongate the process in ways that the affected patients may not be able to understand. The ex-patient would say to state officials: "Since she did this, why haven't you pulled her license?" As the opioid crisis has impacted on the practice of medicine, there has been more attention to the over-prescribing of these medications by "pill mills"[6] and by individual physicians.[7]

II. HHS OFFICE OF INSPECTOR GENERAL

The role of the Office of Inspector General (OIG) of the U.S. Department of Health & Human Services (HHS) is to detect fraud in Medicare and Medicaid programs. The OIG works with the Justice Department and FBI to prosecute violations by healthcare providers,[8] and counsel for providers must be aware of the scrutiny that these programs place on doctors and institutions.[9] Fraud is the primary reason why a person would be "excluded" from federal healthcare programs. This section deals with the federal exclusion authority and its consequences.

The healthcare provider who receives federal money is forced to cooperate with program audits and investigations, under threat

---

[4]Perez v. Texas Med. Bd., 556 F. App'x 341(5th Cir. 2014).
[5]Rorick v. State Med. Bd. of Ohio, 2016 -Ohio- 7070, 2016 WL 5628820 (Ohio App. Sept. 29, 2016).
[6]Texas Med. Bd. v. Wiseman, 2015 WL 410330 (Tex. App. 2015).
[7]*See e.g., Rorick*, 2016 Ohio 7070, 2016 WL 5628820.
[8]See Chapter 25 of this text.
[9]DEPARTMENT OF HEALTH AND HUMAN SERVICES & DEPARTMENT OF JUSTICE HEALTH CARE FRAUD AND ABUSE CONTROL PROGRAM, ANNUAL REPORT FOR FISCAL YEAR 2015 (Feb. 2016).

of being "blackballed." Once excluded from receiving Medicare or Medicaid payments, the provider may become virtually unemployable by many hospitals, which depend on those programs' reimbursements for their financial stability and so cannot risk dealing with the provider who has been excluded.

That prudent provider must obtain legal counsel as soon as the targeting is evident—you are the potential defendant. When the OIG is considering excluding an individual or entity under Section 1128 of the Social Security Act, a standard process is used. For all proposed mandatory exclusions that are longer than the mandatory minimum five-year period,[10] and for most proposed permissive exclusions, the administrative process is the same. The OIG sends out to the targeted individual a written Notice of Intent to Exclude, which "includes the basis for the proposed exclusion and a statement about the potential effect of an exclusion." The Notice of Intent to Exclude is predecisional and allows the individual 30 days to respond in writing with any information or evidence relevant to whether the exclusion is warranted and to raise any other related issues, such as mitigating circumstances. The OIG considers all available information in making a final decision about whether to impose the exclusion.[11]

The List of Excluded Individuals & Entities (LEIE) is the means by which physicians and other practitioners are barred from receiving payments from Medicare and Medicaid.[12] The LEIE contains all individuals and entities that are currently excluded. Once an individual or entity has been reinstated, they are removed from the LEIE.

The LEIE exclusion has a real impact on employability. The "effect of an OIG exclusion, and appearance on the General Services Administration's System for Award Management (SAM) website as a result of such exclusion, is that no payment will be made by any Federal health care program for items or services furnished, ordered, or prescribed by the excluded individual in any capacity."[13] The Online Searchable Database enables users to enter the name of an individual or entity and determine whether they are currently excluded. If a match is made on an individual, the database can verify

---

[10]Social Security Act §§1128(a)(1)–(4).
[11]*Exclusions FAQ*, HHS OIG, https://oig.hhs.gov/faqs/exclusions-faq.asp.
[12]*Id.*
[13]*Id.*

with an individual's Social Security Number (SSN) that the match is unique. Employer Identification Numbers (EINs) are available for verification of excluded entities.

The OIG's exclusion process is governed by regulations that implement sections of the Social Security Act. When an individual or entity gets a Notice of Intent to Exclude, a hearing commences. "OIG will carefully consider all material provided by the person who received the Notice before making a decision."[14]

All exclusions implemented by the OIG may be appealed to an HHS Administrative Law Judge (ALJ), and any adverse decision may be appealed to the HHS Departmental Appeals Board (DAB). Judicial review in federal court is also available after a final decision by the DAB.

III. TRACKING THE PROVIDERS OF FEDERALLY REIMBURSED HEALTHCARE

The national provider identifier (NPI) is the unique number used to identify healthcare providers for payments from the Centers for Medicaid & Medicare Services (CMS).[15] This is a unique provider identifier in lieu of the SSN. CMS created a National Provider System.[16] A "provider" is an entity or individual covered by CMS rules for billing federal programs for health services. Identifying numbers were assigned to physicians as well as certain nonphysician practitioners and medical group practices. Part of the normal review of an incoming professional employee will be verification of their NPI number.[17]

IV. NATIONAL PRACTITIONER DATA BANK

The punishment fits the crime, in some but not all cases. The National Practitioner Data Bank[18] (NPDB) was adopted and later

---

[14]*Id.*
[15]*See* HHS Final Rule, 69 Fed. Reg. 3434 (Jan. 23, 2004) (codified at 45 C.F.R. pt. 162).
[16]45 C.F.R. § 162.408.
[17]45 C.F.R. § 162.406.
[18]NATIONAL PRACTITIONER DATA BANK, https://www.npdb.hrsa.gov.

modified by Congress and is housed in the Department of Health and Human Services.[19] The NPDB is intended to be a catalog that captures the entire list of regulatory and legal charges and convictions against a provider. The NPDB contains information on both exclusions and reinstatement actions taken by the OIG, as well as criminal convictions and malpractice verdicts. It is governed by rules that seek to balance enforcement needs with legitimate concerns about errors.[20] The NPDB has been examined by scholars as a potential "blacklist."[21] An error in a private proceeding may be translated into a career-ending entry on an electronic listing: "Physicians are blacklisted after being 'found' to have provided poor quality of care through a highly subjective, and oft-times summary, peer review process conducted by private hospitals."[22]

Though the HHS Office of Inspector General "exclusion" list on LEIE, discussed in Section II, above, is one of several distinct listings for physicians who have had problems, it is not the only listing. NPDB contains records on additional providers who have not been excluded by the OIG and therefore would not appear in the LEIE. Ideally there could be recourse or remedies against errors.

NPDB listings will include:

- medical malpractice payments;
- licensure actions taken by Boards of Medical Examiners;
- licensure and certification actions taken by states;
- federal licensure and certification actions, such as actions by the Drug Enforcement Administration (DEA) or Food and Drug Administration (FDA);
- negative actions or findings taken by peer review organizations or private accreditation entities;
- adverse actions taken against clinical privileges;

---

[19]Pub. L. 111-148, §6403 (2010); Title IV of P.L. 99-660, Health Care Quality Improvement Act of 1986, as amended; the Social Security Act §1921 (§5(b) of P.L. 100-93, Medicare and Medicaid Patient and Program Protection Act of 1987, as amended); Social Security Act §1128E (P.L. 104-191, Health Insurance Portability and Accountability Act of 1996).

[20]45 C.F.R. pt. 60.

[21]K. Van Tassel, *Blacklisted: The Constitutionality of the Federal System for Publishing Reports of "Bad" Doctors in the National Practitioner Data Bank*, 33 CARDOZO L. REV. 2031 (2012).

[22]*Id.*

- federal or state criminal convictions related to the delivery of a healthcare item or service;
- civil judgments related to the delivery of a healthcare item or service;
- exclusions from participation in federal or state healthcare programs; and
- "other adjudicated actions or decisions."

Part 3

How Other Healthcare Personnel Interact with Employers

CHAPTER 14

NURSES AND COLLECTIVE BARGAINING

I. INTRODUCTION

A healthcare worker's status as a "supervisor" has numerous implications. These include his or her exemption from overtime pay requirements, discussed in Chapter 19 of this text. A healthcare "supervisor" also has special status in that the workers in a unit are to be allowed to collectively bargain apart from their supervisors. The U.S. Supreme Court became involved with the issue of nurse supervisors and did not accept the prior National Labor Relations Board (NLRB or the Board) dividing lines.[1] Multiple NLRB decisions and advice documents have discussed the distinctions between nursing supervisors and the nurses who will be part of the bargaining unit.[2]

---

[1] *See* NLRB v. Kentucky River Cmty. Care, 532 U.S. 706 (2001).

[2] NLRB Memorandum OM 99-44 (Aug. 24, 1999) (specifically on issue of nurse supervisors); NLRB Advice Memorandum OM 04-09, Evidentiary Guidelines for Determining Supervisory Status (Oct. 31, 2003); Oakwood Healthcare, Inc., 348 NLRB 686 (2006) (re "charge nurses"); *see also* NLRB, Labor Relations Explanations, Guideline Memorandum Concerning Oakwood Healthcare, Inc., 348 NLRB No. 37 (2006); Memo GC-07-11 (2007); Oak Park Nursing Care, Case No. 14-RC-12485 (Sept. 26, 2007).

II. NLRB CONFLICTS OVER NURSES AS EXCLUDED "SUPERVISORS" AND MEMBERSHIP IN COLLECTIVE BARGAINING UNITS

In 2012, the U.S. Court of Appeals for the D.C. Circuit upheld an NLRB finding that registered nurses, charge nurses, and shift supervisors at a nursing home were not statutory "supervisors," and thus concluded that the nursing home operator's refusal to bargain with a union violated the National Labor Relations Act (NLRA).[3] In *735 Putnam Pike Operations, LLC v. NLRB*, the D.C. Circuit held that the NLRB finding was supported by substantial evidence.[4]

The Board determined that the nurses in question were not "supervisors" excluded from collective bargaining, even though registered nurses directed staff in performance of patient-care tasks and resolved minor disputes between staff members, and even though the nurses were the highest-ranking nursing employees on the nursing home premises from 4:30 p.m. to 6:00 a.m. The following factors were relevant to the determination that the nurses were not exempt "supervisors":

- they did not exercise disciplinary authority and therefore could have no negative effect on reviewed employees' job status or pay;
- there was no evidence that registered nurses were held accountable if staff failed to perform as directed;
- when these "charge nurses" assigned staff or reallocated staff to equalize workloads, they did not exercise independent judgment, a necessary element for finding supervisory authority under NRLA Section 2(11); and
- as shift supervisors, the nurses could only seek volunteers to replace absent employees, and in doing so the nurses had to follow procedures and criteria set by the operator of the nursing home.[5]

The D.C. Circuit determined that, for example, the NLRB "could reasonably conclude that the one instance where a charge nurse denied an employee's request to leave early in a non-emergency

---

[3] 735 Putnam Pike Operations, LLC v. NLRB, 474 F. App'x 782 (D.C. Cir. 2012).
[4] *Id.*
[5] *Id.*

situation, and the employee renewed her request before the Director of Nursing, indicated the charge nurse lacked final authority."[6]

Given the evidentiary gaps, the Board in *735 Putnam Pike* had reasonably concluded that the employer failed to carry its burden of proving its registered nurses were statutory supervisors.[7] In the absence of evidence of primary indicia of supervisory authority, the employer "cannot salvage its challenge by pointing to secondary indicia of supervisory status."[8] The employer's objection that the charge nurses were the highest-ranking nursing employees on the premises from 4:30 p.m. to 6:00 a.m. and therefore *must* be deemed statutory supervisors failed. The objecting employer did not acknowledge exclusions from the bargaining unit for registered nurses who were in fact supervisors, including "floating shift supervisors." The absence from the nursing home of a statutory supervisor does not automatically confer supervisory status on the highest-ranking person present, so the D.C. Circuit upheld the NLRB's ruling.[9]

Another litigated dispute, *Schnurmacher Nursing Home v. NLRB*, arose in a nursing home. Here, at issue was whether the exercise of the charge nurses' authority to direct the certified nursing assistants (CNAs) required the "exercise of independent judgment."[10] Examining the evidence, the Second Circuit found that the charge nurses directed the CNAs in more than just routine tasks. The charge nurses were responsible to direct staff in providing all aspects of patient care, including the administration of emergency oxygen and the handling of life-threatening situations. The court concluded that in directing the CNAs, the charge nurses had to use independent judgment in assessing the condition of patients. The court emphasized that the charge nurses had to determine patients' treatment and make sure other employees administered it properly. So the court of appeals held that the charge nurses were supervisors and were properly excluded from the bargaining units at issue.

In so holding, the *Schnurmacher* court explained that to be a supervisor under the NLRA, an employee must have the authority to exercise at least one of the listed powers, and the employee must

---

[6] *Id.*

[7] *See* NLRB v. Kentucky River Cmty. Care, 532 U.S. 706, 712 (2001).

[8] *735 Putnam Pike Operations*, 474 F. App'x at 784 (citing Jochims v. NLRB, 480 F.3d 1161, 1173 (D.C. Cir. 2007)).

[9] *Id.*

[10] Schnurmacher Nursing Home v. NLRB, 214 F.3d 260 (2d Cir. 2000).

exercise that power using independent judgment and in the interest of the employer. Such judgments must be other than routine and clerical judgments. The court noted that it can be difficult to assert that an individual is not a supervisor when that person is responsible for the actions of another employee.[11]

Disciplinary roles of supervisors are another significant factor. The record in *Jochims v. NLRB*, a 2007 case in the D.C. Circuit, supported the NLRB's finding that the employer's registered nurses did not exercise disciplinary authority.[12] In *Jochims*, the "write-ups" and performance evaluations that the nurses completed regarding other staff members were not "final and authoritative" disciplinary actions and had no negative effects on the reviewed employees' job status or pay.[13] The appeals court held that the NLRB had a reasonable basis for excluding evidence about workplace conditions under prior employers from its review, because the record showed that the responsibilities of the nurses under the operation of the prior management company had differed from their responsibilities under their current management company.[14]

Nor, in other cases, did inclusion in the employee handbook of a progressive disciplinary system establish that charge nurses exercised disciplinary authority under NLRA Section 2(11); no evidence was presented to indicate that the system was in effect.[15]

An employer's contentions regarding NLRB "supervisor" exclusions concerning nurses' authority to direct and assign work also failed. Although the record indicated that the registered nurses directed staff in the performance of patient-care tasks and resolved minor disputes between staff members, there was no evidence that the nurses were held accountable if the staff failed to perform as directed. A party cannot establish "responsibility to direct" supervisory authority under Section 2(11) without demonstrating accountability.[16]

---

[11] *Id.*

[12] Jochims v. NLRB, 480 F.3d 1161, 1173 (D.C. Cir. 2007).

[13] *Id.*

[14] *Id.*

[15] *See* Oil, Chem. & Atomic Workers Int'l Union v. NLRB, 445 F.2d 237, 243 (D.C. Cir. 1971); Berthold Nursing Care Center, Inc., 351 NLRB 27, 29 (2007).

[16] *See* Oakwood Healthcare, Inc., 348 NLRB 686, 691–92 (2006); Beverly Enters.–Minn., Inc., 348 NLRB 727, 730–31 (2006).

CHAPTER 15

IMPACTS OF THE NLRB HEALTHCARE UNIT CLASSIFICATION RULES

I. INTRODUCTION

Workers who want to "collectively" bargain must define the boundaries of their "collective" cohort or "unit." Consolidation within one employer is essential, but consolidation at one site is not essential. For example, all nurses in a five-hospital chain could be members of the same union. The union initiates the collective definition that it seeks, and then begins the process of being recognized as the collective bargaining representative at a clinical site for a unit of nurses or other workers.

This chapter addresses a very special circumstance. In 1989, responding to Congress, the National Labor Relations Board (NLRB or the Board) adopted a special final regulation that defines the permitted collective bargaining units within an "acute care" hospital.[1] The 1989 rule virtually prevents the formation of a "mingled" unit, in which all of a hospital's nurses and technicians, for example, are combined in the same bargaining unit (except where certain exceptions apply). The regulation was later upheld by the Supreme Court.[2]

II. BACKGROUND: CREATION OF THE BARGAINING UNIT

Creation of a labor bargaining unit is a task of definitional inclusion and the essential foundation of the collective bargaining process. As in any "collective" activity, there must be "collecting in" of workers by job position and "excluding out" of some other workers. There must be a definition of which positions are to be considered inside the unit. Payroll records for a typical small hospital might show there are 100 registered nurses, 10 radiologic technicians, 25 patient care assistants, 20 kitchen workers, etc.

The first step in shaping the unit is to define a common employer and one or more common site(s). With rare and special exceptions, a unit is intended to affect one employer with whom these employees can bargain. The unit does not include multiple employer groups, unless joint bargaining arrangements are specially constructed.

As the next step, the employees identified in the first step must define what workplace positions or job titles they wish to have included in their units before petitioning for recognition, e.g., all assemblers, all packing crew members, all waiters. Typically, the workers who want to have bargaining rights will talk first with a union organizer. The organizer will quietly and informally train the core group of union proponents. The core group determines which people can be counted upon to support their efforts, which sets of workers are likely to agree, and which workers appear to be very friendly with management and so would be unlikely to join in the collective effort.

Three-way conversations then begin between the union's field organizer, the central office union specialists in organizing, and the core group of active employees. It may be that the core group is too small to be attractive to the union. In that case, the core group may

---

[1] 29 C.F.R. §103.30 (2016).
[2] American Hosp. Ass'n v. NLRB, 499 U.S. 606 (1991).

be told to recruit new participants and come back to the union later. Or it may be that the central union staff identifies a problem—either in practical terms or based on legal precedent—with including some of the suggested job titles and employees in the unit. Or it may be that a rival union is recruiting among these workers, and the central office of the union declines to interfere with that rival's efforts, for various reasons.

Collecting information at the factory or shop requires the core group of employees to gather specific numbers of workers and to categorize the unit inclusion by titles or assigned work. Then the group informally "sniffs out" the likely support within the several job titles through informal conversations. The messages back to the union field organizer lay out the potential support—for example, 6 of 8 device assemblers agree, 10 of 15 device testers agree, but 3 of 4 device shift leaders dislike unions. In that situation, the factory unit probably would be composed of assemblers and testers and would not include device shift leaders.

Labor protections in bargaining are intended to assist workers and not the company's managers. Collective bargaining units are composed of workers, and not factory foremen or employees' supervisors. In the healthcare context, where people-intensive workloads often require a little assistance from "all hands," it is more likely that workers will want the rules governing unit creation to have a broader reach so that more workers will be covered in their "unit."

It is not simple to define the inclusion or exclusion norms for collective bargaining units composed of workers in a hospital. Successfully defining a collective bargaining unit requires finding a group of workers with common interests who can be expected to benefit from their collective power in the course of bargaining with management. The criteria for defining a unit also include exceptions that exclude some persons. The combination of the statute, rules, and definitions of roles applicable to defining hospital worker bargaining units make for some specialized analysis. The NLRB acute care hospital rule,[3] discussed below, is one essential element of the process.

---

[3] 29 C.F.R. §103.30.

III. THE NLRB ACUTE CARE HOSPITAL UNIT RULE

In 1989, the NLRB adopted a rule that fixed the appropriate bargaining units in the "acute care" sector of the healthcare industry.[4] Under the NLRB rule, so long as an acute care hospital is the employer, the "*only* appropriate units" for recognition petitions are these eight categories:

(1) All registered nurses.
(2) All physicians.
(3) All professionals except for registered nurses and physicians.
(4) All technical employees.
(5) All skilled maintenance employees.
(6) All business office clerical employees.
(7) All guards.
(8) All nonprofessional employees except for technical employees, skilled maintenance employees, business office clerical employees, and guards.[5]

Three important exceptions apply to the general rule. These are discussed in Section III.B., below.

A. Definition of Acute Care Hospital

A "hospital" is defined in the federal Medicare Act[6] and the NLRB labor unit regulation[7] as an institution that, inter alia, "is primarily engaged in providing, by or under the supervision of physicians, to inpatients (A) diagnostic services and therapeutic services for medical diagnosis, treatment, and care of injured, disabled, or sick persons, or (B) rehabilitation services for the rehabilitation of injured, disabled, or sick persons"; maintains clinical records on all of its patients; and "provides 24-hour nursing service rendered or supervised by a registered professional nurse, and has a licensed practical nurse or registered professional nurse on duty at all times."[8]

---

[4] *Id.*
[5] *Id.* §103.30(a) (emphasis added).
[6] 42 U.S.C. §1395x(e) (2012 & Supp. 2016).
[7] 29 C.F.R. §103.30(f)(1) (incorporating Medicare Act definition by reference).
[8] 42 U.S.C. §1395x(e).

Within the "hospital" category, an "acute care" hospital is defined in the NLRB labor unit rule as "a short term care hospital in which the average length of patient stay is less than thirty days, or ... in which over 50% of all patients are admitted to units where the average length of patient stay is less than thirty days."[9] The unit rule applies to these acute care facilities only.[10]

The NLRB's unit-limiting rule expressly excludes facilities that are "primarily nursing homes, primarily psychiatric hospitals, or primarily rehabilitation hospitals."[11] The effect of this exclusion is that, for example, nursing home employees who are registered nurses (RNs), advanced registered nurse practitioners (ARNPs), and certified nursing assistants (CNAs) could all be in the same bargaining unit if the normal criteria for unit formation were met, unlike similar employees at an acute care hospital.

The NLRB rule has established a presumption that a hospital is covered as an "acute care" facility unless the hospital management produces evidence showing contrary facts, e.g., as to much longer patient stays.[12] For all healthcare facilities other than acute care hospitals, the NLRB will determine appropriate units by its usual process of receiving union petitions, holding adjudicatory hearings, and adjudication.

Not all healthcare facilities fit the in-or-out status for which the acute care hospital rules were designed. The NLRB retains discretion to consider the actual makeup of healthcare entities in order to determine the appropriate units for those facilities and whether the NLRB must apply the eight defined bargaining unit categories to them.[13]

B. Exceptions to the Rule

When it approved the NLRB rule, the U.S. Supreme Court clearly summarized the rule and its three exceptions:

> The rule is applicable to acute care hospitals and provides, with three exceptions, that eight, and only eight, units shall be appropriate in any such hospital. The three exceptions are for cases that present

---

[9]29 C.F.R. §103.30(f)(2).
[10]*Id.* §103.30(a).
[11]*Id.* §103.30(f)(2).
[12]*See id.*
[13]*Id.* §103.30(g).

extraordinary circumstances, cases in which nonconforming units already exist, and cases in which labor organizations seek to combine two or more of the eight specified units. The extraordinary circumstances exception applies automatically to hospitals in which the eight-unit rule will produce a unit of five or fewer employees.[14]

Exceptions exist, but are infrequently used. For example, if the unit would consist of five or fewer employees, such an "extraordinary circumstance" could be debated in a separate hearing. A hospital claiming an extraordinary circumstance must show that its circumstances and arguments are substantially different from those already considered by the NLRB in its rulemaking process.[15] Where there are existing nonconforming units in acute care hospitals and a petition for additional units is filed, the existing units remain in place. Any new units, however, must match the lists of job titles above, unless the management and union make a "consent agreement" otherwise.

IV. PETITIONS

A. Official Definition of a Unit

The union prepares a petition for a representation election on NLRB Form 502-RC.[16] This form then is filed electronically with the regional office of the NLRB. (Alternatively, if public employees are involved, the filing is made with the state labor entity, on that state's form.) The NLRB form identifies the employer, the title(s) of the job categories to be included in the proposed unit, and the excluded job categories. The NLRB's field investigator sets up meetings with the employer and the union and gathers lists of workers who are in those job classifications.

B. Employer Objections to the Unit

The formal delivery to the employer of a copy of the petition for representation election should not be a surprise if the employer has

---

[14] American Hosp. Ass'n v. NLRB, 499 U.S. 606, 608 (1991).
[15] St. Margaret Mem'l Hosp. v. NLRB, 991 F.2d 1146 (3d Cir. 1993).
[16] Form NLRB-502 (RC) (Apr. 2015), *available at* https://www.nlrb.gov/sites/default/files/attachments/basic-page/node-3040/Form%20NLRB-502%20%28RC%29%20-%20RC%20Petition.pdf.

been listening to the rumors circulating among workers at the healthcare facility. The employer's attorney will review the union petition, and will pay particular attention to its attachments, which must show 30 percent or more employee support for the petition. The employer's counsel then can be expected to file objections, likely one or more of three types:

- failure to follow proper process;
- failure to exclude employees who cannot be in the unit; or
- failure to demonstrate adequate support for the petition among at least 30 percent of the workers with the selected job titles.

Sometimes the workforce is fluid and easily changing, and if the collection of worker cards seeking a union has been delayed, the persons who signed the petition might not constitute the required 30 percent of the actual workforce as of the date of decision. Turnover in lower paid healthcare jobs is an unfortunate reality. Intentional additions and accretions over time may change the unit's shape and size, but a unit that had been recognized long ago, and which has experienced great turnover, is not likely to serve as a barrier to a current petition.[17]

Prudent healthcare employers recognize that preferences among some groups can be balanced out by "salting" the unit with opponents of unions. The employer is likely to use personal relationships between some supervisors and some workers to predict their views and then to "lobby" for inclusion of those workers, because their inclusion in the unit can be predicted to bring votes against unionization. These are sometimes called "carve-outs" or "seed ins" because the strategy is to write a unit definition that looks ahead to the probable outcome of the election vote.

The effects of geographic dispersal of the unit members around the healthcare employer's network should also be considered. In a typical case, the NLRB has ruled against breaking up a unit when a union pressed for a change. In *Presbyterian University Hospital v. NLRB*, for example, the Board properly found that geographic proximity of the facilities did not substantially impact the skilled maintenance employee unit's operations, there was lack of contact between

---

[17]*See* NLRB v. Saint Mary Home, 358 F. App'x 255 (2d Cir. 2009); *see also* NLRB v. Long Island Coll. Hosp., 20 F.3d 76 (2d Cir. 1994).

employees at the two facilities, the employees maintained their respective faculties, material purchases were made by the respective facilities, job openings were posted within one facility before openings were posted employer-wide, the employer hired outside contractors for a certain task rather than using workers from its other facility, and the existing skilled maintenance employee unit had bargained successfully and peacefully for 20 years.[18]

C. NLRB Procedures for Deciding Unit Determinations

The process for filing unit petitions was updated in 2014, and the process can be summarized from the NLRB's lists of procedural requirements:[19]

- Representation petitions may be filed with the Board electronically. They must be served on the employer by the petitioner, which will afford the other parties (e.g., another union) the earliest possible notice of the petition.
- The petitioner must provide evidence that employees support the petition (the "showing of interest"). The petitioner must also provide the name and contact information of its representative.
- When a petition is filed, the employer must post and distribute to employees a Board notice about the petition and the potential for an election to follow.
- The pre-election hearing will generally be scheduled to open eight days from notice of the hearing.
- The pre-election hearing will continue from day to day until completed, absent extraordinary circumstances. Nonpetitioning parties are required to state a position responding to the petition in writing one day before the pre-election hearing is set to open.
- The statement must identify the issues the nonpetitioning parties wish to litigate before the election; litigation inconsistent with the statement will not be permitted. Timely amendments to the statement may be made on a showing of good cause.

---

[18]Presbyterian Univ. Hosp. v. NLRB, 88 F.3d 1300 (1996).
[19]Representation—Case Procedures, 79 Fed. Reg. 74,308 (Dec. 15, 2014) (codified at 29 C.F.R. pts. 101, 102 & 103).

- The employer must also provide a list of the names, shifts, work locations, and job classifications of the employees in the petitioned-for unit, and of any other employees that it seeks to add to the unit. The statement must also identify the party's representative for purposes of the proceeding.
- At the start of the hearing, the petitioner is required to respond on the record to the issues raised by the other parties in their statements of position.
- If there is a dispute between the parties, the hearing officer has discretion to ask each party to describe what evidence it has in support of its position, i.e., to make an offer of proof.
- The purpose of the pre-election hearing, to determine whether there is a "question of representation," is clearly identified.[20]
- Once the issues are presented, the regional director will decide which, if any, voter eligibility questions should be litigated before an election is held. These decisions will be made bearing in mind the purpose of the hearing. Generally, only evidence that is relevant to a question that will be decided may be introduced at the pre-election hearing.
- The hearing will conclude with oral argument, and no written briefing will be permitted unless the regional director grants permission to file such a brief. The regional director must decide the matter and may not sua sponte transfer it to the Board.
- Absent a waiver, a party may request NLRB review of the action of a regional director delegated under National Labor Relations Act (NLRA) Section 3(b).[21] Requests will only be granted for compelling reasons.
- Requests for Board review may be filed any time during the proceeding, or within 14 days after a final disposition of the case by the regional director.
- The 2014 changes to the final rule improved the process for Board review by giving parties an option to wait and see whether election results will moot a request for review.
- A request for Board review will not operate as a stay unless specifically ordered by the Board. Stays and/or requests for

---

[20] 29 U.S.C. § 159 (2012).
[21] 29 U.S.C. § 153(b) (2012).

expedited consideration will only be granted when necessary. A stay should not be routine, but should be an extraordinary form of relief.

- The regional director will ordinarily specify in the "direction of election" the election details, such as the date, time, place, and type of election and the payroll period for eligibility, e.g., "X-ray technicians employed as of date 1/1/18."
- Parties will take positions (for or against) on these matters, in writing, in the statement of position and on the record before the close of the hearing.
- The NLRB regional director will set the election for the earliest date practicable. The regional director will ordinarily transmit the notice of election at the same time as the direction of election. Both may be transmitted electronically.
- If the employer customarily communicates with its employees electronically, it must distribute all election notices to employees electronically, in addition to posting paper notices at the workplace. Within two business days of the direction of election, employers must electronically transmit to the other parties (such as a rival union) and to the regional director a list of eligible employees with contact information, including personal email addresses and phone numbers if the employer has such contact information in its possession. The list should also include shifts, job classifications, and work locations. The list may only be used for certain purposes. Recognizing the potential sensitivity of the information, however, the rules also restrict its use in order to guard against potential abuse.
- When a charge is filed alleging the commission of unfair labor practices that could compromise the fairness of the election, the regional director has discretion to delay (or "block") the election until the issue can be resolved.
- Any party seeking to block the election must simultaneously file an offer of proof and promptly make witnesses available.
- After the election, parties have seven days to file both objections and offers of proof in support. Objections, but not offers, must be served by the objector on other parties. If necessary, a post-election hearing on challenges and/or objections will be scheduled to open 21 days after the tally of ballots or as soon as practicable thereafter.

- In every case, the NLRB regional director will be required to issue a final decision. Where applicable, the regional director's decision will be subject to requests for review, where necessary. Any Board decisions on review are likely to be improved by having the parties first obtain the final decision of the regional director before their request for review.

V. CONTESTED UNIT CASES

Employers can be expected to object to the unit size selected by the union. In a 2012 case, the NLRB appropriately certified a very broad "wall-to-wall" bargaining unit combining a hospital's professional and nonprofessional employees, without requiring the union to show extraordinary circumstances under the NLRB's acute care bargaining unit rule. This certification was upheld because the rule contains an exception allowing the union to seek a combination of specified units without showing extraordinary circumstances.[22]   But there are literally hundreds of unit determination cases each year, so the reader who wishes to predict an outcome will start with the 1989 NLRB rule and then study the exceptions and exclusions which have appeared in subsequent individual cases.[23]

VI. ADDING MEMBERS TO A HEALTHCARE UNIT

The NLRB and the U.S. Court of Appeals for the D.C. Circuit have wrestled with the question of how a merged or expanded hospital could add certain non-unit workers into a particular "unit." The NLRB rule's language applicable to this question only applies when "a petition for additional units is filed."[24] The appellate court ruled:

> An election to add unrepresented employees to an existing unit, by its nature, does not involve the creation of any "additional units." Rather, it involves the inclusion of additional unrepresented employees in an already-existing unit. Consequently, the Board's exemption of such

---

[22]San Miguel Hosp. Corp. v. NLRB, 697 F.3d 1181 (D.C. Cir. 2012).

[23]For a discussion on whether the healthcare rule applies to subcontractors operating in an acute care hospital, see *Fair Oaks Anesthesia Assocs., P.C. v. NLRB*, 975 F.2d 1068 (4th Cir. 1992). For a discussion of the single facility presumption in acute care hospitals, see *CPMC-St. Lukes Hosp.*, 357 NLRB No. 21 (July 29, 2011).

[24]29 C.F.R. § 103.30(c) (2016).

elections from the regulation was entirely compatible with the regulation's terms.[25]

VII. EFFECTS OF DELAYS IN REPRESENTATION ELECTIONS WITHIN A UNIT

When an election is held, its results can become "stale" if management delays the eventual outcome. There can be delays while disputed issues such as unit size are determined. For example, in *NLRB v. Long Island College Hospital*,[26] the Second Circuit ruled in 1994 that a hospital should not have been ordered to bargain with a union on the basis of results of a 15-year-old union election, where only 20 of 56 employees currently within that unit had been employed at the time of the election. Because of great delay, extraordinary turnover in employees and NLRB membership, genuine confusion in the law regarding hospital bargaining units, and "the fact that the majority of the present employees did not vote in the relevant election," that case presented "unique circumstances" favoring hospital management and warranting denial of enforcement of the NLRB's bargaining order.[27]

---

[25]Rush Univ. Med. Ctr. v. NLRB, 833 F.3d 202 (D.C. Cir. 2016).
[26]NLRB v. Long Island Coll. Hosp., 20 F.3d 76 (2d Cir. 1994).
[27]*Id.* at 83.

CHAPTER 16

ISSUES FOR NON-MD, NON-RN EMPLOYEES

I. INTRODUCTION

The great majority of the daily work in healthcare institutions is performed by knowledgeable and well-motivated people who happen to not have medical or nursing licenses. Healthcare workers who are engaged in patient care but who are not registered nurses (RNs) present a variety of issues related to collective bargaining. This chapter discusses issues related to these non-MD, non-nurse healthcare workers.

II. SUPPORTIVE CAREGIVERS

Many workers who support the delivery of patient care are not physicians or nurses. The roles of these workers include: physician assistant (PA), certified nursing assistant (CNA), emergency medical technician (EMT), radiology technician (RT), respiratory therapist (RT), registered dietician (RD), physical therapist (PT), health aide, and others. Many of these workers have excellent hands-on experience and training. Some have been examined by state licensing boards and received credentials designated for specific assignments.

These state-regulated employees have a defined set of tasks, for which they have special training and state licensure.

PA licensure is widespread. That particular category of healthcare professional appears to be integrating well into the healthcare system's formerly rigid doctor/nurse exclusive dichotomy.[1] CNAs are a recognized population within hospitals and skilled nursing facilities and can form their own bargaining units.[2] Workload "restructuring" sometimes aims to reduce the registered nurse cohort and replace some of them with lower skilled CNAs.[3]

Some non-RN employees have a state license, but their occupations have a lower barrier to qualify than nurses and some others. For this reason, there are likely to be more CNAs and EMTs employed around a healthcare employer's facilities and clinics, compared to the number of registered nurses. These non-RN employees are likely to be categorized by the NLRB healthcare unit classification rule as appropriate for a unit that consists of "[a]ll professionals except for registered nurses and physicians."[4]

Other occupations are likely to have fewer than five members in the average healthcare facility (e.g., X-ray technicians). For those employees, the NLRB rule would allow the acute care hospital to seek one combined unit of all comparable roles.

III. WHY NON-NURSE EMPLOYEES ARE LESS LIKELY TO BECOME A UNIT

Non-nurse workers at a hospital or other healthcare facility tend to be splintered into small subgroups of technical specialists, often outsourced, so that the hospital places expertise in the hands of a contract provider, like the radiation department or the anesthesia team or an infection control contractor. This can result in a higher frequency of multiple employers on the hospital premises, making

---

[1] J. Hinkel et al., *Practice & Productivity of Physician Assistants & Nurse Practitioners in Outpatient Oncology Clinics at National Comprehensive Cancer Network Institutions*, 6 J. ONCOLOGY PRACTICE, no. 4, at 182–87 (2010).

[2] Specialty Healthcare & Rehabilitation Ctr. of Mobile, 357 NLRB No. 82 (2011).

[3] E. Appelbaum et al., *The Effects of Work Restructuring on Low-Wage, Low-Skilled Workers in U.S. Hospitals, in* LOW-WAGE AMERICA: HOW EMPLOYERS ARE RESHAPING OPPORTUNITY IN THE WORKPLACE (E. Appelbaum et al. eds., 2003).

[4] 29 C.F.R. §103.30 (2016). See discussion of the rule in Chapter 16.

it less likely that a single bargaining contract would be established "across the board."

Non-nurse workers are not likely to share the same goals in bargaining, e.g., reduction in mandatory overtime. Where only a handful of specialized workers are employed in a single healthcare setting, they may decline to join a union, and so a prudent union will be less likely to spend effort recruiting them. The NLRB rule allowing healthcare bargaining units to be structured in response to worker petitions does not mean that there will necessarily be any particular group wishing to be aligned with others. The actual administrative overhead cost to the union compared to the dues that could be collected from the unit would be another reason for a union not to wish to organize five or eight specialty employees who, for example, might operate the ultrasound equipment for a smaller hospital.

Temporary or transient status of the workers is an additional factor. For example, there will be some locations where vacationers account for a high seasonal flow of patients. There will be less cohesion to a unit of workers if their expectations are for six months of work and substantial periods of furloughs.

Moreover, if an individual worker is an EMT working for a fire department or other health emergency public service, his or her public employer has been established under different laws in the public sector, and the EMT would not be eligible to combine into an NLRB-recognized unit of private-sector hospital employees.

Studies of hospital management's use of temporary employees as leverage to control low-wage employee groups are also interesting. "When hospital managers had difficulty recruiting and retaining staff in low-skilled positions, they often turned to temporary help agencies, on the grounds that the agencies were better at recruiting workers."[5]

IV. HEALTH CARE TECHNOLOGY STAFF

Within an acute care hospital, information technologist (IT) workers can form a union, and they will be treated as part of the hospital's "skilled maintenance" workers. NLRB decisions in the past

---

[5]G. Erickeck et al., *The Effects of Temporary Services & Contracting Out on Low-Skilled Workers*, LOW-WAGE AMERICA: HOW EMPLOYERS ARE RESHAPING OPPORTUNITY IN THE WORKPLACE (E. Applebaum et al. eds., 2003).

have regarded ITs' skills as being closer to maintenance operations.[6] Though no specific measurements of IT staff attitudes are able to be generalized, IT technical talent are more likely to be individualists and are inclined not to join collective entity bargaining. This will vary, of course.

Defining which job titles are in or out can be complex, because the systems and job titles vary. Technologists are likely to have training and functional subspecialties ("Mary is our go-to person when we have problems with Epic EHRs"). But their title may be the same as a less-skilled person who is just entering the IT group. Reward systems also vary. Flat compensation arrangements are not as common as in conventional work, especially in a job market where ITs' skills are easily transferred out of the hospital to a tech startup or school setting.

Another factor dissuading union recruitment efforts is the massive use of IT outsourcing. Embedded contractors are very frequently used to solve a need such as a surge in records demand or preparing for changes in the hospital's system. To the extent that an SAP skill set will be needed for six months, for example, the IT role is more likely to be contracted out. The rise of temporary tasks performed by "gig workers" has an effect in reducing the sense of permanence of "loyalty" of IT workers.

In *St. Anthony Hospital Systems, Inc. v. NLRB*,[7] a case that was decided before the NLRB unit rule was finalized, the U.S. Court of Appeals for the Tenth Circuit held that the NLRB had properly applied a "disparity of interests" test in certifying the bargaining unit of a hospital's technical employees as separate from service/maintenance employees. That distinction drew upon significant differences in training and education of employees within the two classes, as well as the fact that these employees did not have common supervision and that there was not substantial integration of their job duties. The court recognized that the Board in this case adopted the "disparity of interests" test in the healthcare field rather than the traditional "community of interests" standard to abide by direction

---

[6]*See, e.g.*, Presbyterian Univ. Hosp. v. NLRB., 88 F.3d 1300 (D.C. Cir. 1996); *see also* 9 C.F.R. §103.30(a)(5).
[7]884 F.2d 518 (10th Cir. 1989).

from Congress[8] to prevent undue proliferation of bargaining units in healthcare.[9]

In *St. Anthony*, the Tenth Circuit stated that the adoption of the "disparity of interests" test did not affect the statutory definition of "professional" as applied in the healthcare field. The court then upheld the NLRB decision that radiologic technologists and respiratory therapists were technical, rather than professional, employees for collective bargaining unit purposes as being supported by substantial evidence.[10]

V. SPECIALIZED SUBCONTRACTORS

Fair Oaks Anesthesia Associates, P.C. v. NLRB[11] provided an interesting test of the NLRB rule on hospital worker "units"[12] when a hospital subcontracts the function of surgical anesthesia. In this case, the anesthesia service was delivered at an acute care hospital by a corporate entity, and the anesthesia entity had some nurses, some doctors who were not yet partner/owners, and some doctors who were partner/owners.

The NLRB rule required all registered nurses to be included in one single bargaining unit at an acute care hospital. The underlying theory was that an acute care hospital, for which the anesthesia corporation provided services, would be adversely affected by a proliferation of bargaining units, and the proliferation would happen if the Board certified a unit consisting solely of the limited subspecialty of registered nurses who provided anesthesia. The specialized corporation was deemed a separate employer from that hospital, and that corporation employed only two categories of employee.[13]

"Sharper than usual differences" existed between the interests of the registered nurse anesthetists and the non-partner physician anesthetists. Therefore, a small unit consisting solely of nurse

---

[8]The 1974 Amendments to the National Labor Relations Act spurred the court in *St. Anthony* to adopt the disparity of interests rule, and the amendments also spurred adoption of the NLRB's healthcare unit rule. *See* 884 F.2d at 519–20 & n.3; *see also 1974 Health Care Amendments*, NATIONAL LABOR RELATIONS BOARD, https://www.nlrb.gov/who-we-are/our-history/1974-health-care-amendments.

[9]884 F.2d at 520.

[10]*Id.* at 522–24.

[11]975 F.2d 1068 (4th Cir. 1992).

[12]29 C.F.R. §130.30 (2016).

[13]*Fair Oaks*, 975 F.2d 1068.

anesthetists was the appropriate bargaining unit. One distinction was that the physicians earned a yearly salary that was significantly higher than nurses' hourly wage. In addition, the physicians expected eventually to become partners in the anesthesia company, but the nurses were not eligible for partnership, even though there was considerable functional integration between nurses and physicians at the time of delivery of the anesthesia.[14]

Size of the employer is relevant. In *Fair Oaks*, the Fourth Circuit declined to hold a small employer with only two categories of employees to the NLRB rule that was developed for large facilities. A corporate service provider supplied anesthetists employed by that professional corporation to an acute care hospital, and the court reasoned that the situation of a small employer providing services to an acute care hospital was different than the situation of employees of that large-scale acute care hospital. The NLRB regional director had set forth in great detail factual evidence to support his conclusions concerning appropriateness of the small bargaining unit.[15]

VI. CLERICAL WORKERS

Medical records clerks and transcribers have sometimes sought to have an individual collective bargaining unit created for their function, and the NLRB has adjudicated several such cases. In 1975, the Board held that such workers did not need a separate bargaining unit because of the small number of clerks/transcribers, the low technical skills required by clerks/transcribers, and the "community of interest" with other employees in matters such as similar hours and benefits.[16] More recent Board decisions have found it appropriate for a bargaining unit to include medical records clerks and transcribers along with a variety of other employees.[17] The changed orientation of newly selected NLRB members in the Trump administration would suggest a far more pro-employer view, even less receptive to formation of small units.

---

[14] *Id.*

[15] *Id.*

[16] Levine Hosp. of Hayward, 219 NLRB 327 (1975).

[17] *See* Specialty Hosp. of Washington-Hadley, 357 NLRB No. 77 (2011); South Hills Health Sys., 336 NLRB No. 80 (2001); *see also* NLRB v. Fairmont General Hosp. 261 F. App'x 534 (4th Cir. 2001).

VII. THE "UNDERCLASS" AS A POOL OF DISSATISFIED WORKERS

This is not a sociology text, of course, but decades of experience with medical venues shows that the dividing line between workers who might be called the "underclass" and the "elite" is in the professional credential of MD and RN.

Nursing homes, rehabilitation hospitals, and urgent care centers have a substantial pool of non-MD, non-RN workers who can be disaffected by the many external economic pressures on management to restrain wage increases. Some have asserted that more spending of government funds on training courses will bring advancement for the lowest range of wage workers. "The 'bad jobs' have low skill, pay and prospects, and often become a job-trap for migrant and female workers."[18] A text on this category of healthcare workers quoted one nursing home assistant as describing her group of workers as "professional butt cleaners."[19] "These jobs require hard and dirty work, often without breaks, have poorly enforced job descriptions and are undervalued, making workers feel worthless, as well as low paid."[20] Training was less valuable than expected and allowed management to "dump on us more."[21] A reviewer of the text said that its view that "more training does not deliver better jobs or even save existing jobs" makes for "uncomfortable reading for those who see skills as the answer to poor job quality."[22]

Cost controls within a hospital sometimes take the form of substitution of a less skilled laborer for a licensed person such as a registered nurse. Restructuring plans by management may undercut the registered nursing staff and even encourage and anticipate their displacement.[23]

Unlike registered nurses, the more transient healthcare work force may be less interested in permanent, secure positions. For those workers who are coming into the healthcare field after layoffs in fields such as manufacturing, however, the utility of the union as

---

[18]Chris Warhurst, *Reviews*, 40 CONTEMPORARY SOC. no. 5, at 576 (2010).

[19]ARIEL DUCEY, NEVER GOOD ENOUGH: HEALTH CARE WORKERS AND THE FALSE PROMISE OF JOB TRAINING (Cornell Press 2008).

[20]*Id.*

[21]*Id.*

[22]Warhurst at 576.

[23]LOW-WAGE AMERICA: HOW EMPLOYERS ARE RESHAPING OPPORTUNITY IN THE WORKPLACE (E. Applebaum et al. eds., 2003).

a collective bargaining agent will be familiar in its ability to assist workers in organizing and negotiating. These lower paid workers' knowledge of the benefits of organizing may fuel their willingness to organize, strike, and picket their employers.

Since 2013, the NLRB has filed multiple charges against a Pittsburgh hospital system for its actions to restrict workers from organizing. A 2016 strike among housekeepers, shuttle drivers and other non–health care workers at a Pittsburgh hospital to protest wages and the employer's efforts to prevent union organizing is an example of lower paid workers' interest in organizing.[24]

---

[24]Maria Castelluci, *UPMC Hourly Workers Strike to Protest Wages, Union Rights*, MODERN HEALTHCARE (Nov. 29, 2016).

CHAPTER 17

STRIKES AND LOCKOUTS IN HEALTHCARE LABOR CONFLICTS

I. INTRODUCTION

Unions collectively bargain with employers under the implicit threat that workers may go on strike at the end of their contract. The law protects "concerted activities for the purpose of collective bargaining or other mutual aid or protection."[1] The National Labor Relations Act (NLRA) provides that nothing in the Act, "except as specifically provided for herein, shall be construed so as either to interfere with or impede or diminish in any way the right to strike, or to affect the limitations or qualifications on that right."[2] The right to strike is further protected under extensive National Labor Relations Board (NLRB) and federal court case law.[3] At times, the announcement of a strike may result in a lockout by the employer, as discussed in the last section of this chapter.

---

[1] 29 U.S.C. §157 (2012).

[2] *Id.* §163.

[3] *See e.g.*, NLRB v. Erie Resistor Corp., 373 U.S. 221 (1963); Ahearn v. Jackson Hosp. Corp., 351 F.3d 226 (6th Cir. 2003); Pirelli Cable Corp. v. NLRB, 141 F.3d 503 (4th Cir. 1998). For a description of the types of protected strikes, see *Right to Strike*, NATIONAL LABOR RELATIONS BOARD, https://www.nlrb.gov/strikes.

The law requires advance notice—an "8(g) notice"—to announce the union's intent to strike.[4] The pre-strike period is typically a scramble for the union as well as for the hospital.[5]

II. PICKETING THE HEALTHCARE INSTITUTION

In the healthcare context, hospital strikes by doctors or nurses are especially problematic. Patients may die if a substitute stand-in worker does not have the necessary skills and the specific patient information needed to make appropriate clinical decisions. For example, nurses in a neonatal intensive care unit (NICU) are legally entitled to collectively bargain and to strike. But will the temporary nurse brought into the NICU at midnight when the strike begins be able to protect the lives of the premature infants whose care had been managed for days or weeks by a nurse who is now on the picket line outside?

Picketing draws attention to a healthcare institution's problems.[6] Accordingly, management talks tough to the union but is gentle with the news media. News reports about hospital strikes are often initially focused on the picket lines outside the front door, but as the strike lengthens, reporters tend to focus on the rates of deaths of patients within the facility. Losing patients to a nearby rival hospital, wherever that is possible, is a significant deterrent to a long strike. In a 2016 confrontation in New York, the nurses' union announced a one-day strike, and the hospital responded with the threat of a five-day lockout of any worker who went on strike. These events forced a settlement after 14 months without a contract.[7]

News media coverage of strikes in healthcare institutions tends to be skewed. Some reporters may leave the reader with the impression that the strikers wanted harm to occur to their "abandoned" patients as some form of visible punishment for the greed of the management. The reader should discount these claims; truly committed nurses and other hospital personnel want to save lives, and they tend to view strikes as a last resort. Unions likewise see the

---

[4]NLRA §8(g), *codified at* 29 U.S.C. §158(g).

[5]*See* G. King et al., *Is "Ten Days" Really Ten Days?—The National Labor Relations Act's Strike Notice Requirement in the Healthcare Industry*, 37 J. HEALTH L. 473 (2004).

[6]Matthew Sturdevant & Mara Lee, *Nursing Home Owner: Union Pickets Illegal Despite Lockout*, HARTFORD COURANT (Dec. 14, 2011).

[7]J. Mulder, *Utica Nurses Drop Strike Threat*, SYRACUSE POST-STANDARD (Aug. 29, 2016).

greed of some managers as a sideline problem that interferes with delivery of good patient care.

There are limitations on the ability of a union to picket a health-care institution, and they are more stringent than constraints on pickets at a tire store or factory. In the 2016 *Capital Medical Center* case, the NLRB concluded that the hospital violated NLRB rules by prohibiting the type of nondisruptive picketing that fell within these limitations. The NLRB said that the Capital Medical Center improperly attempted "to prevent off-duty employees from publicizing a contract dispute at its nonemergency entrances by carrying picket signs and acting in a non-confrontational manner that did not disturb patients or disrupt hospital operations."[8] Supreme Court decisions[9] on freedom of picketers applied, and it was an unfair labor practice for the hospital to summon the police to the facility in response to the picketing.

In the acute care hospital setting, the NLRB held in *Capital Medical Center*, restrictions on picketing activity "in non-patient care areas are valid if the employer shows that the prohibition is needed to prevent patient disturbance or disruption of health care operations."[10] The hospital in that case "did not meet its burden of showing that prohibiting the type of picketing that occurred in this case [—a quiet, stationary two-person picket outside of the hospital building—] was necessary to prevent patient disturbance or disruption of health care operations."[11]

III. STRIKES AS A NEGOTIATING WEAPON

An example of a strike used as a spur to negotiations is the strike at the 13-hospital Allina Health group in Minnesota. The strike, which cost the hospital an estimated $20.4 million,[12] continued for five weeks and ended only after the state governor convened a 17-hour negotiating session. "Under the three-year contract, nurse-

[8]Capital Med. Ctr. & UFCW Local 21, 364 NLRB No. 69, 207 LRRM (BNA) 1426 (2016).

[9]NLRB v. Baptist Hosp., 442 U.S. 773, 781–787 (1979); Beth Israel Hosp. v. NLRB, 437 U.S. 483, 500 (1978); Republic Aviation Corp. v. NLRB, 324 U.S. 793 (1945).

[10]*Capital Med. Ctr.*, 364 NLRB No. 69, at *4.

[11]*Id.*

[12]Bob Herman, *Nurse Strike Costs Allina Health $20.4 Million; New Strike Looms*, MODERN HEALTHCARE (Aug. 15, 2016).

only health insurance plans [would] be phased out completely by the end of 2018, and Allina [would] provide nurses with additional contributions to their health reimbursement arrangements or health savings accounts, depending on the plan, in 2017, 2019, 2020, and 2021."[13]

It seems ironic that health insurance rates were the source of substantial conflict among the personnel of that large Minnesota health services provider, but in the absence of wage rate flexibility, any employer may be tempted to change the employee contribution to health insurance as a way to control its costs.

IV. STRIKES OVER SAFETY ISSUES

Labor contracts routinely include a pledge by the union not to strike during the term of the contract. But there is an exception recognized in the law of labor relations: workers are able to walk off the job if a real safety risk is present and the workers need to immediately get away from the threat. Section 502 of the NLRA[14] exempts workers who objectively fear remaining in the workplace during "abnormally dangerous" activities. Dangerous gas releases or falling rock within a mine are typical "safety strike" occasions. Safety strikes are an exception to the usual rules, which forbid strikes during the term of a contract.[15]

Safety strikes are not often used in a hospital environment, since so many other options exist for protecting the worker from imminent harm. A complaint to the Occupational Safety and Health Administration (OSHA), a call to state agencies that regulate hospitals, or an appeal to the local health department would be used first and most routinely. Intervention in the specific safety risk at the specific work station or department within the hospital would be simpler, through the intervention by a health-related external regulator.

---

[13]Shelby Livingston, *Allina Nurses Reach Tentative Contract Agreement, End Strike*, MODERN HEALTHCARE (Oct. 11, 2016).

[14]NLRA §502, *codified at* 29 U.S.C. §143.

[15]TNS, Inc. v. NLRB, 296 F.3d 384 (6th Cir. 2002). Although an employer does not violate Section 8(a)(1) of the Act if it discharges employees for their breach of a no-strike clause of a collective-bargaining agreement, where employees refuse to do work that is "abnormally dangerous," Section 502 of the Act protects that refusal. The test for determining if conditions are "abnormally dangerous" under Section 502 is an objective one. Gateway Coal Co. v. United Mine Workers, 414 U.S. 368, 386–87 (1974); Redwing Carriers, 130 NLRB 1208, 1209 (1961), *enforced as modified*, 325 F.2d 1011 (D.C. Cir. 1963), *cert. denied*, 377 U.S. 905 (1964).

But the NLRB recognizes rights of the union (not of the individual worker alone) to "strike" by withholding services at a site in which workers are in serious physical risk of injury or death.[16] In doing so, the union is taking the risk that its decision to pull its workers away could result in expensive litigation and create the potential for pay damages for the effects of a wrongful walkout.

V. EMPLOYER "LOCKOUTS"

Health care employer lockouts of union workers are a possible response to threats of a union's threat to strike the hospital. A lockout means that the employer acts unilaterally to stop the union members' presence at the site. The union members can be prevented from entering the workplace and can be replaced by temporary workers, provided such actions do not violate a current labor contract or provision of the NLRA.[17]

Employers who face a potential strike can shut down the workers' jobs and "lock them out" while using substitute nurses or other healthcare workers.[18] Numerous lockouts have been used to pressure unions not to resist management direction.[19] A lockout is distinct from an employer changing workforce contractors when the contract

---

[16]*Cf.* TNS, Inc. v. NLRB, 296 F.3d 384 (6th Cir. 2002) (union led work stoppage by union employees, asserting it was not a strike but fell under Section 502 exemption); *In re* Publishers' Ass'n of N.Y.C., 139 NLRB 1092, 1120, 51 LRRM (BNA) 1434 (1962) ("I do not conceive that an employee or union representative acting in good faith upon ground not patently unreasonable is required by this Act to risk honestly apprehended injury or else be held to have violated his contract.").

[17]*See* Doug Ray, *Revisiting the Offensive Bargaining Lockout*, 31 ABA LAB. & EMP. J. 325 (2016).

[18]*See, e.g.*, Martha Kessler, *AFT Members Ratify Contracts After Strike, Lockout at Connecticut Hospital Last Fall*, DAILY LAB. REP. (BNA) No. 23, at A-10 (Feb. 4, 2014); Martha Kessler, *Hospital in Connecticut to Lift Lockout, Despite Parties' Failure to Reach New Deal*, DAILY LAB. REP. (BNA) No. 244, at A-12 (Dec. 18, 2013) (New London hospital locked out 800 registered nurses, licensed nurse practitioners, and healthcare technicians); John Stucke, *Valley Hospital to Lock Out Strikers for Two Days*, SPOKESMAN REV. (Dec. 5, 2013) (Spokane hospital locked out 1,110 nurses and technicians for two days); Damon Stetson, *21 Nursing Homes in City Lock Out Their Employees*, N.Y. TIMES (Apr. 4, 1984) (nurses' aides, orderlies, porters, and maids locked out at 21 New York City nursing homes); Matthew Sturdevant & Mara Lee, *Nursing Home Owner: Union Pickets Illegal Despite Lockout*, HARTFORD COURANT (Dec. 14, 2011) (100 employees locked out of nursing center in Milford, Connecticut).

[19]Michelle Amber, *NLRB Issues Fourth Complaint Against Nursing Home Chain for Bad Faith Bargaining*, DAILY LAB. REP. (BNA) No. 42, at A-11 (Mar. 2, 2012).

with a provider ends, a relatively frequent commercial change that has been noted more recently in healthcare settings.[20]

An employer need not continue to use workers whose short-term threat of a walkout has put the employer's business at risk from that threat. The 2005 *Sutter Health* case involved management's threat that any worker participating in a one-day walkout would be "locked out" for five days.[21] Hospitals have a more urgent need to settle employee disputes than most employers, for reasons of patient safety, but they do have the legal right to use lockouts as a part of the bargaining process.

The cumbersome steps of preparing for a lockout, including finding state-licensed nurses or other healthcare workers willing to cross active picket lines and training these substitutes to a level appropriate to patient safety, makes the lockout a rare event in healthcare union bargaining.[22] A hospital lockout can result in calls for the intervention of safety regulators, which state and local health officials may find disturbing. Further, "backup nurses" may be scrutinized for clinical care judgments, and families of patients are likely to react with alarm at picket signs informing them that only "temps" are providing healthcare for their hospitalized child or other loved one. Nevertheless, at times healthcare employers choose to use this crude weapon in their efforts to rein in what they consider to be unreasonable demands by a union. In January 2016, a hospital in New York State locked out 130 nurses after a one-day strike.[23] Similarly, in July 2017, members of the Massachusetts Nurses Association who tried to return to work were locked out for four days after their strike ended, because their temporary replacements had a five-day contract.[24]

---

[20] A. Garrett, *Summa Health Bringing in New Doctor Group to Staff its ERs Starting New Year's Day*, AKRON BEACON J. (Jan. 3, 2017).

[21] Sutter Health Inc., NLRB Advice Mem., 2005 WL 6715511 (Aug. 4, 2005).

[22] For a discussion on the legality of hiring permanent replacement workers, *see* American Baptist Homes of the West d/b/a Piedmont Gardens, 364 NLRB No. 13, 206 LRRM (BNA) 1501 (May 31, 2016). As of the July 2016 publication of this book, the case was not yet precedential.

[23] *Nathan Littauer to Pay Back Nurses After Illegal Lock-Out*, NEWS10.COM (July 21, 2016), http://news10.com/2016/07/21/nathan-littauer-to-pay-back-nurses-after-illegal-lock-out/.

[24] Boston Hospital Locks Out Striking Nurses, www.abcnews.com (July 14, 2017).

CHAPTER 18

EMPLOYMENT EFFECTS OF CHANGES OF OWNERS AND EMPLOYERS

I. OVERVIEW

Given the high numbers of mergers, acquisitions, and consolidations in the healthcare sector,[1] along with the increased numbers of employed and unionized physicians and other healthcare workers, it is worth assessing the effects of ownership changes on the labor rights of these employees. Here the key initial question is whether

---

[1] *See Healthcare Mergers, Acquisitions and Joint Ventures in 2017: Running List,* HEALTHCARE FINANCE (May 12, 2017) (noting that mergers and acquisitions in the industry "have been on a tear in the past few years," as companies seek savings from economies of scale in the face of tightening profit margins), http://www.healthcare financenews.com/slideshow/healthcare-mergers-and-acquisitions-2017-running-list.

under the National Labor Relations Act (NLRA) the post-merger entity will be deemed a "successor."[2] If so (more on that question below), and if an existing unit of employees has achieved collective bargaining representative status, preserving the workers' collective bargaining rights following a merger or other ownership change will follow reasonably standard processes—albeit not necessarily standard outcomes.

II. Hospital Mergers—Notice and Duty to Bargain

A. Notice of Ownership Change

An employer bound by an existing labor contract and undergoing an ownership change must promptly notify the union of the impending change and describe it as a merger, sale, or whatever applies.[3] The employer should state in the notice whether the successor employer has agreed to assume the obligations of the existing contract. If not, the effects on labor agreements of acquisition and merger follow norms that are set out in hundreds of NLRB cases.[4] These principles are discussed in more detail below. The precise outcome of the new entity's disavowal of the contract depends on the particular facts of the ownership change.[5]

---

[2]There are five principal U.S. Supreme Court cases that bear on this question: Fall River Dyeing & Finishing Corp. v. NLRB, 482 U.S. 27 (1987) (affirming basic principle that new employer must bargain with union representing predecessor's employees); Howard Johnson v. Detroit Local Joint Exec. Bd., 417 U.S. 249 (1974) (no duty to arbitrate dispute under original contract where there is no successorship); Golden State Bottling Co. v. NLRB, 414 U.S. 168 (1973) (successor employer must address unfair labor practices of predecessor even if predecessor contract is not assumed); NLRB v. Burns Int'l Sec. Servs., 406 U.S. 272 (1972) (successor need not assume union contract of predecessor; successor may negotiate its own contract with new employment terms and conditions); John Wiley & Sons, Inc. v. Livingston, 376 U.S. 543 (1964) (successor to unionized company may be required to arbitrate a dispute arising out of previous labor contract even if successor chooses not to assume contract).

[3]See Mergers and Acquisitions: WARN and the NLRA, FINDLAW (2004), http://corporate.findlaw.com/human-resources/mergers-and-acquisitions-warn-and-the-nlra.html.

[4]See, e.g., Howard Johnson Co. v. Detroit Local Joint Exec. Bd., 417 U.S. 249 (1974); NLRB v. Burns Int'l Sec. Servs., Inc., 406 U.S. 272 (1972); Pressroom Cleaners, Inc., 361 N.L.R.B. 57 (Dec. 15, 2014).

[5]See The Tricky Concept of Labor Law Successorship, LAW360 (Jan. 9, 2012), https://www.law360.com/articles/295667/the-tricky-concept-of-labor-law-successorship.

The notice obligation is founded on Section 8(a)(1) and (5) of the NLRA.[6] Absent "particularly unusual or emergency circumstances," an employer undergoing a merger or other ownership transfer must provide the union representing the employees notice of the transaction "prior to implementation."[7] As the court held in *NLRB v. Compact Video Services, Inc.*: "An employer must provide express notice of changes in terms and conditions of employment before implementing such changes unilaterally."[8] Absent "unusual or emergency circumstances," an employer must give pre-implementation notice in order to allow the union the opportunity to bargain.[9]

B. Duty to Bargain

Under Section 8(a)(5) and 8(b)(3) of the NLRA, it is an unfair labor practice if an employer (or a union) fails to bargain collectively.[10] Section 8(d) of the Act lays out the duty to bargain as "the performance of the mutual obligation of the employer and the representative of the employees to meet at reasonable times and confer in good faith with respect to wages, hours, and other terms and conditions of employment. ..."[11] An employer may have no duty to negotiate concerning the business decision to terminate its services contract, e.g., but still have the obligation to negotiate with its employees' union concerning the effects of that decision.[12]

The duty to bargain will definitely arise where a successor company hires or retains a majority of the unionized employees of the predecessor company.[13] It also potentially applies where there is a "continuity of the business enterprise" from the predecessor to the successor, although this test is less clear, especially in light of the Supreme Court's decision in *Howard Johnson Co. v. Detroit Local Joint Executive Board*.[14] *Howard Johnson* held that there is no duty to bargain in circumstances where "no substantial continuity of iden-

---

[6]NLRB v. Compact Video Servs., Inc., 121 F.3d 478 (9th Cir. 1997).
[7]*Id.* at 481.
[8]*Id.* (citing Am. Distrib. Co. v. NLRB, 715 F.2d 446, 449–51 (9th Cir.1983).
[9]*Id.* at 482 (citing Raskin Packing Co., 246 N.L.R.B. 78 (1979); Nat'l Terminal Baking Corp., 190 N.L.R.B. 465, 465 (1971)).
[10]29 U.S.C. §§ 158(a)(5) and 158(b)(3) (2011).
[11]*See* First Nat'l Maintenance Corp. v. NLRB, 452 U.S. 666 (1981).
[12]*Id.*.
[13]*See* B. Glenn George, *Successorship and the Duty to Bargain*, 63 NOTRE DAME LAW REVIEW 277, 279 (1988),
[14]417 U.S. 249 (1974).

tity in the work force" exists, and where there is an absence of any assumption of the obligation to do so.[15]

C. Section 10(j) Injunction

In situations where the new entity constitutes a "successor" for NLRA purposes, and where the union makes a timely request for bargaining, a refusal to bargain may be met with an injunction. In such circumstances, the NLRB can seek a Section 10(j) injunction from federal court to halt the merger or ownership change.[16] Section 10(j) of the National Labor Relations Act authorizes the Board to receive temporary injunctions against employers in federal district courts to stop unfair labor practices while the case is being litigated before administrative law judges and the Board. "These temporary injunctions are needed to protect the process of collective bargaining and employee rights under the Act, and to ensure that Board decisions will be meaningful."[17] This is a powerful remedy, the threat of which gives the new entity's management strong incentives to deal with the union's bargaining rights and status fairly and in a fashion that makes the issuance of an injunction unlikely.[18]

III. SUCCESSORS GENERALLY INHERIT EXISTING WORKER CONTRACTS

As discussed above, mergers or sales of hospitals to new operating entities or owners have been quite frequent in recent years. Economic stresses in the healthcare market are pushing companies into these consolidations. No prudent hospital manager, however, should rush into a final contract of merger or purchase without paying due attention to the existence of active labor contracts with employee units. Such combinations of employer-entities often must address the consolidation of multiple bargaining units at multiple sites. Achieving merger or other combination prior to expiration of

---

[15]*Id.*
[16]29 U.S.C. § 160(j) (2011).
[17]NLRB, RIGHTS WE PROTECT: 10(J) ACTIVITY, www.nlrb.gov/rights-we-protect/10j-activity.
[18]*See* Katharine J. Liao & Maria C. Rodriguez, *NLRB Will Focus on Injunctions in Successor Cases: For Potential Buyers, 6 Questions About Their Labor Obligations,* DLA PIPER (June 2, 2014), https://www.dlapiper.com/en/us/insights/publications/2014/06/nlrb-will-focus-on/.

the labor contract requires good-faith bargaining by the employer, especially with respect to the disclosure of the planned layoffs of workers by the "successor entity," as that term is defined under the NLRA.[19]

A. Successor Status Under the NLRA

Successor status under federal labor law turns on, among other things, whether there is "substantial continuity of identity in the business enterprise." Where a new employer operates essentially the same business without substantial change and hires a majority of its employees from the predecessor, it is generally deemed a successor under federal labor law. This applies to healthcare as it does to other fields. Hospitals rarely move locations and rarely cease caring for patients. Thus, many mergers or other combinations of hospitals and other entities meet the substantial continuity test and therefore are subject to the requirements imposed on successor entities by the NLRB.

B. Union Majority Status

A union's majority status is measured at the time the successor has hired a "substantial and representative complement of its employees."[20] If, at the specific moment of the transaction, "a majority of the successor's employees had been employed by its predecessor, then the successor has an obligation to bargain with the union that represented these employees."[21] These norms are routinely followed in case law.[22] In addition, that obligation is backed by the union's potential request for the NLRB to seek a 10(j) injunction in federal district court, as noted above. Given this leverage, the union's timely request to bargain over the effects of the merger is critical to whether the merger will go forward.[23] For example, suppose a

---

[19] See NLRB, BASIC GUIDE TO THE NATIONAL LABOR RELATIONS ACT, at 24 (1997), https://www.nlrb.gov/sites/default/files/attachments/basic-page/node-3024/basic guide.pdf.

[20] Fall River Dyeing & Finishing Corp. v. NLRB, 482 U.S. 27, 47; NLRB v. Hosp. San Rafael, Inc., 42 F.3d 45 (1st Cir. 1994).

[21] Asseo v. Centro Medico Del Turabo, 900 F.2d 445, 451–52 (1st Cir. 1990) (quoting Fall River, 482 U.S. at 47).

[22] Fall River, 482 U.S. at 47; Hatfield v. A+ Nursetemps, Inc., 2016 WL 3099085, at *4 (11th Cir. June 3, 2016).

[23] See Pascarell v. Orit Corp., 705 F. Supp. 200 (D.N.J. 1988).

hospital management company changes ownership, but no other changes occur. In this situation, the new manager of the hospital is a successor employer because of the "substantial continuity" in the operations of the hospital under both employers. If the predecessor manager had a union contract with its nurses, for example, a court will ask whether a majority of the nurses at the new entity were in the nurse bargaining unit at the prior hospital.[24] If so, the successor will either have to assume the contract or begin good-faith negotiations with the nurses' union.

The existence of a bargaining relationship, however, "does not compel either party to agree to a proposal or require the making of a concession."[25] Rather, "Congress left those matters to free collective bargaining."[26]

IV. OTHER LABOR STATUTES

In addition to NLRA bargaining duties, the parties to the merger or sale should also consider the various obligations under pension and wage-and-hour issues. The Labor Department applies eight non-exhaustive factors for evaluating whether an employer qualifies as a successor-in-interest for purposes of the Fair Labor Standards Act.[27] These factors derive from *EEOC v. MacMillan Bloedel Containers, Inc.*, which set out a nine-factor test:

1) whether the successor company had notice of the charge, 2) the ability of the predecessor to provide relief, 3) whether there has been a substantial continuity of business operations, 4) whether the new employer uses the same plant, 5) whether he uses the same or substantially the same work force, 6) whether he uses the same or substantially the same supervisory personnel, 7) whether the same jobs exist under substantially the same working conditions, 8) whether he uses the same machinery, equipment and methods of production, and 9) whether he produces the same product.[28]

---

[24]Small v. Avanti Health Sys., LLC, 661 F.3d 1180, 1188 (9th Cir. 2011).
[25]29 U.S.C. § 158(d) (2012).
[26]NLRB v Burns Sec. Servs., 406 U.S. 272, 282 (1972).
[27]29 C.F.R. § 825.107 (2016).
[28]EEOC v. MacMillan Bloedel Containers, Inc., 503 F.2d 1086, 1094 (1974). Note that although *MacMillan* was a Title VII case, courts have applied its nine-factor test to a wide variety of labor and employment laws, including the NLRA, the FLSA, and the Family and Medical Leave Act (FMLA). *See* Sullivan v. Dollar Tree Stores, 623 F3d 770 (9th Cir. 2010) (FMLA); Thompson v. Bruister & Assoc., Inc., 967 F. Supp. 2d 1204 (M.D. Tenn. 2013) (FLSA).

Under the *MacMillan* test and the Department of Labor's rules, a successor employer may be held liable for its predecessor's failure to pay overtime,[29] ERISA violations,[30] or FMLA breaches.[31] New owners should be diligent in investigating whether the target company has any such liabilities.

V. DUTY TO DISCLOSE MERGER-RELATED INFORMATION TO THE UNIONS

As explained above, when a merger or other shift among the employer's entities is announced, the union is likely to insist that the employer must bargain about the effects, beginning with the duty to provide information to the union about the effects of the change on the workers. Given that the union request is likely to be enforced by the NLRB and the courts,[32] delays may frustrate the closing of the merger transaction,[33] placing additional pressure on the new company to provide information and negotiate.

In cases where the NLRB is asked to order disclosures and bargaining, courts have urged the NLRB to be case-specific in applying its remedies: "by specifying the information that the Hospitals must disclose, the Board limits the remedy and leaves future transactions untouched. This step fits neatly with [the court's] belief that each situation is sui generis, and that pending mergers may or may not be a proper subject of effects bargaining (depending on the individualized circumstances)."[34] In other words, employer A should tell the workers of A about the expectations of layoffs and displacement of A's jobs to the acquiring employer B, as effects of the pending takeover of A by employer B, while employer C and acquirer D may have very different disclosures to make to their affected employees.

---

[29] *See* Teed v. Thomas & Betts Power Solutions, 711 F.3d 763 (7th Cir. 2013).
[30] Einhorn v. M.L. Ruberton Construction, 632 F.3d 89 (3d Cir. 2011).
[31] Cobb v. Contract Transport Inc., 452 F.3d 543 (6th Cir. 2006).
[32] 29 U.S.C. § 158(d) (2012).
[33] Providence Hospital v NLRB, 93 F.3d 1012 (1st Cir. 1996).
[34] *Id.* at 1022.

VI. TIMING AND EXTENT OF MERGER DISCLOSURES TO UNIONS

A. Timing of Disclosures

Providence Hospital v. NLRB, a Massachusetts hospital merger, provides a useful guidepost for the duty of the merging employer to disclose useful information.[35] *Providence Hospital* involved a group of not-for-profit Catholic hospitals, the Sisters of Providence Health System (SPHS), whose nursing staffs were represented by the Massachusetts Nurses Association (MNA). After hearing "rumors of an impending consolidation," a union representative requested information, but the hospital "responded that it was too early to predict the changes that might result from a consolidation, and that in all events a reduction in force would likely be restricted to management personnel."[36] Soon afterward, SPHS "announced plans to consolidate the Hospitals' administrations."[37] In a letter sent to the union, the new hospital management reiterated the earlier assurances that there were "no definite plans to downsize the bargaining units," and stated that it was "too early to determine the nature and extent of any potential impact on employee working conditions."[38] About six months later, however, the new administration informed the nursing staff of a planned reduction in jobs. At about the same time, SPHS and a competitor, Holyoke-Chicopee Area Health Resources, entered into a memorandum agreement to pursue a merger. The union's representative requested more information multiple times, but the hospitals stalled, first claiming lack of access to the requested plans, and later needing more time to prepare "a meaningful response."[39]

After months of waiting for the hospitals to disclose their plans regarding staffing levels and the possible effects of the merger, with little or no disclosures by the hospitals, MNA filed charges with the NLRB. The NLRB ruled in MNA's favor, holding that "the Hospitals had breached their duty to bargain in good faith by withholding information relevant to the performance of the union's undertakings as a collective bargaining representative, and had thereby violated

---

[35]*Id.*
[36]*Id.*
[37]*Id.* at 1015.
[38]*Id.* at 1016.
[39]*Id.* at 1019.

the National Labor Relations Act (NLRA), specifically, 29 U.S.C. § 158(a)(1) & (5)."[40] The hospitals then sought review of the NLRB decision in federal court, arguing that any disclosures and related bargaining must follow the finalization of the transaction and that "the prospects of this particular merger are too dim and its outline too amorphous to warrant a finding of relevancy."[41] The First Circuit found in favor of the union, upholding the NLRB determination that the hospitals be required to furnish the requested information about the proposed merger in order to support the union's right to demand bargaining over its effects.[42]

This is not universal; a union cannot demand bargaining over effects that are purely speculative, ephemeral, or too far removed from the underlying activity. But where the hospitals themselves presented the planned merger to their employees and to the media as a *fait accompli*, the hospital's union is entitled to plan in advance for likely contingencies. Under the totality of the circumstances that existed in the *Providence Hospital* case—especially the employer's expressed confidence that the merger would take place "soon," and the emphasis in its handouts on the reallocation of personnel—it was within the NLRB's authority to find that the union's professed need for specifics about the merger's probable impact on the bargaining unit was reasonable. In other words, "given management's professed near-certainty that the merger would eventuate and its broad hints that it already had formulated some ideas relative to future staffing of the new system, the Board reasonably could find—as it did—that MNA needed information both about the proposed merger (for the purpose of bargaining over its effects, if and when necessary) and the structural attributes of the new system (to determine whether the collective bargaining agreements would survive the realignment)."[43] Thus, substantial evidence supported the Board's endorsement of the union's requests for merger-related information. As long as a pending merger is adequately developed, a union is entitled to request information that has been shown by the totality of the circumstances to be relevant in order to prepare for "effects" bargaining.[44]

---

[40] *Id.* at 1022.
[41] *Id.* at 1020.
[42] *Id.* at 1019.
[43] *Id.* at 1017.
[44] *Id.* at 1019.

Moving from timing to describing the duty to disclose, the *Providence Hospital* court held that the "requested information should be deemed relevant if it is likely to be of material assistance in evaluating strategies that may be open to the union as part of its struggle to minimize the adverse effects of the employer's decisionmaking process on persons within the bargaining unit."[45] The "relevancy threshold is low" and the standard for the union to have access "is neither onerous in nature nor stringent in application. This is as it should be, for a union cannot be expected to chart a prudent course without reliable and reasonably specific information about the employer's plans."[46]

B. Confidentiality Concerns

The hospital employer's "commitment to, or genuine need for, confidentiality sometimes can constitute an appropriate reason for keeping documents—even documents that are potentially relevant to the collective bargaining process—out of a union's hands. And when confidentiality is properly put in issue, the Board must carefully balance the employer's need for privacy against the union's need to make informed decisions in its capacity as the employees' bargaining representative."[47] Because "confidentiality is in the nature of an affirmative defense," however, "it is the employer's burden to demonstrate that the requested information is shielded by a legitimate privacy claim. Moreover, to permit the requisite balancing, the employer normally must advance its claim of confidentiality in its response to the union's information request. Only in that way will the parties have a fair opportunity to confront the problem head-on and bargain for a partial disclosure that will satisfy the legitimate concerns of both sides."[48] With very evident skepticism about the hospitals' contentions, the *Providence Hospital* appellate court said "the Hospitals' position boils down to a naked assertion that the union had to take management at its word that the organizational changes portended no further alterations in staffing. That is not the way the world works: a union is not bound to accept management's

---

[45]*Id.* at 1017..
[46]*Id.*
[47]*Id.* at 1020 (citing NLRB v. New England Newspapers, 856 F.2d 409, 413 (1st Cir. 1988).
[48]*Id.* (citing Mary Thompson Hosp., 943 F.2d 741, 747 (7th Cir. 1991)).

ipse dixit, especially when, as now, the totality of the circumstances indicates that something else may be afoot."[49] And where "extensive layoffs had followed past assurances from management, … the union had every reason to probe. It requested information which, if extant, had undeniable relevance for the purpose of effects bargaining." So the union "had a statutory right to receive this information in a timely fashion, or in lieu thereof to receive a contemporaneous written statement as to some legally sufficient reason why it could not be produced (say, that no such information existed or that it was somehow privileged)."[50]

C. Limits on Duty to Engage in Effects Bargaining

In the *Providence Hospital* case, the hospital nurses' union was entitled to timely disclosure of relevant information despite the employers' claims that disclosure was premature and that the requested information was confidential. But each takeover situation is unique, so pending mergers "may or may not be a proper subject of effects bargaining (depending on the individualized circumstances)."[51] For example, in *First National Maintenance Corp. v. NLRB*, the Supreme Court held that an employer's decision to shut down part of its operations and terminate its employees was not subject to the requirement to engage in effects bargaining.[52] Even when a particular managerial decision is not itself a mandatory subject of bargaining, however, the decision's forecasted impact on salaries, employment levels, or other terms and conditions of employment may still constitute a mandatory subject of collective bargaining.[53]

VII. CONCLUSION

The concomitant rise of both mergers and acquisitions and unionization in the healthcare sector has made it critical for counsel on either union or management side to be knowledgeable regarding the law applicable to successorship and effects bargaining. Hospitals and other employers must determine when and if to disclose merger

---

[49] *Id.* at 1021.
[50] *Id.*
[51] *Id.* at 1022.
[52] 452 U.S. 666 (1981).
[53] *Id.* at 672.

or other ownership change information to the affected union—a complicated and uncertain exercise in many circumstances—and the union must be diligent in requesting information and demanding bargaining where there is a duty for the employer to engage in it. Failure on the part of the employer to comply with its obligations could subject it to an injunction and doom the proposed transaction. Failure on the part of the union to press for information and make the case for a duty to bargain could leave its members without a remedy for negative effects of the deal.

CHAPTER 19

EXEMPT EMPLOYEES: ISSUES WITH OVERTIME PAY AND COLLECTIVE BARGAINING

I. INTRODUCTION

If an existing unit of employees has achieved collective bargaining representative status, and thereafter the employing entity changes as the result of a sale or merger, there are reasonably standard processes for preserving the workers' collective bargaining rights. The employer that is bound by an existing labor contract notifies the union of the change and describes it as a merger, sale, or other occurrence. The employer states in the notice whether the successor employer has agreed to assume the obligations of the existing contract. If the successor employer has not so agreed, norms that are well defined in hundreds of National Labor Relations Board (NLRB or Board) cases will determine the effects of the merger or sale on the labor agreement. Some of these norms are discussed in the sections below.

II. OBLIGATIONS OF SUCCESSOR EMPLOYERS INHERITING EXISTING HOSPITAL WORKER CONTRACTS

Hospital mergers and sales of hospitals to new operating entities or owners have been frequent in recent years. Consolidation of multiple bargaining units at multiple sites prior to the expiration of existing labor contracts requires good-faith bargaining by the current employer. A particularly sensitive matter is the disclosure of planned layoffs of workers by the "successor" employer. No prudent hospital manager would rush into a final contract of merger or purchase without paying due attention to the existence of active labor contracts with employee units.

A successor employer has an obligation to bargain with a union if "the new employer is in fact a successor of the old employer and the majority of its employees were employed by its predecessor."[1] A union's majority status is measured at the time the successor has hired a "substantial and representative complement of its employees."[2]

An employer's "successor" status under federal labor law turns on whether there is "substantial continuity of identity in the business enterprise."[3] Where a new employer operates essentially the same business without substantial change and hires a majority of its employees from the predecessor, it is generally deemed a successor under federal labor law.[4]

The successor rule applies to healthcare as it does to other fields.[5] Hospitals rarely change locations and rarely cease caring for patients. A new manager of a hospital is a successor employer because of the "substantial continuity" in the operations of the hospital under both employers. A court would consider whether a majority of the nurses at the new entity were in the nurse bargaining unit at the prior hospital.[6]

A successor employer may be compelled by an NLRB order to bargain with an incumbent union or to arbitrate the extent of its

---

[1]Fall River Dyeing & Finishing Corp. v. NLRB, 482 U.S. 27, 47 (1987).
[2]*Id.*; NLRB v. Hospital San Rafael, Inc., 42 F.3d 45 (1st Cir. 1994).
[3]John Wiley & Sons v. Livingston, 376 U.S. 543, 551 (1964).
[4]*Fall River Dyeing*, 482 U.S. at 41.
[5]United Steelworkers of Am. v. St. Gabriel's Hosp., 871 F. Supp. 335, 338 (D. Minn. 1994); *see also* Community Hosp. of Central Cal. v. NLRB, 355 F.3d 1079 (D.C. Cir. 2003).
[6]Small v. Avanti Health Sys., LLC, 661 F.3d 1180, 1188 (9th Cir. 2011).

obligations.[7] The existence of a bargaining relationship, however, "does not compel either party to agree to a proposal or require the making of a concession."[8] Rather, "Congress left those matters to free collective bargaining."[9]

In addition to NLRB bargaining duties, the parties to a merger or sale should also consider their various obligations related to pension and wage-and-hour issues. The U.S. Department of Labor has provided eight nonexhaustive factors for evaluating whether an employer qualifies as a successor in interest for purposes of the Fair Labor Standards Act.[10]

III. DUTY TO DISCLOSE MERGER-RELATED INFORMATION TO UNIONS

When a merger or other shift among the employer's entities is announced, the union is likely to insist that the employer must provide information about the effects of the change on the workers. The union request is likely to be enforced by the NLRB and the courts, though these delays may frustrate the closing of the merger transaction.[11] Responding to such requests requires both employers and the Board to balance confidentiality concerns against the union's need for information to make informed decisions.

A. Nature of the Duty to Disclose

Courts have urged the NLRB to be case specific in its remedies. The First Circuit in *Providence Hospital v. NLRB* stated:

> by specifying the information that the Hospitals must disclose, the Board limits the remedy and leaves future transactions untouched. This step fits neatly with [the court's] belief that each situation is *sui generis,* and that pending mergers may or may not be a proper

---

[7]*Fall River Dyeing*, 482 U.S. at 41; NLRB v. Burns Sec. Servs., 406 U.S. 272, 278–81 (1972) (duty to recognize and bargain with union representing predecessor's employees); *John Wiley & Sons*, 376 U.S. at 548–51 (duty to arbitrate).

[8]29 U.S.C. §158(d).

[9]*Burns Sec. Servs.*, 406 U.S. at 282.

[10]Siciliano v. Cambridge Home Health Care Inc./Private, 65 F. App'x 542, 543 (6th Cir. 2003).

[11]*Cf.* Providence Hosp. v. NLRB, 93 F.3d 1012, 153 LRRM (BNA) 2097 (1st Cir. 1996).

subject of effects bargaining (depending on the individualized circumstances).[12]

In other words, a hospital should be required to disclose information relevant to only a merger, affiliation, or consolidation that is determined and fairly immediate. For example, employer A should tell the union for workers of A about the expectations of layoffs and displacement of A's jobs to the acquiring employer B as effects of the pending takeover of employer A by employer B. A Board order to disclose information should not be so broad that it includes all mergers or future indeterminate mergers. The *Providence* court said that the "requested information should be deemed relevant if it is likely to be of material assistance in evaluating strategies that may be open to the union as part of its struggle to minimize the adverse effects of the employer's decisionmaking process on persons within the bargaining unit."[13] The relevancy threshold is low, and the standard for the union to have access "is neither onerous in nature nor stringent in application. This is as it should be, for a union cannot be expected to chart a prudent course without reliable and reasonably specific information about the employer's plans."[14]

B. Timing and Extent of Merger Disclosures to Unions

The Massachusetts hospital merger at issue in the *Providence* case provides a useful guidepost for the duty of the merging employer to disclose relevant information to the union for its employees. The court stated that "even when a particular managerial decision is not itself a mandatory subject of bargaining, the decision's forecasted impact on salaries, employment levels, or other terms and conditions of employment may constitute a mandatory subject of collective bargaining."[15] Moreover, "as long as a pending merger is sufficiently advanced, a union is entitled to request information [that has been] shown by the totality of the circumstances to be relevant in order to prepare for effects bargaining."[16]

This is not universal; "a union cannot demand bargaining over effects that are purely speculative, ephemeral, or too far removed

---

[12]*Id.* at 1022.
[13]*Id.* at 1017.
[14]*Id.*
[15]*Id.* at 1018.
[16]*Id.* at 1019.

from the underlying activity."[17] But where a hospital itself has presented a planned merger to its employees and to the media as a *fait accompli*, its union is entitled to plan in advance for likely contingencies.

The First Circuit stated that

> [u]nder the totality of the circumstances that existed [in the *Providence* case]—especially the employer's expressed confidence that the merger would take place soon and the emphasis in its handouts on the reallocation of personnel—[it was within the NLRB's] authority to find that the union's professed need for specifics about the merger's probable impact on the bargaining unit was reasonable.[18]

In other words,

> given management's professed near-certainty that the merger would eventuate and its broad hints that it already had formulated some ideas relative to future staffing of the new system, the Board reasonably could find—as it did—that [the union] needed information both about the proposed merger (for the purpose of bargaining over its effects, if and when necessary) and the structural attributes of the new system (to determine whether the collective bargaining agreements would survive the realignment).[19]

Thus, in *Providence*, "substantial evidence supported the Board's endorsement of the union's requests for merger-related information."[20]

The *Providence* court explained that the hospital "employer's commitment to, or genuine need for, confidentiality sometimes can constitute an appropriate reason for keeping documents—even documents that are potentially relevant to the collective bargaining process—out of a union's hands."[21] The First Circuit further stated that event "when confidentiality is properly put in issue, the Board must carefully balance the employer's need for privacy against the union's need to make informed decisions in its capacity as the employees' bargaining representative."[22]

Because "confidentiality is in the nature of an affirmative defense," the employer has the burden of establishing a legitimate privacy claim justifying nondisclosure of the requested information.[23]

---

[17] *Id.*
[18] *Id.* at 1020.
[19] *Id.*
[20] *Id.*
[21] *Id.*
[22] *Id.*
[23] *Id.*

Moreover, to permit the requisite balancing, the employer normally must advance its claim of confidentiality in its response to the union's information request. Only in that way will the parties have a fair opportunity to confront the problem head-on and bargain for a partial disclosure that will satisfy the legitimate concerns of both sides.[24]

With very evident doubt, the First Circuit said that:

[Providence] Hospitals' position boils down to a naked assertion that the union had to take management at its word that the organizational changes portended no further alterations in staffing. That is not the way the world works: a union is not bound to accept management's *ipse dixit*, especially when, as now, the totality of the circumstances indicates that something else may be afoot.[25]

And where past assurances from management had been followed by extensive layoffs, "the union had every reason to probe. It requested information which, if extant, had undeniable relevance for the purpose of effects bargaining."[26] So the union "had a statutory right to receive this information in a timely fashion, or in lieu thereof to receive a contemporaneous written statement as to some legally sufficient reason why it could not be produced (say, that no such information existed or that it was somehow privileged)."[27]

In *Providence*, the hospital nurses' union was entitled to timely disclosure of relevant information. But each takeover situation is unique, so pending mergers "may or may not be a proper subject of effects bargaining (depending on the individualized circumstances)."[28]

---

[24] *Id.*
[25] *Id.* at 1021.
[26] *Id.*
[27] *Id.*
[28] *Id.* at 1022.

Part 4

Issues for All Healthcare Personnel

CHAPTER 20

SAFETY ISSUES IN HEALTHCARE SETTINGS

I. SAFETY ISSUES AND COMPLIANCE REVIEW

Safety issues in the healthcare employment context are a matter of life and death. Mistakes risk patient deaths, and errors are significantly involved in worker injuries. In fact, human error is the principal cause of injuries in hospitals.[1] Healthcare worker injury patterns indicate that training and staffing upgrades are needed in many healthcare venues.[2]

Part of a union organizing push at a healthcare facility will likely arise from workers' negative expressions regarding workplace safety on social media. In workplaces where employers fear that safety lapses may trigger inspections by the Occupational Safety and Health Administration (OSHA), Medicare or Medicaid sanctions, and bad outcomes from Joint Commission[3] inquiries, the workers' level of concern about their safety is a significant barrier.

Some employers view employee criticism of safety practices as a form of disloyalty. But when a rating agency team asks, front-line employees are likely to be vocal if a safety risk has gone without remediation. The healthcare rating agencies include

---

[1] JAMES O'REILLY, JOLENE SOBOTKA & PHILIP HAGAN, A PRACTITIONER'S GUIDE TO HOSPITAL LIABILITY (ABA Press 2011).

[2] Safe Patient Handling and Mobility, AMERICAN NURSES ASSOCIATION, http://www.nursingworld.org/MainMenuCategories/WorkplaceSafety/SafePatient.

[3] See the Joint Commission website at https://www.jointcommission.org.

- state licensure survey teams
- contractors for the Centers for Medicare and Medicaid Services (CMS)
- teams representing the Joint Commission
- the Bureau of Primary Health Care (the federal overseer of thousands of local Federally Qualified Health Centers)
- and the facility's liability insurers.

Each of these auditors of safety wants to discern the experience of the employees who actually see the risk situations. Employee interviews during the inspection are commonplace.

Feedback about safety practices is important. Lifting obese patients is a source of back injuries for nurses, for example. Managers demanding speedy results while ignoring the safeguards for exposure to bloodborne pathogens is a likely source of OSHA complaints leading to penalties.[4] Issuance of inadequate protective gear in the face of likely assault by mental patients will be a source of serious criticism of management's practices. Loss of accreditation by the Joint Commission can be a serious outcome of a failed inspection, and inspections by their accreditors cover 77 percent of the nation's hospitals.[5]

There is broad consensus that healthcare organizations must improve occupational safety and health for nurses. The most current guidelines for safe patient handling and mobility should be followed. A national expert told *Modern Healthcare* magazine in 2016:

> Nurses originally were educated to think that body mechanics were the answer. We now know that's really not true at all. Particularly as patients are getting heavier, we know that nurses really are at risk. They're the fourth highest occupational category that misses days from work because of musculoskeletal injuries, so this is a key area.[6]

Examples of safety-related problems include lack of protective gear, falls, musculoskeletal strains, and even inadequate access to shields against biting by an aggressive mental patient.

---

[4] 29 C.F.R. pt. 1910 (2017).
[5] *What is Accreditation?*, THE JOINT COMMISSION, https://www.jointcommission. org/accreditation/accreditation_main.aspx.
[6] P. Cipriano, *Future of Nursing & Healthcare*, MODERN HEALTHCARE 20 (Jan. 16, 2017).

II. SAFETY AND WORKER "WHISTLEBLOWING"

Numerous healthcare cases have involved allegations of workplace discrimination or retaliation against a nurse for speaking out / complaining / "whistleblowing" about unsafe practices. Several of these cases are discussed in this section.

Termination of a healthcare worker from employment at an Illinois nursing home triggered anti-retaliation provisions of the state Nursing Home Care Act. Section 3–608[7] of the Act provides that a nursing home may not

> transfer, discharge, evict, harass, dismiss, or retaliate against a resident, a resident's representative, or an employee or agent who makes a report under Section 2–107, brings or testifies in an action under Sections 3–601 through 3–607, or files a complaint under Section 3–702, because of the report, testimony, or complaint.[8]

The first query must be whether or not there is a material issue as to whether plaintiffs engaged in "protected activity." A plaintiff's complaint to the state's health agency must be both made in good faith and have a subjectively reasonable basis to qualify for protection.[9]

In a California case, the worker "asserted, inter alia, that she had undergone adverse employment action in retaliation for reporting unsanitary and unsafe practices at UCLA hospital, where she worked."[10]

The whistleblower in a Pennsylvania hospital case lost where she failed to establish a causal connection and did not meet the elements under the applicable whistleblower law.[11]

A court upheld the discharge of a nurse for refusing to administer kidney dialysis to a terminally ill patient. The termination did not violate a clear mandate of public policy because the nurse acted on the basis of her own "moral, medical and philosophical objections."[12]

---

[7]210 ILLINOIS CONS. STAT. 45/3–608.

[8]Fisher v. Lexington Health Care, Inc., 188 Ill. 2d 455, 459, 722 N.E.2d 1115, 1117 (1999).

[9]Smith v. Gentiva Health Servs. (USA) Inc., 296 F. Supp. 2d 758, 762–63 (E.D. Mich. 2003).

[10]Jones v. Regents of Univ. of Cal., 164 Cal. App. 4th 1072, 1074, 79 Cal. Rptr. 3d 817, 818 (2008).

[11]Evans v. Thomas Jefferson Univ., 81 A.3d 1062, 1064 (Pa. Commw. Ct. 2013).

[12]Warthen v. Toms River Cmty. Mem'l Hosp., 199 N.J. Super. 18, 488 A.2d 229 (1985).

A licensed practical nurse brought an action in state court against her former employer, which operated a nursing facility, alleging she was terminated for reporting concerns about a supervisor's alleged drug use, in violation of Maine's Whistleblowers' Protection Act (WPA).[13]

An employer defendant's argument that a worker merely reached the end of a finite contract that the employer opted not to renew simply ignored the plain words of a statute that protects employees not only from retaliatory discharge, but also from other types of discrimination.[14]

III. BLOODBORNE PATHOGEN STANDARD COMPLIANCE

Millions of healthcare dollars have been spent on the protection of workers from infection by bloodborne pathogens. As the risk of acquired immune deficiency syndrome (AIDS) and hepatitis infections became manifest, attention to accidental splashes and needle sticks grew and protection costs increased. Other texts are available on the intensive details of the OSHA Bloodborne Pathogens Standard[15] and its enforcement.[16] For the healthcare employee and manager, the "devil is in the details" of actual compliance.

For purposes of this employment text, it is sufficient to note that workers have multiple routes to vent their dislike for the employer's handling of exposure to the bodily fluids of their patients. In some cases, the workers themselves resent the degree to which compliance with the bloodborne pathogens standard is an encumbrance to faster or more efficient operations.

One response to a workplace concern about exposures is a complaint to OSHA or its state-level enforcement entity. Some state OSHA programs are more robust than others, and the state must apply at least as strong a protection as is the norm for the federal standard. Most of the OSHA complaints from healthcare workers do not result in a penalty enforcement action, but a call or visit from OSHA will induce the safety manager or operational staff of the healthcare

---

[13]Murray v. Kindred Nursing Ctrs. W. LLC, 789 F.3d 20 (1st Cir. 2015).

[14]Johnson v. Government of Virgin Islands, 1996 WL 663976, at *2 (Terr. V.I. Nov. 6, 1996).

[15]29 C.F.R. §1910.1030.

[16]See, e.g., NATIONAL SAFETY COUNCIL, BLOODBORNE & AIRBORNE PATHOGENS (2d ed. 2009).

facility to immediately review the practices of that particular clinic, service, or other medical operation. The remedial actions could include training, new equipment, new rules for patient handling, and in some cases a civil penalty against the hospital or healthcare institution. Numerous examples have been decided against the employer.[17]

An alternate response would be a complaint to the state licensing agency that regulates hospitals, since hospital-associated infections are a major expense, and especially problematic for the rapid return to hospitals of discharged Medicaid and Medicare patients. When staff and nurses can assert credibly that their management is not following standard safety practices for bloodborne pathogens, a state survey team visit may follow. A complaint to the Joint Commission could put the hospital's accreditation at risk, if the complaint had substance. More than one unit or department has risked a potential infection problem because of inadequate safeguards.

IV. HEALTHCARE-ASSOCIATED INFECTIONS

The Centers for Disease Control and Prevention (CDC) reported that there were an estimated 722,000 healthcare-associated infections (HAI; also known as "hospital-acquired infections") in U.S acute care hospitals in 2011. About 75,000 hospital patients with HAIs died during their hospitalizations. More than half of all HAIs occurred outside of the intensive care unit.[18] The Joint Commission has current data on hospital goals and performance against HAIs.[19]

The CDC's HAI Action Plan in 2015 stated:

> Health care-associated infections, or HAIs, are infections that people acquire while they are receiving treatment for another condition in a health care setting. HAIs can be acquired anywhere health care is delivered, including inpatient acute care hospitals. ... HAIs may be

---

[17]*See, e.g.*, Secretary of Labor v. Genesis Healthcare Corp., OSHRC Docket No. 03-0300 (Aug. 23, 2004) (ALJ Schoenfeld), https://www.oshrc.gov/decisions/html_2004/03-0300.html; Secretary of Labor v. Thoroughgood Inc., OSHRC Docket No. 97-0023 (Feb. 11, 1999) (ALJ Spies), https://www.oshrc.gov/decisions/html_1999/97-0023.html. Other decisions may be found at the Occupational Safety & Health Review Commission website, https://www.oshrc.gov.

[18]*HAI Data and Statistics*, CENTERS FOR DISEASE CONTROL AND PREVENTION, https://www.cdc.gov/hai/surveillance/index.html.

[19]*EC.02.05.01 – Clinical Impact*, THE JOINT COMMISSION, https://www.jointcommission.org/topics/ec020501_clinical_impact.aspx.

caused by any infectious agent, including bacteria, fungi, and viruses, as well as other less common types of pathogens.[20]

CDC has reported that healthcare-associated infections are associated with a variety of risk factors, including:

- Use of in-dwelling medical devices such as bloodstream, endotracheal, and urinary catheters
- Surgical procedures
- Injections
- Contamination of the healthcare environment
- Transmission of communicable diseases between patients and healthcare workers
- Overuse or improper use of antibiotics.[21]

Could a nurse who contracted an HAI sue the hospital from whose patient she or he became infected? Probably not. The state workers compensation exclusion of liability lawsuits probably prevents most employees in healthcare settings from litigating an infection claim.

Can the hospital or skilled nursing facility compel each employee to be vaccinated? A careful review of the mandatory nature of the immunization program and of the concept of worker "informed consent" suggests that there may be limits to the command approach to employee vaccination programs.[22]

V. INJURIES FROM LIFTING AND MOVING PATIENTS

The nursing profession recognizes the significant risk of musculoskeletal injuries from patient movement in healthcare sites.[23] Nursing positions often involve movement of obese patients, and lifting is a real risk in the nursing field.[24] Obesity is a well-recognized

[20]*Id.* (quoting CDC, National Healthcare Safety Network (NHSN) Web Page (May 13, 2015)).

[21]*Id.*

[22]Christine Nero Coughlin, Nancy M.P. King & Kathi Kemper, *When Doctors Become "Patients": Advocating a Patient-Centered Approach for Health Care Workers in the Context of Mandatory Influenza Vaccinations and Informed Consent*, 45 WAKE FOREST L. REV. 1551 (2010).

[23]*Safe Patient Handling and Mobility*, AMERICAN NURSES ASSOCIATION, http://www.nursingworld.org/MainMenuCategories/WorkplaceSafety/SafePatient.

[24]Taylor v. Health, ___ F. App'x ___, 2017 WL 83493 (9th Cir. Jan. 10, 2017).

"co-morbidity" for elders who have chronic illnesses, and even for those who are hospitalized after an accident.[25]

The greater body mass index of the average patient means a correspondingly larger risk of injury to the healthcare workers who move him or her around.[26] Lower back injuries, cervical sprains, and bruises are "part of the territory" in larger healthcare sites, especially the residential care facilities that house and treat elders. Worker complaints about broken or missing equipment for the lifting of immobile obese patients is another potential source of OSHA or state complaints. Nursing leaders explained in a 2017 article that "[p]articularly as patients are getting heavier, we know that nurses really are at risk. They're the fourth highest occupational category that misses days from work because of musculoskeletal injuries, so this is a key area."[27]

VI. RISKS ASSOCIATED WITH UNDERSTAFFING?

Experts believe that the lack of adequate nursing staff members at a healthcare facility is a source of risk to the remaining nurses on duty at that facility. The physical exertion needed to operate in the fast-paced hospital environment is stressful, and the stress worsens when the management has decided to allow operational conditions to continue without the adequate number of nurses or doctors.

Understaffing also affects patient well-being.[28] A California nursing union was harsh: "St. Joseph's understaffing has contributed to patient falls, bedsores, risk of infection, and increased possibility of errors in patient care, and state investigators documented multiple injuries suffered by patients at the two St. Joseph hospitals."[29] Each situation would need to be evaluated on its own merits, of course.

---

[25]These issues are addressed in detail in JAMES O'REILLY, JOLENE SOBOTKA AND PHILIP HAGAN, A PRACTITIONER'S GUIDE TO HOSPITAL LIABILITY (ABA Press 2011).
[26]*Safe Patient Handling and Mobility*, AMERICAN NURSES ASSOCIATION, http://www.nursingworld.org/MainMenuCategories/WorkplaceSafety/SafePatient.
[27]P. Cipriano, *Future of Nursing & Healthcare*, MODERN HEALTHCARE 20 (Jan. 16, 2017).
[28]*See* P. Cipriano, *You Have to Maintain Adequate Staffing to Preserve Safety*, MODERN HEALTHCARE (May 9, 2015).
[29]NUHW, What Has Become of Memorial Hospital?, http://nuhw.org/wp-content/uploads/2016/05/20160425-St.-Joseph-Sonoma-public-leaflet-FINAL.pdf.

CHAPTER 21

EMPLOYMENT DISCRIMINATION IN HEALTHCARE*

*The authors thank Lorene Schaefer-Hooi, Esq., of Schaefer & Associates, LLC in Atlanta, for contributing this chapter.

I. INTRODUCTION

Physicians who are employees of hospitals, clinics and other sites enjoy the same whistleblower, discrimination, and retaliation protections as other employees under federal law. This chapter provides a basic overview of the legal analysis under the federal laws enforced by the Equal Employment Opportunity Commission (EEOC), as well as a general discussion of the administrative remedies process. There is also provided a basic overview of the legal analysis and process for pursuing a retaliation claim brought under the three most common federal fraud and abuse statutes that provide whistleblowers protection from retaliation: the False Claims Act, the Anti-Kickback Statute, and the Physician Self-Referral Law.

In reviewing this chapter, practitioners should be aware that in addition to the laws discussed in this chapter, employees are protected by a number of other laws governing the workplace. For example, there are a number of laws enforced by the Department of Labor (DOL) that are not discussed here, and state laws may also provide additional or different protections to employees.

In today's healthcare market, of course, it is not always clear who is an "employee." It is not uncommon, for example, for a physician working in a hospital or clinic setting to be employed not directly by the hospital or clinic but by another entity, or to be paid as an independent contractor with an Internal Revenue Service (IRS) Form 1099 issued to that person.

In such instances, whether the physician is considered an "employee" of the hospital or clinic for purposes of protection from discrimination and retaliation under the relevant federal law requires a deeper analysis of the day-to-day working conditions of the physician. As such, this chapter will provide practical guidance for evaluating whether a physician working at a hospital or clinic as a contractor also qualifies as an "employee" under the federal laws enforced by the EEOC.

II. FEDERAL LAWS PROHIBITING DISCRIMINATION AND RETALIATION

There are six federal laws that protect employees from discrimination and retaliation and that are enforced by the Equal Employment Opportunity Commission.

A. Title VII of the Civil Rights Act of 1964

Title VII of the Civil Rights Act of 1964[1] applies to employers with 15 or more employees. It prohibits discrimination against someone on the basis of race, color, religion, national origin, or sex. Pursuant to the amendment of Title VII by the Pregnancy Act of 1978, Title VII also prohibits discrimination against a woman

---

[1] Civil Rights Act of 1964, 42 U.S.C. §§2000e, et seq.

because of pregnancy, childbirth, or a medical condition related to pregnancy or childbirth.

Title VII requires that employers reasonably accommodate applicants' and employees' sincerely held religious practices, unless doing so would impose an undue hardship on the operation of the employer's business. The law prohibits retaliation against a person because the person complained about discrimination, filed a charge of discrimination, or participated in an employment discrimination investigation or lawsuit.

B. Equal Pay Act

The Equal Pay Act (EPA)[2] of 1963 prohibits employers from paying unequal wages because of the employee's gender for work requiring equal skill, effort, and responsibility that is performed under similar working conditions. The law protects men and women equally.

The EPA is a part of the Fair Labor Standards Act (FLSA), and it applies to all employers who are covered by the FLSA. There are two ways in which an employee can be covered by the EPA/FLSA: "enterprise coverage" and "individual coverage." In the healthcare industry, most employees will be protected by the EPA under the theory of "enterprise coverage." Under this theory, the law applies to employees who work for businesses or organizations (i.e., "enterprises") that have at least two employees and have either (1) an annual dollar volume of sales or business done of at least $500,000; or (2) are a hospital, business providing medical or nursing care for residents, a school/preschool, or government agency.

Even when there is no enterprise coverage, employees regularly involved in interstate commerce will also be protected by the EPA/FLSA.

C. Age Discrimination in Employment Act

The Age Discrimination in Employment Act (ADEA)[3] of 1967 applies to employers with 20 or more employees. It prohibits employers from discriminating against applicants or employees 40 years of age and older on the basis of age in hiring, promotion, discharge,

---

[2] Equal Pay Act of 1963, 29 U.S.C. §206(d).
[3] 29 U.S.C. §621 et seq.

compensation, or terms, conditions, or privileges of employment. The ADEA also prohibits employers from retaliating against a person because the person engaged in "protected activity" by opposing any practice made unlawful by the ADEA, or because such individual, member, or applicant for membership has made a charge, testified, assisted, or participated in any manner in an investigation, proceeding, or litigation involving an alleged violation of the ADEA.

D. Americans with Disabilities Act

The Americans with Disabilities Act (ADA)[4] of 1990 applies to employers with 15 or more employees for each working day in each of 20 or more calendar weeks in the current or preceding calendar year. It prohibits discrimination against a qualified person with a disability, in the private sector and in state and local governments. It also prohibits retaliation against a person because the person complained about discrimination, filed a charge of discrimination, or participated in an employment discrimination investigation or lawsuit. The law also requires that employers reasonably accommodate the known physical or mental limitations of an otherwise qualified individual with a disability who is an applicant or employee, unless doing so would impose an undue hardship on the operation of the employer's business.

E. Genetic Information Nondiscrimination Act

The Genetic Information Nondiscrimination Act (GINA)[5] of 2008 applies to employers with 15 or more employees. GINA prohibits discrimination against employees or applicants because of genetic information. Genetic information includes information about an individual's genetic tests and the genetic tests of an individual's family members, as well as information about any disease, disorder, or condition of an individual's family members (i.e., an individual's family medical history). Retaliation against a person because the person complained about discrimination, filed a charge of discrimination, or participated in an employment discrimination investigation or lawsuit is also prohibited.

---

[4] Americans with Disabilities Act of 1990, 42 §§12101 et seq.
[5] 42 U.S.C. §§21F et seq.

F. Sections 501 and 505 of the Rehabilitation Act

Sections 501 and 505 and of the Rehabilitation Act[6] of 1973 prohibit discrimination in the federal government against a qualified person with a disability. The law also makes it illegal to retaliate against a person because the person complained about discrimination, filed a charge of discrimination, or participated in an employment discrimination investigation or lawsuit. The law also requires that employers reasonably accommodate the known physical or mental limitations of an otherwise qualified individual with a disability who is an applicant or employee, unless doing so would impose an undue hardship on the operation of the employer's business.

III. Who Is an "Employee" Under Laws Enforced by the EEOC?

There are two threshold questions to resolve in analyzing whether the federal laws enforced by the EEOC are applicable in a particular circumstance. First, the employer must "employ" the requisite number of "employees" to trigger the law. Second, the individual seeking protection under the applicable law must be a "covered individual."

Unfortunately, resolving the first question—who is an "employee" under these laws—is not always easily answered. In fact, as the United States Supreme Court has noted, the common definition of an employee under federal law—"an individual employed by an employer"—is "completely circular and explains nothing."[7] This is particularly true in the healthcare industry, where worker relationships are increasingly complex, as Chapters 4 and 9 of this text have explained. For example, physicians working in hospitals may be direct employees, temporary workers, or independent contractors, or may be employed through a staffing company or other entity that in turn contracts with the hospital to provide physician services.

In its 2003 opinion in *Clackamas Gastroenterology v. Wells*,[8] the United States Supreme Court held that the common-law element of control is the principal guidepost to be followed in deciding

---

[6]29 U.S.C. §§791 et seq.

[7]Nationwide Mut. Ins. Co. v. Darden, 504 U.S. 318, 323 (1992) (discussing definition of "employee" in the ADA).

[8]538 U.S. 440 (2003).

whether an individual is an "employee." The *Wells* case was brought by an employee alleging violation of the ADA by her employer, a professional corporation owned by four physician shareholders and operating as a medical clinic. The clinic argued it was not covered by the ADA because it did not have 15 or more employees for the 20 weeks as required by the ADA. More specifically, the clinic argued that its four physician shareholders were more analogous to partners in a partnership than to shareholders in a corporation and, therefore, were not employees under the ADA.

In *Wells*, Justice Stevens opened his majority opinion by rejecting the application of names and labels as a way to classify individuals as employees vs. owners. "The mere fact that a person has a particular title—such as partner, director, or vice president—should not necessarily be used to determine whether he or she is an employee or a proprietor. ... Nor should the mere existence of a document styled 'employment agreement' lead inexorably to the conclusion that either party is an employee."[9]

In rejecting the analysis offered by both parties, the Supreme Court adopted an analysis closely aligned with the EEOC's guidance[10] and its focus on the "common-law touchstone of control."[11]

PR actioners advising on the issue of who is an employee for purposes of federal EEO laws should be aware that the EEOC has an expansive interpretation of "joint employer" in its *Compliance Manual*[12] and guidance publications.[13] Neither the *Compliance Manual* nor guidance, of course, has the force of law, nor are they universally followed by the federal courts, and practitioners will need to review current case law developments in the applicable jurisdiction. However, a strong policy analysis can be made by referring back to the practical application of the EEOC contained within the manual.

In the EEOC's Strategic Enforcement Plan for fiscal years 2017–2021, complex employment relationships were identified as a new area of enforcement focus. In describing this area of its enforcement focus, the EEOC said that it will be "[c]larifying the employment

---

[9]*Id.*

[10]EEOC COMPLIANCE MANUAL §605:0009.

[11]*Id.*

[12]*Who is an Employee?*, EEOC COMPLIANCE MANUAL §2-III.A.1 (2009).

[13]EEOC Enforcement Guidance: Application of EEO Laws to Contingent Workers Placed by Temporary Employment Agencies and Other Staffing Firms (Dec. 3, 1997).

relationship and the application of workplace civil rights protections in light of the increasing complexity of employment relationships and structures, including temporary workers, staffing agencies, independent contractor relationships, and the on-demand economy."[14]

In light of this new focus by the EEOC, it is important for PR actioners in this area to know that even though an individual is classified and paid as an "independent contractor" or "partner" by an entity/employer, that individual may still be protected and counted as an "employee" under the federal EEO laws. It is not the employer/ entity's classification of the worker that controls. Rather, a determination of whether an employer-employee relationship exists under federal EEO laws requires a fact-specific analysis and depends on whether the employer controls the means and manner of the worker's work performance. PR actioners advising clients on this issue will need to scrutinize workforce relationships carefully for indicia of potential for indirect as well as direct control over the terms and conditions of employment of the workforce.

Pursuant to the EEOC's *Compliance* Manual[15] the following factors indicate that a worker is in an employment relationship with an employer and these factors would be used to analyze the above scenarios, which are common in the healthcare industry:

- The employer has the right to control when, where, and how the worker performs the job.
- The work does not require a high level of skill or expertise.
- The employer furnishes the tools, materials, and equipment.
- The work is performed on the employer's premises.
- There is a continuing relationship between the worker and the employer.
- The employer has the right to assign additional projects to the worker.
- The employer sets the hours of work and the duration of the job.
- The worker is paid by the hour, week, or month rather than the agreed cost of performing a particular job.
- The worker does not hire and pay assistants.

---

[14]EEOC Strategic Enforcement Plan for Fiscal Years 2017–-2021, §II.C.3.d.
[15]*Who is an Employee?*, EEOC COMPLIANCE MANUAL §2-III.A.1.

- The work performed by the worker is part of the regular business of the employer.
- The employer is in business.
- The worker is not engaged in his/her own distinct occupation or business.
- The employer provides the worker with benefits such as insurance, leave, or workers' compensation.
- The worker is considered an employee of the employer for tax purposes (i.e., the employer withholds federal, state, and Social Security taxes).
- The employer can discharge the worker.
- The worker and the employer believe that they are creating an employer-employee relationship.

In setting out the above factors, the EEOC also cautions that:

This list is not exhaustive. Other aspects of the relationship between the parties may affect the determination of whether an employer-employee relationship exists. Furthermore, not all or even a majority of the listed criteria need be met. Rather, the determination must be based on all of the circumstances in the relationship between the parties, regardless of whether the parties refer to it as an employee or as an independent contractor relationship.[16]

As to the second threshold question, the general answer is that the term "covered individual" includes: (1) employees and applicants for employment; (2) former employees; and (3) applicants to, and participants in, training and apprenticeship programs.[17]

IV.   THE ADMINISTRATIVE REMEDIES PROCESS

As discussed above, the EEOC is responsible for enforcing Title VII, the ADEA, the EPA, parts of the ADA, and GINA. Generally, prior to filing a claim in court alleging a violation of Title VII, the ADEA, the ADA, or GINA, an individual must first file an administrative charge with the EEOC or the state agency responsible for handling such complaints. This is referred to as the requirement to "exhaust administrative remedies." If an individual fails to file an

---

[16]*Id.* (emphasis in original).
[17]*Threshold Issues*, EEOC COMPLIANCE MANUAL, §2.

314   HEALTHCARE EMPLOYMENT GUIDE   CH. 21.IV.

314   HEALTHCARE EMPLOYMENT GUIDE   CH. 21.IV.

administrative charge, a court complaint may be dismissed for failure to exhaust administrative remedies.[18]

Equal Pay Act claimants, unlike Title VII, ADEA, ADA and GINA claimants, are not required to file an administrative charge with the EEOC to be able to file a lawsuit.[19]

After an individual (referred to as the "charging party") has filed a charge with the EEOC, the EEOC will notify the employer and begin an investigation. As a general matter, the EEOC's investigation begins with the EEOC sending the employer a questionnaire and may also include an on-site visit by the EEOC to interview witnesses and collect documents.

Generally, the employer submits a position statement to the EEOC that responds to the allegations and provides a legitimate, nondiscriminatory reason for the employment action at issue. The employer will often attach relevant documents to its position statement. A thorough position statement will often result in the EEOC deciding not to pursue an on-site investigation. Care must be taken, however, to ensure the accuracy of everything contained and submitted with the position statement; if there is a lawsuit ultimately filed, the plaintiff will be entitled to a copy of the position statement. Any inaccuracies in the position statement may well be used by the plaintiff as evidence of pretext.[20]

Once the EEOC concludes its investigation, it will inform the parties in writing of its finding. As a general matter, in charges where it has not found probable cause, the EEOC will issue a "Dismissal and Notice of Rights"[21] in which the agency will check a box advising the parties that the EEOC, "based on its investigation ... is unable to conclude that the information obtained establishes violations of the statutes" but will not make any specific findings. If the EEOC finds that there was more likely than not a violation, it will issue a "cause" determination and may include specific facts supporting the decision.[22]

---

[18]See United Air Lines v. Evans, 431 U.S. 553, 557 (1977).
[19]See County of Washington v. Gunther, 452 U.S. 161, 175 n.14 (1981); Miranda v. B&B Cash Grocery Store, Inc. 975 F.2d 1518, 1527 (11th Cir. 1992).
[20]See McDonnell Douglas Corp. v. Green, 411 U.S. 792 (1973).
[21]EEOC Form 161(11/09).
[22]See 29 C.F.R. §1601.21.

Regardless of whether the EEOC finds that there was more likely than not a violation, it will issue a "right-to-sue" notice. All plaintiffs in Title VII, ADEA, and ADA cases must have a right-to-sue notice before filing a lawsuit against the employer. The only situation in which this would not be the case is in the rare instance where the EEOC itself decides to file a lawsuit on behalf of the individual. The plaintiff/charging party has 90 days from receipt of the right-to-sue to file a lawsuit.

V. MAKING A CLAIM OF DISCRIMINATION/RETALIATION UNDER TITLE VII

Under Title VII, an employer may be found liable for unlawful discrimination under one of two theories: disparate treatment and disparate impact. As a general matter, disparate treatment occurs when an employer treats some people less favorably than others because they are members of a protected category. Disparate impact occurs when an employer's facially neutral practice impacts one group more harshly than another. Disparate treatment requires proof of discriminatory intent, while disparate impact does not.

A. Disparate Treatment

There are two ways to prove disparate treatment under Title VII: by direct evidence and by indirect evidence.

Proof by direct evidence is rare. Direct evidence shows discriminatory animus without any inference or presumption. Examples include sexist, racial, or other discriminatory remarks by the decisionmaker related to the decisionmaking process or made by a supervisor in the process of influencing the decisionmaking.

Indirect evidence is the most common. Indirect evidence shows that the wrongful action occurred under circumstances suggesting a discriminatory motive. When a plaintiff is relying on indirect evidence, a burden-shifting framework is used. Under this framework, a plaintiff has the burden of proving a prima facie case of discrimination by showing by a preponderance of the evidence that

- he or she is a member of a protected class (race, color, religion, sex, or national origin, as well as pregnancy or pregnancy-related conditions);

- he or she applied and was qualified for a job (or other employment opportunity or benefit) for which the employer was seeking applicants;
- despite the plaintiff's qualifications, he or she was rejected or suffered some other adverse employment action; and
- after the plaintiff's rejection, the position was awarded to a person outside of the protected class or the position remained open and the employer continued to seek applications from persons with the plaintiff's qualifications (or provide the benefit to other persons).

Once the plaintiff establishes a prima facie case of discrimination, the burden then shifts to the employer to "articulate some legitimate, non-discriminatory reason"[23] for the decision at issue. Note, however, that the employer does not have the burden of proving that it was actually motivated by the proffered reasons. Rather, the employer meets its burden by raising a genuine issue of fact as to whether it discriminated against the plaintiff.

Once the employer articulates a legitimate, nondiscriminatory reason, the plaintiff must show by a preponderance of the evidence that the employer's stated reason was, in fact, pretext. The plaintiff can persuade the fact finder of this by either directly persuading the fact finder that a discriminatory reason more likely than not motivated the employer, or indirectly, by showing that the employer's proffered explanation is unworthy of credence.

B. Disparate Impact

Disparate impact (also referred to as "adverse impact") discrimination is an unintentional form of discrimination. As such, unlike Title VII disparate treatment discrimination, it does not require proof of an intention to discriminate. To prevail under a theory of disparate impact discrimination under Title VII, plaintiff must first prove by a preponderance of the evidence that

- plaintiff is a member of a protected class; and
- plaintiff's employer has a specific employment practice or policy that appears neutral on its face, but which disparately

---

[23]*McDonnell Douglas Corp. v. Green*, 411 U.S. 792.

impacts a protected group more harshly as compared to an unprotected group.

Once an employee proves the above, the burden of proof shifts to the employer, who must prove that the challenged practice is job related and consistent with business necessity.[24]

If the employer establishes a sufficient business justification for the policy or practice, the burden shifts back to the plaintiff, who must then prove that there was a policy or practice the employer could have used that would have a less discriminatory impact that the employer refused to adopt.

C. Sexual Harassment

Prohibited sexual harassment[25] under Title VII can take the form of unwelcome sexual advances, requests for sexual favors, and other verbal or physical conduct of a sexual nature that explicitly or implicitly adversely affects an individual's employment. Sexual harassment is not limited by gender; anyone can be a victim or a perpetrator of sexual harassment. Moreover, the victim and the perpetrator do not have to be of the opposite sex.[26]

As such, it is possible for males to sexually harass other males, and females can sexually harass other females. The critical question to ask is whether the conduct itself would have occurred if the victim had been of a different sex. Put another way, is a male harasser harassing a male employee in a way that he would not harass a female, or is a female harasser harassing a female employee in a way that she would not harass a male employee?

---

[24]42 U.S.C. §2000e-2(k)(1)(A)(i).

[25]This overview of harassment claims under Title VII is focused on claims of sexual harassment, as it is the most common type of harassment litigation, but it is also applicable to harassment of members of other protected classes under Title VII, as well as harassment that offends other statutes such as the ADA or the ADEA. *See* Faragher v. City of Boca Raton, 524 U.S. 775, 787 n.1 (1998) ("Although racial and sexual harassment will often take different forms, and standards may not be entirely interchangeable, we think there is good sense in seeking generally to harmonize the standards of what amounts to actionable harassment."); Brennan v. Metro. Opera Ass'n, 192 F.3d 310, 318 (2d Cir. 1999) ("The analysis of the hostile working environment theory of discrimination is the same under the ADEA as it is under Title VII.").

[26]Oncale v. Sundowner Offshore Servs., Inc., 523 U.S. 75 (1998).

1. Plaintiff's Burden: Four Elements

There are four elements of proof required to prevail on a claim of sexual harassment under Title VII:

(1) The offensive conduct must be "because of sex." Put another way, the plaintiff must prove by a preponderance of the evidence that "but for" his or her sex, he or she would not have been the object of harassment. Note, however, that "[a]lthough sexual harassment must be based on sex, it need not be motivated by sexual desire."[27]

(2) The unwelcome conduct was so "severe or pervasive" that it "create[d] an objectively hostile or abusive work environment"[28] evaluated from the perspective of a "reasonable person."[29] Under relevant case law, a determination of whether offensive conduct is "severe or pervasive" is made using "common sense" and an "appropriate sensitivity to social context."[30] As such, there are few "rules" about what constitutes "severe or pervasive." Nonsexual, ordinary "horseplay," however, does not generally give rise to a Title VII claim, especially when it occurs between people of the same gender.[31]

(3) The behavior is "unwelcome." Not all conduct of a sexual nature in the workplace is prohibited by Title VII. It is only conduct of a sexual nature that is "unwelcome" that is prohibited.[32] Whether conduct is "unwelcome" is evaluated on a case-by-case basis.[33]

(4) There is a legal basis for employer liability. Once the plaintiff proves the above three elements of a sexual harassment claim and thereby establishes a prima facie case, whether the harassment was committed by the plaintiff's supervisor, a co-worker, or a third party determines the next step in the legal analysis.

---

[27]EEOC v. Boh Brothers Const. Co., 731 F.3d 444 (5th Cir. 2013).

[28]Harris v. Forklift Sys., Inc., 510 U.S. 17, 21 (1993); *see also* Meritor Sav. Bank v. Vinson, 477 U.S. 57, 67 (1986).

[29]Oncale v. Sundowner Offshore Servs., Inc., 523 U.S. 75, 82 (1998).

[30]*Id.* at 81–82.

[31]*See* Shafer v. Kal Kan Foods, 417 F.3d 663 (7th Cir. 2005).

[32]29 C.F.R. §160.411(a).

[33]EEOC Enforcement Guidance on Current Issues of Sexual Harassment (1990).

2. Harassment by Supervisor

If the plaintiff's "supervisor" committed the harassment, the employer has the burden of proving by a preponderance of the evidence that there was no "tangible employment action" in order to avoid vicarious liability. Put another way, if the harassment was by the plaintiff's supervisor, then the only way that the employer can avoid vicarious liability is by proving that (1) the harasser was not the plaintiff's "supervisor" as defined by Title VII; or (2) there was no "tangible employment action."

For purposes of the harassment analysis under Title VII, the legal definition of a "supervisor" is someone "with immediate (or successively higher) authority"[34] whom "the employer has empowered … to take tangible employment actions against the victim."[35] As such, it is not whether the harasser has "supervisor" in his or her title, it is whether the harasser has the requisite authority.

A "tangible employment action" requires proof of "a significant change in employment status, such as hiring, firing, failing to promote, reassignment with significantly different responsibilities, or a decision causing a significant change in benefits."[36]

3. Harassment by Co-worker

Where the alleged hostile work environment harassment is perpetrated by a co-worker, the employer will be held liable for the harassment only where plaintiff proves by a preponderance of the evidence that the employer knew or should have known about the harassment and failed to take prompt remedial action reasonably calculated to end the harassment.[37]

---

[34]Burlington Indus., Inc. v. Ellerth, 524 U.S. 742, 765 (1998); Faragher v. City of Boca Raton, 524 U.S. 775, 807 (1998).

[35]Vance v. Ball State Univ., 133 S. Ct. 2434, 2443 (2013) (internal quotation marks and citations omitted).In *Vance*, the Supreme Court specifically disapproved the EEOC's guidance that someone who has the "authority to direct the employee's daily work activities" is a "supervisor" for purposes of Title VII.

[36]*Burlington Industries*, 524 U.S. at 761.

[37]*See* 29 C.F.R. §1604.11(d)(1992); Baldwin v. Blue Cross/Blue Shield, 480 F.3d 1287, 1302 (11th Cir. 2007) (employer liable for co-worker harassment liable only if employer "knew or should have known of the harassing conduct but failed to take prompt remedial action"); Hitchens v. Montgomery County, 2008 U.S. App. LEXIS 10688 (3d Cir. May 19, 2008) (unpublished decision) (affirming judgment in favor of employer where plaintiff failed to show employer knew or should have known of the alleged harassment since the first time she notified the employer of the alleged

4. Harassment by Third Party

Under developing law, employers can be liable for harassment by a third party when the employer knew or reasonably should have known about the harassment and failed to take prompt, remedial action reasonably calculated to end the harassment.[38] In the healthcare industry, where it is not uncommon for patients to make unwelcome racist and sexist comments to healthcare providers, this development is one for practitioners to watch closely.

D. Retaliation

To successfully establish a claim of retaliation under Title VII, plaintiff must show:

- plaintiff engaged in a "protected activity"[39];
- employer subjected plaintiff to an "adverse employment action"[40]; and
- employer's retaliatory motive was the "but for" cause of the adverse employment action.[41]

As the EEOC points out in its 2016 Guidance,[42] however, the "but for" causation standard does not require that retaliation be the "sole cause" of the action. In making this point, the EEOC quotes from a 2014 Supreme Court decision as follows:

---

harassment was when she filed her administrative charge with the EEOC; "because her employer did not know or have reason to know of the alleged sexual harassment, there was no opportunity for her employer to promptly remedy the situation and defendants cannot be held liable").

[38]Freeman v. Dal-Tile Corp., 750 F.3d 413 (4th Cir. 2014) (employer liable for third-party racial and sexual harassment of an employee harassed by third-party sales representative where employee's supervisor took no action to stop the harassment for three years other than ineffectively telling the harasser to stop using inappropriate language; court concluded that employer's response to complaints was neither prompt nor adequate). See also EEOC v. Costco Wholesale Corp., 14-cv-6553 (N.D. Ill. Dec. 22, 2016) (jury awarded Costco employee $250,000 for third-party harassment after employer failed to take steps to protect employee from a customer who was harassing her, had inappropriately touched her, and was stalking her).

[39]Reserved.

[40]As a general matter, any action that would have persuaded a reasonable person from complaining is considered an "adverse employment action" in retaliation claims.

[41]University of Tex. Sw. Med. Ctr. v. Nassar, 570 U.S. ___, 133 S. Ct. 2517, 2534 (2013).

[42]EEOC Enforcement Guidance on Retaliation and Related Issues (Aug. 25, 2016).

"[W]here A shoots B, who is hit and dies, we can say that A [actually] caused B's death, since but for A's conduct B would not have died." *LaFave* 467–468 (italics omitted). The same conclusion follows if the predicate act combines with other factors to produce the result, so long as the other factors alone would not have done so—if, so to speak, it was the straw that broke the camel's back. Thus, if poison is administered to a man debilitated by multiple diseases, it is a but-for cause of his death even if those diseases played a part in his demise, so long as, without the incremental effect of the poison, he would have lived.[43]

E. Failure to Accommodate Religion

Title VII has a specific provision requiring the "reasonable accommodation" of an employee's "religious observance or practice."[44] To prevail on a claim of discrimination under Title VII based on a failure to accommodate a religious observance or practice, an individual must show:

- plaintiff requested an accommodation for a religious observance or practice;
- employer failed to
  - engage in a sufficient exploration of possible accommodations;
  - offer an accommodation that adequately addressed plaintiff's needs; or
  - state a legitimate basis for its inability to accommodate plaintiff based on an undue hardship to its business operations.

F. Administrative Procedure and Statute of Limitations

In general, individuals must file a charge with the EEOC within 180 days of the alleged discriminatory act. Where a state has an anti-discrimination law and a state agency authorized to grant or seek relief, the individual must file the administrative charge with the state agency. In such states, the individual has 300 days, or 30 days after

---

[43]*Id.* (quoting Burrage v. United States, 134 S. Ct. 881, 888–89 (2014) (citing State v. Frazier, 339 Mo. 966, 974–75, 98 S.W.2d 707, 712–13 (1936))).

[44]42 U.S.C. §2000e(j).

receiving notice that the state or local agency has terminated the proceeding, to file a charge with the EEOC.[45]

VI. MAKING A CLAIM OF AGE DISCRIMINATION/RETALIATION UNDER THE ADEA

As with Title VII claims, age discrimination claims can be brought under two legal theories: disparate treatment and disparate impact.

A. Disparate Treatment

The majority of ADEA claims are brought under the disparate treatment theory. To prevail under this theory, a plaintiff must prove intentional age discrimination and that "but for" his or her age, he or she would not have been treated less favorably.[46] Note that this is significantly different from a Title VII claim, where the plaintiff only has to prove that his or her protected class status was "a motivating factor."

As with Title VII claims, a plaintiff can prove discriminatory intent using either direct or circumstantial evidence. Direct evidence of age discrimination is evidence that proves, without a need to make inferences, that plaintiff was adversely treated for an illegal reason.[47]

Where direct evidence of age discrimination is unavailable, the courts will utilize the *McDonnell Douglas* framework for Title VII claims, discussed in Section V, above. Under this framework, the plaintiff has the initial burden of establishing a prima facie case which, if unrebutted, would be sufficient to raise an inference of unlawful age discrimination. Once a prima facie case is established, the burden shifts to the employer to articulate a legitimate, nondiscriminatory business reason for the adverse employment action. If the employer meets this burden, the burden shifts back to the plaintiff to prove that the proffered reason is in reality a "pretext" for discrimination.[48]

---

[45]42 U.S.C. §2000e-5(e)(1).

[46]Hazen Paper Co. v. Biggins, 507 U.S. 604, 610 (1993).

[47]*See* EEOC v. City of Independence, 471 F.3d 891 (8th Cir. 2006) (direct evidence of age discrimination found where policy prohibited only employees eligible for "regular retirement" from participating in a leave donation program).

[48]Reeves v. Sanderson Plumbing Prods., Inc., 530 U.S. 133 (2000).

Generally, a plaintiff establishes a prima facie case in a case alleging that a termination violated the ADEA by proving that

(1) plaintiff is a member of the protected class, i.e., age 40 or older;

(2) plaintiff was qualified for the job and met the employer's legitimate expectations;

(3) plaintiff was discharged despite plaintiff's qualifications and performance; and

(4) following the discharge, plaintiff was replaced by a substantially younger individual with comparable qualifications.[49]

In evaluating whether a plaintiff has established that the employer's reason was a "pretext" for discrimination, the U.S. Supreme Court has held that a

> plaintiff bringing a disparate treatment claim pursuant to the ADEA must prove, by a preponderance of the evidence, that age was the "but-for" cause of the challenged adverse employment action. The burden of persuasion does not shift to the employer to show that it would have taken the action regardless of age, even when a plaintiff has produced some evidence that age was one motivating factor in that decision.[50]

The plaintiff must show both that the employer's reason is false and that age discrimination was the real reason for the adverse action.[51]

B. Disparate Impact

As with Title VII disparate impact claims, under the ADEA a plaintiff seeking to prove age discrimination under the disparate impact theory must prove the employer has a facially neutral policy that

---

[49]Note that unlike in Title VII cases, ADEA plaintiffs are not required to prove they were replaced by someone outside the protected age group to establish a prima facie case. O'Connor v. Consolidated Coin Caterers Corp., 517 U.S. 308, 312 (1996) (holding that "the fact that a replacement is substantially younger than the plaintiff is a far more reliable indicator of age discrimination than is the fact that the plaintiff was replaced by someone outside the protected class").

[50]Gross v. FBL Fin. Servs., Inc., 557 U.S. 167, 180 (2009).

[51]*Reeves*, 530 U.S. at 148 (explaining why proof an employer gave a false reason for the employment acting will not always be sufficient to prove pretext by pointing out possibility of case where plaintiff presents "weak issue of fact as to whether the employer's reason was untrue" while the employer presents "abundant and uncontroverted evidence that no discrimination had occurred").

affects employees age 40 or older differently than employees age 39 and younger.

Under the ADEA, once a plaintiff proves age-based disparate impact, the employer then bears the burden of showing a "reasonable factor other than age" is the cause of the disparate impact.[52] Under the EEOC's regulations, to establish the "reasonable factor other than age" affirmative defense, an employer must show:

(1)   that the employment practice was reasonably designed to further or achieve a legitimate business purpose; and

(2)   that it was administered in a way that reasonably achieves that purpose in light of the particular facts and circumstances that were known, or should have been known, to the employer.[53]

The EEOC's regulation provides a nonexclusive list of considerations that the EEOC considers relevant in determining whether an employment practice is based on a reasonable factor other than age:

- the extent to which the factor is related to the employer's stated purpose;
- the extent to which the employer defined the factor accurately and applied the factor fairly and accurately, including whether or not managers were given guidance or training about how to apply the factor and avoid discrimination;
- the extent to which the employer limited the discretion of supervisors in applying the factor;
- the extent to which the employer assessed the adverse impact of its employment practices on older workers; and
- the degree of harm to individuals within the protected age group, in terms of both the extent of injury and the numbers of persons adversely affected, and the extent to which the employer took steps to reduce the harm, in light of the burden of undertaking such steps.[54]

In listing these factors for consideration, the EEOC cautioned that the presence or absence of any one of the factors does not necessarily determine whether the defense has been established. Rather,

---

[52]Meacham v. Knolls Atomic Power Lab., 554 U.S. 84, 128 S. Ct. 2395 (2008).
[53]29 C.F.R. pt. §1625.
[54]Id.

whether an employment practice in based on reasonable factors other than age must be decided based on all of the particular facts and circumstances in each situation.

C. Hostile Work Environment/Harassment

Whether the ADEA covers claims for age-based hostile work environment remains an unresolved area of the law. Some courts have entertained hostile environment claims under the ADEA, although they have rejected the claim in question.[55] Other courts have held that the ADEA does not recognize a cause of action for hostile environment age discrimination.[56]

D. Retaliation

As with Title VII retaliation claims, to successfully establish a claim of retaliation under the ADEA, a plaintiff must show:

- plaintiff engaged in a "protected activity";[57]
- employer subjected plaintiff to an "adverse employment action";[58] and
- employer's retaliatory motive was the "but for" cause of the adverse employment action.[59]

E. Administrative Procedure and Statute of Limitations

Unlike Title VII claims, an ADEA plaintiff does not need to obtain a Notice of Right to Sue from the EEOC before filing a lawsuit. Rather, an ADEA plaintiff can file a lawsuit 60 days after filing an EEOC charge. The statute of limitations for filing an ADEA lawsuit is no later than 90 days after the EEOC gives notice that it has completed its investigation.

---

[55]*See* Breeding v. Arthur J. Gallagher & Co., 164 F.3d 1151 (8th Cir. 1999); Crawford v. Medina Gen. Hosp., 96 F.3d 830 (6th Cir. 1996).

[56]*See* Burns v. AAF-McQuay, 166 F.3d 292 (4th Cir. 1999).

[57]Reserved.

[58]As a general matter, any action that would have dissuaded a reasonable person from complaining is considered an "adverse employment action" in retaliation claims.

[59]University of Tex. Sw. Med. Ctr. v. Nassar, 570 U.S. ___, 133 S. Ct. 2517, 2534 (2013).

VII. Making a Claim of Discrimination/Retaliation
Under the Equal Pay Act

A. Burden of Proof

To successfully raise a discrimination claim under the Equal Pay Act, a plaintiff must show by a preponderance of the evidence that plaintiff and an employee of the opposite sex are:

- working in the same "establishment" (meaning a "distinct physical place of business" rather than an "entire business or enterprise");[60]
- doing "equal work on jobs the performance of which requires equal skill, effort, and responsibility,[61] and which are performed under similar working conditions";[62] and

---

[60]29 C.F.R. §1620.9. Note, therefore, that as a general rule under the EPA wages cannot be compared in different hospital, practice, or clinic locations. Some courts, however, have made exceptions to this distinct physical place of business test where an employer's operations are integrated and the administration of the different locations is centralized. See Erickson v. Mike Finnin Motors, Inc., 2001 WL 1243166, 2001 U.S. Dist. LEXIS 11628 (N.D. Iowa 2001) ("The regulations, however, also indicate that two or more physical locations may be treated as a single establishment, 'for example, when a central administration unit ... hire[s] all employees, set[s] wages, and assign[s] the location of employment; employees ... frequently interchange work locations; and daily duties [are] virtually identical and performed under similar working conditions."). Under Title VII, however, such a comparison might be relevant and allowed as the comparison of work standard under Title VII wage discrimination cases is less restrictive than the "equal work" standard under the EPA. See Miranda v. B&B Cash Grocery Store, Inc., 975 F.2d 1518, 1525 (11th Cir. 1992).

[61]Courts have interpreted the requirements of equal skill, equal effort, and equal responsibility as constituting three separate tests, each of which must be met in order to bring a successful EPA claim. See Christopher v. State of Iowa, 559 F.2d 1135, 1138 (8th Cir. 1977). Pursuant to 29 C.F.R. §1620.15, whether two jobs require "equal skill" depends on the experience, training, education, and ability required in the performance of the job. "Equal effort" is measured by the physical or mental exertion needed in the performance of the job. 29 C.F.R. §1620.16. The degree of accountability required to perform the job is analyzed when determining whether the jobs being compared have "equal responsibility." 29 C.F.R. §1620.17.

[62]In evaluating whether the jobs being compared have "similar working conditions," the focus is on the surroundings and hazards. 29 C.F.R. §1620.18. To assert successfully a claim under the EPA, it is not necessary that the jobs be identical, only substantially equal. Determining whether employees are performing substantially equal work requires a fact-intensive analysis as well as "a practical judgment on the basis of all the facts and circumstances of a particular case, including factors such as level of experience, training, education, ability, effort and responsibility." Lawrence v. CNF Transp., Inc., 340 F.3d 486, 492 (8th Cir. 2003). Significantly, it is the job content that is controlling, not the job title or job description. 29 C.F.R. §1620.13.

- receiving unequal pay.[63]

The elements of a successful retaliation claim under the EPA are the same as for the ADEA and Title VII. As such, please see the discussion in Sections V and VI, above.

B. Statute of Limitations

The statute of limitations for a lawsuit under the EPA is two years from the day plaintiff received the last discriminatory pay-check. The limitations period is extended to three years in the case of willful discrimination.

Pursuant to the Lilly Ledbetter Fair Pay Act, enacted on January 29, 2009, in cases involving allegations of pay discrimination, an unlawful employment practice occurs (1) when the discriminatory pay decision is made; (2) when "an individual" becomes subject to the discriminatory pay decision; or (3) when "an individual is affected by the discriminatory compensation decision or other practice." This is significant because it means that in pay discrimination cases the deadline for filing a claim starts anew each time an employee receives wages, benefits, or other compensation that is tainted by the discriminatory pay decision. As such, an employee can reach back as far as two years from the date on which a charge is filed with the EEOC or state administrative agency.

C. Process for Making the Claim

Unlike Title VII, the EPA does not require a plaintiff to exhaust administrative remedies by first filing with the EEOC. Instead, an aggrieved employee can proceed directly to federal court. The statute of limitations under the EPA is two years, unless there are allegations of "willful violations," in which case a three-year limitations period applies. See Section VII.B, above.[64]

---

[63]If, however, the employer can show that the wage disparity is the result of an existing and legitimate (1) seniority system, (2) merit system, (3) system that measures earnings by quantity or quality of production, or (4) differential based on any other factor than gender, the claim will be defeated.

[64]29 U.S.C. §255.

VIII. MAKING A CLAIM OF DISCRIMINATION/RETALIATION
UNDER THE ADA

A. Disparate Treatment

In order to establish a prima facie case of employment discrimination under Title I of the Americans with Disabilities Act, an individual must prove three elements:

(1) the individual's impairment qualifies as a disability within the meaning of the ADA;
(2) the individual is qualified to perform the job-essential functions with or without reasonable accommodations; and
(3) the individual has suffered an adverse employment action owing to the employer's act or omission against the individual.

As a general matter, a person is a qualified individual with a disability if that person has a physical or mental impairment that substantially limits one or more of his or her major life activities. In determining whether an individual's impairment substantially limits a major life activity, courts will consider (1) the nature and severity of the impairment, (2) its duration or anticipated duration, and (3) its actual or expected long-term impact.

The most common way for an employer to defend against a claim of disability discrimination is to argue that the plaintiff is not a "qualified individual." As defined by the ADA, a "qualified individual" is an "individual who with or without reasonable accommodation, can perform the essential functions of the employment position that such individual holds or desires."[65] The EEOC regulations define "essential functions" to mean "the fundamental job duties" and provide that the term does not include the "marginal" functions of the position.[66]

The employer has substantial leeway in determining a job's "essential functions." "[C]onsideration shall be given to the employer's judgment as to what functions of a job are essential, and if an employer has prepared a written description before advertising or interviewing applicants for the job, this description shall be considered

---

[65]42 U.S.C. §12111(8).
[66]29 C.F.R. §1630.2(n)(1). *See* Dean v. Pocono Med. Ctr., 142 F.3d 138 (3d Cir. 1998) (ADA requires proof only of plaintiff's ability to perform "essential functions" of the job, not all functions, in order to be "qualified").

evidence of the essential functions of the job."[67] The frequency of a particular function, however, does not necessarily control whether the function is "essential." The appendix to the EEOC's regulations provides an instructive example on this point: "although a firefighter may not regularly have to carry an unconscious adult out of a burning building, the consequence of failing to require the firefighter to perform this function would be serious."[68]

An employer may also argue the individual is not a "qualified individual" because no reasonable accommodation for the person's disability exists that would not cause the employer undue hardship. According to the EEOC's Enforcement Guidance,[69] whether "undue hardship" exists requires "an individualized assessment of current circumstances that show that a specific reasonable accommodation would cause significant difficulty or expense." That assessment includes an analysis of several factors, including

- the nature and cost of the accommodation needed;
- the overall financial resources of the facility making the reasonable accommodation;
- the number of persons employed at the facility;
- the effect on expenses and resources of the facility;
- the overall financial resources, size, number of employees, and type and location of facilities of the employer (if the facility involved in the reasonable accommodation is part of a larger entity);
- the type of operation of the employer, including the structure and functions of the workforce, the geographic separateness, and the administrative or fiscal relationship of the facility involved in making the accommodation to the employer; and
- the impact of the accommodation on the operation of the facility.[70]

Once the plaintiff makes the above-described prima facie case, the burden shifts to the employer to prove that:

---

[67]42 U.S.C. §12111(8).
[68]29 C.F.R. pt. 1630, app.
[69]Enforcement Guidance: Reasonable Accommodation and Undue Hardship Under the Americans with Disabilities Act (Oct. 17, 2001).
[70]*Id.*; *see also* 42 U.S.C. §12111(10)(B) (2012); 29 C.F.R. §1630.2(p)(2) & app. (2017); 8 FEP Manual (BNA) 405:7005-07.

• the employer had a legitimate, nondiscriminatory reason for its actions; or

• the employee posed a direct threat that could not be eliminated by reasonable accommodation, which justified the adverse action taken by the employer.[71]

B. Disparate Impact

Disparate impact claims under the ADA are not common. With that said, the ADA prohibits employers from "utilizing standards, criteria, or methods of administration—(A) that have the effect of discrimination on the basis of disability; or (B) that perpetuate the discrimination of others who are subject to common administrative control."[72] The ADA also prohibits:

> [U]sing qualification standards, employment tests or other selection criteria that screen out or tend to screen out an individual with a disability or a class of individuals with disabilities unless the standard, test or other selection criteria, as used by the covered entity, is shown to be job-related for the position in question and is consistent with business necessity. ...[73]

C. Retaliation

As with the other federal discrimination laws enforced by the EEOC, individuals may assert claims for retaliation for exercising rights under the ADA in good faith. The absence of a disability does not translate into absence of protection from the anti-retaliation provisions of the ADA.[74]

D. Statute of Limitations

Administrative charges of disability discrimination under the ADA must be filed with the EEOC within 180 calendar days from the date the discrimination took place. The 180-day filing deadline is extended to 300 calendar days if a state or local agency enforces a law that prohibits employment discrimination on the same basis.

---

[71]29 C.F.R. §1630.2(r).
[72]42 U.S.C. §12112(b)(3).
[73]42 U.S.C. §12112(b)(6).
[74]Shellenberger v. Summit Bancorp Inc., 318 F.3d 183 (3d Cir. 2003).

The individual claiming disability discrimination has 90 days after receiving a Notice of Right to Sue to file a lawsuit.

IX. MAKING A CLAIM UNDER GINA

Under GINA, it is illegal for an employer to discriminate against employees or applicants because of genetic information. GINA also prohibits the use of genetic information in making employment decisions; prohibits employers from requesting, requiring, or purchasing genetic information; and strictly limits the disclosure of genetic information.

GINA took effect in 2009. To date, the majority of the cases have involved not claims of discrimination but alleged violations of the provision that forbids companies to "request, require, or purchase genetic information with respect to an employee."[75]

X. FEDERAL LAWS PROTECTING HEALTHCARE WHISTLEBLOWERS FROM RETALIATION

In the healthcare world, the three most common federal fraud and abuse laws that protect whistleblowers from retaliation are the False Claims Act (FCA), the Anti-Kickback Statute (AKS), and the Physician Self-Referral Law (the "Stark Law"). For a more in-depth overview of these three laws, please refer to Chapter 25.

Individuals with information about violations of the AKS or Stark Law can file a qui tam lawsuit under the FCA, which protects them from retaliation. The following sections discuss (1) burden of proof; (2) damages and relief available; and (3) the statute of limitations for claims of whistleblower retaliation.

---

[75]*See* Lowe v. Atlas Logistics Grp. Retail Servs. (Atlanta), LLC, 102 F. Supp. 3d 1360 (N.D. Ga. 2015) ($2.2 million jury award to two employees forced to undergo DNA test as part of grocery distributor's internal investigation into who was leaving feces in the aisle and on top of canned goods). *See also* Press Release, EEOC, Founder Pavilion Will Pay $370,000 to Settle EEOC Genetic Information Discrimination Lawsuit (Jan. 13, 2014) (EEOC alleged employer violated GINA when it requested family history as part of its post-offer, pre-employment medical exams of patients); Press Release, EEOC, Joy Mining Machinery Settles EEOC Genetic Information Non-Discrimination Act Lawsuit (Jan. 7, 2016) (EEOC alleged employer violated GINA by requesting family medical history during its post-offer, preplacement physical form asking applicants if they had family medical history for tuberculosis, cancer, diabetes, epilepsy, or heart disease).

A. Burden of Proof

To prevail on a claim of whistleblower retaliation under the FCA (as amended in 2009),[76] the plaintiff must prove that he or she

- engaged in lawful acts in furtherance of an action under the FCA or engaged in other efforts to stop a violation of the FCA; and
- was discharged, demoted, harassed, or otherwise discriminated against because of those lawful acts.[77]

In decisions interpreting the FCA following its amendment in 2009, courts have held the FCA's whistleblower retaliation provision protects

- internal reporting of fraudulent activity to a supervisor;[78]
- complaints made in good faith, even if they do not turn out to prove a violation of the FCA by a preponderance of the evidence;[79]
- steps taken in furtherance of a potential or actual qui tam action;[80] and
- steps taken to remedy fraudulent activity or to stop an FCA violation.[81]

In *Marbury v. Talladega College*,[82] Marbury alleged that Talladega terminated her employment because she opposed requests to allocate federal funds in an unlawful manner. The college argued (among other things) that Marbury was not protected from retaliation under the FCA because she engaged only in internal complaints to her supervisor and did not file a formal grievance or a qui tam

---

[76]31 U.S.C. §3730(h).

[77]*Id.* §3730(h)(i) ("Any employee, contractor, or agent shall be entitled to all relief necessary to make that employee, contractor, or agent whole, if that employee, contractor, or agent is discharged, demoted, suspended, threatened, harassed, or in any other manner discriminated against in the terms and conditions of employment because of lawful acts done by the employee, contractor, agent or associated others in furtherance of an action under this section or other efforts to stop 1 or more violations of this subchapter.").

[78]*See* Marbury v. Talladega Coll., 2014 WL 234667 (N.D. Ala. Jan. 22, 2014).

[79]*See* Ickes v. Nexcare Health Sys., L.L.C., 178 F. Supp. 3d 578 (E.D. Mich. 2016).

[80]*See* United States v. Northern Adult Daily Health Care Ctr., 205 F. Supp. 3d 276 (E.D.N.Y. 2016).

[81]*Id.*

[82]2014 WL 234667.

complaint to the government. The federal district court rejected the college's narrow construction of the FCA's whistleblower protection provision, concluding Marbury's complaint to her supervisor and refusal to complete requisition forms for unauthorized uses of the federal funds could qualify as protected whistleblowing.

In *Ickes v. NexCare Health Systems, LLC*,[83] a case alleging FCA retaliation filed by a physical therapist against a rehabilitation center, the employer argued that the therapist did not engage in protected conduct for two reasons: (1) "violations of patient transfer and discharge rules ... are violations of a condition of participation not payment," and (2) "Plaintiff did not have a good-faith basis for her concerns."[84] The federal district court rejected the first argument, stating in relevant part that "[t]he Act protects an employee who is punished for his or her 'efforts to stop' violations of the FCA; its protection is not limited to only those employees whose complaints turn out to prove a violation of the FCA by a preponderance of the evidence."[85] The court similarly rejected the defendants' second argument, finding that Ickes clearly had a good-faith basis for her concerns based on her conversations with others, including other therapists and patients, an elder-law attorney, and the ombudsperson, that confirmed the rehabilitation center was engaging in an unlawful practice.

In another notable FCA healthcare case, *United States v. Northern Adult Daily Health Care Center*,[86] the federal district court denied an adult day care's motion to dismiss a claim of FCA retaliation, holding that a plaintiff need not plead an FCA retaliation claim with particularity because no showing of fraud is required. Rather, to be protected the plaintiff must show his conduct constituted "lawful acts done by the employee ... in furtherance of an action under the FCA," as well as "other efforts to stop one or more violations of the FCA."[87] The court also noted that under the FCA complaining of regulatory violations may qualify as an "effort[] to stop 1 or more violations" under the 2009 amendments to the FCA.[88] In explaining its analysis, the court noted that such complaints made in an effort

---

[83] 178 F. Supp. 3d 578.
[84] *Id.* at 593.
[85] *Id.* at 594 (internal quotation marks omitted).
[86] 205 F. Supp. 3d 276.
[87] *Id.* at 298 (internal quotation marks omitted).
[88] *Id.* at 299 (internal quotation marks omitted).

to stop a violation of the FCA are protected "even if the employee's actions were not necessary in furtherance of an FCA claim."[89]

B. Damages and Available Relief

Relief available to FCA retaliation plaintiffs includes the following:

- reinstatement;
- double back pay;
- compensation for any special damages, including litigation costs and reasonable attorneys' fees.

C. Statute of Limitations for FCA Whistleblower Retaliation Claims

The statute of limitations for filing an FCA retaliation case is different from that for filing a qui tam recovery case. An FCA retaliation case must be filed under the statute of limitations applicable to the most closely analogous state statute.

---

[89]*Id.* at 298 (internal quotation marks omitted).

XI. EMPLOYMENT LAWS ENFORCED BY EEOC: SIMPLE CHART

Name of Federal Law	No. of "Employees"[90] Needed to Trigger the Law	Purpose of the Law
Title VII of the Civil Rights Act of 1964, as amended ("Title VII")	15	Prohibits employers from discriminating in the employee's compensation, terms, conditions, or privileges of employment and from creating a hostile work environment on the basis of race, color, religion, sex or national origin as well as pregnancy or pregnancy-related conditions. The prohibition on pregnancy discrimination was added in the Pregnancy Discrimination Act of 1978. Requires employers to promulgate a comprehensive policy to ensure that sexual harassment complaints are impartially, promptly and thoroughly investigated. Requires employers to reasonably accommodate an applicant's and employee's sincerely held religious practices, unless doing so would impose an undue hardship on the operation of the employer's business.

---

[90]*Cautionary note for counsel:* How a worker is classified and paid is not the controlling factor in determining whether that worker is an "employee" for purposes of the federal laws discussed in this chapter. A determination of whether a worker is an "employee" for purposes of these federal laws requires a fact-based analysis as described further in Section III of this chapter.

Name of Federal Law	No. of "Employees"[90] Needed to Trigger the Law	Purpose of the Law
		Prohibits employers from retaliating against a person because the person engaged in "protected activity" by complaining about discrimination, filing a charge of discrimination, or participating in an employment discrimination investigation or lawsuit.
Age Discrimination in Employment Act of 1967, as amended (ADEA)	20	Prohibits employers from discriminating against applicants or employees 40 years of age and older on the basis of age in hiring, promotion, discharge, compensation, or terms, conditions or privileges of employment. Prohibits employers from retaliating against a person because the person engaged in "protected activity" by opposing any practice made unlawful by the ADEA, or because such individual, member or applicant for membership has made a charge, testified, assisted, or participated in any manner in an investigation, proceeding, or litigation involving an alleged violation of the ADEA.
Equal Pay Act of 1963, as amended (EPA)	15	Prohibits employers from engaging in sex-based discriminatory rates of pay. Men and women are protected equally.
Genetic Information Nondiscrimination Act of 2008 (GINA)	15	Prohibits employers from discriminating against employees on the basis of genetic information.

Name of Federal Law	No. of "Employees"[90] Needed to Trigger the Law	Purpose of the Law
Americans with Disabilities Act, as amended by ADA Amendments Act (ADA)	15	Prohibits employers from discriminating against someone based on their actual, perceived or record of disability.

Requires employers to accommodate someone with a known qualified disability, except where there is undue hardship to the company.

Requires employers to engage in the interactive process. |

CHAPTER 22

BARGAINING UNIT RULES APPLIED TO PUBLIC SECTOR WORKERS

I. INTRODUCTION

The development of workplace bargaining protections for state and federal employees came into existence long after the private-sector union protections of the National Labor Relations Act.[1] In the states, the history of public-sector collective bargaining has involved multiple variations, adopted in several waves over different periods of time.[2] Labor union strength in the private sector of a state has historically been a good predictor of the state legislature's receptivity toward empowering public-sector bargaining rights for public workers.

The assertion of rights and the conflicts of worker versus supervisor are quite comparable in the public and private sectors. For purposes of this text, numerous parallels exist: workers at the veteran's hospital, at the state hospital next door, and at the private rehabilitation facility down the street will have roughly comparable concerns in the administration of fair employment practices. Each of the three employers would want compatible and cooperative spirits among

---

[1] *See e.g.*, JAMES O'REILLY, OHIO PUBLIC EMPLOYEE COLLECTIVE BARGAINING (2d ed. 1995).

[2] For a comprehensive article that includes statutes and helpful categorizations for every state, see Center for Economic & Policy Research, Regulation of Public Sector Collective Bargaining in the States (Mar. 2014), http://cepr.net/documents/state-public-cb-2014-03.pdf. For a list of statutes from each state, see the AFSCME (American Federation of State, County & Municipal Employees) website, https://www.afscme.org/news/publications/for-leaders/public-sector-collective-bargaining-laws.

their workforce members. It is when conflicts arise that distinctions among federal, state, and private-sector healthcare entities become most significant.

II. FEDERAL EMPLOYEE RIGHTS

Special status for healthcare workers who are employed directly by federal government agencies, and who fall outside the realm of the National Labor Relations Board (NLRB) but inside the parallel Merit Systems Protection Board coverage, is a topic of great interest, particularly for thousands of nurses and doctors employed by the U.S. Department of Veterans Affairs. Federal employee rights cover healthcare workers as "employees" of that and other federal agencies, such as the National Institutes of Health, the Indian Health Service, the Bureau of Prisons, and the various subentities of the Public Health Service. "Unfair practices" norms for federal employees roughly parallel NLRB norms of behavior for private-hospital supervisors and managers. Remedial orders for federal agencies can include reinstatement and back pay of the individual. The federal employer is not subject to forced closure or mandatory remedial actions, as a tire store or steel mill would be, but there is a basic incentive for the employer to come into compliance with Merit Systems Protection Board requirements.

The federal Office of Personnel Management has the leading policy setting role impacting federal healthcare workers,[3] while the employer agency itself determines many of the ways in which its hospital and healthcare employment efforts are managed. It is important to pay attention to jurisdictional lines. Entities that receive federal funds are not automatically outside the scope of private-sector NLRB requirements, and federal employee protections do not cover the employees of health-related contractors or grant recipients such as Federally Qualified Health Centers.

---

[3] *See Labor-Management Relations,* OPM.gov, https://www.opm.gov/policy-data-oversight/labor-management-relations/.

III. STATE AUTHORITY

Public-sector employees in a state are subject to the state's set of labor laws. Some states have enacted separate laws governing hospitals and healthcare employment sites. Advising public-sector employees is not simple: in addition to protecting a worker's state law collective bargaining rights, the worker's legal advisor must be wary of the special status of medical personnel under exceptions provided in state bargaining laws.[4] State laws may allow cost constraints on hospitals, for example, which may indirectly influence how hospitals bargain for wages.[5]

Great variations exist in state labor law coverage and exclusions. Practitioners should review the union and employee remedies and protections applicable to a particular state, and check for state laws specific to hospital labor relations. For example, some states decline to allow advanced practice registered nurses (APRNs) to operate outside the supervision of a licensed physician, while other states allow it.[6] On the federal level, the Department of Veterans Affairs allows broad discretion in the practice by APRNs.[7]

---

[4] See the discussion of relative powers of state hospitals in *Washington State Nurses Ass'n v. Washington State Hosp. Comm'n*, 773 F.2d 1044, 120 LRRM (BNA) 2788 (1985) (holding that state hospital commission did not unlawfully restrain collective bargaining rights when it set maximum rates that state hospitals could charge patients and used guidelines to measure reasonableness of wage increases as component of overall hospital costs).

[5] *Id.*

[6] *See, e.g., Tapping Nurse Practitioners to Meet Rising Demand for Primary Care,* KAISER FAMILY FOUNDATION (Jan. 2015), http://files.kff.org/attachment/issue-brief-tapping-nurse-practitioners-to-meet-rising-demand-for-primary-care.

[7] 38 C.F.R. §17.415 (2017).

CHAPTER 23

BARGAINING UNIT RULES APPLIED TO NON-HEALTHCARE WORKERS IN HOSPITALS

I. INTRODUCTION

Hospitals and healthcare facilities need maintenance workers, heating technicians, plumbers, and security guards. For these employees, their workplace is a healthcare facility but their duties do not intersect with patient care. This section discusses cases involving appropriate collective bargaining units for non-healthcare workers in healthcare settings.

II. NLRB FINAL RULE ON HEALTHCARE BARGAINING UNITS

In *Presbyterian University Hospital v. NLRB*,[1] the U.S. Court of Appeals for the Second Circuit held that a healthcare center's telecommunication workers were properly categorized as "skilled maintenance employees" for purposes of the National Labor Relations Board (NLRB) rule on appropriate bargaining units in the healthcare industry.[2] This status applied even though these telecommunication workers were unlicensed and uncertified and had different immediate supervisors than the health center's other skilled maintenance employees. Significant factors were that the telecommunication workers performed work functions related to the maintenance of the physical plant; their jobs required one to three years' experience and

---

[1] 88 F.3d 1300 (2d Cir. 1996).
[2] 29 C.F.R. §103.30(a)(5) (2016). See discussion of the NLRB rule in Chapter 16.

343

a high school diploma; their wage rates compared to those of skilled maintenance employees; and they interacted regularly with skilled maintenance employees.[3]

The court in *Presbyterian University Hospital* upheld the NLRB determination that an existing skilled maintenance employee unit at one facility within a healthcare center remained an appropriate multifacility healthcare unit, distinct from unrepresented skilled maintenance employees at another one of the center's facilities. The court therefore concluded that unrepresented skilled maintenance employees were properly excluded from a union election, even though both facilities were part of a healthcare center that operated under a single state license. The court upheld NLRB findings that there was no interaction between skilled maintenance employees at the two facilities; that skilled maintenance employees maintained their respective facilities; that material purchases were performed by respective facilities; and that the existing unit of skilled maintenance employees had a 20-year history of successful and peaceful bargaining.[4]

III. COMMUNITY OF INTERESTS STANDARD

In an earlier case, *NLRB v. Long Island College Hospital*, the Second Circuit had approved the NLRB's discretion to apply a test of the employees' "community of interests" when determining whether a hospital's skilled maintenance and engineering employees were an appropriate bargaining unit.[5] The court applied the older NLRB standards that preceded the adoption of the NLRB final rule[6] governing bargaining units to hold that the skilled maintenance and engineering employees were an appropriate bargaining unit.[7] Once the NLRB rule was in place, that rule decided the issue and further adjudications for a specific determination were unnecessary.[8]

---

[3] *Presbyterian Univ. Hosp. v. NLRB*, 88 F.3d 1300.
[4] *Id.*
[5] NLRB v. Long Island Coll. Hosp, 20 F.3d 76 (2d Cir. 1994).
[6] 29 C.F.R. §103.30.
[7] *Id.*
[8] St. Margaret Mem. Hosp. v. NLRB, 991 F.2d 1146 (3d Cir. 1993).

CHAPTER 24

OUTSOURCING THE STAFFING OF HEALTHCARE INSTITUTIONS

I. INTRODUCTION

Increases in labor costs, combined with equipment and infrastructure changes and upgrades, have negatively impacted many hospitals in recent years. Labor cost increases were cited as part of the reason for a 6.8 percent increase in costs for a Massachusetts hospital system in 2016, for example.[1] Many hospitals are finding that reduction of their labor costs through outsourcing seems like an attractive option. Outsourcing brings with it a range of issues, however, from its impact on union relations to its ability to shield health care providers from liability in certain situations.

II. COSTS OF BACK OFFICE TECHNOLOGY UPGRADES

Although administrative details are still referred to as "paperwork," the adaptation of healthcare to the digital age has made it much easier for healthcare providers to operate with no paper and many fewer clerical employees. The check-in kiosk may be replacing the friendly and reassuring smile of the greeter.

---

[1] Maria Castelluci, *UMass Memorial Posts Earnings Loss Due to Massive EHR Rollout*, MODERN HEALTHCARE (Dec. 28, 2016).

Those who study hospital administrative costs are aware that health information technology upgrades are hugely expensive. At UMass Memorial Hospital, for example, the hospital's

> system-wide switch to an Epic Systems network contributed to $26.1 million in additional expenses in fiscal 2016. The rollout has cost the system a total of about $64 million so far, according to the earnings report. The rollout has added $23.3 million in labor expenses, $23.9 million in consulting fees and $14.2 million in implementation fees.[2]

Such technology upgrades can result in budget shortfalls, which in turn can reduce the hiring of new workers—or even trigger lay-offs. A layoff of 250 employees in a health insurance company may offer insights.[3] In nonunion companies, the sudden action will likely cause a backlash among the suddenly discharged workers, whose responsive actions may make for a rougher transition. In a company with union representation, budget shortfalls may increase the employer's resistance to wage or benefit increases in collective bargaining, extending and worsening disputes with workers.[4]

III. LABOR CONTRACTS AND OUTSOURCING

In facilities with an existing union contract, unilateral termination of the contract and replacement of workers would be an unfair labor practice,[5] and a union could ask the National Labor Relations Board (NLRB) to obtain an injunction halting the outsourcing. The hospital workers also could strike against the hospital because of the unfair labor practice.[6] If a court finds that a strike is an unfair labor practice strike, the striking workers have significant job protection.[7]

---

[2]Id.
[3]Jonathan LaMantia, Anatomy of a Layoff: How an Embattled New York Health Insurer Broke the News, CRAIN's N.Y. BUS. (Apr. 21, 2016).
[4]Castelluci, UMass Memorial Posts Earnings Loss.
[5]29 U.S.C. §158(d) (2012).
[6]See, e.g., Jeremy Olson, Allina Nurses Set Labor Day as Date for Hospital Strike, STAR TRIBUNE (Aug. 26, 2016).
[7]29 U.S.C. §§152(3), 158(a)(1) (2012); see Pirelli Cable Corp. v. NLRB, 141 F.3d 503 (4th Cir. 1998) (discussing employee rights in event of unfair labor practice); see also Ahearn v. Jackson Hosp. Corp., 351 F.3d 226 (6th Cir. 2003) (hospital committed unfair labor practices when it threatened to discharge striking nurses).

IV. OUTCOMES FROM SUBDIVIDING AND OUTSOURCING TASKS

From the outside, a brick façade might seem to house a typical nursing home. But today, the risk of liability verdicts has driven the operators of many skilled nursing facilities to contract for multiple functions, which they outsource to various corporations. In this way, the liability for errors is placed upon the limited liability company (LLC) that controlled the tortious actions.

Six to eight LLCs may provide services for one health care provider, making it difficult for litigants to reach the correct defendant in a death or serious accident case involving that provider.[8] Surgeons performing complex surgery are themselves likely to be part of an LLC or professional service corporation (PSC). At the same time, the technicians supporting the surgical devices used are employees of the technology corporation, the remote radiologist consultant has her own LLC, and the anesthesia provider is employed by a separate LLC.

In at least one state, some courts have not allowed the license holder to shield itself behind independent contractors.[9] However, the U.S. Supreme Court's 2017 decision in *Kindred Nursing Centers*[10] may reduce the likelihood that potential litigants will be able to reach a court at all. Nursing facilities often include binding arbitration clauses in their patient contracts. The Supreme Court considered a state contract rule that required power of attorney documents to specifically authorize representatives to waive the principal's right to access the courts in order for an arbitration agreement signed by the representative to be enforceable. The *Kindred* Court held, however, that the state rule violated the Federal Arbitration Act because the rule was not applicable to all contracts; instead, the rule singled out arbitration agreements in a disfavored way.

Outsourcing of hospital physicians can have other consequences as well. For example, using a national service provider to manage its provision of physician services may reduce a hospital's cost, but hospital doctors employed by outsourcing services tend to be

---

[8]*See* JAMES O'REILLY, LITIGATING THE NURSING HOME CASE (ABA 2d ed. 2015).
    [9]*Id.* at 228; *see* NME Props., Inc. v. Rudich, 840 So. 2d 309 (Fla. Dist. Ct. App. 2003) (nursing home license holder liable for punitive damages based on vicarious liability).
    [10]Kindred Nursing Ctr. Ltd. P'ship. v. Clark, 137 S. Ct. 1421 (2017).

compensated according to how many patients they treat each day.[11] This in turn may reduce the time available for front-line physicians to properly diagnose their patients' subtle symptoms. At an Oregon hospital, physicians protested the hospital's plan to outsource management of its hospital physicians to an outside employer.[12] The doctors feared they would have to go from seeing no more than 15 patients per day to 18 to 20, which they regarded as unsafe. Some of the doctors formed a union. The hospital abandoned the management company approach, and the parties entered a "long, grinding negotiation ... over the proper role of the hospital doctor."[13]

---

[11]Noam Schriber, *Doctors Unionize to Resist the Medical Machine*, N.Y. TIMES (Jan. 9, 2016).
[12]*Id.*
[13]*Id.*

CHAPTER 25

TELEMEDICINE

The introduction of telemedicine has invited new scrutiny of the definitions of the practice of medicine and healthcare. Telemedicine is the use of technology to undertake activity constituting the practice of medicine when the healthcare provider and patient are not in the same physical location. There is no single definition of telemedicine; indeed, a 2007 World Health Organization study had found 107 definitions in peer-reviewed publications.[1] This is a broadly changing field, in which the definitions are changing alongside the rapid evolution of technology. The American Telemedicine Association uses a definition that is as broad as the information network at the physician's disposal, including email, telephone, and fax: "*[T]he use of medical information exchanged from one site to another via electronic communications to improve a patient's clinical health status. Telemedicine includes a growing variety of applications and services using two-way video, email, smart phones, wireless tools and other forms of telecommunications technology.*"[2]

The legal definition of telemedicine in the U.S. varies based on the location of the act and the governmental agencies that have authority to regulate the act. The definitions are crucial for legal counsel in advising physicians because they describe, specifically and by implication, what a physician can and cannot do across state lines without having a license to practice medicine in that jurisdiction.[3] For example, CMS defines telemedicine to include two-way,

---

[1] WORLD HEALTH ORG., TELEMEDICINE: OPPORTUNITIES AND DEVELOPMENTS IN MEMBER STATES: REPORT ON THE SECOND GLOBAL SURVEY ON EHEALTH 8 (2010).

[2] American Telemedicine Ass'n, www.americantelemed.org.

[3] A very useful comparative chart compiled by state licensure agencies can be found on the website of the Federation of State Medical Boards (FSMB) at http://www.fsmb.org/Media/Default/PDF/FSMB/Advocacy/Agency%20Jurisdiction%20Chart--Internet.pdf.

real-time interactive communication between the patient and distant-site physician,[4] but not communication via telephone, email, or fax.[5]

Many state laws follow CMS's lead in this definition of tele-medicine for the purposes of state Medicaid participation, but other state law definitions of telemedicine include telephone calls, emails, or faxes. The definition of telemedicine can even vary within a given state, depending on the regulatory authority or purpose of the par-ticular law in question, such as medical licensure, pharmaceuticals, private health insurance, or rural utilities services. To further com-plicate the issue, telemedicine laws and regulations do not always explicitly refer to "telemedicine" and may use other words, such as "telehealth," "practicing medicine across state lines," or "practicing medicine by electronic means," to name a few.[6]

Any physician or medical group interested in a telemedicine practice should be aware of their "duty of care"[7] under state health-care practitioner licensing statutes or regulations, which may create heightened licensing or practice requirements for each jurisdiction that the physician seeks to reach through telemedicine.[8] Physicians should be aware of not only any additional permits or licenses that may be required by a given state, but also the additional practice requirements that may be imposed on any physician who uses tele-medicine within the state or reaches into the state through telemedi-cine. Physicians should also be aware of any additional licensing or practice requirements on those healthcare practitioners whom they supervise in relation to a telemedicine activity.

States have developed their medical licensing laws indepen-dently of one another, and the lack of state consistency in regulating the practice of medicine presents a significant barrier to any multi-state telemedicine program.[9] One of the initial questions when think-ing about a telemedicine practice is whether a license to practice medicine is required in each state. Some states explicitly address telemedicine in their state medical licensing laws and define the

---

[4]CMS, Telehealth Services (Nov. 2016), https://www.cms.gov/Outreach-and-Education/Medicare-Learning-Network-MLN/MLNProducts/downloads/TelehealthSrvcsfctsht.pdf.

[5]CMS, Next Generation ACO Model Telehealth Waiver (May 2017), https://innovation.cms.gov/Files/x/nextgenaco-telehealthwaiver.pdf.

[6]FSMB.org.

[7]See White v. Harris, 190 Vt. 647, 36 A.3d 203 (2011).

[8]FSMB.org.

[9]Id.

practice of telemedicine to include telemedicine that reaches into their state. Some states indirectly address telemedicine by including the act of diagnosing or recommending treatment through any "electronic" means in the practice of medicine in their state. Other states use broader language such as "by any means or instrumentality" to implicitly subject out-of-state telemedicine physicians to their medical licensing laws. Still other states do not address telemedicine, directly or indirectly, in their state physician licensing statutes or regulations. Even for those states that do not directly or indirectly address telemedicine in their medical licensing laws or define the location of the practice of medicine, it is generally assumed that any act of diagnosing or recommending treatment constitutes the practice of medicine in the state where the patient is located for the purpose of medical licensing and falls within the state's interest in protecting public health. The Federation of State Medical Boards has the best current charts of legal obligations on its website.[10]

All state physician licensing boards explicitly require a license granted by the board to practice medicine in their state. In the absence of licensure exceptions for telemedicine, each state medical board would likely require a physician to obtain a license to practice medicine in their state before allowing the physician to provide telemedicine services to a patient physically located in their state. Physicians should reconsider their medical licensing law coverages even when they only seek to provide telemedicine services within their licensed state. This is because many states have special telemedicine licensing or permitting requirements for currently-licensed physicians seeking to commence telemedicine activities within the state.

It is important to review the statutes and administrative codes for each state where your client may want to practice electronically. Obtaining valid licenses to practice medicine can be expensive, time consuming, and burdensome. The healthcare provider will be subject to multiple state medical boards, statutes, and regulations whenever they participate in out-of-state licensing processes or exceptions.[11]

Another alternative to obtaining licenses in multiple states is the common exception for out-of-state doctors. Some states follow

---

[10]FSMB.org.
[11]*See generally* FSMB.org.

Alaska, where medical licensing boards offer a consultation exception for those physicians who are licensed in another state.

Telemedicine activities often are intertwined with technologies providing pharmaceutical prescribing and dispensing. Many state and federal regulations and enforcement efforts have been aimed at telepharmacies, and each year more laws are passed. The regulations relate to informed consent, medical records, credentialing and regulating telemedicine licenses, standard of care, transmitting orders for medicines, and contractual arrangements. The federal government has enacted requirements concerning the reimbursement to the distant site practitioner if the services are provided to a Medicare patient at an acceptable site.[12]

Minimum requirements will apply for physicians who use physician practice websites, Internet advertising, or email for patient communications. For example, physicians who use email for patient communications must have periodically evaluated policies for email management, processing, responses, privacy, archiving, and hours of operation. Physician-practice websites must include numerous disclosures, such as website ownership, in-office contact information, licensure and qualifications of affiliated physicians and healthcare professionals, complaint and feedback processes, and disclosure of any financial interest the physicians may have in any products or services discussed or advertised on the website.

Existing state malpractice case law, tort law, and civil procedure govern telemedicine malpractice issues not directly addressed by a specific telemedicine statute or case.[13] The standard of care to which the physician's actions is compared to determine negligence is not always clear, even in traditional medical encounters. Some courts prefer using a local or community standard of care, while others use a national standard of care.

In addition to pre-existing standards of care based on the type of physician or disorder being treated, states and private organizations have taken proactive steps to create standards of care specific to telemedicine encounters. For example, some states have created telemedicine-specific informed consent standards, privacy

---

[12]CMS, Telehealth Services (Nov. 2016), https://www.cms.gov/Outreach-and-Education/Medicare-Learning-Network-MLN/MLNProducts/downloads/TelehealthSrvcsfctsht.pdf.

[13]*See* JAMES O'REILLY & MICHELLE YOUNG, MEDICAL MALPRACTICE, ch.7 (ABA Press 2014).

standards, and general telemedicine standards of care. This may create an additional, heightened standard of care to which the physician's actions might be compared in a telemedicine malpractice case.[14] Controlled substances prescribing rules apply under Drug Enforcement Administration (DEA) requirements.[15] Finally, professional healthcare and technology organizations and the U.S. Food and Drug Administration (FDA) have published standards and guidelines for various aspects of telemedicine that are good reference material to review on the standard of care for telemedicine.

Of course, traditional rules on joint and several liability will apply to telemedicine encounters in which more than one physician is involved and is found to be responsible for an indivisible injury to a patient during a single encounter.[16] However, it would be better for the physicians involved in the telemedicine encounter to communicate their respective responsibilities at the outset rather than waiting for something to go unattended and result in a jury's determination of who was responsible. In addition to negligence, once the relationship is established, physicians can be held liable for patient abandonment if the physician unilaterally severs the relationship with the patient without reasonable notice or without providing adequate alternative medical care at a time when there is a necessity of continuing medical attention. Telemedicine encounters are often one-time encounters for a specific purpose. Failed communication between the consulting or referring physician's role in the ongoing care of the patient could result in an unintentional patient abandonment case, in which both physicians assumed that the other was responsible for the ongoing care of the patient.

Again, communication at the outset could prevent these unnecessary risks that arise in telemedicine. Thus, counsel should identify the range of risks presented by the particular telemedicine activity and preempt these issues by developing processes to ensure continuity of care, coordination of care, creation and termination of the physician-patient relationship, and ultimate responsibility over the patient among multiple healthcare providers and facilities.[17]

---

[14]*Medical Malpractice and Liability*, TELEHEALTH RESOURCE CENTERS, http://www.telehealthresourcecenter.org/toolbox-module/medical-malpractice-and-liability.
    [15]21 C.F.R. § 1300.04.
    [16]*See* MEDICAL MALPRACTICE, ch. 7.
    [17]Tara Kepler & Charlene L. McGinty, *Telemedicine: How to Assess Your Risks and Develop a Program That Works*, PHYSICIANS & JUDICIAL ORGS. L. INST., AM. HEALTH LAW. ASS'N (Feb. 2009),

Telemedicine is challenging the tradition of independent state control over medical malpractice.[18] States have significant variances in statutory and common law authority governing the elements of medical malpractice, including standards of care, statutes of limitations, informed consent requirements, arbitration requirements, burden of proof, joint and comparative liability, immunity, and damage caps. The Federation of State Medical Boards has a useful compilation.[19]

Another issue to consider is whether the physician's malpractice insurance covers multi-state telemedicine encounters. Insurance policies vary from state to state, and some policies may only cover malpractice claims in the state in which the physician is licensed to practice, even though the physician may qualify for an exception to practice medicine in the state without a license. Malpractice insurance policies should be examined to determine if multi-state telemedicine encounters are directly addressed, or if additional coverage is necessary. Counsel should first identify the possible states where the specific telemedicine is practiced, and then review the similarities and differences in medical malpractice law for the identified states. These variances allow for increased attention to potential telemedicine claims and the need for heightened risk management.[20]

The intensity of regulatory control for telemedicine practices within a state and throughout different states is increasing daily.[21] CMS reimbursement issues are also evolving rapidly.[22] Besides considering licensure requirements for each state in which the physician is involved, there are ethical guidelines applicable to the physician's activities. There are many new areas of regulation, conflicts, and legal principles about which attorneys must become knowledgeable and advise their clients. These issues go beyond conventional employment counseling and require counsel to be continuing learners.

---

[18]*See* American Telemedicine Ass'n, http://www.americantelemed.org.

[19]See the FSsMB website at http://www.fsmb.org/Media/Default/PDF/FSMB/Advocacy/Agency%20Jurisdiction%20Chart--Internet.pdf.

[20]*See generally* Medical Malpractice.

[21]*See* American Telemedicine Ass'n, http://www.americantelemed.org.

[22]CMS, Telehealth Services (Nov. 2016), https://www.cms.gov/Outreach-and-Education/Medicare-Learning-Network-MLN/MLNProducts/downloads/TelehealthSrvcsfctsht.pdf.

CHAPTER 26

STARK AND ANTI-KICKBACK COMPLIANCE*

I. INTRODUCTION: THE ROLE OF FRAUD AND ABUSE LAWS

Physicians practicing medicine today are faced with a multitude of operational, financial, and legal issues that far exceed what their counterparts encountered in years past. In particular, the development and enforcement of stringent fraud and abuse laws at both the federal and state level have significantly complicated what was once a simple goal of providing quality patient care while making a respectable living doing so. While it was enough at one point in time to avoid violating the law by maintaining a good moral character, this is not necessarily the case in today's age of "strict liability" laws and vigorous government enforcement.

---

*The authors thank Megan C. Phillips, Senior Counsel, and Cori Casey Turner, Partner, Husch Blackwell LLP, for contributing this chapter.

The purpose of this chapter is to familiarize the reader with the major fraud and abuse laws impacting practicing physicians today, including the federal physician self-referral law (commonly referred to as the "Stark Law") and the federal anti-kickback statute ("Anti-Kickback Statute"). These laws regularly come into play with respect to many common arrangements that physicians enter into while practicing medicine, not the least of which are employment, independent contractor, and practice ownership arrangements that may serve as a physician's primary source of income. There are key requirements that must be met in order for these types of arrangements to avoid a violation of the Stark Law and Anti-Kickback Statute. This chapter will provide guidance regarding these requirements in order to give the reader a workable understanding of the issues that must be considered when entering into these types of arrangements.

II. OVERVIEW OF THE IMPACTS OF THE STARK LAW

One of the most significant laws that impacts arrangements between physicians and healthcare entities is the Stark Law. The Stark Law generally provides that

- a *physician*
- may not make a *Medicare referral*
- for the provision of a *designated health service (DHS)*
- to an *entity* (e.g., a hospital)
- if the physician and the entity have a *financial relationship*
- unless the relationship fits within a Stark Law *exception*.[1]

Before delving into a discussion of each of these elements, it is important to note that the Stark Law is a strict liability statute. In other words, the government does not have to prove that the physician and healthcare entity who are parties to the arrangement have improper intent or willful knowledge. It is also important to note that violations of the Stark Law can result in significant fines and other penalties. These penalties include civil monetary penalties of up to $15,000 for *each* bill or claim that should not have been submitted and $100,000 for engaging in a scheme to circumvent the Stark Law; fines for failing to report an entity's ownership, investment,

---

[1] *See* 42 U.S.C. §1395nn.

and compensation arrangements when required; and/or exclusion from participation in Medicare, Medicaid, and other federal government healthcare programs.[2] Therefore, any financial relationships between physicians and the healthcare entities to which they refer should be carefully examined to determine whether the Stark Law is implicated.

The first element of the Stark Law clarifies that it only applies to referrals made by "physicians." However, the term "physician" is defined under the Stark Law to include not just medical and osteopathic physicians, but also dentists, dental surgeons, podiatrists, optometrists, and chiropractors.[3] Notably, the term "physician" does not include nurse practitioners, physician assistants, or other mid-level providers, and therefore these individuals are not subject to the Stark Law's restrictions on referrals.

The next element relates to the referral requirement of the Stark Law. For purposes of the Stark Law, a "referral" generally includes any request or order by a physician for DHS, which are discussed in more detail below.[4] It is important to note that referrals are not deemed to occur with respect to any DHS that are "personally performed" by a physician. Therefore, to the extent a physician directly provides a DHS to a patient, such service would not be subject to the restrictions of the Stark Law. Personal performance truly means that the physician must provide the service himself or herself—services provided by the physician's nurses, mid-level providers, or fellow physician practice members do not qualify as being personally performed.[5]

In addition, the prohibition in the statutory and regulatory text applies only to referrals of Medicare patients, not referrals of Medicaid patients or patients who are covered by commercial insurance.[6] However, with respect to Medicaid, it is important to note that several federal district courts have indicated that noncompliance with the Stark Law may also impact Medicaid claims.[7] In light of

---

[2] *Id.*
[3] 42 C.F.R. §411.351.
[4] *Id.*
[5] *Id.*
[6] *See* 42 U.S.C. §1395nn; 42 C.F.R. §411.353(a).
[7] In *United States ex rel. Schubert v. All Children's Health System, Inc.*, 2013 U.S. Dist. LEXIS 163075 (M.D. Fla. Nov. 15, 2013), the federal district court held that even though the Stark Law and its regulations only reference Medicare claims, the reach of the Stark Law is extended to Medicaid claims through Section 1903(s) of the Social

this development, physicians who refer or provide DHS to Medicaid patients should be cognizant of the potential application of the Stark Law to this patient population.

As noted above, physicians are prohibited under the Stark Law from making referrals for certain types of services, which are referred to under the Stark Law as "designated health services" or DHS. The current list of DHS includes the following types of services:

- Clinical laboratory services
- Physical therapy, occupational therapy, and speech-language pathology services
- Radiology and certain other imaging services
- Radiation therapy services and supplies
- Durable medical equipment and supplies
- Parenteral and enteral nutrients, equipment, and supplies
- Prosthetics, orthotics, and prosthetic devices and supplies
- Home health services
- Outpatient prescription drugs
- Inpatient and outpatient hospital services

Many of the services that qualify as DHS may be viewed as ancillary services. The Centers for Medicare & Medicaid Services (CMS) has developed detailed definitions for these DHS, some of which are based on lists of Current Procedural Terminology (CPT) codes.[8] Notably, DHS do not include Evaluation and Management (E/M) services, or many other types of professional services (with the primary exception of certain radiology professional services), and therefore referrals of such services are not subject to the Stark Law.

Security Act, which prohibits the federal government from making federal financial participation (FFP) payments to state Medicaid programs for claims that would have been prohibited under Medicare due to the Stark Law. Even though Section 1903(s) only appears on its face to apply to the FFP payment obligation of the federal government, the court held that a provider's act of "[c]ertifying compliance with the Stark Amendment to ensure that CMS pays FFP for Medicaid claims that violate the Stark [Law] would be a violation of the False Claims Act in the same manner that certifying compliance for full reimbursement under Medicare would be." *Id.* at *17 (footnote omitted). *See also* United States v. Halifax Hosp. Med. Ctr., 2012 U.S. Dist. LEXIS 36304 (M.D. Fla. Mar. 19, 2012); United States *ex rel.* Parikh v. Citizens Med. Ctr., 977 F. Supp. 2d 654 (S.D. Tex. 2013).

[8]42 C.F.R. §411.351. These CPT code lists are updated periodically and can be found on the CMS website at http://www.cms.gov/PhysicianSelfReferral/.

The "entity" element of the Stark Law is very broad. Entities—typically referred to as "DHS Entities"—include any person, sole proprietorship, public or private agency or trust, corporation, partnership, limited liability company, foundation, nonprofit corporation, or unincorporated association that performs or bills for DHS. A DHS Entity does not include the referring physician himself or herself, but does include his or her sole or group medical practice to the extent the medical practice performs or bills for DHS.[9] DHS Entities also include hospitals, laboratories, DME suppliers, and any other entities to which the physician refers DHS.

The final element of the Stark Law relates to the existence of a "financial relationship" between the physician (or an immediate family member of the physician)[10] and the DHS Entity. *If there is no financial relationship between a physician/immediate family member of a physician and a DHS Entity, then the physician is free to refer to the DHS Entity without regard to the Stark Law.* However, if a financial relationship exists, then the relationship must be structured to meet an applicable exception to the Stark Law in order to avoid violating the statute. The term "financial relationship" is defined very broadly under the Stark Law to include the exchange of remuneration (which includes any payment or benefit) between the referring physician and DHS Entity, and includes ownership, investment, and compensation relationships.[11] Due to this broad definition, the Stark Law may apply to employment agreements, independent contractor agreements, space and equipment leases, and ownership/partnership interests involving physicians and the DHS Entities to which they refer.

The Stark Law may also apply to financial relationships that are not directly between a referring physician and a DHS Entity. These types of relationships are referred to as "indirect financial relationships." They involve situations where another entity or entities (such as a management company or a physician practice of which the referring physician is not an owner) is a part of a chain of

---

[9]42 C.F.R. §411.351.

[10]For purposes of the Stark Law, an immediate family member of a physician includes the physician's husband or wife; birth or adoptive parent, child, or sibling; stepparent, stepchild, stepbrother, or stepsister; father-in-law, mother-in-law, son-in-law, daughter-in-law, brother-in-law, or sister-in-law; grandparent or grandchild; and spouse of a grandparent or grandchild. 42 C.F.R. §411.351.

[11]42 C.F.R. §§411.351, .354.

financial relationships that ultimately connect the DHS Entity to the referring physician. The illustration below depicts a potential indirect compensation relationship between a referring physician and a DHS Entity:

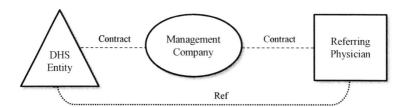

Arrangements such as these require careful analysis to determine whether or not a financial relationship subject to the Stark Law truly exists, and if so, what exceptions may be available to protect it.

If all of the elements discussed above are met and the Stark Law is therefore implicated, the analysis next turns to whether the financial relationship between the physician and the DHS Entity can be structured to meet one of the exceptions available under the Stark Law. If an exception can be satisfied, then referrals may continue to be made by the physician to the DHS Entity subject to the requirements of the exception.

III. STARK LAW EXCEPTIONS

The Stark Law includes various exceptions that can help protect financial relationships between DHS Entities and the physicians who refer to them. As noted above, the Stark Law is a strict liability statute, and therefore *all* requirements of an applicable exception must be met in order for an arrangement to avoid violating the Stark Law. It is important to note that if an exception to the Stark Law is not met, regardless of whether the referral relationship is innocent or the conduct is unintentional, a violation of the Stark Law may be found. While a detailed discussion of all of the exceptions available under the Stark Law is beyond the scope of this chapter, several of the most frequently used exceptions and the types of arrangements to which they may apply are discussed below.

A. Employment Arrangements With Hospitals

The "Employment Exception" to the Stark Law is typically utilized when a DHS Entity other than a physician practice (e.g., a hospital) directly employs a physician.[12] While physician practices may also utilize this exception, many instead take advantage of the more generous physician compensation provisions available by meeting the definition of a "group practice" and satisfying the requirements of the "In-Office Ancillary Services Exception" to the Stark Law, which are discussed in Section III.B, below.[13]

The Employment Exception includes, without limitation, the following requirements:

- Productivity bonuses paid to the employed physician may be calculated and paid only on the physician's *personally performed* services. In other words, the physician's compensation may not take into account revenue from technical services or facility fees provided by other entities or individuals.

- The compensation amount paid to the physician under the employment agreement must be consistent with the *fair market value*[14] of the services provided, not the volume or value of any referrals by the physician, and be commercially reasonable.

- If the employer will require the physician to make certain referrals to the employer, the agreement must be documented in writing and the compensation under the agreement must be set in advance. Note that referrals may *not* be required by an employee under the following circumstances: (1) if the patient expresses a preference for a different provider, practitioner, or supplier; (2) the patient's insurer determines the provider, practitioner, or supplier; or (3) the referral is not in the patient's best medical interests in the physician's judgment. In addition, the physician cannot be required to make

---

[12]*See* 42 C.F.R. §411.357(c).
[13]*See* 42 C.F.R. §411.355(b).
[14]Methods for determining fair market value will be discussed in Section V. of this chapter.

referrals that are unrelated to services provided under the scope of the physician's employment.[15]

B. Employment Arrangements and/or Ownership Interests in Physician Practices

Many physician practices that perform or bill for DHS utilize the In-Office Ancillary Services Exception (the IOAS Exception) to the Stark Law in order to protect referrals made by their employed physicians and/or physicians who hold a partnership or other ownership interest in the practice. In addition to meeting the requirements of this exception, if the physician practice is not a solo practice and desires to credit its physician employees and/or its partners/owners with revenue for DHS *not* personally performed by the credited physician (including DHS that are either independently billed or performed incident to the physician's services by a mid-level provider or nurse), the practice must also be structured as a "group practice" under the Stark Law. The IOAS Exception and the group practice requirements are commonly regarded as some of the most complex aspects of the Stark Law to navigate. However, structuring the practice in this manner also allows group practices to avoid the fair market value and commercial reasonableness limitations on compensation that are present in the Employment Exception.

1. Group Practice Requirements

In order to be considered a "group practice" for purposes of the Stark Law, a physician practice must satisfy all of the following requirements:

- Be a single legal entity operating primarily for the purpose of being a physician group practice;
- Have at least two physician "members" (which may include the practice's physician owners and employees);
- Ensure that each of its members furnish substantially the full range of patient care services that the physician routinely furnishes through the joint use of shared office space, facilities, equipment, and personnel;

---

[15]*See* 42 C.F.R. §411.354(d).

- Ensure that "substantially all" (i.e., at least 75 percent) of the total patient services of the group members are furnished through the practice and billed under the practice's billing number;
- Ensure that the group members personally conduct no less than 75 percent of the physician-patient encounters through the group practice;
- Be a "unified business" having centralized decision-making and consolidated operations;
- Comply with specific distribution of expense/income and physician compensation requirements.[16]

While a detailed discussion of all of these requirements is beyond the scope of this chapter, it is important to have a general understanding of the last requirement related to how physicians may be paid DHS revenue in a physician practice context. Compliance with this requirement is critical in assessing whether or not a physician practice's compensation plan is compliant with the Stark Law.

The DHS payment methodologies permitted for a group practice under the Stark Law include profit shares and productivity bonuses, provided that certain conditions are met. With respect to profit sharing, a physician may be paid a share of a group practice's *entire* profits derived from DHS payable by Medicare or Medicaid, or the profits derived from DHS payable by Medicare or Medicaid to any *component* of the group practice that consists of at least five physicians. In either case, these profits should be divided in a reasonable and verifiable manner that is not *directly* related to the volume or value of the physicians' DHS referrals.[17]

The component approach is commonly used by larger group practices when they want to segregate DHS compensation based on certain specialties. For example, different specialists in a practice could be segregated into separate components (e.g., family practice physicians, orthopedic surgeons, physiatrists, etc.)—assuming there are at least five physicians in each specialty component—and such physicians' profits within the component could be shared among them, provided they are not divided in a manner that directly relates to their DHS referrals to the group practice as a whole. While

---

[16]42 C.F.R. §411.352.
[17]42 C.F.R. §411.352(i)(2).

the Stark Law does not mandate specific procedures that must be followed in order for profit shares not to violate this direct relation requirement, it does provide "safe harbors" that provide assurance of meeting this requirement if followed. These safe harbors include:

(1) dividing the group practice/component's profits per capita among the physicians in the group practice/component;

(2) distributing revenue from DHS based on the distributions of the group practice's revenues attributed to non-DHS services; or

(3) distributing DHS revenue based on any method, provided that the revenue derived from DHS constitutes less than 5 percent of the group practice's total revenues and the allocation portion of that revenue to each physician in the group practice constitutes 5 percent or less of his or her total compensation from the group practice.[18]

In addition to the profit share methodology, another way to distribute DHS revenue in a group practice context is through productivity bonuses. Specifically, physicians may be paid productivity bonuses based on DHS that they have personally performed *and* DHS that are performed incident to his or her services, provided that the bonus is not determined in any manner that directly relates to the volume or value of DHS referrals made by the physician.[19] As with profit shares, there are safe harbors for productivity bonus distribution methods, which include the following: (1) basing the bonus on a physician's total patient encounters or relative value units (RVUs); (2) basing the bonus on the allocation of the physician's compensation attributable to non-DHS; or (3) basing the bonus on any method, if less than 5 percent of the revenue the bonus is based on is related to DHS, and the allocated portion of the DHS revenue to each physician in the group practice constitutes 5 percent or less of his or her total compensation from the group practice.[20]

In addition to DHS revenue, a group practice may also credit the physicians with revenue for any non-DHS services provided at the practice, which includes, without limitation, all revenue from commercial payors and revenue from Medicare for non-DHS services such as E/M and other appropriate professional services.

---

[18]42 C.F.R. §411.352(i)(2)(i)–(iii).
[19]42 C.F.R. §411.352(i)(3).
[20]42 C.F.R. §411.352(i)(3)(i)–(iii).

Group practices have significant flexibility with respect to determining how to distribute such revenue to their physicians, provided that such compensation is not allocated in a manner that directly or indirectly relates to the physician's DHS referrals.[21]

2. *In-Office Ancillary Services Exception*

Although the group practice requirements discussed in the previous section dictate how group practices must be structured and how they may compensate their employed physicians and/or partners/owners, a physician practice must still meet a separate exception to the Stark Law in order for its physicians to make in-office referrals of DHS. The exception utilized by most physician practices is the IOAS Exception.

It is important to note that the IOAS Exception includes specific limitations with respect to a physician practice's ability to supply certain types of durable medical equipment (DME).[22] To the extent DME will be supplied by a physician practice, the requirements of the IOAS Exception pertaining to DME should be carefully reviewed to ensure the IOAS Exception can be satisfied.

The IOAS Exception includes numerous requirements, which primarily relate to three different concepts: (1) which providers in the practice may provide the referred DHS; (2) who may bill for the referred DHS; and (3) where the referred DHS may be provided. In addition, the IOAS Exception includes specific patient disclosure requirements for physician practices that provide certain imaging services.

With respect to the first concept, the IOAS Exception requires that the referred DHS must be provided by the referring physician himself or herself, by another physician in the referring physician's group practice, or by an individual who is supervised by the referring physician or another physician in the physician's group practice (subject to applicable Medicare billing and supervision rules).[23] With respect to the second requirement, the referred DHS must generally be billed by:

(1)   the physician performing or supervising the DHS;

(2)   the physician's group practice;

---

[21] 42 C.F.R. §411.352(g).
[22] 42 C.F.R. §411.355(b).
[23] 42 C.F.R. §411.355(b)(1).

(3) an entity wholly owned by the performing or supervising physician or the physician's group practice; or

(4) an independent third-party billing company acting as an agent and billing under the physician or the physician's group practice billing number.[24]

The third concept, which relates to the locations where the DHS may be provided, is the most complicated and requires the most attention when structuring or analyzing a physician practice's compliance with the IOAS Exception. The exception states that referred DHS may be provided only in two alternative locations, the first being the "same building" (meaning the same street address), but not necessarily in the same space or part of the building, where the referring physician's "office" is located.[25] A physician will be deemed to have an "office" in the building if *one* of the conditions below is satisfied:

• The office is normally open at least 35 hours per week, and the physician (or one or more members of his or her group practice) regularly practices medicine and furnishes physician services (including at least some services unrelated to DHS) there at least 30 hours per week.

• The office is normally open at least eight hours per week, and the physician regularly practices medicine and furnishes physician services (including at least some services unrelated to DHS) there at least six hours per week. In addition, the building must be one in which the patient receiving the DHS usually sees the physician or other members of the physician's group practice.

• The office is normally open at least eight hours per week, and the physician (or one or more members of his or her group practice) regularly practices medicine and furnishes physician services (including at least some services unrelated to DHS) there at least six hours per week. In addition, either (1) the physician must be present and order the DHS in connection with a patient visit during the time the office is open in the building, or (2) the physician (or a member of his or her group practice) must be present while the DHS is furnished

---

[24]42 C.F.R. §411.355(b)(3).
[25]42 C.F.R. §411.355(b)(2); *see also* 42 C.F.R. §411.351.

during the time the office is open in the building. This test requires presence in the building, but not necessarily in the same space or part of the building.[26]

In lieu of meeting one of the same building tests, DHS may also be provided in a "centralized building" that is used by the referring physician or the referring physician's group practice to provide some or all of its DHS. A building will be deemed to be a centralized building if it is owned or leased on a full-time basis (that is, 24 hours per day, seven days per week, for a term of not less than six months) and used exclusively by the referring physician or the referring physician's group practice.[27]

As noted above, the IOAS Exception also includes specific patient disclosure requirements for physicians who provide in-office MRI, CT, or PET services. In particular, the IOAS Exception requires the physician referring the patient for the imaging service to inform patients, in writing, at the time the referral is made that the patient may receive the same services from a person other than the referring physician, a physician member of the same group practice as the referring physician, or someone directly supervised by the referring physician or another physician in the group practice. The exception goes on to require that the written notice include a list of at least five other suppliers that provide the imaging service for which the patient is being referred (including their name, address, and telephone number) within a 25-mile radius of the referring physician's office location. If there are fewer than five other suppliers located within this area, the physician must list all of the other suppliers of the imaging service that are present within the area (unless there are no other suppliers, in which case the written list of alternate suppliers is not required to be provided).[28]

C. Service Agreements / Independent Contractor Agreements

Physicians may be offered many opportunities throughout their careers to enter into various service agreements with DHS Entities, including but not limited to professional service agreements, medical director agreements, call coverage agreements, consulting

---

[26]42 C.F.R. §411.355(b)(2).
[27]42 C.F.R. §411.355(b)(2); *see also* 42 C.F.R. §411.351.
[28]42 C.F.R. §411.355(b)(7).

agreements, management agreements, and others. When these types of agreements are entered into between a DHS Entity and a physician on an independent contractor basis, they should typically be structured to comply with either the Personal Service Arrangements Exception or the Fair Market Value Exception to the Stark Law.[29] The key elements of these exceptions include, but are not limited to, the following:

- The arrangement must be in writing, signed by the parties, and specify the services covered.
- The services must be reasonable and necessary.
- The compensation must be *fair market value*,[30] set in advance, and not take into account the volume or value of any referrals or other business generated between the parties. Compensation will be considered to be "set in advance" if the aggregate compensation, a per-service rate, or a specific formula for calculating the compensation is set in the agreement before any services are provided.[31]
- The term of the agreement must be at least one year (or for a shorter time frame, provided that the parties do not terminate the agreement and enter into a replacement agreement for the same services within a one-year period).

While some of these requirements appear fairly innocuous, failure to comply with the strict terms of a Stark exception can have dire consequences, given the strict liability nature of the statute. Therefore, it is extremely important to have a complete understanding of the requirements of an applicable Stark Law exception when structuring any contractual arrangement between a DHS Entity and an independent physician.

---

[29]See 42 C.F.R. §411.357(d) and (l), respectively. Note that, in certain circumstances, the physician may be deemed to have an indirect financial relationship with the DHS Entity, in which case the arrangement should be structured in accordance with the Indirect Compensation Arrangement Exception available at 42 C.F.R. §411.357(p).

[30]Methods for determining fair market value will be discussed in Section V. of this chapter.

[31]*See* 42 C.F.R. §411.354(d).

D. Space Leases/Office Share Arrangements

As noted above with respect to service agreements, the Stark Law comes into play with respect to any financial relationship between physicians and the DHS Entities to which they refer, including relationships involving the lease of, license, or other right to use space. Generally, there are two exceptions that physicians and DHS Entities may potentially utilize for arrangements of this type, which are the Rental of Office Space Exception and the more recently implemented Timeshare Arrangement Exception.[32]

Before delving into an overview of these two exceptions, it is important to note that not all arrangements involving a third party's space, equipment, or staff would constitute a lease, license, or right of use arrangement. In many cases, the relevant inquiry is whether the party using the space or other resources is being conferred a benefit through use of such space or resources. For example, an employed physician using space, equipment, or staff provided by his or her employer under the physician's employment arrangement would not be considered to be leasing or licensing such items, as the employee is using these items for the benefit of his or her employer. Similarly, a physician practice that reassigns its right to bill for services to a hospital under a professional services agreement would not be considered to be leasing or licensing space, equipment, and staff provided by the hospital under the agreement to the extent it uses such resources to provide services to the hospital's patients. (Note, however, that in both this and the previous example, the employment and professional *service* relationship between the parties would need to meet an exception applicable to service agreements under the Stark Law.) In addition, CMS has indicated that in situations where a physician uses examination rooms, nursing personnel, and supplies of a DHS Entity, and the physician bills for the professional services and the hospital bills for a facility fee, there is no need for a lease arrangement or lease payment between the parties. In particular, CMS has stated:

> We do not believe that such an arrangement involves remuneration between the parties, because the physician and the DHS entity do not provide items, services, or other benefits to one another. Rather, the physician provides services to the patient and bills the payor for his or her services, and the DHS entity provides its resources and services

---

[32]42 C.F.R. §411.357(a), (y).

to the patient and bills the payor for the resources and services. There is no remuneration between the parties for the purposes of [the Stark Law].[33]

On the other hand, if a physician practice is utilizing a hospital-owned medical office building to run a full-time independent medical practice, then that use of space would likely be considered a lease arrangement that would need to comply with the Rental of Office Space Exception.

The Rental of Office Space Exception includes several strict requirements, including but not limited to the following:

- The lease must be set out in writing, signed by the parties, and specify the premises covered.
- The term of the lease must be at least one year.
- The space leased must be used *exclusively* by the lessee during the leased periods (except for certain shared common areas). Rental payments for any shared common areas must also be calculated in a certain manner.
- The rental payment must be set in advance, be consistent with fair market value, and not be determined in a manner that takes into account the volume or value of any referrals or other business generated between the parties. In addition, the rental payment may not be determined using a percentage-based or per-unit formula under certain circumstances.[34]

The exclusive-use requirement noted above can make structuring a space lease arrangement very difficult, particularly if the arrangement is a part-time lease or involves an office-sharing component. For example, if a DHS Entity's employed physicians will share space with an independent physician, the arrangement must be structured to meet the requirements noted above. This may require the parties to schedule in advance blocks of time during which they will each have exclusive use of exam and procedure rooms. Note that the parties would not need to have exclusive use of certain common areas, which CMS has indicated may include foyers, central waiting rooms, break rooms, vending areas, and hallways with limited

---

[33]Department of Health & Human Services, CMS, Medicare Program; Revisions to Payment Policies Under the Physician Fee Schedule and Other Revisions to Part B for CY 2016, 80 Fed. Reg. 70,886, 71,321 (Nov. 16, 2015).

[34]42 C.F.R. §411.357(a).

equipment that is not typically separately leased (e.g., scales).[35] However, any rental payments for common areas made by the lessee would need to be calculated in accordance with the specific requirements of the Rental of Office Space Exception.

Due to these difficulties, CMS has implemented an exception to the Stark Law for "timeshare arrangements." The Timeshare Arrangement Exception applies to part-time space use arrangements between physicians and hospitals, and addresses many of the concerns noted above for office sharing arrangements. The requirements of this exception include, without limitation, the following:

- The arrangement must be set out in writing, signed by the parties, and specify the premises covered.
- The arrangement may only be between a physician or the referring physician's practice and a hospital or unrelated physician practice.
- The premises, equipment, personnel, items, supplies, and services covered by the arrangement must be used predominantly for the provision of E/M services to patients and be provided on the same schedule.
- The equipment covered by the arrangement must be located in the same building where the E/M services are furnished, and may be used only to provide DHS that are incidental to the E/M services. In addition, the equipment cannot be advanced imaging equipment, radiation therapy equipment, or clinical or pathology lab equipment (other than equipment used to perform lab tests for which Clinical Laboratory Improvement Amendments (CLIA) requirements have been waived).
- The compensation under the arrangement must be set in advance, consistent with fair market value, and not determined in a manner that takes into account the volume or value of any referrals or other business generated between the parties. In addition, the compensation generally may not be determined using a percentage-based or per-unit formula.

[35]Department of Health & Human Services, Medicare Program; Physicians' Referrals to Health Care Entities With Which They Have Financial Relationships (Phase III), 72 Fed. Reg. 51,012, 51,045 (Sept. 5, 2007).

- The arrangement may not convey a possessory leasehold interest in the office space being used.[36]

IV. OVERVIEW OF THE FEDERAL ANTI-KICKBACK STATUTE

In addition to structuring their financial relationships to comply with the Stark Law, physicians should ensure that their financial relationships do not run afoul of the Anti-Kickback Statute. Unlike the Stark Law, the Anti-Kickback Statute is not limited to Medicare referrals for DHS between physicians and DHS Entities. Instead, it is potentially implicated by referrals for any type of federal healthcare program services (e.g., Medicare, Medicaid, TRICARE/CHAMPUS, Veterans Health Administration (VHA), etc.) made by physicians and non-physicians alike. In particular, the Anti-Kickback Statute makes it a civil and criminal offense to knowingly and willfully solicit or receive any remuneration in return for "purchasing, leasing, ordering, or arranging for or recommending purchasing, leasing, or ordering any good, facility, service, or item for which payment may be made in whole or in part under a Federal health care program."[37]

For purposes of the Anti-Kickback Statute, the term "remuneration" has been defined to include the transfer of anything of value, directly or indirectly, overtly or covertly, in cash or in kind. The statute has been interpreted to cover arrangements where just *one purpose* of the remuneration was to obtain money for the referral of services or to induce further referrals.[38] Violations of the Anti-Kickback Statute often relate to the failure to pay fair market value for items and services and can result in significant criminal and civil penalties, including criminal fines of up to $25,000 per violation, up to five years' imprisonment, or both. In addition, an Anti-Kickback Statute violation can result in civil monetary penalties of up to $50,000 per violation plus up to three times the total amount of remuneration offered, paid, solicited, or received; exclusion from participation in Medicare, Medicaid, and other federal government healthcare programs; or both.[39] Therefore, it is important to ensure that any contractual arrangements involving payments to potential

---

[36]42 C.F.R. §411.357(y).

[37]42 U.S.C. §1320a-7b(b)(1)(B).

[38]*See* United States v. Kats, 871 F.2d 105 (9th Cir. 1989); United States v. Greber, 760 F.2d 68 (3rd Cir.), *cert. denied*, 474 U.S. 988 (1985).

[39]*See* 42 U.S.C. §§1320a-7a(a), 42 U.S.C. §1320a-7b(b).

federal healthcare program referral sources do not implicate the Anti-Kickback Statute.

Due to the broad nature of the Anti-Kickback Statute, the Office of Inspector General (OIG) has promulgated various "safe harbors" designed to protect certain types of arrangements, provided that specific conditions are met. Some of the safe harbors, such as the Employees Safe Harbor, are relatively easy to meet.[40] In other cases, the safe harbors track the requirements of the corresponding exception to the Stark Law. Other safe harbors relevant to healthcare service contracts contain stringent requirements that make them difficult to satisfy. For example, the Personal Services and Management Contracts Safe Harbor requires, among other things, that the *aggregate* compensation paid under an independent contractor agreement be a fixed amount for each one-year term of the agreement.[41] This type of compensation structure can be very difficult to implement in many service agreements when the services are provided in a manner more in line with a per-service rate or other variable methodology, for which the total annual aggregate compensation may not be determined up front.

Unlike the need to meet an exception under the Stark Law due to its strict liability nature, it is not necessarily fatal if a particular arrangement does not meet every element of the applicable safe harbor. This is because the Anti-Kickback Statute is an intent-based statute, which means that the parties must have provided remuneration with the *intent* to induce or reward referrals of federal healthcare program business for a violation to occur. Therefore, failure to satisfy a safe harbor does not necessarily mean that the arrangement violates the Anti-Kickback Statute, unless the requisite intent to violate the statute is also present.

When structuring arrangements where one or both parties is a referral source of federal healthcare program business, care should be taken to ensure that none of the parties have any intent—meaning not one purpose—to induce or reward referrals or otherwise violate the Anti-Kickback Statute. In addition, it would be beneficial to structure the arrangement to meet as many elements of an applicable safe harbor as possible in order to help demonstrate the appropriate

---

[40]*See* 42 C.F.R. §1001.952(i). Note that the Employees Safe Harbor to the Anti-Kickback Statute simply requires a bona fide employment agreement, which has generally been interpreted to require fair market value compensation.

[41]42 C.F.R. §1001.952(d).

intent of the parties. At the very least, the parties to any arrangement involving the provision of services by a referral source should ensure that compensation for the services is consistent with fair market value. When determining intent and the propriety of an arrangement between entities that refer to one another, the OIG has indicated that it will typically focus its attention on whether the payment or other benefit provided under the arrangement is consistent with fair market value for the items or services provided in the absence of any referrals.[42]

V. WHAT IS "FAIR MARKET VALUE"?

As discussed above, fair market value is a key requirement of many exceptions to the Stark Law and safe harbors to the Anti-Kickback Statute. The Stark Law defines "fair market value" to mean "the value in arm's-length transactions, consistent with the general market value."[43] "General market value" is defined to mean "the compensation that would be included in a service agreement as the result of *bona fide* bargaining between well-informed parties to the agreement who are not otherwise in a position to generate business for the other party … at the time of the service agreement."[44] Fair market value usually will be "the compensation that has been included in *bona fide* service agreements with comparable terms at the time of the agreement, where the price or compensation has not been determined in any manner that takes into account the volume or value of anticipated or actual referrals."[45]

In commentary to the Stark Law regulations, CMS has stated that "reference to multiple, objective, independently published salary surveys remains a prudent practice for evaluating fair market value."[46] However, CMS has also indicated that salary surveys are not the only means to establish fair market value. CMS specifically stated that:

---

[42]See OIG, Special Fraud Alert: Laboratory Payments to Referring Physicians (June 25, 2014).

[43]42 C.F.R. §411.351.

[44]*Id.*

[45]*Id.*

[46]Department of Health & Human Services, Medicare Program; Physicians' Referrals to Health Care Entities With Which They Have Financial Relationships (Phase III), 72 Fed. Reg. 51,012, 51,015 (Sept. 5, 2007).

nothing precludes parties from calculating fair market value using any commercially reasonable methodology that is appropriate under the circumstances and otherwise fits the definition at section 1877(h) of the Act and § 411.351. Ultimately, fair market value is determined based on facts and circumstances. The appropriate method will depend on the nature of the transaction, its location and other factors.[47]

CMS also indicated that "although a good faith reliance on an independent valuation (such as an appraisal) may be relevant to a party's intent, it does not establish the ultimate issue of the accuracy of the valuation figure itself."[48] Therefore, the relevant inquiry appears to be whether the fair market value determined by an independent valuation is supportable, not whether or not a valuation was obtained in the first place. This provides valuable insight in that (1) an independent valuation is not required to support the fair market value of an arrangement, and possibly more importantly, (2) the act of obtaining an independent valuation in and of itself does not mean an arrangement is consistent with fair market value.

In addition to the guidance provided by CMS with respect to the Stark Law, the OIG has issued guidance regarding the meaning of fair market value in conjunction with its advisory opinion process.[49] When an entity requests an advisory opinion from the OIG, it is encouraged to answer a set of preliminary questions published by the OIG in connection with such request, including answering whether or not the remuneration involved with the transaction was consistent with fair market value. The preliminary questions define fair market value to mean "the value that would be assigned to the item or service in question by individuals or entities who have an arm's-length relationship and who have no ability to influence referrals of any health care business to each other."[50] It is important to note that even though the OIG has provided a definition of fair market value in the preliminary questions, it is not permitted to provide an opinion on whether remuneration described in an advisory opinion request

---

[47]*Id.* at 51,015–16.

[48]*Id.* at 51,015.

[49]An "advisory opinion" is a legal opinion issued by the OIG to a requesting party about the application of the Anti-Kickback Statute (or other fraud and abuse laws under the purview of the OIG) to an existing or proposed business arrangement of the party.

[50]Recommended Preliminary Questions and Supplementary Information for Addressing Requests for OIG Advisory Opinions In Accordance With Section 1128D of the Social Security Act and 42 CFR Part 1008, http://oig.hhs.gov/fraud/docs/advisoryopinions/prequestions.htm.

actually constitutes fair market value. In fact, the OIG is precluded by statute from issuing an advisory opinion that speaks to "[w]hether the fair market value shall be, or was paid or received for any goods, services or property."[51]

In addition to guidance contained in the advisory opinion procedures, the OIG has indicated in its Supplemental Compliance Program Guidance for Hospitals ("Compliance Guidance") that

> [t]he general rule of thumb is that any remuneration flowing between hospitals and physicians should be at fair market value for actual and necessary items furnished or services rendered based upon an arm's-length transaction and should not take into account, directly or indirectly, the value or volume of any past or future referrals or other business generated between the parties.[52]

The Compliance Guidance also gives specific factors that hospitals should consider when assessing fair market value, including but not limited to the following:

- Are the items and services obtained from a physician legitimate, commercially reasonable, and necessary to achieve a legitimate business purpose of the hospital (apart from obtaining referrals)? Assuming that the hospital needs the items and services, does the hospital have multiple agreements with different physicians, so that in the aggregate the items or services provided by all physicians exceed the hospital's actual needs (apart from generating business)?

- Does the compensation represent fair market value in an arm's-length transaction for the items and services? Could the hospital obtain the services from a nonreferral source at a cheaper rate or under more favorable terms? Does the remuneration take into account, directly or indirectly, the value or volume of any past or future referrals or other business generated between the parties? Is the compensation tied, directly or indirectly, to Federal health care program reimbursement?

- Is the determination of fair market value based upon a reasonable methodology that is uniformly applied and properly documented? If fair market value is based on comparables, the hospital should ensure that the market rate for the comparable

---

[51]42 U.S.C. §1320a-7d(b)(3)(A).
[52]Department of Health & Human Services, OIG Supplemental Compliance Guidance for Hospitals, 70 Fed. Reg. 4858, 4866 (Jan. 31, 2005).

service is not distorted (*e.g.*, the market for ancillary services may be distorted if all providers of the service are controlled by physicians).

• Is the compensation commensurate with the fair market value of a physician with the skill level and experience reasonably necessary to perform the contracted services?[53]

These factors are important considerations in determining whether compensation is fair market value. If any of these factors is called into question with respect to a proposed compensation arrangement, then the arrangement would likely be suspect under the Anti-Kickback Statute.

VI. STATE LAWS RELATED TO SELF-REFERRALS AND KICKBACKS

In addition to the Stark Law and Anti-Kickback Statute, some states have implemented their own specific laws and regulations regarding self-referrals and kickbacks that may have similar or additional requirements for service agreements as those noted above. While a comprehensive review of state laws is beyond the scope of this chapter, it is important to remember that applicable state law should always be consulted when structuring a service agreement or other relationship involving healthcare providers and their potential referral sources in order to determine whether any state-level requirements must be met.

---

[53]*Id.* at 4866–67.

Chapter 27

CONFLICT RESOLUTION THROUGH MEDIATION OR ARBITRATION

I. INTRODUCTION

Healthcare employee conflicts should be resolved amicably and constructively. But experience teaches that a small percentage of such conflicts will require external decisionmakers to become involved. This chapter addresses the mediation and arbitration methods for resolving these conflicts.

II. DRAWING THE CONTRAST: CHOOSING AMONG METHODS OF CONFLICT RESOLUTIOn

Counsel needs to consult with the client when deciding whether to mediate, arbitrate, or litigate. There is no single "right way" to resolve a pending dispute.

Let's summarize the options as we would for a doctor or other professional client. At a mediation, the parties decide whether to settle and what to pay. At an arbitration, a neutral outsider decides which party wins and how much compensation is due, and that decision is final and binding. Once in litigation, virtually all cases settle rather than undergo the judge and jury decision processes (including hearings, motion practice, and trial), which otherwise could eat up the available funds as the parties wait for several years to receive a final judicial award (or no award).

Mediation is fastest. The parties negotiate a settlement of a dispute in an informal and usually confidential situation, with a mediator going between the parties. The settlement contract entered into at the end of the negotiations is binding. The process takes one-half to one day to accomplish, and is an inexpensive method to resolve a case. When the settlement documents are signed, the matter is over and there are no other proceedings, discovery, or appeals.

At an arbitration, the proceedings are private, with no visitors or observers, and the arbitration hearing proceeds based upon an agreement to rules that the parties had accepted in their original contract. For example, the American Arbitration Association rules to resolve disputes may have been referenced in the contract clause in the parties' employment agreement.[1] The arbitration result is usually final. That finality can be binding, depending on the rules that have been stipulated by the parties or stated in a clause of the contract in dispute. The arbitration can be held quickly. Once an arbitrator is chosen, the parties are ready, and limited discovery and hearing preparation is completed, the arbitration hearing usually lasts one to two days. Arbitration is both less expensive and less formal than a trial.

Litigation is tried to a judge or a jury. The proceedings are open to the public and are not confidential. The verdict is binding, but the parties may appeal the final verdict to a higher court. There is no trial until all of the pretrial document discovery is conducted, many motions are heard, trial preparation is completed, and the judge orders a trial date, which all can take up to two years, depending on the court. The actual trial may last a week or more, is formal, and follows the court's rigid rules of procedure. The litigation option can be very

---

[1] The American Arbitration Association website, https://www.adr.org, has considerable background information that may be useful for client education.

expensive due to the cost of experts and witnesses, delays that occur in the judge's schedule, and the attorney fees.

Confidentiality is one important factor for parties to consider when deciding whether to mediate or arbitrate a matter. Unlike mediation and arbitration, litigation is not private and creates a public record. In a mediation or arbitration, the negotiations are not revealed by either party, and the plaintiff usually executes a confidential settlement forbidding discussion of the amount and terms of the settlement.

Before deciding which approach to take, each party's attorneys must know their side of the case. They should undertake an objective assessment regarding the pros and cons of taking the matter to trial, and the likely worth of an award for the claim, before choosing to mediate, arbitrate, or litigate the matter.

III. Pre-Arbitration Procedures

A. Nature of Arbitration

Arbitration is a form of alternative dispute resolution that is widely used to avoid trials. Many employment contracts that doctors sign contain arbitration clauses stipulating that the parties must resort to arbitration rather than litigation to resolve disputes. Such clauses are also found in collective bargaining agreements, employment contracts, business deals, and shareholder agreements. Arbitration may be the best approach to resolution if neither side is willing or able to make concessions. Arbitration awards do not create legal precedent, so the award typically only binds the parties to the specific dispute and can be confidential.

Arbitrations can be arranged in any manner chosen by the parties. The parties enter into an arbitration agreement, which is a contract outlining the procedures and timeline for the arbitration. The individual who will act as arbitrator is selected from a list. See Section III.A, below, for further discussion of arbitrator selection.

Some state and federal courts require the use of pre-trial mandatory arbitrations, which are non-binding and are based upon the economic worth of the claim. In a court-affiliated arbitration, the parties may appeal to the court for a trial de novo if they are dissatisfied with the arbitration award. The party requesting the trial de novo must pay the other side's costs if their ultimate cash award does not exceed the arbitration award amount.

B. The Arbitration Agreement

Before the arbitration can begin, the parties must prepare and sign an arbitration agreement. The final agreement should include a summary of the issues to be decided by the arbitrator and all arbitration deadlines. The arbitrator will rule only on those issues that are listed in the arbitration agreement.

The final arbitration agreement must be completed and executed at a prehearing conference, or shortly thereafter. When completed, the original final arbitration agreement is given to the local administrator for the mandatory arbitration program, if one exists, or the original is sent to the arbitrator. The agreement serves as a binding contract, although it is not filed with any court.

Sample arbitration agreement forms can be found at most court websites and at the websites of the American Arbitration Association[2] and the American Health Lawyers Association.[3]

C. Selecting an Arbitrator

The parties must select an arbitrator as they are preparing the arbitration agreement. Many states and third-party neutral organizations maintain lists of qualified and experienced attorneys to choose as an arbitrator. Usually, the courts and the organizations offering arbitration services will set a deadline by which the parties must agree upon an arbitrator.

When the parties cannot agree on an arbitrator in a mandatory court-ordered arbitration, a list of potential arbitrators will be provided by the court to the parties, who then will each strike two of the five possible arbitrators from the list. This results in the selection of an arbitrator who will hear the matter.

Selection of the decision maker is a key difference between contractual arbitration and litigation. In court, each case is assigned randomly to a judge. The motions and trial will be heard by a judge, who may have had no experience in trying a lawsuit dealing with

---

[2]*See Rules, Forms, Fees*, AMERICAN ARBITRATION ASSOCIATION, https://adr.org/Forms.

[3]AMERICAN HEALTH LAWYERS ASSOCIATION, https://www.healthlawyers.org.

healthcare issues. Certainly, a jury is not expected to understand the complexity of health law. But in an arbitration, the parties will typically select an arbitrator who is experienced in health law and who is qualified to devise a remedy that makes sense in the particular case. By selecting an experienced and qualified arbitrator, the parties will save money, will make the hearing less argumentative, and will benefit from the arbitrator's practical understanding of the health care field.

A tool that is very effective for arbitrator selection is provided by the Bloomberg BNA Analytics Service, in the form of the Labor Arbitration Award Navigator,[4] which provides parties the ability to evaluate arbitrators and discover trends.

D. Paying the Arbitrator

The parties should discuss payment arrangements with the arbitrator at a pre-hearing conference. Most of the time, the parties agree that the compensation fee for the arbitrator is to be split evenly between the parties. The arbitrator is compensated for his or her time spent in the hearing, in reviewing evidence, and in writing the final order. The arbitrator is also reimbursed for reasonable expenses such as mileage, hotels, and meals. Organizations that sponsor arbitrations establish the hourly fees for the arbitrator.

E. Preparing for the Arbitration Hearing

Pursuant to Rules of Civil Procedure for each jurisdiction, the parties are responsible for issuing and serving any subpoenas needed to compel the appearance of witnesses at an arbitration hearing or for obtaining documentary evidence.

Exchange and preparation of exhibits is less formal than in litigation. Parties can share information at any time. The parties may perform limited discovery before the arbitration, which then can be presented at the hearing as evidence. Copies of documentary evidence and written notice of a party's intent to offer them must be served on opposing parties prior to the arbitration hearing, usually on a certain date set forth in the final arbitration agreement.

Parties may object to the admission of any piece of evidence into the record, but objections must be served on the other parties

---

[4]See the Bloomberg BNA website at https://www.bna.com.

before the hearing. Although neither the notices nor the objections need to be filed with a court, a copy of the item with a proof of service should be sent to the arbitrator.

Each party must mark its own hearing exhibits and should prepare marked copies of the exhibits for the arbitrator and opposing parties.

IV. THE ARBITRATION HEARING

A. Hearing Procedures

All parties and their counsel should be present to participate in the arbitration hearing. The arbitrator may proceed with the hearing in the absence of any party who received written notice of the hearing but does not appear.

The arbitrator determines the mode and order of presentation of issues, arguments, and evidence. The process is less formal than a court trial. The arbitrator will decide only those issues covered in the arbitration agreement (absent a stipulation by the parties to also reach other issues). The parties can stipulate that a witness or party will not need to appear at the arbitration, or a motion can be made to the arbitrator to determine if a party must attend the hearing.

The hearing is conducted in general conformity with the applicable state or federal Rules of Evidence. However, the arbitrator may receive evidence that is generally inadmissible in a court if the arbitrator finds the evidence relevant and trustworthy and not unfairly prejudicial to any party against whom it is offered. The plaintiff presents its case first and, with the arbitrator's approval, may reserve a limited time for a reply after the defendant's presentation. The arbitrator will enforce previously established time limits for each side's presentation. Absent extenuating circumstances, the hearing should be completed in one to two days.

B. The Arbitration Award

At the conclusion of the hearing, the arbitrator may choose to orally announce the award. A party must ask for a written decision in the arbitration agreement or at the beginning of the arbitration. In practice, an arbitrator is required to file a written arbitration award pursuant to most arbitration rules or arbitration agreements. Usually the written award must be produced within 30 days after the hearing and copies of the award are distributed to the parties by the arbitrator or administrator. Any party who intends to ask for a trial de novo must obtain a copy of the final decision and provide it to the coordinator of the mandatory arbitration program or to the court, where the decision is retained in a sealed non-public file.

The decision whether to divulge the reasons for a monetary award lies within the discretion of the arbitrator. When an arbitrator finds that equitable or other non-monetary relief is appropriate, the arbitrator should require the parties to obtain court approval of such award, if the arbitration was part of the court process. This is not a necessary step for non-court arbitrations. In non-court arbitrations, the enforcement of the final award proceeds under state laws or the Federal Arbitration Act.

In cases where the court has sent the matter to arbitration and the parties have stipulated to binding arbitration, the arbitration award is final and a judgment will be entered on the award by the court. Recommendations for equitable relief are awarded if approved by the court. If the parties did not stipulate to binding arbitration, the parties will have 30 days to file a demand for a trial de novo.

If any party demands a trial de novo, the award is vacated and the case is returned to litigation. However, if the clerk does not receive a request for trial de novo within a 30-day period, a judgment will be entered on the award. The party requesting the trial de novo must pay the other party's costs of the trial if the requesting party does not improve their economic position after a trial. For example, a party who received an arbitration award of $10,000 and then requested a de novo trial, receiving a jury award of $8,000, would be required to pay for the trial costs that otherwise would have fallen on the defending side.

In most cases, the arbitrator closes the record and addresses all claims raised in the arbitration order. The arbitrator may keep the record open at the end of the hearing for a number of reasons, including to accept additional documentary evidence that was unavailable at the hearing; to allow the parties a final opportunity to argue their positons in writing; or to receive briefs on a specific issue that may have come up during the hearing.

V. MEDIATION

Mediation is voluntary and requires the agreement and cooperation of both parties. The potential for settlement is enhanced when the parties seek to resolve the claim with a minimum of expenses and acrimony. If mediation is successful, it will result in a settlement of a lawsuit without the parties having to arbitrate or go to trial.

The parties agree upon a mediator, who may be trained in mediation or be a former judge. The medical context for mediation is typical: the health care defendant must have money to resolve the patient/plaintiff's claim and the physician must consent to settle before mediation can occur. Once the parties have selected a mediator, the mediation can be scheduled within weeks or months. It is typically a one-day process at a chosen location, such as the mediator's office.

At the mediation, the parties discuss the discovery that has been conducted before the mediation and what else needs to be performed. They also examine the position of the parties, the expert witnesses, the monetary demands of the plaintiff, and the requests of both parties to resolve the matter. If the plaintiff agrees to settle, the parties sign a contract requiring each of them to do certain actions as part of the settlement. There is no appeal and the lawsuit or dispute is resolved. If a settlement agreement is reached, the matter is resolved with less expense than through arbitration or litigation, and both sides are generally satisfied with the mediation process and the settlement. Some mediations, however, end in an impasse, often because of inflated and unrealistic client or attorney expectations. Then the claim must be resolved through arbitration or litigation.

CHAPTER 28

FUTURE TRENDS

The demographic trends in healthcare employment are frightening, especially for those patients who face chronic illness and long-term needs for medical care. In the coming years, the United States will have fewer physicians than needed, and fewer nurses than needed, and there is a demographic slant away from lower-skilled healthcare professionals who deliver bedside care.

Doctors are leaving active professional service, driven away by issues such as the documentation and enumeration hassles. "The burden of bureaucracy may also explain why so many physicians, when asked what they plan to do with their career in the next few years, anticipate either reducing their time in clinic or switching to alternative practice models, like concierge care, that reduce bureaucratic hassles."[1] The slight increases in physician numbers compared to the large increases in aging residents makes for a graphic visualization of pressures on the medical profession.[2]

From 2014 to 2024, the Bureau of Labor Statistics (BLS) projects the healthcare industry to grow by 19 percent, adding about 2.3 million jobs to the economy.[3] The Affordable Care Act has increased demand for healthcare services among insured persons, just as the baby boomer population begins to leave the workforce. In Montana, for example, that state's healthcare industry is expected to grow by 1.8 percent each year, or 1,300 jobs annually, until 2024, but data suggests there will not be enough people to fill those positions.[4]

---

[1]Peter Ubel, M.D., *Doctors Are Facing Incredible Bureaucratic Hassles— But Healthcare Leaders Could Take Steps to Cut the Paperwork Burden*, MODERN HEALTHCARE (Aug. 31, 2016).

[2]*Chartbook: Trends Affecting Hospitals and Health Systems*, AMERICAN HOSPITAL ASSOCIATION, ch. 5, chart 5.1, http://www.aha.org/research/reports/tw/chartbook/2016/chapter5.pdf.

[3]Statistics are available at the BLS website, https://www.bls.gov.

[4]Maria Castelluci, *Montana Projects Healthcare Labor Shortage in 10 Years*, MODERN HEALTHCARE (May 24, 2016).

The immigration changes of the Trump Administration may have an impact on that inflow of qualified and willing workers from other nations.

A *Modern Healthcare* magazine interview with nursing thought leaders produced a concise expert opinion:

We're graduating about 150,000 nurses per year, and we expect those numbers to go up. (But) we also know the demand is going to go up. Our biggest concern right now is that in pockets across the country many nurses are telling us that they are very understaffed, and we know that that creates a serious risk for patients.[5]

Employer responses to dissatisfaction vary tremendously, from the largest urban hospital groups to the local retail store's "mini-clinic" nursing stations.[6] On the physician side of healthcare employment, staffing trends demonstrate a shortfall in licensed physicians and a trend of displacing physicians who were direct hospital employees with the equivalent of temporary contract doctors who work for staffing companies as a hospital cost savings.[7]

---

[5]P. Cipriano, *Interview*, MODERN HEALTHCARE 20 (Jan. 16, 2017).

[6]V. Lelli et al., *Retail Clinics Versus Traditional Primary Care: Employee Satisfaction Guaranteed?*, 27 J. AM. ASS'N OF NURSE PRACTITIONERS no. 9, at 514–20 (Sept. 2015).

[7]D. Barkholz, *Herding Hospital Docs: Staffing Firms Buy MD Groups*, MODERN HEALTHCARE (Dec. 12, 2015).

Appendices

TABLE OF STATUTES AND
CASE LAW BY STATE

This appendix is an update to *Restrictive Covenants in Physician Employment Relationships* © 2013, published by the American Health Lawyers Association, and used with permission. The article in which the original 2013 appendix appeared is 8 Robert W. Horton, Esq., *Restrictive Covenants in Physician Employment Relationships*, AM. HEALTH L. ASS'N. Apr. 2013, available at http://www.bassberry.com/~/media/Files/Publications/2013/05/AHLA.

This appendix is provided for guidance only and is not a substitute for checking the primary state statute sources, state case law or consulting a comprehensive source such as Brian M. Malsberger's *Covenants Not to Compete: A State-by-State Survey* (11th ed. 2017), with annual updates, which is a thorough compilation of:

- the latest state statutes, latest case law (often down to the trial court level and identified by the worker's profession), and summaries on such matters as:
- what an employer's protectable business interest is and how that is defined;
- who has the burden of proof that the restraint is reasonable and no greater than necessary to protect the employer's legitimate business interest;
- judicial findings as to reasonableness or unreasonableness of covenants not to compete;
- what time or geographic restrictions the courts in the specific jurisdiction have found to be reasonable or unreasonable;
- whether continued employment will support a covenant not to compete after an employment relationship starts;
- developments as to what the employer must prove to obtain a preliminary injunction to enforce a covenant not to compete;

- the elements of proof for irreparable harm;
- whether the courts in the state will 'blue pencil' the contract provision or not;
- whether liquidated damages will be enforced;
- what must the employer prove to obtain a preliminary injunction enforcing a covenant not to compete?
- If the employer terminates the employment relationship is the covenant enforceable?
- what rule the state applies when considering a choice of law provision in a covenant not to compete;
- assignment of employment agreements as it affects covenants not to compete; successor employers; attorney's fees; etc.

Please always check primary statutes and case authority sources!

I. STATES WITH STATUTES SPECIFICALLY REGARDING PHYSICIAN RESTRICTIVE COVENANTS

State & Statute	Statute Language
Colorado Colo. Rev. Stat. § 8-2-113	Any covenant not to compete provision of an employment, partnership, or corporate agreement between physicians which restricts the right of a physician to practice medicine, as defined in section 12-36-106, C.R.S., upon termination of such agreement, shall be void; except that all other provisions of such an agreement enforceable at law, including provisions which require the payment of damages in an amount that is reasonably related to the injury suffered by reason of termination of the agreement, shall be enforceable. Provisions which require the payment of damages upon termination of the agreement may include, but not be limited to, damages related to competition.
Connecticut Conn. Gen. Stat. 20-14p. (eff. July 1, 2016)	**Covenants not to compete involving physician.** (a) For purposes of this section: (1) "Covenant not to compete" means any provision of an employment or other contract or agreement that creates or establishes a professional relationship with a physician and restricts the right of a physician to practice medicine in any geographic area of the state for any period of time after the termination or cessation of such partnership, employment or other professional relationship; (2) "physician" means an individual licensed to practice medicine under this chapter; and (3) "primary site where such physician practices" means (A) the office, facility or location where a majority of the revenue derived from such physician's services is generated, or (B) any other office, facility or location where such physician practices

State & Statute	Statute Language
Connecticut (con't) CONN. GEN. STAT. 20-14p. (eff. July 1, 2016)	and mutually agreed to by the parties and identified in the covenant not to compete. (b) (1) A covenant not to compete is valid and enforceable only if it is: (A) Necessary to protect a legitimate business interest; (B) reasonably limited in time, geographic scope and practice restrictions as necessary to protect such business interest; and (C) otherwise consistent with the law and public policy. The party seeking to enforce a covenant not to compete shall have the burden of proof in any proceeding. (2) A covenant not to compete that is entered into, amended, extended or renewed on or after July 1, 2016, shall not: (A) Restrict the physician's competitive activities (i) for a period of more than one year, and (ii) in a geographic region of more than fifteen miles from the primary site where such physician practices; or (B) be enforceable against a physician if (i) such employment contract or agreement was not made in anticipation of, or as part of, a partnership or ownership agreement and such contract or agreement expires and is not renewed, unless, prior to such expiration, the employer makes a bona fide offer to renew the contract on the same or similar terms and conditions, or (ii) the employment or contractual relationship is terminated by the employer, unless such employment or contractual relationship is terminated for cause. (3) Each covenant not to compete entered into, amended or renewed on and after July 1, 2016, shall be separately and individually signed by the physician.

State & Statute	Statute Language
Connecticut (con't) CONN. GEN. STAT. 20-14p. (eff. July 1, 2016)	(c) The remaining provisions of any contract or agreement that includes a covenant not to compete that is rendered void and unenforceable, in whole or in part, under the provisions of this section shall remain in full force and effect, including provisions that require the payment of damages resulting from any injury suffered by reason of termination of such contract or agreement.
Delaware 6 DEL. CODE ANN. § 2707 (eff. July 13, 1983)	Any covenant not to compete provision of an employment, partnership or corporate agreement between and/or among physicians which restricts the right of a physician to practice medicine in a particular locale and/or for a defined period of time, upon the termination of the principal agreement of which the said provision is a part, shall be void; except that all other provisions of such an agreement shall be enforceable at law, including provisions which require the payment of damages in an amount that is reasonably related to the injury suffered by reason of termination of the principal agreement. Provisions which require the payment of damages upon termination of the principal agreement may include, but not be limited to, damages related to competition.
Massachusetts MASS. GEN. LAW CH. 112, § 12X (eff. Nov. 23, 1977)	Section 12X. Restrictive covenants upon physicians rendered unenforceable. Any contract or agreement which creates or establishes the terms of a partnership, employment, or any other form of professional relationship with a physician registered to practice medicine pursuant to section two, which includes any restriction of the right of such physician to practice medicine in any geographic area for any period of time after the termination of such partnership, employment or

State & Statute	Statute Language
Massachusetts (con't) MASS. GEN. LAW CH. 112, §12X (eff. Nov. 23, 1977)	professional relationship shall be void and unenforceable with respect to said restriction; provided, however, that nothing herein shall render void or unenforceable the remaining provisions of any such contract or agreement.
New Hampshire N. H. Rev. Stat. Ann § 329:31-a (eff. Aug. 5, 2016)	**Certain Contract Restrictions upon Physicians Unenforceable**. Any contract or agreement which creates or establishes the terms of a partnership, employment, or any other form of professional relationship with a physician licensed by the board to practice in this state, which includes any restriction to the right of such physician to also practice medicine in any geographic area for any period of time after the termination of such partnership, employment, or professional relationship shall be void and unenforceable with respect to said restriction; provided however, that nothing herein shall render void or unenforceable the remaining provision of any such contract or agreement. The requirements of this section shall apply to new contracts or renewals of contracts entered into on or after the effective date of this section.
New Mexico New Mexico Statutes Annotated §§ 24-1I-1 through 24-1I-5	As used in Chapter 24, Article 1I NM Stat. Definitions (2016 Edition): A. "agreement" means a written contract to which a health care practitioner is a party; and B. "health care practitioner" means: (1) a dentist; (2) an osteopathic physician; (3) a physician; (4) a podiatrist; (5) a certified registered nurse anesthetist; (6) a certified nurse practitioner; and (7) a certified nurse-midwife.

State & Statute	Statute Language
New Mexico (con't) New Mexico Statutes Annotated §§ 24-1I-1 through 24-1I-5	**NM Stat. 24-1I-2** Enforceability of a Non-compete Provision--other Provisions Void. (New Mexico Statutes (2016 Edition)) A. A non-compete provision in an agreement, which provision restricts the right of a health care practitioner to provide clinical health care services in this state, shall be unenforceable upon the termination of: (1) the agreement; (2) a renewal or extension of the agreement; or (3) a health care practitioner's employment with a party seeking to enforce the agreement. B. A provision in an agreement for clinical health care services to be rendered in this state is void, unenforceable and against public policy if the provision: (1) makes the agreement subject to the laws of another state; or (2) requires any litigation arising out of the agreement to be conducted in another state. **NM Stat. 24-1I-3** Enforceability of other provisions. (New Mexico Statutes (2016 Edition)) Nothing in this act shall be construed to limit the enforceability of: A. a provision in an agreement requiring a health care practitioner who has worked for an employer for an initial period of less than three years to repay all or a portion of: (1) a loan; (2) relocation expenses; (3) a signing bonus or other remuneration to induce the health care practitioner to relocate or establish a health care practice in a specified geographic area; or (4) recruiting, education and training expenses;

State & Statute	Statute Language
New Mexico (con't) New Mexico Statutes Annotated §§ 24-1I-1 through 24-1I-5	B. a nondisclosure provision relating to confidential information and trade secrets; C. a nonsolicitation provision with respect to patients and employees of the party seeking to enforce the agreement for a period of one year or less after the last date of employment; or D. any other provision of an agreement that is not in violation of law, including a provision for liquidated damages. **NM Stat. 24-1I-4 Liquidated damages.** (New Mexico Statutes (2016 Edition)) A. An agreement may provide for liquidated damages in an amount that is reasonable at the time the agreement is executed and in light of anticipated harm and difficulty of proving the amount of loss resulting from breach of the agreement by any party. B. A provision in an agreement fixing unreasonably large liquidated damages is void as a penalty. **NM Stat. 24-1I-5 Applicability.** (New Mexico Statutes (2016 Edition)) A. Chapter 24, Article 1I NMSA 1978 does not apply to agreements between health care practitioners who are shareholders, owners, partners or directors of a health care practice. B. Except as provided by Subsection C of this section, the provisions of Chapter 24, Article 1I NMSA 1978 apply to agreements, or renewals or extensions of agreements, executed on or after July 1, 2015. C. The provisions of Subsection B of Section 24-1I-2 NMSA 1978 apply to agreements, or renewals or extensions of agreements, executed on or after the effective date of this 2017 act.

State & Statute	Statute Language
Rhode Island (R.I. GEN. LAWS §5-37-33) (eff. July 12, 2016)	**§ 5-37-33 Restrictive covenants.** (a) Any contract or agreement that creates or establishes the terms of a partnership, employment, or any other form of professional relationship with a physician licensed to practice medicine pursuant to this chapter that includes any restriction of the right of such physician to practice medicine shall be void and unenforceable with respect to said restriction; provided, however, that nothing herein shall render void or unenforceable the remaining provisions of any such contract or agreement. (b) Restrictions rendered void under subsection (a) of this section shall include, but shall not be limited to, the following: (1) The right to practice medicine in any geographic area for any period of time after the termination of such partnership, employment, or professional relationship; and (2) The right of such physician to provide treatment, advise, consult with, or establish a physician/patient relationship with any current patient of the employer; and (3) The right of such physician to solicit or seek to establish a physician/patient relationship with any current patient of the employer. (c) Notwithstanding the foregoing, the prohibition on physician covenants shall not apply in connection with the purchase and sale of a physician practice, provided the restrictive covenant and/or non-compete covenant is for a period of time of no more than five (5) years.

State & Statute	Statute Language
Tennessee TENN. CODE ANN. §§ 63-1-148, 68-11-205, 63-6-204(f)(2)	TENN. CODE ANN. § 63-1-148: (a) (1) A restriction on the right of an employed or contracted healthcare provider to practice the healthcare provider's profession upon termination or conclusion of the employment or contractual relationship shall be deemed reasonable if: (A) The restriction is set forth in an employment agreement or other written document signed by the healthcare provider and the employing or contracting entity; and (B) The duration of the restriction is two (2) years or less and either: (i) The maximum allowable geographic restriction is the greater of: (a) A ten-mile radius from the primary practice site of the healthcare provider while employed or contracted; or (b) The county in which the primary practice of the healthcare provider while employed or contracted is located; or (ii) There is no geographic restriction, but the healthcare provider is restricted from practicing the healthcare provider's profession at any facility at which the employing or contracting entity provided services while the healthcare provider was employed or contracted with the employing or contracting entity. (b) An agreement entered into in conjunction with the purchase or sale of a healthcare provider's practice, or all or substantially all of the assets of the healthcare provider's practice, may restrict the healthcare provider's right to practice the healthcare provider's profession; provided, that the duration of the restriction and the allowable area of the restriction are

State & Statute	**Statute Language**
Tennessee (con't) Tenn. Code Ann. §§ 63-1-148, 68-11-205, 63-6-204(f)(2)	reasonable under the circumstances. There shall be a rebuttable presumption that the duration and area of restriction agreed upon by the parties in such an agreement are reasonable.

(c) This section shall apply to healthcare providers licensed under chapters 3, 4, 5, 6, 8, 9 and 11 of this title.

(d) This section shall not apply to physicians who specialize in the practice of emergency medicine.

[Emphasis added.]

68-11-205. Practice in healing arts or medicine by partnership, person, association or corporation unauthorized.

(a) Nothing in this part shall authorize any person, partnership, association, corporation, or any state, county, or local governmental unit, or any division, department, board or agency of the governmental unit, to engage, in any manner, in the practice of the healing arts, or the practice of medicine, as defined by law; provided, that nothing in this section shall prohibit a person, corporation, organization, or other entity from employing a physician to treat only its own employees, the entity's retirees, or dependents of the entity's employees or retirees, in accordance with § 63-6-204.

(b) (1) Notwithstanding this section, nothing shall prohibit a hospital licensed under this chapter or an affiliate of a hospital from employing physicians, other than radiologists, anesthesiologists, pathologists, or emergency physicians, licensed under title 63, chapter 6 or 9, subject to the following conditions:

State & Statute	Statute Language
Tennessee (con't) TENN. CODE ANN. §§ 63-1-148, 68-11-205, 63-6-204(f)(2)	(A) Employing entities shall not restrict or interfere with medically appropriate diagnostic or treatment decisions; (B) Employing entities shall not restrict or interfere with physician referral decisions, unless: (i) The physician so employed has agreed in writing to the specific restrictions at the time that the contract is executed; (ii) The restriction does not, in the reasonable medical judgment of the physician, adversely affect the health or welfare of the patient; and (iii) The employing entity discloses any such restrictions to the patient; and (C) In the event that there is any dispute relating to subdivision (b)(1)(A) or (B), the employing entity shall have the burden of proof. (b) (2) Employing entities[1] shall not restrict the employed physician's right to practice medicine upon the termination or conclusion of the employment relationship, except as allowed by § 63-6-204(f)(2). (b) (3) Notwithstanding subdivision (b)(2), in the event that the employment contract with a physician employed independently of a bona fide practice purchase is terminated by the employing entity for reasons other than breach by the employee, any such restrictions shall be void.

[1]"'Employing entity'" means a hospital licensed under this chapter or title 33, chapter 2, or an affiliate of such an entity that employs one or more physicians. 'Employing entity' does not mean, however, a health maintenance organization licensed under title 56, chapter 32." TENN. CODE ANN. § 68-11-205(e)(4)(A).

State & Statute	Statute Language
Tennessee (con't) TENN. CODE ANN. §§ 63-1-148, 68-11-205, 63-6-204(f)(2)	**TENN. CODE ANN. § 63-6-204(f)(2):**

(f)(2) Employing entities[2] shall not restrict the employed physician's right to practice medicine upon the termination or conclusion of the employment relationship, except as follows:

(A) For physicians from whom the employing entity has made a bona fide purchase of the physician's practice, the employing entity may impose reasonable geographic restrictions upon the employed physician's practice; provided, that:

(i) The maximum allowable area of the restriction is the greater of:

(a) The county in which the primary practice site is located; or

(b) A ten (10) mile radius from the primary practice site;

(ii) The duration of the restriction is two (2) years or less, unless a longer period, not to exceed five (5) years, is determined by mutual agreement of the parties in writing to be necessary to comply with federal statutes, rules, regulations, or IRS revenue rulings or private letter rulings;

(iii) Any employment agreement or medical practice sale agreement restricting the right of a physician to practice shall:

(a) Allow the physician to buy back the physician's medical practice for the original purchase price of the practice, or, in the alternative, if the parties agree in writing, at a price not to exceed the fair market value of the practice at the time of the

---

[2] "'Employing entity' means a hospital licensed under title 68, chapter 11, or title 33, chapter 2, or an affiliate of such an entity, that employs one or more physicians. 'Employing entity' does not mean, however, a health maintenance organization licensed under title 56, chapter 32." TENN CODE ANN. § 63-6- 204(f)(7)(D).

State & Statute	Statute Language
Tennessee (con't) TENN. CODE ANN. §§ 63-1-148, 68-11-205, 63-6-204(f)(2)	buyback, at which time any such restriction on practice shall be void; and (b) Not require that the physician give more than thirty-day's notice to exercise the repurchase option; provided, that this provision shall not otherwise affect the contract termination notice requirements; and (iv) If the buyback provision is dependent upon a determination of the fair market value of the practice, the contract shall specify the method of determining fair market value by independent appraisal, in the event that the parties cannot agree as to the fair market value. The contract shall also include the following language: "In the event that the employing entity and the physician cannot agree upon the fair market value of the practice within ten (10) business days of the physician's notice of intent to repurchase the practice, the physician may remove any contractual restrictions upon the physician's practice by tendering to the employing entity the amount that was paid to the physician for the practice. The employing entity or the physician may then seek a determination of the fair market value of the practice by the independent appraisal method specified by contract." (B) For physicians employed independently of a bona fide practice purchase, employing entities shall not restrict the employed physician's right to practice medicine upon the termination or conclusion of the employment relationship, except as allowed by § 63-1-148 or any successor section.

State & Statute	Statute Language
Texas Tex. Bus. & Com. Code § 15.50(a)-(c); Tex. Bus. & Com. Code §15.52; Tex. Gov't Code § 848.101(c)	**15.50 Criteria for Enforceability of Covenants Not to Compete** (a) Notwithstanding Section 15.05 of this code, and subject to any applicable provision of Subsection (b), a covenant not to compete is enforceable if it is ancillary to or part of an otherwise enforceable agreement at the time the agreement is made to the extent that it contains limitations as to time, geographical area, and scope of activity to be restrained that are reasonable and do not impose a greater restraint than is necessary to protect the goodwill or other business interest of the promisee. (b) A covenant not to compete relating to the practice of medicine is enforceable against a person licensed as a physician by the Texas Medical Board if such covenant complies with the following requirements: (1) the covenant must: (A) not deny the physician access to a list of his patients whom he had seen or treated within one year of termination of the contract or employment; (B) provide access to medical records of the physician's patients upon authorization of the patient and any copies of medical records for a reasonable fee as established by the Texas State Board of Medical Examiners under Section 5.08(o), Medical Practice Act (Article 4495b, Vernon's Texas Civil Statutes); and (C) provide that any access to a list of patients or to patients' medical records after termination of the contract or employment shall not require such list or records to be provided in a format different than that by which such records are maintained except by mutual consent of the parties to the contract; (2) the covenant must provide for

State & Statute	Statute Language
Texas (con't) TEX. BUS. & COM. CODE § 15.50(a)-(c); TEX. BUS. & COM. CODE §15.52; TEX. GOV'T CODE § 848.101(c)	a buyout of the covenant by the physician at a reasonable price or, at the option of either party, as determined by a mutually agreed upon arbitrator or, in the case of an inability to agree, an arbitrator of the court whose decision shall be binding on the parties; and (3) the covenant must provide that the physician will not be prohibited from providing continuing care and treatment to a specific patient or patients during the course of an acute illness even after the contract or employment has been terminated. (c) Subsection (b) does not apply to a physician's business ownership interest in a licensed hospital or licensed ambulatory surgical center. **TEX. BUS. & COM. CODE §15.52 Preemption of Other Law.** The criteria for enforceability of a covenant not to compete provided by Section 15.50 of this code and the procedures and remedies in an action to enforce a covenant not to compete provided by Section 15.51 of this code are exclusive and preempt any other criteria for enforceability of a covenant not to compete or procedures and remedies in an action to enforce a covenant not to compete under common law or otherwise. **TEX. GOV'T CODE § 848.101(c):** A health care collaborative may not use a covenant not to compete to prohibit a physician from providing medical services or participating in another health care collaborative.

II. STATES WITH STATUTES GENERALLY CONCERNING EMPLOYEE RESTRICTIVE COVENANTS

State & Statute	Statute Language	Case Law
Alabama ALA. CODE § 8-1-1 for covenants entered into *before* Jan. 1 2016	ALA. CODE § 8-1-1(a). Every contract by which anyone is restrained from exercising a lawful profession, trade, or business of any kind otherwise than is provided by this section is to that extent void. **Exceptions:** (1) sale of the good will of a business; (2) in connection with an employment relationship; or (3) upon or in anticipation of dissolution of the partnership. ALA. CODE §8-1-1(b)–(c).	Section 8-1-1(a) places a broad general ban on every contract that restrains anyone from exercising a lawful profession. There are only "two exceptions [Sections 8-1-1(b) and (c)] to this otherwise uncompromising provision." *Walker Reg'l Med. Ctr., Inc. v. McDonald*, 775 So. 2d 169, 171 (Ala. 2000). The practice of medicine is a profession under the terms of this statute. However, the inclusion of a covenant not to compete in a contract does not necessarily render void the entire contract. The statute itself provides that a contract containing a covenant not to compete "is to that extent void." The contract remains otherwise valid. Therefore, the entire agreement in this case was not made
ALA. CODE §8-1-190 -197 for covenants entered into *after* Jan. 1, 2016	ALA. CODE §8-1-190. Void contracts; contracts allowed to preserve protectable interests. (a) Every contract by which anyone is restrained from exercising a lawful profession, trade, or business of any kind otherwise than is provided by this section is to that extent void. (b) Except as otherwise prohibited by law, the following contracts are allowed	

State & Statute	Statute Language	Case Law
Alabama **(con't)**	to preserve a protectable interest: (1) A contract between two or more persons or businesses or a person and a business limiting their ability to hire or employ the agent, servant, or employees of a party to the contract where the agent, servant, or employee holds a position uniquely essential to the management, organization, or service of the business. (2) An agreement between two or more persons or businesses or a person and a business to limit commercial dealings to each other. (3) One who sells the good will of a business may agree with the buyer to refrain from carrying on or engaging in a similar business and from soliciting customers of such business within a specified geographic area so long as the buyer, or any entity deriving title to the good will from that business, carries on a like business therein, subject to reasonable time and place restraints. Restraints of one year or less are presumed to be reasonable. (4) An agent, servant, or employee of a commercial entity may agree with such entity to refrain from	void by the fact that it included the disputed clause. *Salisbury v. Semple*, 565 So. 2d 234, 236 (Ala. 1990). Not every contract that imposes a restraint on trade or competition is void. The fact that a contract may affect a few or several individuals engaged in a like business does not render it void under ALA. CODE § 8-1-1(1975). Every contract to some extent injures other parties; that is, it necessarily prevents others from making the sale or sales consummated by such contract. The court held that the fact that Southeast's physicians are denied staff privileges at certain facilities did not restrain them from practicing their profession in violation of § 8-1-1, ALA. CODE 1975. *Southeast Cancer Network, P.C. v. DCH Healthcare Auth., Inc.*, 869 So. 2d 452, 458 (Ala. 2003). It is well settled in Alabama that to the extent a contract restrains the practice

State & Statute	Statute Language	Case Law
Alabama **(con't)**	carrying on or engaging in a similar business within a specified geographic area so long as the commercial entity carries on a like business therein, subject to reasonable restraints of time and place. Restraints of two years or less are presumed to be reasonable. (5) An agent, servant, or employee of a commercial entity may agree with such entity to refrain from soliciting current customers, so long as the commercial entity carries on a like business, subject to reasonable time restraints. Restraints of 18 months or for as long as post-separation consideration is paid for such agreement, whichever is greater, are presumed to be reasonable. (6) Upon or in anticipation of dissolution of a commercial entity, partners, owners, or members, or any combination thereof, may agree that none of them will carry on a similar commercial activity in the geographic area where the commercial activity has been transacted. **Ala. Code 8-1-191** **Protectable interests.** **(a)** A protectable interest includes all of the following:	of a lawful profession, it is void, under § 8-1-1(a), as against public policy. There is universal agreement that the law looks with disfavor upon contracts that restrain employment. A contract that requires the payment of damages in the event one of the contracting parties competes with the other is a contract "by which ... one is restrained from exercising a lawful profession." *Anniston Urologic Assocs., P.C. v. Kline*, 689 So. 2d 54, 57 (Ala. 1997).

State & Statute	Statute Language	Case Law
Alabama **(con't)**	(1) Trade secrets, as defined in Section 8-27-2.	
	(2) Confidential information, including, but not limited to, pricing information and methodology; compensation; customer lists; customer data and information; mailing lists; prospective customer information; financial and investment information; management and marketing plans; business strategy, technique, and methodology; business models and data; processes and procedures; and company provided files, software, code, reports, documents, manuals, and forms used in the business that may not otherwise qualify as a trade secret but which are treated as confidential to the business entity, in whatever medium provided or preserved, such as in writing or stored electronically.	
	(3) Commercial relationships or contacts with specific prospective or existing customers, patients, vendors, or clients.	
	(4) Customer, patient, vendor, or client good will associated with any of the following: a. An ongoing business, franchise,	

State & Statute	Statute Language	Case Law
Alabama (con't)	commercial, or professional practice, or trade dress. b. A specific marketing or trade area.	

(5) Specialized and unique training involving substantial business expenditure specifically directed to a particular agent, servant, or employee; provided that such training is specifically set forth in writing as the consideration for the restraint.

(b) Job skills in and of themselves, without more, are not protectable interests.

Ala. Code 8-1-193 Voidable restraints.

If a contractually specified restraint is overly broad or unreasonable in its duration, a court may void the restraint in part and reform it to preserve the protectable interest or interests. If a contractually specified restraint does not fall within the limited exceptions set out in subsection (b) of Section 8-1-190, a court may void the restraint in its entirety.

Ala. Code 8-1-194 Burden of proof.

The party seeking enforcement of the covenant has the burden of proof on every element. The party resisting

State & Statute	Statute Language	Case Law
Alabama (con't)	enforcement of the covenant has the burden of proving the existence of undue hardship, if raised as a defense.	

**Ala. Code 8-1-195
Remedies and defenses.**

a) The remedies available for breach of an agreement subject to this article are:

(1) Such injunctive and other equitable relief as may be appropriate with respect to any actual or threatened breach.

(2) The actual damages suffered as a result of the breach or lawful liquidated damages if provided in the contract.

(3) Any remedies available in contract law, including attorneys' fees or costs, if provided for in the contract or otherwise provided for by law.

(b) Nothing in this article shall limit the availability of any defense otherwise available in law or equity.

**Ala. Code 8-1-196
Professional exemptions.**

Nothing in this article shall be construed to eliminate any professional exemption recognized by Alabama law.

State & Statute	Statute Language	Case Law
Alabama (con't)	**Ala. Code 8-1-197** **Legislative intent** It is hereby declared that this article expresses fundamental public policies of the State of Alabama. Therefore, this article shall govern and shall be applied instead of any foreign laws that might otherwise be applicable in those instances when the application of those foreign laws would violate a fundamental public policy expressed in this article.	
ARK. Code § 4-70-207 **Editor's Note: Be aware that the Arkansas statute governing covenants not to compete in the employment context specifically excludes numerous licensed health care professionals.** §4-70-207 **(j)(2).**	**ARK. Code § 4-70-207** Covenant not to compete agreements. (a) A covenant not to compete agreement is enforceable if the agreement is ancillary to an employment relationship or part of an otherwise enforceable employment agreement or contract to the extent that: (1) The employer has a protectable business interest; and (2) The covenant not to compete agreement is limited with respect to time and scope in a manner that is not greater than necessary to defend the protectable business interest of the employer. (b) For the purposes of subsection (a) of this	Important Note: The Arkansas statute governing covenants not to compete in the employment context specifically does not apply to a very long list of individuals who are licensed health care professionals! Including, without limitation, physicians, nurses, pharmacists, dentists, therapists, hygienists, chiropractors, etc., per §4-70-207 (j)(2). In *Mercy Health Sys. of Northwest Ark., Inc. v. Bicak*, 2011 Ark. App. LEXIS 341 (Ark. Ct. App. May 11, 2011), the

State & Statute	Statute Language	Case Law
ARK. Code § 4-70-207 (con't)	section, the protectable business interest of the employer includes the employer's: (1) Trade secrets; (2) Intellectual property; (3) Customer lists; (4) Goodwill with customers; (5) Knowledge of his or her business practices; (6) Methods; (7) Profit margins; (8) Costs; (9) Other confidential business information that is confidential, proprietary, and increases in value from not being known by a competitor; (10) Training and education of the employer's employees; and (11) Other valuable employer data that the employer has provided to an employee that an employer would reasonably seek to protect or safeguard from a competitor in the interest of fairness. (c) (1) The lack of a specific or defined geographic descriptive restriction in a covenant not to compete agreement does not make the covenant not to compete agreement overly broad under subdivision (a)(2) of this section if the covenant not to compete agreement is limited with respect to time and scope in a manner that is not greater than necessary to defend the protectable business interest of the	Arkansas Court of Appeals held that "[t]he circuit court did not err in granting partial summary judgment to [defendant-physician] on [his] covenant-not-to-compete claim because [the hospital] did not counter [defendant-physician's] evidence demonstrating that it had no interest sufficient to warrant its enforcement; that it was designed only to eliminate competition; and that it would unreasonably interfere with the public's right of access to the physicians of their choice and [defendant physician's] ability to earn a living." In *Jaraki v. Cardiology Assocs. of Northeast Ark.*, 55 S.W.3d 799 (Ark. Ct. App. 2001), a doctor and the corporation entered into an employment agreement under which the doctor agreed not to practice within a 75-mile radius of the corporation's principal office for a period of

State & Statute	Statute Language	Case Law
ARK. Code § 4-70-207 (con't)	employer. (2) The reasonableness of a covenant not to compete agreement shall be determined after considering: (A) The nature of the employer's protectable business interest; (B) The geographic scope of the employer's business and whether or not a geographic limitation is feasible under the circumstances; (C) Whether or not the restriction placed on the employee is limited to a specific group of customers or other individuals or entities associated with the employer's business; and (D) The nature of the employer's business. (d) A post-termination restriction of two (2) years is presumptively reasonable as to length of time under subdivision (a)(2) of this section unless the facts and circumstances of a particular case clearly demonstrate that two (2) years is unreasonable compared to the employer's protectable business interest. (e) (1) In a private court action, a court may award the employer damages for a breach of a covenant not to compete agreement, appropriate injunctive relief, or both, if appropriate. (2)	two years if he terminated his employment before the end of the contract term. The court held that covenants not to compete are not looked upon with favor by the law. In order for such a covenant to be enforceable, three requirements must be met: (1) the covenantee must have a valid interest to protect; (2) the geographical restriction must not be overly broad; (3) a reasonable time limit must be imposed. A party challenging the validity of a covenant is required to show that it is unreasonable and contrary to public policy. Without statutory authorization or, some dominant policy justification, a contract in restraint of trade is unreasonable if it is based on a promise to refrain from competition that is not ancillary to a contract of employment or to a contract for the transfer of goodwill or other property. However, the law will

State & Statute	Statute Language	Case Law
ARK. Code § 4-70-207 (con't)	The immediate harm associated with the breach of a covenant not to compete agreement shall be considered irreparable to establish the appropriateness of a preliminary injunction. (3) This subsection does not limit: (A) Any other defense available to a party against a claim for preliminary injunctive relief; or (B) An employer's right to monetary damages for breach of a covenant not to compete agreement. (f) (1) If restrictions in a covenant not to compete agreement are found to be unreasonable and impose a greater restraint than is necessary to protect the protectable business interest of the employer under subdivision (a)(1) of this section, the court shall reform the covenant not to compete agreement to the extent necessary to: (A) Cause the limitations contained in the covenant not to compete agreement to be reasonable; and (B) Impose a restraint that is not greater than necessary to protect the protectable business interest. (2) The court shall enforce the covenant not to compete agreement under the reformed terms and conditions.	not protect parties against ordinary competition. Covenants not to compete in employment contracts are subject to stricter scrutiny than those connected with a sale of a business. *Id.* The court stated that it is contrary to public policy to unduly restrict the public's right of access to the physicians of their choice. *Id.* Where a covenant not to compete grows out of an employment relationship, the courts have found an interest sufficient to warrant enforcement of the covenant only in those cases where the covenantee provided special training, or made available trade secrets, confidential business information, or customer lists, and then only if it is found that the associate was able to use information so obtained to gain an unfair competitive advantage. *Id.*

State & Statute	Statute Language	Case Law
ARK. Code **§ 4-70-207** **(con't)**	(g) An employee's continued employment is sufficient consideration for a covenant not to compete agreement. (h) (1) This subsection does not apply to a covenant not to compete agreement that is ancillary to other contractual relationships, including any type of agreement for the sale and purchase of a business, franchise agreement, and any other agreement not ancillary to an employment relationship or employment contract. (2) Existing common law standards governing a covenant not to compete agreement outside the employment background shall remain in effect. (i) (1) This subsection shall not apply to other types of agreements between employers and employees that do not concern competition or competitive work, including: (A) Agreements not to solicit, recruit, or hire employees; (B) Confidentiality agreements; (C) Nondisclosure agreements; and (D) The terms and conditions of an employment or employment agreement. (2) Existing common law standards governing these types of	The geographic area in a covenant not to compete must be limited in order to be enforceable. The restraint imposed upon one party must not be greater than is reasonably necessary for protecting the other party. In determining whether the geographic area is reasonable, the trade area of the former employer is viewed. Where a geographic restriction is greater than the trade area, the restriction is too broad and the covenant not to compete is void. *Id.*

State & Statute	Statute Language	Case Law
ARK. Code § 4-70-207 (con't)	agreements shall remain in effect. **(j) This section shall not:** (1) Be read to impair, limit, or change a party's protections and rights under the Arkansas Trade Secrets Act, § 4-75-601 et seq.; or **(2) Apply to a person holding a professional license under Arkansas Code Title 17, Subtitle 3. [Emphasis Added].**	
California CAL. BUS. & PROF. CODE §§ 16600–16602.5	Except as provided in this chapter, every contract by which anyone is restrained from engaging in a lawful profession, trade, or business of any kind is to that extent void. CAL. BUS. & PROF. CODE § 16600. **Exceptions:** (1) sale of goodwill or corporate shares; (2) the dissolution of the partnership or dissociation of the partner from the partnership; or (3) agreements by members of LLCs not to carry on similar business within specified locality so long as any other member of the limited liability company carries on a like business. CAL. BUS. & PROF. CODE §§ 16600–16602.5.	CAL. BUS. & PROF. CODE § 16600 presently sets out the general rule in California—covenants not to compete are void. This provision is an expression of public policy to ensure that every citizen shall retain the right to pursue any lawful employment and enterprise of their choice. CAL. BUS. & PROF. CODE §§ 16600 and 16601 do not exclude professional medical corporations. *Hill Med. Corp. v. Wycoff*, 2001 Cal. App. LEXIS 58 (Cal. App. 2d Dist. 2001). In *Hill Med. Corp.*, the court concluded that

State & Statute	Statute Language	Case Law
Cal. Labor § 925 (eff. Jan. 1, 2017) *Forum Selection, closure of Loophole with respect to Restrictive Covenants.*	Cal. Labor § 925 essentially provides that Employers shall not require employees, as a condition of employment, to agree to a provision that: requires the employee to adjudicate a dispute outside California; or deprives the employee of the substantive protection of California law. *Exception*—contracts with employees who were individually represented by counsel when negotiating the agreement.	the covenant not to compete at issue was void and unenforceable. As defendant's professional practice consisted solely of providing radiology and associated medical imaging services, the noncompetition provision effectively excluded him from the practice of his profession and was void. Substantial evidence supported the trial court's finding that the covenant not to compete did not fall within the exception of § 16601. This was not a situation in which an otherwise valid covenant covered an unreasonably large geographical area or was unreasonably long in duration. Since there had been no compensation for goodwill, it was impossible to re-write this void covenant. To re-write the covenant would have undermined California's public policy of open competition as set forth in § 16600. *Id.*

State & Statute	Statute Language	Case Law
District of Columbia D.C. CODE § 28-4502	D.C. CODE § 28-4502 Every contract, combination in the form of a trust or otherwise, or conspiracy in restraint of trade or commerce all or any part of which is within the District of Columbia is declared to be illegal.	*Deutsch v. Barsky*, 795 A.2d 669, 674 (D.C. 2002) (holding that covenant not to compete between dentists was not a *per se* violation of public policy; restraint must be no greater than necessary to protect a legitimate business interest); *Erikson v. Hawley*, 56 App. D.C. 268, 12 F.2d 491 (D.C. Cir. 1926) (upholding preliminary injunction restraining orthodontist from violating restrictive covenant).
D.C. CODE §7-751.07	D.C. CODE §7-751.07: Non-compete clauses are prohibited in all contracts for the District of Columbia Health Professional Recruitment Program. (Covering physicians, dentists, or other health professionals as defined in § 7-751.01).	
Florida FLA. STAT. § 542.335 (For covenants entered into on or after July 1, 1996)	Due to the extreme length of Florida Statute 542.335. *Valid restraints of trade or commerce*, it is set forth in Endnote No 1 on Page 470 of this Appendix A.	So long as the covenant not to compete fits within the parameters of FLA. STAT. Ch. 542.335 (1999), it may be enforced by the injunctive power of the courts. One applying for a temporary injunction to enforce a noncompete agreement must show, among other things, a likelihood of success on the merits. The person against whom the injunction is sought may offer as a defense that the moving party has materially

State & Statute	Statute Language	Case Law
Florida (con't) FLA. STAT. § 542.335		breached the contract. If the employee introduces evidence of the employer's breach, as the employee is entitled to do pursuant to FLA. STAT. ch. 42.335(g)3 (1999), the employer must then demonstrate that it is likely to succeed on the merits of the proffered defense, as well. *Supinski v. Omni Healthcare*, 853 So. 2d 526 (Fla. Dist. Ct. App. 5th Dist. 2003). Where a non-competition restraint is neither six months or less, nor more than two years in duration, it is neither presumed reasonable nor unreasonable. FLA. STAT. ch.542.335(1)(h) (2003) directs that a court shall construe a restrictive covenant in favor of providing reasonable protection to all legitimate business interests established by the person seeking enforcement. *Southernmost Foot & Ankle Specialists v. Torregrosa*, 891 So. 2d 591 (Fla. Dist. Ct. App. 3d Dist. 2004).

State & Statute	Statute Language	Case Law
Florida (con't) FLA. STAT. § 542.335		In Florida, the enforceability of restrictive covenants is controlled in large part by FLA. STAT. § 542.335 (2004). Under § 542.335, a restrictive covenant is not enforceable unless supported by a legitimate business interest. If the party seeking to enforce the restrictive covenant pleads and proves a legitimate business interest, it must also then demonstrate that the contractually specified restraint is reasonably necessary to protect its identified business interest. With respect to patients of a medical practice, FLA. STAT. § 542.335 (2004) expressly defines "legitimate business interest" to include only those specific prospective or existing patients with whom a party has a substantial relationship. *Florida Hematology & Oncology v. Tummala*, 927 So. 2d 135 (Fla. Dist. Ct. App. 5th Dist. 2006).

State & Statute	Statute Language	Case Law
Georgia GA. CONST. Art. III, Sec. VI, Par. V(c)1; GA. CODE ANN. § 13-8-50 *et seq.* *For covenants entered into on or after May 11, 2011.*	Due to the length of GA. CODE ANN. § 13-8-50 – *13-8-59, the full text can be found in* endnote 2 on pages 473–481 of this Appendix A. Relevant portions follow: § 13-8-50 (a) Notwithstanding any other provisions of this chapter, enforcement of contracts that restrict competition during the term of a restrictive covenant, so long as such restrictions are reasonable in time, geographic area, and scope of prohibited activities, shall be permitted. However, enforcement of contracts that restrict competition after the term of employment [as distinguished from a customer nonsolicitation provision or a nondisclosure of confidential information provision in GA. CODE. ANN. § 13-8-53(b) and (e), respectively] shall not be permitted against any employee who does not, in the course of his or her employment: (1) Customarily and regularly solicit for the employer customers or prospective customers; (2) Customarily and regularly engage in making sales or obtaining orders or contracts for products or services to be performed	The RCA [Restrictive Covenants Act] only applies to restrictive covenant agreements entered into after May 11, 2011. *Becham v. Crosslink Orthopedics*, 482 F. App'x 387 (11th Cir. 2011). Prior to the enactment of the RCA, Georgia courts generally treated restrictive covenants in physicians' employment contracts like such clauses in other employment contracts—if they were sufficiently limited and reasonable, considering the interest to be protected and the effects on both parties to the contract, they were upheld. *See Pittman v. Coosa Med. Grp., P.C.*, 300 Ga. App. 529 (Ga. Ct. App. 2009); *see also Peachtree Fayette Women's Specialists, LLC v. Turner*, 699 S.E.2d 69 (Ga. Ct. App. 2010) (declining to enforce a restrictive covenant that prohibited physician from providing obstetric and gynecological

State & Statute	Statute Language	Case Law
Georgia (con't) GA. CONST. Art. III, Sec. VI, Par. V(c)1; GA. CODE ANN. § 13-8-50 *et seq.*	by others; (3) Perform the following duties: (A) Have a primary duty of managing the enterprise in which the employee is employed or of a customarily recognized department or subdivision thereof; (B) Customarily and regularly direct the work of two or more other employees; and (C) Have the authority to hire or fire other employees or have particular weight given to suggestions and recommendations as to the hiring, firing, advancement, promotion, or any other change of status of other employees; or (4) Perform the duties of a key employee or of a professional. ... §13-8-51(5) (b) Notwithstanding any other provision of this chapter, an employee may agree in writing for the benefit of an employer to refrain, for a stated period of time following termination, from soliciting, or attempting to solicit, directly or by assisting others, any business from any of such employer's customers, including actively seeking prospective customers, with whom the employee had material contact during his or her	services in a geographic area where she had never worked during her employment and where her former employer did not maintain an office); *Keeley v. Cardiovascular Surgical Assocs.*, 510 S.E.2d 880 (Ga. Ct. App. 1999) (finding that in order to be enforceable, a non-compete covenant must be reasonably necessary to protect the interests of the party in whose favor it is imposed); *Augusta Eye Ctr. v. Duplessie*, 506 S.E.2d 242 (Ga. Ct. App. 1998) (finding that one-year duration of a non-competition clause is well within the time frame permitted by law).

State & Statute	Statute Language	Case Law
Georgia (con't) GA. CONST. Art. III, Sec. VI, Par. V(c)1; GA. CODE ANN. § 13-8-50 *et seq.*	employment for purposes of providing products or services that are competitive with those provided by the employer's business. No express reference to geographic area or the types of products or services considered to be competitive shall be required in order for the restraint to be enforceable. Any reference to a prohibition against "soliciting or attempting to solicit business from customers" or similar language shall be adequate for such purpose and narrowly construed to apply only to: (1) such of the employer's customers, including actively sought prospective customers, with whom the employee had material contact; and (2) products or services that are competitive with those provided by the employer's business. ... §13-8-52 (e) Nothing in this article shall be construed to limit the period of time for which a party may agree to maintain information as confidential or as a trade secret, or to limit the geographic area within which such information must be kept confidential or as a trade secret, for so long as	

State & Statute	Statute Language	Case Law
Georgia (con't) GA. CONST. Art. III, Sec. VI, Par. V(c)1; GA. CODE ANN. § 13-8-50 *et seq.*	the information or material remains confidential or a trade secret, as applicable.	
Hawaii HAW. REV. STAT. § 480-4(c)-4(d)	**HAW. REV. STAT. 480-4(c)** … [I]t shall be lawful for a person to enter into any of the following restrictive covenants or agreements ancillary to a legitimate purpose not violative of this chapter, unless the effect thereof may be substantially to lessen competition or to tend to create a monopoly in any line of commerce in any section of the State: (1) A covenant or agreement by the transferor of a business not to compete within a reasonable area and within a reasonable period of time in connection with the sale of the business; (2) A covenant or agreement between partners not to compete with the partnership within a reasonable area and for a reasonable period of time upon the withdrawal of a partner from the partnership; (3) A covenant or agreement of the lessee to be restricted in the use of the leased premises to certain business	*Technicolor, Inc. v. Traeger*, 57 Haw. 113, 551 P.2d 163 (1976) (holding that a restrictive covenant is "not reasonable" if (1) it is greater than required for the protection of the employer; (2) it imposes undue hardship on the person being restricted; or (3) injury to the public outweighs the benefit to the employer); *UARCO, Inc. v. Lam.*, 18 F. Supp. 2d 1116, 1121 (D. Haw. 1998) ("[F]or restrictive covenants that are not *per se* illegal, courts should determine as a matter of law whether a restrictive covenant is reasonable. 'In making this analysis, the court must examine such factors as geographical scope, length of time, and breadth of the restriction placed on a given activity.'").

State & Statute	Statute Language	Case Law
Hawaii (con't) Haw. Rev. Stat. § 480-4(c)-4(d)	or agricultural uses, or covenant or agreement of the lessee to be restricted in the use of the leased premises to certain business uses and of the lessor to be restricted in the use of premises reasonably proximate to any such leased premises to certain business uses; (4) A covenant or agreement by an employee or agent not to use the trade secrets of the employer or principal in competition with the employee's or agent's employer or principal, during the term of the agency or thereafter, or after the termination of employment, within such time as may be reasonably necessary for the protection of the employer or principal, without imposing undue hardship on the employee or agent.	Non-Compete Clauses in Physician Employment Contracts are Bad For Our Health. 14 HBJ, No. 13, at 79 (2011).
Haw. Rev. Stat. § 480-4(d) effective for contracts executed on or after July 1, 2015.	**Haw. Rev. Stat. 480-4(d):** Except as provided in subsection (c)(4), it shall be prohibited to include a noncompete clause or a nonsolicit clause in any employment contract relating to an employee of a technology business. The clause shall be void and of no force and effect. As used in this subsection: "Information technology development" means the	

State & Statute	Statute Language	Case Law
Hawaii (con't) HAW. REV. STAT. § 480-4(c)-4(d)	design, integration, deployment, or support services for software. "Noncompete clause" means a clause in an employment contract that prohibits an employee from working in a specific geographic area for a specific period of time after leaving employment with the employer. "Nonsolicit clause" means a clause in an employment contract that prohibits an employee from soliciting employees of the employer after leaving employment with the employer. "Software development" means the creation of coded computer instructions. "Technology business" means a trade or business that derives the majority of its gross income from the sale or license of products or services resulting from its software development or information technology development, or both. A "technology business" excludes any trade or business that is considered by standard practice as part of the broadcast industry or any telecommunications carrier, as defined in section 269-1, that holds a franchise or charter enacted or granted by the legislative or executive authority of	

State & Statute	Statute Language	Case Law
Hawaii (con't) HAW. REV. STAT. § 480-4(c)-4(d)	the State or its predecessor governments. **§607-14.9 Actions to enforce covenants not to compete.** In a civil action which involves the interpretation or enforcement of an agreement or alleged agreement which purportedly restricts an employee from competing with an employer, or former employer, or working for a competitor of an employer or former employer, any employee or former employee who prevails shall be awarded reasonable attorneys' fees and costs.	
Idaho IDAHO CODE § 44-2701–2704	§ 44-2701. A key employee or key independent contractor may enter into a written agreement or covenant that protects the employer's legitimate business interests and prohibits the key employee or key independent contractor from engaging in employment or a line of business that is in direct competition with the employer's business after termination of employment, and the same shall be enforceable, if the agreement or covenant is reasonable as to its duration, geographical area, type of employment or line of business, and	The Idaho Supreme Court addressed physician non-competes in *Intermountain Eye & Laser Ctrs. v. Miller*, 127 P.3d 121 (Idaho 2005), which was decided prior to the enactment of IDAHO CODE § 44-2701 et seq. (2008). In *Intermountain Eye & Laser Centers*, the court found: A non-competition provision must be no more restrictive than necessary to protect the interest or interests at issue.

State & Statute	Statute Language	Case Law
Idaho (con't) IDAHO CODE § 44-2701–2704	does not impose a greater restraint than is reasonably necessary to protect the employer's legitimate business interests. § 44- 2702. Definitions. (1) "Key employees" and "key independent contractors" shall include those employees or independent contractors who, by reason of the employer's investment of time, money, trust, exposure to the public, or exposure to technologies, intellectual property, business plans, business processes and methods of operation, customers, vendors or other business relationships during the course of employment, have gained a high level of inside knowledge, influence, credibility, notoriety, fame, reputation or public persona as a representative or spokesperson of the employer, and as a result, have the ability to harm or threaten an employer's legitimate business interests. (2) "Legitimate business interests" shall include, but not be limited to, an employer's goodwill, technologies, intellectual property, business plans, business processes and methods of operation, customers,	Non-competitive activity is generally not protectable, at least in the medical profession. When considering the degree to which a particular non-compete provision affects the "public interest," courts focus on both the general public's interest in access to care, and the patients' interests in continuity of care and access to the physician of their choice. *Id.* Medical services firms, particularly those providing specialized care, generally have protectable interests in referral sources. *Id.* Doctor-patient relationships are different from most other relationships between service providers and their customers. While the public has a strong interest in freedom of contract, that interest must be balanced against the public interest in upholding the highly personal relationship between the physician and his or her patient.

State & Statute	Statute Language	Case Law
Idaho (con't) IDAHO CODE § 44-2701–2704	customer lists, customer contacts and referral sources, vendors and vendor contacts, financial and marketing information, and trade secrets as that term is defined by chapter 8, title 48, Idaho Code. §44-2703. Construction and Enforcement. To the extent any such agreement or covenant is found to be unreasonable in any respect, a court shall limit or modify the agreement or covenant as it shall determine necessary to reflect the intent of the parties and render it reasonable in light of the circumstances in which it was made and specifically enforce the agreement or covenant as limited or modified. §44-2704. Restriction of Direct Competition – Rebuttable Presumptions. (1) Under no circumstances shall a provision of such agreement or covenant, as set forth herein, establish a postemployment restriction of direct competition that exceeds a period of eighteen (18) months from the time of the key employee's or key independent contractor's termination unless consideration, in addition to	While doctor-patient relationships are somewhat analogous to attorney-client relationships, requiring closer scrutiny than other consumer-provider relationships, regulating the practice of law is the business of the court; regulating the practice of medicine is not. For that reason, an outright ban is unwise. Instead, the reasonableness of a particular non-compete provision should be left to the finder of fact in light of the interests involved. *Id.*

State & Statute	Statute Language	Case Law
Idaho (con't) IDAHO CODE § 44-2701–2704	employment or continued employment, is given to a key employee or key independent contractor. Nothing in this chapter shall be construed to limit a party's ability to otherwise protect trade secrets or other information deemed proprietary or confidential. (2) It shall be a rebuttable presumption that an agreement or covenant with a postemployment term of eighteen (18) months or less is reasonable as to duration. (3) It shall be a rebuttable presumption that an agreement or covenant is reasonable as to geographic area if it is restricted to the geographic areas in which the key employee or key independent contractor provided services or had a significant presence or influence. (4) It shall be a rebuttable presumption that an agreement or covenant is reasonable as to type of employment or line of business if it is limited to the type of employment or line of business conducted by the key employee or key independent contractor while working for the employer.	

State & Statute	Statute Language	Case Law
Idaho (con't) IDAHO CODE § 44-2701–2704	(5) It shall be a rebuttable presumption that an employee or independent contractor who is among the highest paid five percent (5%) of the employer's employees or independent contractors is a "key employee" or a "key independent contractor." To rebut such presumption, an employee or independent contractor must show that it has no ability to adversely affect the employer's legitimate business interests.	
Editor's Note: Subparagraph (6) was added to IDAHO CODE 44-2704(d) in 2016 and became effective July 1, 2017.	(6) If a court finds that a key employee or key independent contractor is in breach of an agreement or a covenant, a rebuttable presumption of irreparable harm has been established. To rebut such presumption, the key employee or key independent contractor must show that the key employee or key independent contractor has no ability to adversely affect the employer's legitimate business interests.	

State & Statute	Statute Language	Case Law
Illinois IL Public Act 099-0860 IL Freedom To Work Act (Illinois Public Acts) (eff. date Jan.1, 2017)	Section 5. Definitions. In this Act: "Covenant not to compete" means an agreement: (1) between an employer and a low-wage employee that restricts such low-wage employee from (A) any work for another employer for a specified period of time; (B) any work in a specified geographical area; or (C) work for another employer that is similar to such low-wage employee's work for the employer included as a party to the agreement; and (2) that is entered into after the effective date of this Act. "Employer" has the meaning given to such term in subsection (c) of Section 3 of the Minimum Wage Law. "Employer" does not include governmental or quasi-governmental bodies. "Low-wage employee" means an employee who earns the greater of (1) the hourly rate equal to the minimum wage required by the applicable federal, State, or local minimum wage law or $13.00 per hour. Section 10. Prohibiting covenants not to compete for low-wage employees. (a) No employer shall enter into a covenant not to compete	Historically, covenants restricting the performance of medical professional services have been held valid and enforceable in Illinois as long as their durational and geographic scope are not unreasonable, taking into consideration the effect on the public and any undue hardship on the parties to the agreement. The vast majority of jurisdictions follow the modern view, which is that restrictive covenants are enforceable if they are supported by consideration, ancillary to a lawful contract, and reasonable and consistent with the public interest. *Mohanty v. St. John Heart Clinic*, 866 N.E.2d 85 (Ill. 2006). When a party seeks to show that a contract term is against the public policy of Illinois, that party bears the burden of showing that the contract term is clearly contrary to what the constitution, the statutes, or the decisions

State & Statute	Statute Language	Case Law
Illinois (con't) IL Public Act 099-0860	with any low-wage employee of the employer. (b) A covenant not to compete entered into between an employer and a low-wage employee is illegal and void.	of the courts have declared to be the public policy or that the contract is manifestly injurious to the public welfare. *Id.*

In determining whether a restraint imposed by a covenant not to compete is reasonable it is necessary to consider whether enforcement will be injurious to the public or cause undue hardship to the promisor and whether the restraint imposed is greater than is necessary to protect the promisee. *Id.*

Restrictive covenants precluding the practice of medicine against physicians who practice a specialty have been upheld as reasonable. *Id.*

See also International Eyecare Ctr., Inc. v. Hayden, 2011 Ill. App. Unpub. LEXIS 615 (Ill. Ct. App. Apr. 7, 2011) (finding covenant not to compete that prohibited optometrist from competing within 20 miles of and soliciting patients and/or interviewing

State & Statute	Statute Language	Case Law
Illinois (con't) IL Public Act 099-0860		or hiring employees from former employer enforceable). Restrictive covenant regarding non-solicitation of patient agreement also requires a legitimate business interest to be enforced. Gastroenterology Consultants of the North Shore, S.C. v. Meiselman (2013 Il. App. 1st 123672). See: Prairie Rheumatology Assocs., S.C. v. Francis, 24 N.E. 3d 58 (Ill. App., 2014).
Louisiana LA. REV. STAT. ANN. §23:921	Due to the extreme length of the full Louisiana statute §23:921 it is set forth in its entirety in End Note 3 on page 481 hereof to this Appendix A. Only §23:921(c). is set forth below: C. Any person, including a corporation and the individual shareholders of such corporation, who is employed as an agent, servant, or employee may agree with his employer to refrain from carrying on or engaging in a business similar to that of the employer and/or from soliciting customers	In *Kimball v. Anesthesia Specialists of Baton Rouge, Inc.*, 809 So. 2d 405 (La. Ct. App. 2001), the plaintiff, a physician, former employee, and shareholder of an incorporated anesthesiology provider, filed suit against defendants, the corporation and the individual doctors/shareholders of the corporation, following his termination from employment. The court of appeals found that the

State & Statute	Statute Language	Case Law
Louisiana (con't) LA. REV. STAT. ANN. §23:921	of the employer within a specified parish or parishes, municipality or municipalities, or parts thereof, so long as the employer carries on a like business therein, not to exceed a period of two years from termination of employment. An independent contractor, whose work is performed pursuant to a written contract, may enter into an agreement to refrain from carrying on or engaging in a business similar to the business of the person with whom the independent contractor has contracted, on the same basis as if the independent contractor were an employee, for a period not to exceed two years from the date of the last work performed under the written contract.	non-compete clause of plaintiff's employment contract was unenforceable as it failed to conform to LA. REV. STAT. ANN. §23:921(C) by not specifying geographic restrictions. *See also West Carroll Health Sys.,LLC v. Tilmon*, 92 So. 3d 1131 (La. App. Ct. 2012) (reversing trial court's enforcement of a noncompetition agreement against a physician's assistant that extended to a named parish and "other surrounding parishes" on the basis that the geographic restriction was too broad). *Regional Urology, L.L.C. v. Price*, 966 So.2d 1087 (La. Ct. App. 2007) (finding that public policy arguments regarding patient choice would not trump a non-compete that complies with LA. REV. STAT. ANN. § 23:921(c)).

State & Statute	Statute Language	Case Law
Maryland	***Editor's Note:*** On January 27, 2017, Maryland lawmakers passed House Bill 506, which would render null and void any non-compete provision in an employment contract that restricts the ability of an employee who earns equal to or less than $15.00 per hour or $31,200 annually to enter into employment with a new employer or to become self-employed in the same or similar business. As of June 2017 it has not been voted on in the Maryland Senate (SB468).	Maryland employers have no protectable interest in preventing an increase in merely ordinary competition. *Intellus Corp. v. Barton, 7 F. Supp.2d 635, 639 (D. Md. 1998); See also Deutsche Post Global Mail, Ltd. v. Conrad, 116 Fed. Appx. 435, 438 (4th Cir 2004) (unpublished opinion), aff'g 292 F. Supp.2d 748, 756 (D. Md. 2003).* *Lofton v. TLC Laser Eye Ctrs., Inc.,* 2001 U.S. Dist. LEXIS 1476, 143 Lab. Cas. (CCH) P59231 (D. Md. Feb. 8, 2001) (evaluating non-compete restrictions with respect to an ophthalmic technician); *Wakefield v. Booth*, 33 Md. 63 (1870).
Michigan MICH. COMP. LAWS § 445.774a	M.C.L. § 445.774a. An employer may obtain from an employee an agreement or covenant which protects an employer's reasonable competitive business interests and expressly prohibits an employee from engaging in employment or a line of business after	In Great Lakes Home Health Servs. Inc. v. Crissman, No. 15-CV-11053, 2015 BL 360368, WL 6667772, (E.D. Mich. Nov. 2, 2015) the court refused to enforce a two year noncompete covenant barring a

State & Statute	Statute Language	Case Law
Michigan (con't) MICH. COMP. LAWS § 445.774a	termination of employment if the agreement or covenant is reasonable as to its duration, geographical area, and the type of employment or line of business. To the extent any such agreement or covenant is found to be unreasonable in any respect, a court may limit the agreement to render it reasonable in light of the circumstances in which it was made and specifically enforce the agreement as limited.	home health and hospice care administrator from working in any capacity in any location for a competitor on the basis, among other things, because of "extreme broadness in the geographical range and type of employment restricted is simply not necessary to protect [the former employer's] interests, especially when viewed in conjunction with the long duration" of the covenant. *Id. p.*15,* The court also ruled that, under the circumstances, it would be unreasonable for the former employer to prevent the former employee from working for a new employer based merely on new employer's status as a competitor. Id. p.*16. In *St. Clair Med., P.C. v. Borgiel,* 715 N.W.2d 914 (Mich. Ct. App. 2006), the employee signed a contract that contained a restrictive covenant. The covenant stated that the employee was prohibited from practicing medicine within

State & Statute	Statute Language	Case Law
Michigan (con't) MICH. COMP. LAWS § 445.774a		a seven mile radius of two clinics. After the employee left, he allegedly breached the agreement by seeing patients within this radius. The employer then filed a breach of contract action, which sought liquidated damages under the contract. The trial court granted summary disposition to the employer, and the employee sought review. In affirming, the appellate court determined that the covenant protected the employer from unfair competition by the employee and therefore protected a reasonable competitive business interest, as required by MICH. COMP. LAWS §445.774a. The restrictive covenant was modest in geographical scope and was not unreasonable in relation to the employer's competitive business interests. *Id.*

State & Statute	Statute Language	Case Law
Minnesota Minn. Stat. § 325D.51	A contract, combination, or conspiracy between two or more persons in unreasonable restraint of trade or commerce is unlawful.	In *Kari Family Clinic of Chiropractic v. Bohnen*, 349 N.W.2d 868 (Minn. Ct. App. 1984), a chiropractor signed an employment agreement with the clinic, three months after he began full time employment. He stated that he signed the contract because he understood he would be fired if he did not. Following a disagreement between the parties, the chiropractor left his employment and began practicing within 20 miles of the clinic. The clinic sought an injunction prohibiting the chiropractor from practicing, alleging that he violated a covenant not to compete contained in the parties' employment agreement. The trial court denied the motion for an injunction, and the clinic appealed. The court affirmed, finding that there were no facts to support a temporary injunction because the covenant was

State & Statute	Statute Language	Case Law
Minnesota (con't) MINN. STAT. § 325D.51		clearly not supported by adequate consideration or by additional consideration for the non-compete agreement as required by Minnesota law.
		Enforcement of restrictive covenants against professional employees is based on the relationship that is created, as for example, between a doctor and his patients. Once this relationship is formed, it is beyond question that a doctor's patients will seek his aid regardless of this doctor's employment situation. *Saliterman v. Finney*, 361 N.W.2d 175, 177 (Minn. Ct. App. 1985).
Missouri MO. REV. STAT. § 431.202 (eff. July 1, 2001)	**Editor's Note:** Missouri has a statute governing covenants not to solicit, recruit, hire or interfere; **however the statute (see §431.202.3) specifically exempts from its coverage covenants not to compete between employers-employees.** §431.202. 1. A reasonable covenant in writing promising not to solicit, recruit, hire or otherwise interfere	Generally, because covenants not to compete are considered restraints on trade, they are presumptively void and are enforceable only to the extent that they are demonstratively reasonable. *Armstrong v. Cape Girardeau Physician Assocs.*, 49 S.W.3d 821 (Mo. Ct. App. 2001).

State & Statute	Statute Language	Case Law
Missouri (con't) Mo. Rev. Stat. § 431.202 (eff. July 1, 2001)	with the employment of one or more employees shall be enforceable and not a restraint of trade pursuant to subsection 1 of section 416.031 if: (1) Between two or more corporations or other business entities seeking to preserve workforce stability (which shall be deemed to be among the protectable interests of each corporation or business entity) during, and for a reasonable period following, negotiations between such corporations or entities for the acquisition of all or a part of one or more of such corporations or entities; (2) Between two or more corporations or business entities engaged in a joint venture or other legally permissible business arrangement where such covenant seeks to protect against possible misuse of confidential or trade secret business information shared or to be shared between or among such corporations or entities; (3) Between an employer and one or more employees seeking on the part of the employer to protect:	The court has held that a permissible purpose of a non-compete agreement is to protect an employer from unfair competition by a former employee without imposing unreasonable restraint on the latter. An employer may only seek to protect certain narrowly defined and well-recognized interests, namely its trade secrets and its stock in customers. The enforcing party must also show that the agreement is reasonable in scope, both as to place and as to time. The burden of demonstrating the covenant's validity is on the party seeking to enforce it. *Id.* Missouri has no *per se* rule against enforcing covenants not to compete between medical practitioners. *Id.* (summarizing Missouri case law addressing physician non-compete agreements).

State & Statute	Statute Language	Case Law
Missouri (con't) MO. REV. STAT. § 431.202 (eff. July 1, 2001)	(a) Confidential or trade secret business information; or (b) Customer or supplier relationships, goodwill or loyalty, which shall be deemed to be among the protectable interests of the employer; or (4) Between an employer and one or more employees, notwithstanding the absence of the protectable interests described in subdivision (3) of this subsection, so long as such covenant does not continue for more than one year following the employee's employment; provided, however, that this subdivision shall not apply to covenants signed by employees who provide only secretarial or clerical services. 2. Whether a covenant covered by this section is reasonable shall be determined based upon the facts and circumstances pertaining to such covenant, but a covenant covered exclusively by subdivision (3) or (4) of subsection 1 of this section shall be conclusively presumed to be reasonable if its postemployment duration is no more than one year. 3. Nothing in subdivision (3) or (4) of subsection 1	

State & Statute	Statute Language	Case Law
Missouri (con't) Mo. REV. STAT. § 431.202 (eff. July 1, 2001)	of this section is intended to create, or to affect the validity or enforceability of, employer-employee covenants not to compete. 4. Nothing in this section shall preclude a covenant described in subsection 1 of this section from being enforceable in circumstances other than those described in subdivisions (1) to (4) of subsection 1 of this section, where such covenant is reasonably necessary to protect a party's legally permissible business interests. 5. Nothing is this section shall be construed to limit an employee's ability to seek or accept employment with another employer immediately upon, or at any time subsequent to, termination of employment, whether said termination was voluntary or nonvoluntary. 6. This section shall have retrospective as well as prospective effect.	

State & Statute	Statute Language	Case Law
Montana MONT. CODE ANN. §§ 28-2-703, 28-2-704, 28-2-705	Any contract, by which anyone is restrained from exercising a lawful profession, trade, or business of any kind, otherwise than is provided for by 28-2-704 or 28-2-705, is to that extent void. MONT. CODE ANN. § 28-2-703. Exceptions: (1) sale of goodwill of business; (2) dissolution of partnership. MONT. CODE ANN. §§ 28-2-704, 28-2-705.	In *Western Mont. Clinic v. Jacobson*, 544 P.2d 807 (Mont. 1976), the court declared a covenant not to compete incident to an orthopedic surgeon's employment contract unenforceable because it violated a Montana statute prohibiting contracts restraining the exercise of a lawful profession. *See also Mungas v. Great Falls Clinic, LLP*, 221 P.3d 1230 (Mont. 2009) (finding that clause in partnership agreement providing for the forfeiture of accounts receivable and certain other capital account amounts if partner-physician left the medical clinic and practiced in the same county or contiguous counties within three years did not constitute the sale of goodwill of a business and thus § 28-2-704 did not apply).

State & Statute	Statute Language	Case Law
Nebraska Neb. Rev. Stat. § 59-801	Every contract, combination in the form of trust or otherwise, or conspiracy in restraint of trade or commerce, within this state, is hereby declared to be illegal. Every person who shall make any such contract or engage in any such combination or conspiracy shall be deemed guilty of a Class IV felony.	See, Mertz v. Pharmacists Mut. Ins. Co., 261 Neb. 704, 625 N.W.2d 197 (Neb., 2001). A licensed physician who purchases the good will and other property of a sanitarium and agrees not to practice his profession within a radius of 150 miles may be enjoined from violating his restrictive agreement, when that remedy is essential to the protection of the seller's contractual rights. *Tarry v. Johnston*, 208 N.W. 615 (Neb. 1926). A licensed physician who purchases the good will and other property of a sanitarium may bind himself by an agreement not to practice his profession within a radius of 150 miles if the restriction is necessary for the protection of the seller's contractual rights and does not injure the public by restraining trade. *Id.* A contract which fails to specify in direct terms the time limit of restraint on

State & Statute	Statute Language	Case Law
Nebraska (con't) NEB. REV. STAT. § 59-801		a physician's right to practice medicine in a restricted area is not for that reason void, a reasonable time being implied. *Id.* *Akkad v. Nebraska Heart Inst., P.C.*, 2012 Neb. App. LEXIS 82 (Neb. Ct. App. Apr. 10, 2012) (finding that depriving the state of Nebraska of the services of a highly specialized cardi-ologist was injurious to the public; thus non-compete that prevented cardiologist from working any-where in the state, regardless of how he secured patients, was overbroad).
Nevada NEV. REV. STAT. §613.200*	*[*EDITORS NOTE: Be advised that as of June 14, 2017 there is a Nevada Senate Bill (A.B.149) under consideration in the Nevada Legislature to amend § 613.200 to, among other things, limit all em-ployment non-competes to 3 months.]* NEV. REV. STAT. 613.200 Prevention of employment of person who has been discharged or who termi-nates employment unlawful;	In *Hansen v. Edwards*, 426 P.2d 792 (Nev. 1967), a podiatrist commenced an action for injunctive relief and damages based upon a breach of a post-employment cov-enant not to engage in the practice of surgical chiropody within 100 miles of the city. The employee ter-minated the contract and opened his own

State & Statute	Statute Language	Case Law
Nevada (con't) NEV. REV. STAT. §613.200*	criminal and administrative penalties; exception. 1. Except as otherwise provided in this section, any person, association, company or corporation within this State, or any agent or officer on behalf of the person, association, company or corporation, who willfully does anything intended to prevent any person who for any cause left or was discharged from his, her or its employ from obtaining employment elsewhere in this State is guilty of a gross misdemeanor and shall be punished by a fine of not more than $5,000. 2. In addition to any other remedy or penalty, the Labor Commissioner may impose against each culpable party an administrative penalty of not more than $5,000 for each such violation. 3. If a fine or an administrative penalty is imposed pursuant to this section, the costs of the proceeding, including investigative costs and attorney's fees, may be recovered by the Labor Commissioner. 4. The provisions of this section do not prohibit a person, association,	office and acquired approximately 180 of podiatrist's customers. The court held that the podiatrist should have the opportunity to recoup his loss and, in addition, to readjust his office routine, which had previously been geared to the employee's association. The court held that a review of the record showed that the covenant was valid, and the court modified it to make it reasonable. The court held that the circumstances warranted a confinement of the area of restraint to the boundary limits of the city and a time interval of one year commencing on the date of the injunction. The court dismissed the arguments of the employee that NEV. REV. STAT. §613.200 prohibited the covenant, holding that the statute concerned only persons seeking employment with someone else, not those who intended self-employment. Where the public interest is not directly involved, the

State & Statute	Statute Language	Case Law
Nevada (con't) NEV. REV. STAT. §613.200*	company, corporation, agent or officer from negotiating, executing and enforcing an agreement with an employee of the person, association, company or corporation which, upon termination of the employment, prohibits the employee from: (a) Pursuing a similar vocation in competition with or becoming employed by a competitor of the person, association, company or corporation; or (b) Disclosing any trade secrets, business methods, lists of customers, secret formulas or processes or if the agreement is supported by valuable consideration and is otherwise reasonable in its scope and duration.	test usually stated for determining the validity of the covenant as written is whether it imposes upon the employee any greater restraint than is reasonably necessary to protect the business and good will of the employer. A restraint of trade is unreasonable, in the absence of statutory authorization or dominant social or economic justification, if it is greater than is required for the protection of the person for whose benefit the restraint is imposed or imposes undue hardship upon the person restricted. The period of time during which the restraint is to last and the territory that is included are important factors to be considered in determining the reasonableness of the agreement. *Id.* at 793; *see also Ellis v. McDaniel*, 596 P.2d 222 (Nev. 1979) (noting that the medical profession is not exempt from a restrictive covenant provided that the covenant meets the test of reasonableness).
NEV. REV. STAT. § 439A.175	Also, NEV. REV. STAT. § 439A.175 provides that contracts between employers and J-1 visa physicians may not include noncompete clauses or restrictive covenants.	

State & Statute	Statute Language	Case Law
North Carolina N.C. GEN. STAT. § 75-4	No contract or agreement hereafter made, limiting the rights of any person to do business anywhere in the State of North Carolina shall be enforceable unless such agreement is in writing duly signed by the party who agrees not to enter into any such business within such territory: Provided, nothing herein shall be construed to legalize any contract or agreement not to enter into business in the State of North Carolina, or at any point in the State of North Carolina, which contract is now illegal, or which contract is made illegal by any other section of this Chapter.	Under North Carolina law, covenants not to compete are valid and enforceable if: (1) in writing; (2) made part of a contract of employment; (3) based on valuable consideration; (4) reasonable both as to time and territory; and (5) not against public policy. *Calhoun v. WHA Med. Clinic*, 632 S.E.2d 563, 571 (N.C. Ct. App. 2006). North Carolina courts have long held covenants not to compete are not *per se* unenforceable, and medical doctors are by no means immune from such agreements. *Id.*
North Dakota N.D. CENT. CODE § 9-08-06	Every contract by which anyone is restrained from exercising a lawful profession, trade, or business of any kind is to that extent void. **Exceptions:** (1) one who sells the goodwill of a business; (2) partners, upon or in anticipation of a dissolution of the partnership.	Spectrum Emergency Care, Inc. v. *St. Joseph's Hosp. & Health Ctr.*, 479 N.W.2d 848 (N.D. 1992) (refusing to enforce physician non-compete and holding that such covenant violated North Dakota statute prohibiting restraints of trade).

State & Statute	Statute Language	Case Law
Ohio OHIO REV. CODE ANN. § 1331.02	No person shall issue or own trust certificates, and no person shall enter into a combination, contract, or agreement, the purpose and effect of which is to place the management or control of such combination, or the product or service thereof, in the hands of a trustee with the intent to limit or fix the price or lessen the production or sale of an article or service of commerce, use, or consumption, to prevent, restrict, or diminish the manufacture or output of such article or service, or refuse to buy from, sell to, or trade with any person because such person appears on a blacklist issued by, or is being boycotted by, any foreign corporate or governmental entity.	A covenant restraining an employee from competing with his former employer upon termination of employment is reasonable if it is no greater than is required for the protection of the employer, does not impose undue hardship on the employee, and is not injurious to the public. The purpose in allowing noncompetition agreements is to foster commercial ethics and to protect the employer's legitimate interests by preventing unfair competition— not ordinary competition. Therefore, the agreement must be reasonable before it will be enforced, and there must be a weighing of the interests of the employer, the employee, and the public to determine what is reasonable. If there is no legitimate interest of the employer to protect, then any non-competition agreement is not reasonable. *Premier Assocs. v. Loper*, 778 N.E.2d 630, 635 (Ohio Ct. App. 2002).
OHIO REV. CODE ANN. §4731.228 eff. March 22, 2013	OHIO REV. CODE §4731.228 (Termination of physician's employment with a health care entity; notice to patients) provides, "a health care entity shall send notice of the termination of a physician's employment to each patient who received physician services from the physician in the two year period immediately preceding the date of employment termination. Only patients of the health care entity who	

State & Statute	Statute Language	Case Law
Ohio (con't) OHIO REV. CODE ANN. §4731.228	received services from the physician are to receive the notice." Specific requirements regarding the content and timing of the notice are set forth in the law.	While covenants not to compete are disfavored in the medical profession, they are not *per se* unreasonable. *Id.*; *see also Owusu v. Hope Cancer Ctr. of Northwest Ohio, Inc.*, 2011 Ohio 4466 (Ohio Ct. App. 2011) (finding that an oncologist's non-compete agreement was reasonably limited to only two years and to his former employer's primary service area; and noting that "Ohio courts have repeatedly rejected the argument that covenants are not enforceable against physicians solely because it impairs the patient's choice"); *General Med., P.C. v. Manolache*, 2011 Ohio 340 (Ohio Ct. App. 2011) (restrictive covenants concerning mobility of physicians are not *per se* unenforceable). However, courts must strictly construe non-compete agreements in favor or professional mobility and access to medical care and facilities. *Riverhills Healthcare, Inc. v. Guo*, 2011 Ohio 4359 (Ohio Ct. App. 2011).

State & Statute	Statute Language	Case Law
Oklahoma 15 OKLA. STAT. §§ 217-219B eff. June 4, 2001)	OKLA. STAT. tit. 15 Sec. 217 Restraint of Trade Void Every contract by which any one is restrained from exercising a lawful profession, trade or business of any kind, otherwise than as provided by Sections 218 and 219 of this title, or otherwise than as provided by Section 2 of this Act, is to that extent void. 15 OKLA. STAT. § 217. **Exceptions:** (1) sale of goodwill of a business but subject to territorial limitations; (2) partners, upon or in anticipation of a dissolution of the partnership, again subject to territorial limitations; (3) nonsolicitation of "established customers." 15 OKLA. STAT. §§ 218- 219. **§15-219A. (Noncompete agreements).** "A. A person who makes an agreement with an employer, whether in writing or verbally, not to compete with the employer after the employment relationship has been terminated, shall be permitted to engage in the same business as that conducted by the former employer or in a similar business as that conducted by the former employer as	*Cardiovascular Surgical Specialist Corp. v. Mammana,* 61 P.3d 210 (Okla. 2002) (decision predating the current non-compete statute and upholding one-year prohibition on physician's active solicitation of former employer's patients, excluding where the patient affirmatively requested continued medical treatment by the physician, rather than the plaintiff employer).

State & Statute	Statute Language	Case Law
Oklahoma (con't) 15 OKLA. STAT. §§ 217-219B eff. June 4, 2001)	long as the former employee does not directly solicit the sale of goods, services or a combination of goods and services from the established customers of the former employer. B. Any provision in a contract between an employer and an employee in conflict with the provisions of this section shall be void and unenforceable." 15 OKLA. STAT. §§ 218-219B (Nonsolicitation agreements) "A contract or contractual provision which prohibits an employee or independent contractor of a person or business from soliciting, directly or indirectly, actively or inactively, the employees or independent contractors of that person or business to become employees or independent contractors of another person or business shall not be construed as a restraint from exercising a lawful profession, trade or business of any kind. Sections 217, 218, 219 and 219A of Title 15 of the Oklahoma Statutes shall not apply to such contracts or contractual provisions."	

State & Statute	Statute Language	Case Law
Oregon OR. REV. STAT. § 653.295	ORS § 653.295 Noncompetition agreements; (1) A noncompetition agreement entered into between an employer and employee is voidable and may not be enforced by a court of this state unless: (a)(A) The employer informs the employee in a written employment offer received by the employee at least two weeks before the first day of the employee's employment that a noncompetition agreement is required as a condition of employment; or (B) The noncompetition agreement is entered into upon a subsequent bona fide advancement of the employee by the employer; (b) The employee is a person described in ORS 653.020 (3); (c) The employer has a protectable interest. As used in this paragraph, an employer has a protectable interest when the employee: (A) Has access to trade secrets, as that term is defined in ORS 646.461; (B) Has access to competitively sensitive confidential business or professional information that otherwise	In *Ladd v. Hikes*, 639 P.2d 1307 (Or. Ct. App. 1982), the plaintiff medical partnership contracted with defendant physician to work as an associate for two years. The contract of employment had a non-competition provision. It did not so provide, but it was contemplated that at the end of the contract period plaintiff, if satisfied with defendant, would offer him a partnership and that defendant, if he then desired, would accept. There was no requirement that a partnership be either offered or accepted. When the contract ended, defendant left plaintiff's practice and started practicing on his own within the prohibited geographical area, attracting a considerable number of plaintiff's former patients. Plaintiff brought an action seeking to enjoin defendant from practicing within the city area. The trial court denied the injunction because defendant

State & Statute	Statute Language	Case Law
Oregon (con't) OR. REV. STAT. § 653.295	would not qualify as a trade secret, including product development plans, product launch plans, marketing strategy or sales plans; or (C) Is employed as an on-air talent by an employer in the business of broadcasting and the employer: (i) In the year preceding the termination of the employee's employment, expended resources equal to or exceeding 10 percent of the employee's annual salary to develop, improve, train or publicly promote the employee, provided that the resources expended by the employer were expended on media that the employer does not own or control; and (ii) Provides the employee, for the time the employee is restricted from working, the greater of compensation equal to at least 50 percent of the employee's annual gross base salary and commissions at the time of the employee's termination or 50 percent of the median family income for a four-person family, as determined by the United States Census Bureau for the most recent year available at the time of the employee's termination; and	was in a weak position in negotiating his contract, so it was unconscionable, and because the restrictive provision was against public policy. On appeal, the court reversed and remanded, concluding that the provision was enforceable because the state supreme court had approved physician covenants not to compete. *Id.*

State & Statute	Statute Language	Case Law
Oregon (con't) OR. REV. STAT. § 653.295	(d) The total amount of the employee's annual gross salary and commissions, calculated on an annual basis, at the time of the employee's termination exceeds the median family income for a four-person family, as determined by the United States Census Bureau for the most recent year available at the time of the employee's termination. This paragraph does not apply to an employee described in paragraph (c) (C) of this subsection.	

(2) The term of a noncompetition agreement may not exceed 18 months from the date of the employee's termination. The remainder of a term of a noncompetition agreement in excess of 18 months is voidable and may not be enforced by a court of this state.

(3) Subsections (1) and (2) of this section apply only to noncompetition agreements made in the context of an employment relationship or contract and not otherwise.

(4) Subsections (1) and (2) of this section do not apply to:

(a) Bonus restriction agreements, which are lawful agreements that may be

State & Statute	Statute Language	Case Law
Oregon (con't) Or. Rev. Stat. § 653.295	enforced by the courts in this state; or (b) A covenant not to solicit employees of the employer or solicit or transact business with customers of the employer. (5) Nothing in this section restricts the right of any person to protect trade secrets or other proprietary information by injunction or any other lawful means under other applicable laws. (6) Notwithstanding subsection (1)(b) and (d) of this section, a noncompetition agreement is enforceable for the full term of the agreement, for up to 18 months, if the employer provides the employee, for the time the employee is restricted from working, the greater of: (a) Compensation equal to at least 50 percent of the employee's annual gross base salary and commissions at the time of the employee's termination; or (b) Fifty percent of the median family income for a four-person family, as determined by the United States Census Bureau for the most recent year available at the time of the employee's termination.	

State & Statute	Statute Language	Case Law
Oregon (con't) OR. REV. STAT. § 653.295	(7) As used in this section: (a) "Bonus restriction agreement" means an agreement, written or oral, express or implied, between an employer and employee under which: (A) Competition by the employee with the employer is limited or restrained after termination of employment, but the restraint is limited to a period of time, a geographic area and specified activities, all of which are reasonable in relation to the services described in subparagraph (B) of this paragraph; (B) The services performed by the employee pursuant to the agreement include substantial involvement in management of the employer's business, personal contact with customers, knowledge of customer requirements related to the employer's business or knowledge of trade secrets or other proprietary information of the employer; and (C) The penalty imposed on the employee for competition against the employer is limited to forfeiture of profit sharing or other bonus compensation that has not yet been paid to the employee.	

State & Statute	Statute Language	Case Law
Oregon (con't) OR. REV. STAT. § 653.295	(b) "Broadcasting" means the activity of transmitting of any one-way electronic signal by radio waves, microwaves, wires, co-axial cables, wave guides or other conduits of communications. (c) "Employee" and "employer" have the meanings given those terms in ORS 652.310. (d) "Noncompetition agreement" means an agreement, written or oral, express or implied, between an employer and employee under which the employee agrees that the employee, either alone or as an employee of another person, will not compete with the employer in providing products, processes or services that are similar to the employer's products, processes or services for a period of time or within a specified geographic area after termination of employment.	
South Dakota S.D. CODIFIED LAWS §§ 53-9-8 et seq.	§ 53-9-8 "Every contract restraining exercise of a lawful profession, trade, or business is void to that extent, *except as* provided by §§ 53-9-9 to 53-9-11, inclusive, and 53-9-12.	*Loescher v. Policky*, 84 S.D. 477, 173 N.W.2d 50 (1969) (holding that a noncompete signed after employment had begun was validated by the employee's continued employment after signing).

State & Statute	Statute Language	Case Law
	S.D. CODIFIED LAWS § 53-9-8-11 Employment contract – Covenant not to compete. "An employee may agree with an employer at the time of employment or at any time during his employment not to engage directly or indirectly in the same business or profession as that of his employer for any period not exceeding two years from the date of termination of the agreement and not to solicit existing customers of the employer within a specified county, city or other specified area for any period not exceeding two years from the date of termination of the agreement, if the employer continues to carry on a like business." Other Exceptions: 1) Sale of good will of a business (§53-9-9), 2) Dissolution of a partnership (§53-9-10), 3) Contracts of independent contractor who is captive insurance agent (§53-9-12).	
Note: S.D. CODIFIED LAWS § 44:63:02:10	**Editor's Note:** Non competes are prohibited in employment contracts for J-1 physicians serving underserved areas. ARSD 44:63:02:10	

State & Statute	Statute Language	Case Law
Utah UTAH CODE ANN 34-51-101, et. seq. (eff. May 10, 2016)	**34-51-101. Title.** This chapter is known as the "Post-Employment Restrictions Act." **34-51-102. Definitions.** As used in this chapter: (1) (a) "Post-employment restrictive covenant," also known as a "covenant not to compete" or "noncompete agreement," means an agreement, written or oral, between an employer and employee under which the employee agrees that the employee, either alone or as an employee of another person, will not compete with the employer in providing products, processes, or services that are similar to the employer's products, processes, or services. b. "Post-employment restrictive covenant" does not include nonsolicitation agreements or nondisclosure or confidentiality agreements. (2) "Sale of a business" means a transfer of the ownership by sale, acquisition, merger, or other method of the tangible or intangible assets of a business entity, or a division or segment of the business entity. **34-51-201. Post-employment restrictive covenants.** In addition to any requirements imposed	*Robbins v. Finlay*, 645 P.2d 623 (Utah 1982) (holding that covenants not to compete are enforceable only to the extent necessary to protect the legitimate interest of the employer; noting that the scope and duration of the restriction will be compared with the nature of the interest the employer seeks to protect); *Microbiological Research Corp. v. Muna*, 625 P.2d 690 (Utah 1981) (holding that employer's customer list was not protectable because customer identities publicly available); *see also Allen v. Rose Park Pharmacy*, 120 Utah 608, 237 P.2d 823 (1951); *Melrose v. Low*, 80 Utah 356, 15 P.2d 319 (1932).

State & Statute	Statute Language	Case Law
Utah (con't) UTAH CODE ANN 34-51-101, et. seq. (eff. May 10, 2016)	under common law, for a post-employment restrictive covenant entered into on or after May 10, 2016, an employer and an employee may not enter into a post-employment restrictive covenant for a period of more than **one year** from the day on which the employee is no longer employed by the employer. A post-employment restrictive covenant that violates this section is void.	
	34-51-202. Exceptions (1) This chapter does not prohibit a reasonable severance agreement mutually and freely agreed upon in good faith at or after the time of termination that includes a post-employment restrictive covenant. A severance agreement remains subject to any requirements imposed under common law. (2) This chapter does not prohibit a post-employment restrictive covenant related to or arising out of the sale of a business, if the individual subject to the restrictive covenant receives value related to the sale of the business	
	34-51-301. Award of arbitration costs, attorney fees and court costs, and damages.	

State & Statute	Statute Language	Case Law
Utah (con't) UTAH CODE ANN 34-51-101, et. seq. (eff. May 10, 2016)	If an employer seeks to enforce a post-employment restrictive covenant through arbitration or by filing a civil action and it is determined that the post-employment restrictive covenant is unenforceable, the employer is liable for the employee's: (1) costs associated with arbitration; (2) attorney fees and court costs; and (3) actual damages.	
Washington WASH. REV. CODE § 49.44.190 **Editor's Note:** As of June 15, 2017 there is a bill that has been passed in the Washington House on March 8, 2017 and is currently in the Washington Senate (HB 1967) which specifically provides that an unreasonable noncompetition agreement is void and unenforceable and, among other things also requires that all the terms of a	RCW §49.44.190 RCW §49.44.190 is only applicable to broadcasting industry employees (and excepting sales and management employees).	The burden of proving reasonableness is on the employer. Sheppard v. Blackstock Lumber Co., 85 Wash. 2d 929, 933, 540 P.3d 1373 (1975). Public policy requires a court to consider possible harm to the public from enforcing the covenant. Such harm may include restraint of trade, limits on employment opportunities, and denial of public access to necessary services. But the court must still balance these concerns against the employer's right to protect his business. *Emerick v. Cardiac Study Ctr., Inc.*, 286 P.3d 689 (Wash. Ct. App. 2012) *["Emerick I"]*.

State & Statute	Statute Language	Case Law
Washington (con't) WASH. REV. CODE § 49.44.190 non-compete contract be disclosed in writing before the employee accepts the employment offer, and that the court "may" reform the agreement to make it reasonable or, if the agreement is entered into after the commencement of employment, the employer must provide independent consideration for the agreement.		*In Emerick v. v. Cardiac Study Ctr., Inc.*, 189 Wash. App. 711, 729 357 P.3d 696, 705 (1st Div. 2015) *[Emerick II]*, after judicial reformation, a 48-month non-competition covenant barring a physician from practicing cardiology within a 2-mile radius of any of the employer's offices in the city of Federal Way and Pierce Co. WA. The court found that the physician was not restricted from practicing cardiology on his former or new patients at any hospital and the restriction would not require his patients to travel inordinate distances to see him. *Boyd v. Davis*, 127 Wash. 2d 256, 897 P.2d 1239 (Wash. 1995) (upholding arbitrator's decision to sever noncompete restrictions from other agreements executed in conjunction with sale of a medical practice); *see also Ashley v. Lance*, 75 Wash. 2d 471 (1969); *Partlow v. Mathews*, 43 Wash. 2d 398, 261 P.2d 394 (1953).

State & Statute	Statute Language	Case Law
Washington (con't) Wash. Rev. Code § 49.44.190		In *Genex Coop., Inc. v. Contreras, et.al.*, No. 2:13-cv-03008-SAB.2014 BL 279888 (E.D. Wash. Oct. 3, 2014) the court found unenforceable as a matter of law an 18-month noncompete barring bovine breeding specialist(s) from engaging in certain practices in the Sunnyside WA. area where he/they had been employed, because the covenant was, among other things, not limited to former employer's customers and because employer appeared to use the covenant "as either a method to eliminate legitimate competition, or to strong-arm its employees to accept ever-dwindling wages and restrict their freedom to work." *Id.* at *11.

State & Statute	Statute Language	Case Law
Wisconsin WIS. STAT. § 103.465	A covenant by an assistant, servant or agent not to compete with his or her employer or principal during the term of the employment or agency, or after the termination of that employment or agency, within a specified territory and during a specified time is lawful and enforceable only if the restrictions imposed are reasonably necessary for the protection of the employer or principal. Any covenant, described in this subsection, imposing an unreasonable restraint is illegal, void and unenforceable even as to any part of the covenant or performance that would be a reasonable restraint.	In *Fox Valley Thoracic Surgical Assocs. v. Ferrante*, 2008 Wisc. App. LEXIS 150 (Wis. Ct. App. 2008), the practice asserted that the circuit court erred by concluding that the covenant not to compete in the surgeon's employment contract was invalid pursuant to WIS. STAT. § 103.465 (2005-06). The appellate court agreed with the circuit court that the covenant was void under the statute. The contract's prohibition was overbroad because it prevented the surgeon from practicing thoracic medicine, not just heart surgery, and because the geographic restraint was greater than reasonably necessary to protect the practice. Because the contract was invalid, there was no basis for the tortuous interference claim. Under WIS. STAT. § 103.465, a covenant not to compete within a specific time and a specific territory is lawful only if the restrictions imposed

State & Statute	Statute Language	Case Law
Wisconsin **(con't)** Wis. Stat. § 103.465		are reasonably necessary for the protection of the employer. Five inquiries are made in evaluating the enforceability of a covenant not to compete. The covenant must: (1) be necessary for the protection of the employer; (2) provide a reasonable time restriction; (3) provide a reasonable territorial limit; (4) be reasonable as to the employee; and (5) be reasonable as to the general public. WIS. STAT. § 103.465 provides that any unreasonable portion of the covenant not to compete voids the entire covenant even if the remaining portions would be enforceable. *Wausau Med. Ctr., S.C. v. Asplund*, 514 N.W.2d 34, 38 (Wis. Ct. App. 1994); *see also Prpa v. Wheaton Franciscan Med. Grp., Inc.*, 2013 Wis. App. LEXIS 57 (Wis. Ct. App. Jan. 23, 2013).

End Note 1: Fla. Stat. Ch. 542.335.

FLORIDA STATUTE LANGUAGE: Valid restraints of trade or commerce. (For covenants executed on or after July 1, 1996)

(1)   Notwithstanding s. 542.18 and subsection (2), enforcement of contracts that restrict or prohibit competition during or after the term of restrictive covenants, so long as such contracts are reasonable in time, area, and line of business, is not prohibited. In any action concerning enforcement of a restrictive covenant:

(a)   A court shall not enforce a restrictive covenant unless it is set forth in a writing signed by the person against whom enforcement is sought.

(b)   The person seeking enforcement of a restrictive covenant shall plead and prove the existence of one or more legitimate business interests justifying the restrictive covenant.

The term "legitimate business interest" includes, but is not limited to:

1.   Trade secrets, as defined in s. 688.002(4).

2.   Valuable confidential business or professional information that otherwise does not qualify as trade secrets.

3.   Substantial relationships with specific prospective or existing customers, patients, or clients.

4.   Customer, patient, or client goodwill associated with: a.   An ongoing business or professional practice, by way of trade name, trademark, service mark, or "trade dress"; b.   A specific geographic location; or c.   A specific marketing or trade area.

5.   Extraordinary or specialized training.

Any restrictive covenant not supported by a legitimate business interest is unlawful and is void and unenforceable.

(c)   A person seeking enforcement of a restrictive covenant also shall plead and prove that the contractually specified restraint is reasonably necessary to protect the legitimate business interest or interests justifying the restriction. If a person seeking enforcement of the restrictive covenant establishes prima facie that the restraint is reasonably necessary, the person opposing enforcement has the burden of establishing that the contractually specified restraint is overbroad, overlong, or otherwise not reasonably necessary to protect the established legitimate business interest or interests. If a contractually specified restraint is overbroad, overlong, or otherwise not reasonably necessary to protect the legitimate business interest or interests, a court shall modify the restraint and grant only the relief reasonably necessary to protect such interest or interests.

(d)   In determining the reasonableness in time of a postterm restrictive covenant not predicated upon the protection of trade secrets, a court shall apply the following rebuttable presumptions:

1.   In the case of a restrictive covenant sought to be enforced against a former employee, agent, or independent contractor, and not associated with the sale of all or a part of: a.   The assets of a business or professional practice, or b.   The shares of a corporation, or c.   A partnership interest, or d.   A limited liability company membership, or e.   An equity interest, of any other type, in a business or professional practice, a court shall presume reasonable in time any restraint 6 months or less in duration and shall presume unreasonable in time any restraint more than 2 years in duration.

2.   In the case of a restrictive covenant sought to be enforced against a former distributor, dealer, franchisee, or licensee of a trademark or service mark and not associated with the sale of all or a part of: a.   The assets of a business or professional practice, or b. The shares of a corporation, or c.   A partnership interest, or d. A limited liability company membership, or e. An equity interest, of any other type, in a business or professional practice, a court shall presume reasonable in time any restraint 1 year or less in duration and shall presume unreasonable in time any restraint more than 3 years in duration.

3.   In the case of a restrictive covenant sought to be enforced against the seller of all or a part of: a.   The assets of a business or professional practice, or b.   The shares of a corporation, or c.   A partnership interest, or d.   A limited liability company membership, or e.   An equity interest, of any other type, in a business or professional practice, a court shall presume reasonable in time any restraint 3 years or less in duration and shall presume unreasonable in time any restraint more than 7 years in duration.

(e)   In determining the reasonableness in time of a postterm restrictive covenant predicated upon the protection of trade secrets, a court shall presume reasonable in time any restraint of 5 years or less and shall presume unreasonable in time any restraint of more than 10 years. All such presumptions shall be rebuttable presumptions.

(f)   The court shall not refuse enforcement of a restrictive covenant on the ground that the person seeking enforcement is a third-party beneficiary of such contract or is an assignee or successor to a party to such contract, provided: 1.   In the case of a third-party beneficiary, the restrictive covenant expressly identified the person as a third-party beneficiary of the contract and expressly stated that the restrictive covenant was intended for the benefit of such person. 2.   In the case of an assignee or successor, the restrictive covenant expressly authorized enforcement by a party's assignee or successor.

(g)   In determining the enforceability of a restrictive covenant, a court: 1.   Shall not consider any individualized economic or other hardship that might be caused to the person against whom enforcement is sought. 2.   May consider as a defense the fact that the person seeking enforcement no longer continues in business in the area or line of business that is the subject of the action to enforce the restrictive covenant only if such discontinuance of business is not the result of a violation of the restriction. 3.   Shall consider all other pertinent legal and equitable defenses. 4.   Shall consider the effect of enforcement upon the public health, safety, and welfare.

(h)   A court shall construe a restrictive covenant in favor of providing reasonable protection to all legitimate business interests established by the person seeking enforcement. A court shall not employ any rule of contract construction that requires the court to construe a restrictive covenant narrowly, against the restraint, or against the drafter of the contract.

(i)   No court may refuse enforcement of an otherwise enforceable restrictive covenant on the ground that the contract violates public policy unless such public policy is articulated specifically by the court and the court finds that the specified public policy requirements substantially outweigh the need to protect the legitimate business interest or interests established by the person seeking enforcement of the restraint.

(j)   A court shall enforce a restrictive covenant by any appropriate and effective remedy, including, but not limited to, temporary and permanent injunctions. The violation of an enforceable restrictive covenant creates a presumption of irreparable injury to the person seeking enforcement of a restrictive covenant. No temporary injunction shall be entered unless the person seeking enforcement of a restrictive covenant gives a proper bond, and the court shall not enforce any contractual provision waiving the requirement of an injunction bond or limiting the amount of such bond.

(k)   In the absence of a contractual provision authorizing an award of attorney's fees and costs to the prevailing party, a court may award attorney's fees and costs to the prevailing party in any action seeking enforcement of, or challenging the enforceability of, a restrictive covenant. A court shall not enforce any contractual provision limiting the court's authority under this section.

(2)   Nothing in this section shall be construed or interpreted to legalize or make enforceable any restraint of trade or commerce otherwise illegal or unenforceable under the laws of the United States or of this state.

(3)   This act shall apply prospectively, and it shall not apply in actions determining the enforceability of restrictive covenants entered into before July 1, 1996.

End Note 2: GEORGIA

GA. Code § 13-8-50 Reasonable restrictive covenants valid

The General Assembly finds that reasonable restrictive covenants contained in employment and commercial contracts serve the legitimate purpose of protecting legitimate business interests and creating an environment that is favorable to attracting commercial enterprises to Georgia and keeping existing businesses within the state. Further, the General Assembly desires to provide statutory guidance so that all parties to such agreements may be certain of the validity and enforceability of such provisions and may know their rights and duties according to such provisions.

GA. Code § 13-8-51. Definitions

As used in this article, the term:

(1) "Affiliate" means: (A) A person or entity that directly, or indirectly through one or more intermediaries, controls or is controlled by or is under common control with another person or entity; (B) Any entity of which a person is an officer, director, or partner or holds an equity interest or ownership position that accounts for 25 percent or more of the voting rights or profit interest of such entity; (C) Any trust or other estate in which the person or entity has a beneficial interest of 25 percent or more or as to which such person or entity serves as trustee or in a similar fiduciary capacity; or (D) The spouse, lineal ancestors, lineal descendants, and siblings of the person, as well as each of their spouses.

(2) "Business" means any line of trade or business conducted by the seller or employer, as such terms are defined in this Code section.

(3) "Confidential information" means data and information: (A) Relating to the business of the employer, regardless of whether the data or information constitutes a trade secret as that term is defined in Code Section 10-1-761; (B) Disclosed to the employee or of which the employee became aware of as a consequence of the employee's relationship with the employer; (C) Having value to the employer; (D) Not generally known to competitors of the employer; and (E) Which includes trade secrets, methods of operation, names of customers, price lists, financial information and projections, route books, personnel data, and similar information; provided, however,

that such term shall not mean data or information (A) which has been voluntarily disclosed to the public by the employer, except where such public disclosure has been made by the employee without authorization from the employer; (B) which has been independently developed and disclosed by others; or (C) which has otherwise entered the public domain through lawful means.

(4) "Controlling interest" means any equity interest or ownership participation held by a person or entity with respect to a business that accounts for 25 percent or more of the voting rights or profit interest of the business prior to the sale, alone or in combination with the interest or participation held by affiliates of such person or entity.

(5) "Employee" means: (A) An executive employee; (B) Research and development personnel or other persons or entities of an employer, including, without limitation, independent contractors, in possession of confidential information that is important to the business of the employer; (C) Any other person or entity, including an independent contractor, in possession of selective or specialized skills, learning, or abilities or customer contacts, customer information, or confidential information who or that has obtained such skills, learning, abilities, contacts, or information by reason of having worked for an employer; or (D) A franchisee, distributor, lessee, licensee, or party to a partnership agreement or a sales agent, broker, or representative in connection with franchise, distributorship, lease, license, or partnership agreements. Such term shall not include any employee who lacks selective or specialized skills, learning, or abilities or customer contacts, customer information, or confidential information.

(6) "Employer" means any corporation, partnership, proprietorship, or other business organization, whether for profit or not for profit, including, without limitation, any successor in interest to such an entity, who or that conducts business or any person or entity who or that directly or indirectly owns an equity interest or ownership participation in such an entity accounting for 25 percent or more of the voting rights or profit interest of such entity. Such term also means the buyer or seller of a business organization.

(7) "Executive employee" means a member of the board of directors, an officer, a key employee, a manager, or a supervisor of an employer.

(8) "Key employee" means an employee who, by reason of the employer's investment of time, training, money, trust, exposure to the public, or exposure to customers, vendors, or other business relationships during the course of the employee's employment with the employer, has gained a high level of notoriety, fame, reputation, or public persona as the employer's representative or spokesperson or has gained a high level of influence or credibility with the employer's customers, vendors, or other business

relationships or is intimately involved in the planning for or direction of the business of the employer or a defined unit of the business of the employer. Such term also means an employee in possession of selective or specialized skills, learning, or abilities or customer contacts or customer information who has obtained such skills, learning, abilities, contacts, or information by reason of having worked for the employer.

(9) "Legitimate business interest" includes, but is not limited to: (A) Trade secrets, as defined by Code Section 10-1-761; (B) Valuable confidential information that otherwise does not qualify as a trade secret; (C) Substantial relationships with specific prospective or existing customers, patients, vendors, or clients; (D) Customer, patient, or client good will associated with: (i) An ongoing business, commercial, or professional practice, including, but not limited to, by way of trade name, trademark, service mark, or trade dress; (ii) A specific geographic location; or (iii) A specific marketing or trade area; and (E) Extraordinary or specialized training.

(10) "Material contact" means the contact between an employee and each customer or potential customer: (A) With whom or which the employee dealt on behalf of the employer; (B) Whose dealings with the employer were coordinated or supervised by the employee; (C) About whom the employee obtained confidential information in the ordinary course of business as a result of such employee's association with the employer; or (D) Who receives products or services authorized by the employer, the sale or provision of which results or resulted in compensation, commissions, or earnings for the employee within two years prior to the date of the employee's termination.

(11) "Modification" means the limitation of a restrictive covenant to render it reasonable in light of the circumstances in which it was made. Such term shall include: (A) Severing or removing that part of a restrictive covenant that would otherwise make the entire restrictive covenant unenforceable; and (B) Enforcing the provisions of a restrictive covenant to the extent that the provisions are reasonable.

(12) "Modify" means to make, to cause, or otherwise to bring about a modification.

(13) "Products or services" means anything of commercial value, including, without limitation, goods; personal, real, or intangible property; services; financial products; business opportunities or assistance; or any other object or aspect of business or the conduct thereof.

(14) "Professional" means an employee who has as a primary duty the performance of work requiring knowledge of an advanced type in a field of science or learning customarily acquired by a prolonged course of specialized intellectual instruction or requiring invention, imagination, originality, or talent in a recognized field of artistic or creative endeavor. Such term

shall not include employees performing technician work using knowledge acquired through on-the-job and classroom training, rather than by acquiring the knowledge through prolonged academic study, such as might be performed, without limitation, by a mechanic, a manual laborer, or a ministerial employee.

(15) "Restrictive covenant" means an agreement between two or more parties that exists to protect the first party's or parties' interest in property, confidential information, customer good will, business relationships, employees, or any other economic advantages that the second party has obtained for the benefit of the first party or parties, to which the second party has gained access in the course of his or her relationship with the first party or parties, or which the first party or parties has acquired from the second party as the result of a sale. Such restrictive covenants may exist within or ancillary to contracts between or among employers and employees, distributors and manufacturers, lessors and lessees, partnerships and partners, employers and independent contractors, franchisors and franchisees, and sellers and purchasers of a business or commercial enterprise and any two or more employers. A restrictive covenant shall not include covenants appurtenant to real property.

(16) "Sale" means any sale or transfer of the good will or substantially all of the assets of a business or any sale or transfer of a controlling interest in a business, whether by sale, exchange, redemption, merger, or otherwise.

(17) "Seller" means any person or entity, including any successor-in-interest to such an entity, that is: (A) An owner of a controlling interest; (B) An executive employee of the business who receives, at a minimum, consideration in connection with a sale; or (C) An affiliate of a person or entity described in subparagraph (A) of this paragraph; provided, however, that each sale involving a restrictive covenant shall be binding only on the person or entity entering into such covenant, its successors-in-interest, and, if so specified in the covenant, any entity that directly or indirectly through one or more affiliates is controlled by or is under common control of such person or entity.

(18) "Termination" means the termination of an employee's engagement with an employer, whether with or without cause, upon the initiative of either party.

(19) "Trade dress" means the distinctive packaging or design of a product that promotes the product and distinguishes it from other products in the marketplace.

GA. Code § 13-8-52. Parties to whom provisions are applicable.

(a) The provisions of this article shall be applicable only to contracts and agreements between or among: (1) Employers and employees; (2) Distributors and manufacturers; (3) Lessors and lessees; (4) Partnerships and partners; (5) Franchisors and franchisees; (6) Sellers and purchasers of a business or commercial enterprise; and (7) Two or more employers.

(b) The provisions of this article shall not apply to any contract or agreement not described in subsection (a) of this Code section.

GA. Code § 13-8-53. Prohibition against unreasonable restrictive covenants against competition.

(a) Notwithstanding any other provision of this chapter, enforcement of contracts that restrict competition during the term of a restrictive covenant, so long as such restrictions are reasonable in time, geographic area, and scope of prohibited activities, shall be permitted. However, enforcement of contracts that restrict competition after the term of employment, as distinguished from a customer nonsolicitation provision, as described in subsection (b) of this Code section, or a nondisclosure of confidential information provision, as described in subsection (e) of this Code section, shall not be permitted against any employee who does not, in the course of his or her employment: (1) Customarily and regularly solicit for the employer customers or prospective customers; (2) Customarily and regularly engage in making sales or obtaining orders or contracts for products or services to be performed by others; (3) Perform the following duties:

(A) Have a primary duty of managing the enterprise in which the employee is employed or of a customarily recognized department or subdivision thereof;

(B) Customarily and regularly direct the work of two or more other employees; and

(C) Have the authority to hire or fire other employees or have particular weight given to suggestions and recommendations as to the hiring, firing, advancement, promotion, or any other change of status of other employees; or

(4) Perform the duties of a key employee or of a professional.

(b) Notwithstanding any other provision of this chapter, an employee may agree in writing for the benefit of an employer to refrain, for a stated period of time following termination, from soliciting, or attempting to solicit, directly or by assisting others, any business from any of such employer's customers, including actively seeking prospective customers, with whom the employee had material contact during his or her employment for purposes of providing products or services that are competitive with those provided by the employer's business. No express reference to geographic area or the types of products or services considered to be competitive shall be required in order for the restraint to be enforceable. Any reference to a prohibition against "soliciting or attempting to solicit business from customers" or similar language shall be adequate for such purpose and narrowly construed to apply only to: (1) such of the employer's customers, including actively sought prospective customers, with whom the employee had material contact; and (2) products or services that are competitive with those provided by the employer's business.

GA. Code 13-8-54. Reasonable intent and expectation standard for construing restrictive covenants.

(a) A court shall construe a restrictive covenant to comport with the reasonable intent and expectations of the parties to the covenant and in favor of providing reasonable protection to all legitimate business interests established by the person seeking enforcement. (b) In any action concerning enforcement of a restrictive covenant, a court shall not enforce a restrictive covenant unless it is in compliance with the provisions of Code Section 13-8-53; provided, however, that if a court finds that a contractually specified restraint does not comply with the provisions of Code Section 13-8-53, then the court may modify the restraint provision and grant only the relief reasonably necessary to protect such interest or interests and to achieve the original intent of the contracting parties to the extent possible.

GA. Code § 13-8-55. Pleading requirements for enforcement of a restrictive covenant.

The person seeking enforcement of a restrictive covenant shall plead and prove the existence of one or more legitimate business interests justifying the restrictive covenant. If a person seeking enforcement of the restrictive covenant establishes by prima-facie evidence that the restraint is in compliance with the provisions of Code Section 13-8-53, then any person opposing enforcement has the burden of establishing that the contractually specified restraint does not comply with such requirements or that such covenant is unreasonable.

GA. Code § 13-8-56. Reasonableness of restrictive covenants limiting competition.

In determining the reasonableness of a restrictive covenant that limits or restricts competition during or after the term of an employment or business relationship, the court shall make the following presumptions:

(1) During the term of the relationship, a time period equal to or measured by duration of the parties' business or commercial relationship is reasonable, provided that the reasonableness of a time period after a term of employment shall be as provided for in Code Section 13-8-57;

(2) A geographic territory which includes the areas in which the employer does business at any time during the parties' relationship, even if not known at the time of entry into the restrictive covenant, is reasonable provided that:

(A) The total distance encompassed by the provisions of the covenant also is reasonable;

(B) The agreement contains a list of particular competitors as prohibited employers for a limited period of time after the term of employment or a business or commercial relationship; or

(C) Both subparagraphs (A) and (B) of this paragraph;

(3) The scope of competition restricted is measured by the business of the employer or other person or entity in whose favor the restrictive covenant is given; provided, however, that a court shall not refuse to enforce the provisions of a restrictive covenant because the person seeking enforcement establishes evidence that a restrictive covenant has been violated but has not proven that the covenant has been violated as to the entire scope of the prohibited activities of the person seeking enforcement or as to the entire geographic area of the covenant; and

(4) Any restriction that operates during the term of an employment relationship, agency relationship, independent contractor relationship, partnership, franchise, distributorship, license, ownership of a stake in a business entity, or other ongoing business relationship shall not be considered unreasonable because it lacks any specific limitation upon scope of activity, duration, or geographic area so long as it promotes or protects the purpose or subject matter of the agreement or relationship or deters any potential conflict of interest.

GA. Code § 13-8-57. Reasonableness in time of restrictive covenants.

(a) In determining the reasonableness in time of a restrictive covenant sought to be enforced after a term of employment, a court shall apply the rebuttable presumptions provided in this Code section.

(b) In the case of a restrictive covenant sought to be enforced against a former employee and not associated with the sale or ownership of all or a material part of:

(1) The assets of a business, professional practice, or other commercial enterprise; (2) The shares of a corporation; (3) A partnership interest; (4) A limited liability company membership; or (5) An equity interest or profit participation, of any other type, in a business, professional practice, or other commercial enterprise, a court shall presume to be reasonable in time any restraint two years or less in duration and shall presume to be unreasonable

in time any restraint more than two years in duration, measured from the date of the termination of the business relationship.

(c) In the case of a restrictive covenant sought to be enforced against a current or former distributor, dealer, franchisee, lessee of real or personal property, or licensee of a trademark, trade dress, or service mark and not associated with the sale of all or a part of: (1) The assets of a business, professional practice, or other commercial enterprise; (2) The shares of a corporation; (3) A partnership interest; (4) A limited liability company membership; or (5) An equity interest or profit participation, of any other type, in a business, professional practice, or other commercial enterprise, a court shall presume to be reasonable in time any restraint three years or less in duration and shall presume to be unreasonable in time any restraint more than three years in duration, measured from the date of termination of the business relationship.

(d) In the case of a restrictive covenant sought to be enforced against the owner or seller of all or a material part of: (1) The assets of a business, professional practice, or other commercial enterprise; (2) The shares of a corporation; (3) A partnership interest; (4) A limited liability company membership; or (5) An equity interest or profit participation, of any other type, in a business, professional practice, or other commercial enterprise, a court shall presume to be reasonable in time any restraint the longer of five years or less in duration or equal to the period of time during which payments are being made to the owner or seller as a result of any sale referred to in this subsection and shall presume to be unreasonable in time any restraint more than the longer of five years in duration or the period of time during which payments are being made to the owner or seller as a result of any sale referred to in this subsection, measured from the date of termination or disposition of such interest.

GA. Code § 13-8-58. Enforceability of Restrictive Covenants.

(a) A court shall not refuse to enforce a restrictive covenant on the ground that the person seeking enforcement is a third-party beneficiary of such contract or is an assignee or successor to a party to such contract.

(b) In determining the enforceability of a restrictive covenant, it is not a defense that the person seeking enforcement no longer continues in business in the scope of the prohibited activities that is the subject of the action to enforce the restrictive covenant if such discontinuance of business is the result of a violation of the restriction.

(c) A court shall enforce a restrictive covenant by any appropriate and effective remedy available at law or equity, including, but not limited to, temporary and permanent injunctions.

(d) In determining the reasonableness of a restrictive covenant between an employer and an employee, as such term is defined in subparagraphs (A) through (C) of paragraph (5) of Code Section 13-8-51, a court may consider the economic hardship imposed upon an employee by enforcement of the covenant; provided, however, that this subsection shall not apply to contracts or agreements between or among those persons or entities listed in paragraphs (2) through (7) of subsection (a) of Code Section 13-8-52.

GA. Code § 13-8-59. No illegal restraint of trade or commerce.

Nothing in this article shall be construed or interpreted to allow or to make enforceable any restraint of trade or commerce that is otherwise illegal or unenforceable under the laws of the United States or under the Constitution of this state or of the United States.

End Note 3: Louisiana

LA. REV. STAT. ANN §23:921. Restraint of business prohibited; restraint on forum prohibited; competing business; contracts against engaging in; provisions for

A. (1) Every contract or agreement, or provision thereof, by which anyone is restrained from exercising a lawful profession, trade, or business of any kind, except as provided in this Section, shall be null and void. However, every contract or agreement, or provision thereof, which meets the exceptions as provided in this Section, shall be enforceable.

(2) The provisions of every employment contract or agreement, or provisions thereof, by which any foreign or domestic employer or any other person or entity includes a choice of forum clause or choice of law clause in an employee's contract of employment or collective bargaining agreement, or attempts to enforce either a choice of forum clause or choice of law clause in any civil or administrative action involving an employee, shall be null and void except where the choice of forum clause or choice of law clause is expressly, knowingly, and voluntarily agreed to and ratified by the employee after the occurrence of the incident which is the subject of the civil or administrative action.

B. Any person, including a corporation and the individual shareholders of such corporation, who sells the goodwill of a business may agree with the buyer that the seller or other interested party in the transaction, will refrain from carrying on or engaging in a business similar to the business being sold or from soliciting customers of the business being sold within a specified parish or parishes, or municipality or municipalities, or parts thereof, so long as the buyer, or any person deriving title to the goodwill from him, carries on a like business therein, not to exceed a period of two years from the date of sale.

C. Any person, including a corporation and the individual shareholders of such corporation, who is employed as an agent, servant, or employee may agree with his employer to refrain from carrying on or engaging in a business similar to that of the employer and/or from soliciting customers of the employer within a specified parish or parishes, municipality or municipalities, or parts thereof, so long as the employer carries on a like business therein, not to exceed a period of two years from termination of employment. An independent contractor, whose work is performed pursuant to a written contract, may enter into an agreement to refrain from carrying on or engaging in a business similar to the business of the person with whom the independent contractor has contracted, on the same basis as if the independent contractor were an employee, for a period not to exceed two years from the date of the last work performed under the written contract.

D. For the purposes of Subsections B and C of this Section, a person who becomes employed by a competing business, regardless of whether or not that person is an owner or equity interest holder of that competing business, may be deemed to be carrying on or engaging in a business similar to that of the party having a contractual right to prevent that person from competing.

E. Upon or in anticipation of a dissolution of the partnership, the partnership and the individual partners, including a corporation and the individual shareholders if the corporation is a partner, may agree that none of the partners will carry on a similar business within the same parish or parishes, or municipality or municipalities, or within specified parts thereof, where the partnership business has been transacted, not to exceed a period of two years from the date of dissolution.

F. (1) Parties to a franchise may agree that:

(a) The franchisor shall refrain from selling, distributing, or granting additional franchises to sell or distribute, within defined geographic territory, those products or services which are the subject of the franchise.

(b) The franchisee shall:

(i) During the term of the franchise, refrain from competing with the franchisor or other franchisees of the franchisor or engaging in any other business similar to that which is the subject of the franchise.

(ii) For a period not to exceed two years following severance of the franchise relationship, refrain from engaging in any other business similar to that which is the subject of the franchise and from competing with or soliciting the customers of the franchisor or other franchisees of the franchisor.

(c) The employee if employed by a franchisor shall:

(i) During the term of his employment by the franchisor, refrain from competing with his employer or any of the franchisees of his employer or engaging in any other business similar to that which is the subject of the franchise.

(ii) For a period not to exceed two years following severance of the employment relationship between the franchisor and the employee, refrain from engaging in any other business similar to that which is the subject of the franchise between the franchisor and its franchisees and from competing with or soliciting the customers of his employer or the franchisees of his employer.

(2) Except as provided in Paragraph (3) of this Subsection, neither a franchisee who is a party to a franchise agreement regulated under the Federal Trade Commission Franchise Disclosure Rule, 16 CFR 436, nor an employee of the franchisee shall be deemed to be an employee of the franchisor for any purpose. A voluntary agreement entered into between the United States Department of Labor and an employer shall not be used by a state department or agency as evidence or for any other purpose in an investigation or judicial or administrative determination, including whether an employee of a franchisee is also considered to be an employee of the franchisor.

(3) Pursuant to Chapter 10 and Chapter 11 of Title 23 of the Louisiana Revised Statutes of 1950, an employee of a franchisee may be deemed to be an employee of the franchisor only where the two entities share or co-determine those matters governing the essential terms and conditions of employment and directly and immediately control matters relating to the employment relationship such as hiring, firing, discipline, supervision, and direction.

(4) As used in this Subsection:

(a) "Franchise" means any continuing commercial relationship created by any arrangement or arrangements as defined in 16 CFR 436.1(h).

(b) "Franchisee" means any person who participates in a franchise relationship as a franchisee, partner, shareholder with at least a ten percent interest in the franchisee, executive officer of the franchisee, or a person to whom an interest in a franchise is sold, as defined in 16 CFR 436.1(h), provided that no person shall be included in this definition unless he has signed an agreement expressly binding him to the provisions thereof.

(c) "Franchisor" means any person who participates in a franchise relationship as a franchisor as defined in 16 CFR 436.1(k).

G.(1) An employee may at any time enter into an agreement with his employer that, for a period not to exceed two years from the date of the termination of employment, he will refrain from engaging in any work or activity to design, write, modify, or implement any computer program that directly competes with any confidential computer program owned, licensed, or marketed by the employer, and to which the employee had direct access during the term of his employment or services.

(2) As used in this Subsection, "confidential" means that which:

(a) Is not generally known to and not readily ascertainable by other persons.

(b) Is the subject of reasonable efforts under the circumstances to maintain its secrecy.

(3) As used in this Subsection, "computer program" means a plan, routine, or set of statements or instructions, including any subset, subroutine, or portion of instructions, regardless of format or medium, which are capable, when incorporated into a machine-readable medium, of causing a computer to perform a particular task or function or achieve a particular result

(4) As used in this Subsection, "employee" shall mean any individual, corporation, partnership, or any other entity which contracts or agrees with an employer to perform, provide, or furnish any services to, for, or on behalf of such employer.

H. Any agreement covered by Subsection B, C, E, F, G, J, K, or L of this Section shall be considered an obligation not to do, and failure to perform may entitle the obligee to recover damages for the loss sustained and the profit of which he has been deprived. In addition, upon proof of the obligor's failure to perform, and without the necessity of proving irreparable injury, a court of competent jurisdiction shall order injunctive relief enforcing the terms of the agreement. Any agreement covered by Subsection J, K, or L of this Section shall be null and void if it is determined that members of the agreement were engaged in ultra vires acts. Nothing in Subsection J, K, or L of this Section shall prohibit the transfer, sale, or purchase of stock or interest in publicly traded entities.

I. (1) There shall be no contract or agreement or provision entered into by an automobile salesman and his employer restraining him from selling automobiles.

(2)(a) For the purposes of this Subsection, "automobile" means any new or used motor-driven car, van, or truck required to be registered which is used, or is designed to be used, for the transporting of passengers or goods for public, private, commercial, or for-hire purposes.

(b) For the purposes of this Subsection, "salesman" means any person with a salesman's license issued by the Louisiana Motor Vehicle Commission or the Used Motor Vehicle and Parts Commission, other than a person who owns a proprietary or equity interest in a new or used car dealership in Louisiana.

J. A corporation and the individual shareholders of such corporation may agree that such shareholders will refrain from carrying on or engaging in a business similar to that of the corporation and from soliciting customers of the corporation within a specified parish or parishes, municipality or municipalities, or parts thereof, for as long as the corporation carries on a similar business therein, not to exceed a period of two years from the date such shareholder ceases to be a shareholder of the corporation. A violation of this Subsection shall be enforceable in accordance with Subsection H of this Section.

K. A partnership and the individual partners of such partnership may agree that such partners will refrain from carrying on or engaging in a business similar to that of the partnership and from soliciting customers of the partnership within a specified parish or parishes, municipality or municipalities, or parts thereof, for as long as the partnership carries on a similar business therein, not to exceed a period of two years from the date such partner ceases to be a partner. A violation of this Subsection shall be enforceable in accordance with Subsection H of this Section.

L. A limited liability company and the individual members of such limited liability company may agree that such members will refrain from carrying on or engaging in a business similar to that of the limited liability company and from soliciting customers of the limited liability company within a specified parish or parishes, municipality or municipalities, or parts thereof, for as long as the limited liability company carries on a similar business therein, not to exceed a period of two years from the date such member ceases to be a member. A violation of this Subsection shall be enforceable in accordance with Subsection H of this Section.

[End LA. REV. STAT. ANN §23:921]

III. STATES WITH NO STATUTE
CONCERNING RESTRICTIVE COVENANTS

State & Statute	Case Law
Alaska	Unlike covenants not to compete ancillary to employment contracts, which "are scrutinized with particular care because they are often the product of unequal bargaining power," this level of scrutiny is not applied to covenants ancillary to

the sale of a business because the contracting parties are more likely to be of equal bargaining power. *Wenzell v. Ingrim*, 228 P.3d 103 (Alaska 2010).

A covenant not to compete is unenforceable on grounds of public policy if it unreasonably restrains trade, either because: (a) the restraint is greater than is needed to protect the promisee's legitimate interest, or (b) the promisee's need is outweighed by the hardship to the promisor and the likely injury to the public. *Id.*

This case, however, presents a rare instance where a party is attempting to enforce a covenant not to compete against a person employed by a federally funded nonprofit organization that provides free or low-cost healthcare services. In such a case, competition will not be presumed and must be proven. *Id.*

It appears from the record that [defendant] is employed by an organization providing an important, low-cost service to a population in need of such care. In a case that implicates such considerations, it is appropriate for a court to closely scrutinize the covenant not to compete to determine whether it is void for public policy reasons. *Id.*

Metcalfe Ins. Invs. v. Garrison, 919 P.2d 1356 (Alaska 1996) (finding that although

State & Statute	Case Law
Alaska (con't)	customer lists are a protectable interest, a customer non-solicitation restriction would be unreasonable if it prevented former employee from practicing his or her "specialty").
Arizona	To be enforced, the restrictive covenants must do more than simply prohibit fair competition by the employee. In other words, a covenant not to compete is invalid unless it protects some legitimate interest beyond the employer's desire to protect itself from competition. Despite the freedom to contract, the law does not favor restrictive covenants. By restricting a physician's practice of medicine, this covenant involves strong public policy implications and must be closely scrutinized. *Valley Med. Specialists v. Farber*, 982 P.2d 1277 (Ariz. 1999).
	This covenant must be put through a reasonableness analysis.
	Reasonableness is a fact-intensive inquiry that depends on the totality of the circumstances. A restriction is unreasonable and, thus, is not enforced: (1) if the restraint is greater than necessary to protect the employer's legitimate interest, or (2) if that interest is outweighed by the hardship to the employee and the likely injury to the public. *Id.*
	The continued success of a specialty practice, which is dependent upon patient referrals, is a legitimate interest worthy of protection. The restriction cannot be greater than necessary to protect VMS's legitimate interests. A restraint's scope is defined by its duration and geographic area. *Id.*

State & Statute	Case Law
Arizona (con't)	Restrictive covenants between physicians are strictly construed. The burden is on the party wishing to enforce the covenant to demonstrate that the restraint is no greater than necessary to protect the employer's legitimate interest, and that such interest is not outweighed by the hardship to the employee and the likely injury to the public. A court must evaluate the extent to which enforcing a covenant would foreclose patients from seeing the departing physician if they desire to do so. *Id.*
Arkansas **Editor's note:** ARK. Code Ann. §4-70-207,(the Arkansas statute governing postemployment noncompete covenants) specifically *excludes* medical professionals listed in Arkansas Code Title 17, Subtitle 3, which is an long laundry list of medical professionals, including, without limitation, physicians, surgeons, nurses, midwives, massage therapists, dentists, physician's trained assistants, podiatrists, psychologists and psychological examiners, veterinarians, social workers, acupuncturists, perfusionists, physician assistants, etc.	In *Mercy Health Sys. of Northwest Ark., Inc. v. Bicak*, 2011 Ark. App. LEXIS 341 (Ark. Ct. App. May 11, 2011), the Arkansas Court of Appeals held that "[t]he circuit court did not err in granting partial summary judgment to [defendant-physician] on [his] covenant-not-to-compete claim because [the hospital] did not counter [defendant-physician's] evidence demonstrating that it had no interest sufficient to warrant its enforcement; that it was designed only to eliminate competition; and that it would unreasonably interfere with the public's right of access to the physicians of their choice and [defendant physician's] ability to earn a living." In *Jaraki v. Cardiology Assocs. of Northeast Ark.*, 55 S.W.3d 799 (Ark. Ct. App. 2001), a doctor and the corporation entered into an employment agreement under which the doctor agreed not to practice within a 75-mile radius of the corporation's principal office for a period of two years if he terminated his employment before the end of the contract term. The court held that covenants not to compete are not looked upon with favor by the law.

State & Statute	Case Law
Arkansas (con't)	In order for such a covenant to be enforceable, three requirements must be met: (1) the covenantee must have a valid interest to protect; (2) the geographical restriction must not be overly broad; (3) a reasonable time limit must be imposed. A party challenging the validity of a covenant is required to show that it is unreasonable and contrary to public policy. Without statutory authorization or, some dominant policy justification, a contract in restraint of trade is unreasonable if it is based on a promise to refrain from competition that is not ancillary to a contract of employment or to a contract for the transfer of goodwill or other property. However, the law will not protect parties against ordinary competition. Covenants not to compete in employment contracts are subject to stricter scrutiny than those connected with a sale of a business. *Id.*

The court stated that it is contrary to public policy to unduly restrict the public's right of access to the physicians of their choice. *Id.*

Where a covenant not to compete grows out of an employment relationship, the courts have found an interest sufficient to warrant enforcement of the covenant only in those cases where the covenantee provided special training, or made available trade secrets, confidential business information, or customer lists, and then only if it is found that the associate was able to use information so obtained to gain an unfair competitive advantage. *Id.*

The geographic area in a covenant not to compete must be limited in order to be enforceable. The restraint imposed upon one party must not be greater than |

State & Statute	Case Law
Arkansas (con't)	is reasonably necessary for protecting the other party. In determining whether the geographic area is reasonable, the trade area of the former employer is viewed. Where a geographic restriction is greater than the trade area, the restriction is too broad and the covenant not to compete is void. *Id.*
Indiana	Non-competition agreements between a physician and a medical practice group are not *per se* void as against public policy and are enforceable to the extent they are reasonable. To be geographically reasonable, the agreement may restrict only that area in which the physician developed patient relationships using the practice group's resources. The Indiana Supreme Court has rejected the claim that public policy precludes medical doctors from entering into or enforcing non-competition covenants, and has adopted a reasonableness standard for physician noncompetition agreements. *Central Ind. Podiatry v. Krueger*, 882 N.E.2d 723 (Ind. 2008).

Regarding the enforceability of non-competition agreements between physicians, the issue is essentially a balancing of policy considerations best left to the legislature. Countervailing reasons exist that would militate against any deviation from the long-standing practice of finding reasonable restrictive covenants in medical employment contracts enforceable. For this reason, prohibiting restrictive covenants in medical practice contracts is a decision better left to the legislature, where the competing interests can be fully aired. Any decision to ban physician non-competition agreements altogether should be left to the legislature. *Id.* |

State & Statute	Case Law
Indiana (con't)	Non-competition covenants in employment contracts are in restraint of trade and disfavored by the law. Courts construe these covenants strictly against the employer and will not enforce an unreasonable restriction. Agreements by physicians should be given particularly careful scrutiny. To be enforceable, a
	non-competition agreement must be reasonable; unlike reasonableness in many other contexts, the reasonableness of a noncompetition agreement is a question of law. In arguing the reasonableness of a non-competition agreement, the employer must first show that it has a legitimate interest to be protected by the agreement. The employer also bears the burden of establishing that the agreement is reasonable in scope as to the time, activity, and geographic area restricted. *Id.*
Iowa	Restrictive covenants regarding physicians have been recognized as valid and enforceable in Iowa. Non-compete agreements, otherwise known as covenants not to compete, are not generally favored, however, because they are viewed as restraints of trade that limit an employee's freedom of movement among employment opportunities. A restrictive covenant is strictly construed against the party seeking injunctive relief. *Board of Regents v. Warren*, 2008 Iowa App. LEXIS 1192 (Iowa Ct. App. Nov. 26, 2008).
	To determine whether a restrictive covenant in an employment contract is enforceable, a court considers: (1) whether the restriction is reasonably necessary for the protection of the employer's business; (2) whether it is unreasonably restrictive of

State & Statute	Case Law
Iowa (con't)	the employee's rights; and (3) whether it is prejudicial to the public interest. The restriction must be no greater than that necessary to protect the employer. Essentially, these rules require a court to apply a reasonableness standard in maintaining a proper balance between the interests of the employer and the employee. The facts and circumstances of each individual case must be carefully considered to determine whether a restrictive covenant is reasonable. The validity of the contract in each case must be determined on its own facts and a reasonable balance must be maintained between the interests of the employer and employee. *Id.*
Kansas	Covenants not to compete restrict competition, disrupt continuity of care, and potentially deprive the public of medical services. Any agreement that restricts the right of a physician to practice medicine for a specified period of time or in a specified area upon termination of an employment, partnership, or corporate agreement is discouraged. Restrictive covenants are unethical if they are excessive in geographic scope and duration in the circumstances presented, or if they fail to make reasonable accommodation of patients' choice of physician.
	The American Medical Association's standards, however, do not make restrictive covenants *per se* unethical but adopt a reasonableness standard similar to that applied by courts. *Idbeis v. Wichita Surgical Specialists*, 112 P.3d 81 (Kan. 2005).
	Any restrictive covenant agreed to by a physician is going to make some limitation on patient choice. The American

State & Statute	Case Law
Kansas (con't)	Medical Association's ethics guidelines condemn only those covenants that fail to make reasonable accommodation for patient choice. In each case, the varying circumstances must be considered in the effort to evaluate that impact. One valid consideration in this case is the nature of the typical relationship between a patient and a cardiovascular surgeon: it is usually short-term, lasting long enough to accommodate the surgical care and follow-up. *Id.* Editor's Note: K.S.A. §50-163 (e) (6) provides that the Kansas restraint of trade act shall not be construed to apply to any franchise agreements or covenants not to compete.
Kentucky	The clinic sought an injunction to prevent defendant physician from violating a restrictive covenant in his employment contract. Plaintiff patients sought an injunction to prohibit enforcement of the restrictive covenant. The trial court found the patients were third-party beneficiaries to the restrictive covenant entitled to notice of termination, which they did not receive. It enjoined enforcement of the restrictive covenant. The court reversed and held that defendant was terminated within the meaning of the restrictive covenant when his contract was not renewed upon expiration. The court also held no inequity would result from enforcing the restrictive covenant. The patients were not third-party beneficiaries to the restrictive covenant; rather, two distinct contracts existed. The first contract was between the clinic and the patients, which required the clinic to provide medical care meeting the

State & Statute	Case Law
Kentucky (con't)	standard of care required of all physicians, but it did not require the clinic to provide a particular doctor or to give notice of personnel changes. The second contract was the employment contract, involving professional service to which the patients were only incidental beneficiaries. *Daniel Boone Clinic, P.S.C. v. Dahhan* 734 S.W.2d 488 (Ky. Ct. App. 1987).

Restrictive covenants are valid and not against public policy unless the particular circumstances of the case would cause serious inequities to result. *Id.* |
| **Maine** | The Supreme Judicial Court of Maine has recognized "existing patients and business good will as legitimate interests that may be protected through a restrictive covenant." *Sisters of Charity Health Sys., Inc.,* 21 A.3d 110 (Me. 2011) (citing *Brignull v. Albert,* 666 A.2d 82, 84 (Me. 1995)).

Liquidated damages clauses in physician non-compete contracts are enforceable in Maine. *Id.* (enforcing $100,000 liquated damages clause against physicians for breach of two-year, 25-mile restrictive covenant).*See also Moshe Myerowitz, D.C., P.A. v. Howard,* 507 A.2d 578 (Me. 1986)(evaluating whether a chiropractic practice was entitled to a preliminary injunction to enforce a restrictive covenant); *Roy v. Bolduc,* 140 Me. 103, 34 A.2d 479 (1943) (holding that protectable confidential information may include trade or business secrets). |

State & Statute	Case Law

Maryland

Editor's Note:

On January 27, 2017, Maryland lawmakers passed House Bill 506, which would render null and void any non-compete provision in an employment contract that restricts the ability of an employee who earns equal to or less than $15.00 per hour or $31,200 annually to enter into employment with a new employer or to become self-employed in the same or similar business.

As of June 2017 it has not been voted on in the Maryland Senate.

Maryland employers have no protectable interest in preventing an increase in merely ordinary competition. *Intellus Corp. v. Barton, 7 F. Supp.2d 635, 639 (D. Md. 1998); See also Deutsche Post Global Mail, Ltd. v. Conrad, 116 Fed. Appx. 435, 438 (4th Cir 2004) (unpublished opinion), aff'g 292 F. Supp.2d 748, 756 (D. Md. 2003).*

Lofton v. TLC Laser Eye Ctrs., Inc., 2001 U.S. Dist. LEXIS 1476, 143 Lab. Cas. (CCH) P59231 (D. Md. Feb. 8, 2001) (evaluating non-compete restrictions with respect to an ophthalmic technician); *Wakefield v. Booth,* 33 Md. 63 (1870).

Mississippi

Field v. Lamar, 822 So.2d 893 (Miss. 2002) (dismissing, on procedural grounds, action seeking to enforce non-compete against physician); *Wilson v. Gamble,* 180 Miss. 499, 177 So. 363 (1937) (holding that a restriction must cover only such territory and such time as to be reasonably necessary for the protection of the employer or principal, without imposing undue hardship on the employee).

State & Statute	Case Law
New Jersey	In New Jersey, restrictive covenants between physicians are not *per se* unreasonable and unenforceable. Instead a three-part test called the Solari/Whitmyer test exists: whether the covenant in question (1) protects the legitimate interests of the employer, (2) imposes no undue hardship on the employee, and (3) is not injurious to the public. A non-exhaustive list of relevant factors to consider exists when determining the enforceability of restrictive covenants among physicians. Those factors include the time the employer physician needs to rebuild the practice following the employee-physician's departure, the reasonableness of the geographic scope, whether the activities the departing physician is prohibited from engaging in are the same as those performed by the employer physician, the hardship on the employee and the reason for the departure, the likelihood that another physician in the area can provide the medical services left vacant by the departing physician, and the effect that enforcement of the covenant would have on the public interest. *Community Hosp. Group, Inc. v. More*, 869 A.2d 884, 894 (N.J. 2005).

Except for attorneys and psychologists, New Jersey courts have consistently utilized a reasonableness test to determine the enforceability of restrictive covenants. There is no logical justification to treat a hospital-employer differently from a physician-employer. If either the hospital-employer or the physician-employer cannot establish that it has a legitimate business interest and, most important, that enforcement of the restriction will not be injurious to patient care, then enforcement of the restriction should be denied. *Id.* |

State & Statute	Case Law
New Jersey (con't)	A restrictive covenant between a physician and a hospital, although not favored, is not *per se* unreasonable and unenforceable. Rather, the trial court must determine whether the restrictive covenant protects the legitimate interests of the employer, imposes no undue hardship on the employee, and is not adverse to the public interest. *Pierson v. Med. Health Ctrs.*, 183 N.J. 65, 69- 70 (N.J. 2005).
New York **Editor's Note:** there is New York Broadcast Employees Right to Work Act., N.Y. Lab. Law §202-k (Consol. 2011) applicable to postemployment restrictions on broadcast employees.	Under New York law, negative covenants restricting competition are enforceable only to the extent that they satisfy the overriding requirement of reasonableness. An employee agreement not to compete will be enforced only if it is reasonable in time and area, necessary to protect the employer's legitimate interests, not harmful to the general public, and not unreasonably burdensome to the employee. This general limitation of reasonableness applies equally to a covenant given by an employee where he quits his employ. *Oak Orchard Cmty. Health Ctr. v. Blasco*, 2005 NY Slip Op. 25221, 3 (N.Y. Sup. Ct. 2005). See also *North Shore Hematology/ Oncology v. Zervos,* 278 A.D.2d 210, 717 N.Y.S.2d 250 (2nd Dept. 2000). Although the rule of reasonableness in cases involving professionals gives greater weight to the interests of the employer in restricting competition within a confined geographical area because professionals are deemed to provide unique or extraordinary services, the New York Court of Appeals nevertheless requires strict scrutiny of the particular facts and circumstances giving context to the agreement in the learned profession cases. Accordingly, even though an agreement is reasonable

State & Statute	Case Law
New York (con't)	as to time and area, there is no *per se* rule of reasonableness arising just because it is a physician's unique or extraordinary services that is involved; a court must still scrutinize whether the covenant, on the facts presented, is being legitimately employed to protect a plaintiff's legitimate interests, would not be harmful to the public, and would not be unduly burdensome to the defendant. New York case precedents do not obviate the need for independent scrutiny of the anti-competitive provisions of an employment agreement under the tripartite common-law standard. *Id.*

"... [e]nforcing a noncompetition provision when the employee has been discharged without cause would be unconscionable because it would destroy the mutuality of obligation on which a covenant not to compete is based." *Morris v. Schroder Capital Mgmt. Int'l, 445 F.3d 525, 529-30 (2d Cir.2006).*

Editor's Note*: In Prime Medical Associates, P.C. v. Ramani, 5 Misc.3d 311, 781 N.Y.S.2d 450 (Sup. Ct. Greene Cty. 2004),* a federal prohibition against enforcement of non compete provisions in physician contracts under a particular federal program was upheld, where a foreign physician studying in the U.S. had applied for such federal program and been assigned by the U.S. Department of Agriculture to an area designated as a health professional shortage area by the U.S. Department of Health and Human Services under a program to encourage foreign medical physicians studying in the U.S. to serve such communities in exchange for certain visa requirements. |

State & Statute	Case Law
New York (con't)	The court found that noncompetition provisions in the physician's employment contract would violate U.S. public policy because they would stop physicians under the program from remaining in the underserved area after expiration of their underlying employment agreement and continue serving the public.
Pennsylvania	Pennsylvania's courts have taken the traditional path in evaluating the enforceability of non-competition agreements involving physicians. Two Pennsylvania cases, *New Castle Orthopedic Assocs. v. Burns*, 392 A.2d 1383 (Pa. 1978), and *West Penn Specialty MSO, Inc. v. Nolan*, 737 A.2d 295 (Pa. Super. Ct. 1999), set the bounds for the traditional view. In Pennsylvania, a plaintiff seeking to enforce such a covenant must show: (1) the covenant relates to the contract for employment; (2) the covenant is supported by adequate consideration; and (3) the covenant is reasonably limited in both duration of time and geographical distance. A plaintiff seeking enforcement must also demonstrate that the court's protection will not detrimentally impact the availability of healthcare services in the restricted area. The *Burns* court emphasized that it attached great weight to this additional public policy prong. Once a legitimate interest is established, a court balances the employer's business interest against the employee's interest in earning a living and also the interests of both the employer and employee against the public interest. In doing so, a court must also determine whether the restrictive covenant is temporally and geographically reasonable in light of the fact that the public interest is

State & Statute	Case Law
Pennsylvania (con't)	of paramount importance in determining whether to enforce a restrictive covenant against a healthcare provider. *A&T Med. Inc. v. Mercadante*, 2011 Pa. Dist. & Cnty. Dec. LEXIS 200 (Pa. Common Pleas Ct. Feb. 28, 2011) (finding a two-year and five-mile radius restriction in chiropractor non-compete agreement reasonable).

[R]etaining patients is a compelling interest as is their interest in preventing existing and former employees from establishing a competing medical practice using their current patients. *Id.*

See also Wound Care Ctrs., Inc. v. Catalane, 2011 U.S. Dist. LEXIS 88136 (W.D. Pa. Aug. 9, 2011) (denying injunction where plaintiffs sought to enjoin for a period of one year within 20 miles several physicians and a hospital from entering into the business of or employing a physician-defendant for the purpose of treating chronic non-healing wounds); *Eckert v. Lehigh Valley Women's Med. Specialties, P.C.*, 2012 Pa. Dist. & Cnty. Dec. LEXIS 226 (Pa. Common Pleas Ct. Feb. 29, 2012) (finding physician's junior position with the practice and relatively brief duration of employment weighed against enforcement, but enforcing non-compete against physician who was officer and shareholder). |
| **Rhode Island** | *Dial Media v. Shiff*, 612 F. Supp. 1483 (D. R.I. 1985) (holding that the employer's good will, special training, and trade secrets are protectable interests); *see also Abbey Med./Abbey Rents, Inc. v. Mignacca*, 471 A.2d 189 (R.I. 1984); *Tillinghast v. Boothby*, 20 R.I. 59, 37 A. 344 (1897); *French v. Parker*, 16 R.I. 219, 14 A. 870 (1888). |

State & Statute	Case Law
South Carolina	*McElveen v. McElveen*, 332 S.C. 583, 506 S.E.2d 1 (S.C. Ct. App. 1998) (enforcing non-compete covenant against former manager of a surgical center); *Stringer v. Herron*, 309 S.C. 529, 424 S.E.2d 547 (S.C. Ct. App. 1992) (refusing to enforce, as overbroad, a restriction preventing a departing veterinarian from competing within a 15-mile radius of his former employer's three practice locations); *see also Hyer v. McRee*, 306 S.C. 210, 410 S.E.2d 604 (1991).
Vermont	*Roy's Orthopedic v. Lavigne*, 142 Vt. 347, 454 A.2d 1242 (1982), and 145 Vt. 324, 487 A.2d 173 (1985) (declining to enforce a restriction prohibiting former employee from competing for three years in any "territories presently served by [the] corporation and those additional territories to which the [employee] knows the corporation intends to extend and carry on business by expansion of its present activities"); *see also Butler v. Burleson*, 16 Vt. 176 (1844).
	Employment contracts, including noncompete covenants contained therein, are not assignable under Vermont law. *Smith, Bell & Hauck, Inc. v. Cullins*,123 Vt. 96, 183 A.2d 528 (1962).

State & Statute	Case Law
Virginia *Editor's Note: Following, *Parikh v. Family Care Ctr., Inc.*, 273 Va. 284, 288 (Va. 2007), Virginia's legislature amended its statute in 2008 (VA. CODE § 54.1-111(D) (amended, 2008) to clarify that both professional corporations and limited liability companies employing physicians are permitted to enforce the terms of employment contracts, including non-competes.	"Virginia law requires that 'non-competition clauses be strictly construed against the employer.'" *Roto-Die, Inc. v. Lesser*, 899 F. Supp. 1515, 1519 (W.D. Va. 1995) quoting *Grant v. Carotek*, Inc., 737 F.2d 410, 411 (4th Cir. 1984) (applying Virginia law)). Strictly construing against the employer can mean "giv[ing] the broadest possible meaning" to covenant language and then holding the covenant unenforceable for overbreadth. *Id.* at 1520. A nonprofessional corporation, which cannot lawfully engage in the practice of medicine in Virginia, does not have a legitimate business interest in enforcing a covenant not to compete in an employment contract with a licensed physician. A covenant not to compete between an employer and an employee will be enforced if the covenant is narrowly written to protect the employer's legitimate business interest, is not unduly burdensome on the employee's ability to earn a living, and does not violate public policy. Restrictive covenants are disfavored restraints on trade and, therefore, the employer bears the burden of proof and any ambiguities in the contract will be construed in favor of the employee. *Parikh v. Family Care Ctr., Inc.*, 273 Va. 284, 288 (Va. 2007).*

State & Statute	Case Law
West Virginia	An 18-month, 30-mile restrictive covenant on a former call center employee was "unreasonable on its face" and did not serve to protect the interest of the call center to retain its confidential information and retain current employees. *JAK Productions, Inc. v Bayer*, 94 F. Supp.3d 777 (S.D.W.Va.), *aff'd*, 616 F. App'x 94 (4th Cir. 2015).

A one-year, 10-mile covenant not to compete executed by an audiologist was found reasonable in *Audiology Distribution, LLC v Hawkins*, No. 5:13CV154, 2014 BL 337686, 2014 WL 6775599, at *12 (N.D. W. Va. Dec. 2, 2014).

An employee covenant not to compete is unreasonable on its face if its time or area limitations are excessively broad, or where the covenant appears designed to intimidate employees rather than to protect the employer's business, and a court should hold any such covenant void and unenforceable, and not undertake even a partial enforcement of it, bearing in mind, however, that a standard of "unreasonable on its face" is to be distinguished from the standard of "reasonableness" used in inquiries adopted by other authorities to address the minor instances of over breadth to which restrictive covenants are naturally prone. *Huntington Eye Assocs. v. LoCascio*, 553 S.E.2d 773, 780 (W. Va. 2001).

In *Gant v. Hygeia Facilities Found.*, 384 S.E.2d 842 (W. Va. 1989), appellant doctor sought review of a decision that denied his motion for declaratory judgment to void a restrictive covenant in his employment contract prohibiting him from practicing within a 30-air-mile radius of any facility |

State & Statute	Case Law
West Virginia (con't)	owned and operated by appellee nonprofit organization for three years. The court held that the restrictive covenant was reasonable on its face because it was included in the contract for a valid business purpose and was not designed to intimidate appellant. The court held that the restrictive covenant was presumptively enforceable because appellee met its burden of proving it had legitimate interests that its covenant was designed to protect. *Id.*
Wyoming	*Hopper v. All Pet Animal Clinic, Inc.,* 861 P.2d 531 (Wyo. 1993) (upholding restriction preventing a veterinarian from practicing small-animal medicine within a five-mile radius but reducing such restriction from three years to one year).
	"A valid and enforceable covenant not to compete requires a showing that the covenant is: (1) in writing; (2) part of a contract of employment; (3) based on reasonable consideration; (4) reasonable in durational and geographical limitations; and (5) not against public policy." *CBM Geosolutions, Inc. v Gas Sensing Tech. Corp.*, 215 P.3d 1054, 1059 (Wyo. 2009).
	The employer must be able to show that the contract is fair, the restrictive covenants reasonable, and that they have a fair relation to, and are really necessary for the protection of employer in the business to which the covenants are an incident. *Tench v. Weaver*, 374 P.2d 27, 29 (Wyo. 1962).

Restrictive Covenants in Physician Employment Relationships © 2013 is published by the American Health Lawyers Association. All rights reserved. No part of this publication may be reproduced in any form except by prior written permission from the publisher. Printed in the United States of America. Any views or advice offered in this publication are those of its authors and should not be construed as the position of the American Health Lawyers Association.

"This publication is designed to provide accurate and authoritative information in regard to the subject matter covered. It is provided with the understanding that the publisher is not engaged in rendering legal or other professional services. If legal advice or other expert assistance is required, the services of a competent professional person should be sought."—*from a declaration of the American Bar Association*

SAMPLE PHYSICIAN EMPLOYMENT AGREEMENT [With Annotations]

This Physician Employment Agreement ("**Agreement**") is effective as of the ___ day of _____, 20__ (the "**Effective Date**") by and between _____, a _____ professional corporation ("**Employer**"), and _____, M.D. ("**Physician**").

WHEREAS, Employer owns and operates a medical clinic located at *[insert full address]* _____;

WHEREAS, Physician is duly licensed as a physician in the state of _____, specializing in _____ medicine (the "**Specialty**"); and

WHEREAS, Employer desires to employ Physician to provide professional medical services in the Specialty to patients of Employer, as further described herein.

NOW, THEREFORE, in consideration of the above premises, which are hereby incorporated by this reference, and the mutual covenants and agreements contained herein, Employer agrees to employ Physician, and Physician hereby accepts employment with Employer, upon the terms and conditions hereinafter set forth.

1. *Term and Renewal.* The term of this Agreement shall begin on the Effective Date, with the actual commencement of Physician's employment to begin on _____, 20__ (the "**Commencement Date**"). This Agreement shall continue in effect for an initial term of one (1) year following the Commencement Date, unless earlier terminated as hereinafter provided. Thereafter, this Agreement shall automatically renew for successive one (1) year periods upon the same terms and conditions as set forth herein, unless earlier terminated as hereinafter provided or unless prior to ninety (90) days before the next succeeding one (1) year renewal term either party notifies the other party in writing that it does not desire to renew this

Agreement. In the event of such notification, this Agreement and any right to automatic renewal shall terminate at the end of the then current term. Each one-year period of this Agreement beginning with the Commencement Date shall be referred to herein as a "**Contract Year**".

    2. *Physician's Employment Responsibilities.* As of the Commencement Date and throughout the term of this Agreement, Physician's employment duties shall include:

    (a) *Services, Work Schedule.* Physician shall provide professional medical services in the Specialty (the "**Services**") to patients of Employer on a full-time basis, which is defined as a minimum of [28] scheduled hours per week in Employer's offices [during Employer's regularly scheduled office hours] OR [on Monday through Friday generally between the hours of ___ A.M and ___ P.M.], with each work shift generally not to exceed 8 hours per working day.

    [**Editors Note:** Wherever possible insert Physician's actual work schedule to avoid disputes later.]

    The above schedule is exclusive of time off for major holidays or vacation days, CME days, illness or other paid time off days, attendance at work related seminars and meetings, unless performing on- call Service coverage as described in Subparagraph 2(d) *On-Call Service Coverage* below.

    [**Editor's Note:** Modify language if Physician shall perform Services on a part time basis. For part time employment, so as to avoid the physician coming in for only an few hours per day and not having a minimum number of employment hours to rely on, include something to the effect that "Physician is expected to be available and Employer shall pay Physician to provide Services for no less than [___] hours per work day. The minimum number of work days per week shall be [___]."

    (b) *Primary Location of Services.* Physician shall perform the Services for the Employer pursuant to this Agreement primarily at the medical office space located at *[Identify medical office by Street Address, City, State, and Zip_____]* or such other medical office location mutually agreed upon by the Employer and Physician in writing as an amendment to this Agreement. Services shall also be provided at the hospital(s) located at *[Identify hospital by name, street address, City, State, Zip _____]* (the "**Hospital(s)**"), or such other hospital mutually agreed upon in writing by Employer and Physician.

(c)   *Required Medical Staff Membership.* The Hospital(s) where Physician shall require medical staff membership(s) and clinical privileges are: _____ *[Identify by hospital name, street address, City, State, Zip]*. Employer shall provide reasonable assistance to Physician in obtaining any medical staff membership(s) and clinical privileges necessary to perform the Services under this Agreement.

(d)   *On-call Service Coverage.* Physician shall furnish on-call coverage for Employer's patients as scheduled by the Employer from time to time on substantially the same basis as required of the other Employer physicians in the Specialty, but such on-call Service coverage shall generally not exceed every *[insert number, e.g. 4th]* weeknight / *[insert number, e.g. one]* calendar week per month or every *[insert number, e.g. 4th]* weekend. Holiday assignments are to be rotated substantially equally between Physician and other physicians in the Specialty. The name and location of the hospitals or other health care facilities where Physician shall provide on-call Service coverage are: _____ *[Identify by hospital name, street address, City, State, and Zip]*.

(e)   *Standard of Practice.* Physician shall provide Services in accordance with the current medical standards in the community applicable to the Specialty and in accordance with the applicable ethical and professional standards of conduct and practice as may from time to time be required or recommended by the American Medical Association or American Osteopathic Association, as applicable.

(f)   *Medical License.* Physician shall maintain an active medical license in good standing without limitation or restriction under the laws of the state of [_____] (the "**State**").

(g)   *Board Certification.* Physician shall maintain board certification or board eligibility in Physician's Specialty if that is a requirement of employment, unless waived by Employer.

(h)   *Other Licenses.* Physician shall obtain and maintain all necessary narcotics and controlled substances registration numbers and licenses for the performance of Physician's duties hereunder. Employer shall provide reasonable assistance to Physician in obtaining and maintaining such registrations and licenses.

(i) *Provider Eligibility.* Physician shall maintain participating provider status in good standing in all federal and state healthcare programs in which Employer participates, including Medicare and applicable state Medicaid programs. Where applicable, Employer shall provide reasonable assistance to Physician in obtaining and maintaining such participating provider status.

(j) *Audits.* If requested, Physician shall assist Employer in any regulatory, billing, and agency reviews relating to the Services.

(k) *Continuing Education and Training.* Physician shall maintain Physician's professional skills through continuing medical education and training programs, including participating in such educational sessions and compliance reviews as Employer reasonably requests.

(l) *Records for Services.* Physician shall timely prepare and update medical records and reports for Services rendered to patients pursuant to this Agreement in accordance with Employer's written medical records policies, as such policies may be amended from time to time, including coding appropriately for Services rendered to patients pursuant to this Agreement, with reasonable assistance therewith from Employer. The obligations described in this Subparagraph 2(l) *Records for Services* shall survive any termination or expiration of the Agreement with respect to Services provided by Physician prior to the effective date of such termination or expiration.

(m) *Compliance with Law.* Physician shall use Physician's best efforts to comply with all relevant federal and state statutes, laws, rules, regulations and ordinances applicable to the licensure and regulation of physicians and the performance of the Services provided by Physician under this Agreement.

(n) *Medical Staff Policies and Procedures.* Physician shall comply with the relevant policies and procedures for the medical staff of Employer and the Hospitals where Physician performs Services under this Agreement.

(o)   *Administrative Tasks.* If requested, Physician shall participate in reasonable amounts of administrative, supervisory, medical education, staff meeting and quality improvement tasks and initiatives, in each case directly relating to the Services and on substantially the same basis as other Employer physicians in the Specialty. Such tasks and initiatives shall generally not exceed more than *[insert number __ e.g. four]* hours cumulative per week; and

(p)   *Notification of Claims.* Physician shall immediately notify Employer of any professional liability or other claim made against the Physician or the Employer related to the Physician's provision of Services under this Agreement, including furnishing copies of any writings reflecting or discussing the same. The notification obligation described in this Subparagraph 2(p) *Notification of Claims* shall survive the termination or expiration of this Agreement.

3.   Employer Responsibilities. Throughout the term of the Agreement, Employer shall have the following duties:

(a)   *Payment of Annual Salary.* Upon and following the Commencement Date, Employer shall pay Physician an annual salary of _____ Dollars ($_____) per Contract Year, which shall be payable in equal bi-monthly installments in accordance with Employer's standard payroll practices. Employer shall withhold from any compensation payable under this Agreement all taxes as required by law or governmental regulation or ruling.

(b)   *Payment of Incentive Compensation*: Upon and following the Commencement Date, in addition to the annual salary and other benefits provided herein, Physician shall receive [annual] incentive compensation beginning *[___(date)____]* equal to *[___]* percent of Physician's billings generated from Physician's professional fees exceeding *[$_____.00]* during the Contract Year, or part thereof, for which Physician was employed. The parties agree that, for purposes of determining compensation, "billings" shall include those Services and other procedures that may be lawfully or contractually billed to and collected from a payor, whether such payor be an individual, governmental payor, insurance company, employer, managed care company or any other third party payor. Physician shall receive billing credit hereunder for all such professional services or procedures, regardless of whether or not Employer (or its designee) bills or collects for such services or procedures. Such incentive compensation shall be payable to Physician no later than [___insert month and day_____] of each calendar year.

[**Editor's Note**: If any part of Physician's compensation is based on wRVUs or on any similar type of production incentives make sure to include a provision such as: "The parties agree that, for purposes of determining compensation, a wRVU shall include those services and procedures that may be lawfully or contractually billed to and collected from a payor, whether such payor be an individual, governmental payor, insurance company, employer, managed care company or any other third party payor. Physician shall receive wRVU credit for all such services or procedures, regardless of whether or not Employer bills or collects for such services or procedures." If at all possible insert examples of exactly how any such production incentive is to be calculated to avoid future disputes. Also make it clear whether Physician is entitled to such incentive compensation on a prorata basis if Physician is employed for a portion of a year.]

(c) *Benefits.* Employer shall provide Physician with the benefits contained in its benefit plan for other similarly situated physicians employed by Employer, including health, dental and vision insurance, life and disability insurance, and participation in 401K or other pension plan benefits, as described in *[Attach or specifically reference such benefit plan]*, as approved and amended from time to time by Employer.

(d) *Vacation, Illness and Personal Leave.* Employer shall provide Physician with the following paid leave during Physician's employment:

(i) three (3) weeks per year of paid vacation during the first Contract Year. Following the first Contract Year Physician shall receive *[insert number___]* additional days of paid vacation leave per additional Contract Year up to a maximum of *[insert number___]* weeks paid vacation leave. Physician and Employer shall arrange reasonably in advance upon such vacation schedule so as to have sufficient coverage and otherwise manage the practice. If not taken, vacation leave may not be accrued unless otherwise agreed upon by the parties.

(ii)   up to *[insert number _]* working days of paid sick leave each Contract Year, which may be accrued up to a maximum of *[insert number___]* days paid sick leave if carried over to subsequent years.

(iii)   5 working days of paid leave each Contract Year for continuing medical education (CME) leave; and

(iv)   other leave as approved by Employer for extraordinary events, including, without limitation, family emergencies, funerals, studying for or taking medical board or certification examinations, teaching, etc.

(e)   *Reimbursable Business Expenses.* In addition to the foregoing, Employer shall reimburse Physician for the following business expenses upon submission of applicable bills, receipts or other sufficient documentation reasonably required by Employer:

(i)   Physician's medical licensure payments in the State(s) where Physician provides Services for Employer;

(ii)   Hospital medical staff dues in hospitals where Physician provides Services;

(iii)   Physician's professional medical membership dues in the following medical societies: [American College of Physicians, and _____];

(iv)   Physician's professional membership fees in any practice association or health care delivery system in which Employer elects to participate as a provider;

(v)   Subscriptions and professional book payments up to [$__] per Contract Year;

(vi)   Continuing medical education expenses up to [$5,000.00] per Contract Year;

(vii)   Business cell phone and monthly service fee and phone insurance;

(viii)   Business mobile computer;

(ix)   Moving or relocation expense reimbursement up to [$_____]; and

(x)   Other approved business expenses as agreed by Physician and Employer.

Editor's Note: Include payment of Director and Officer insurance premiums, if Physician is expected to serve on any administrative board or if Physician does or is expected to act in an executive capacity for Employer. Otherwise include a provision where Employer agrees to defend and indemnify any physician who does or is expected to provide such service - including costs and attorney's fees - for actions taken by Physician in such capacity.

Editor's Note: Signing or Retention Bonuses: Employers frequently help newly employed physicians with signing and/or retention bonuses, however be sure to exclude repayment obligations in the event of Physician's death, disability, or termination of Agreement without cause by Employer, termination of the Agreement with cause by Physician due to breach of Agreement by Employer, etc.;

Editor's Note: Optional: As an employment benefit, increasingly employers are assisting with physician student loan repayment, however, often the terms of such assistance may complicate and often times contradict the terms of the underlying employment agreement. Any such loan repayment assistance must be coordinated with the Physician's employment Agreement and, at a minimum, a priority clause is required stating that the Physician's employment agreement prevails in the event of any conflict in interpretation.

(f)   *Physician Right to Access Books and Records for Compensation Verification.* Upon reasonable written request, Physician and Physician's accountant or attorney shall have the right, at a time during ordinary business hours as reasonably determined by Employer, to inspect and copy records relevant to the calculation of Physician's compensation hereunder. Employer may impose a reasonable charge for the expenses, including labor, associated with providing such inspection and copying. The right to inspect shall survive the termination or expiration of this Agreement, and the legal representative of

Physician if deceased or under a legal disability shall have the same rights as Physician to access to Employer's books and records for proper purposes to the extent they pertain to the period during which Physician was entitled to any type of incentive or formula compensation.

(g)   *Facilities, Equipment, Supplies.* Upon and following the Commencement Date, the Employer shall provide and maintain throughout the term of the Agreement, or shall cause to be provided and maintained throughout the term of the Agreement, at employer's expense, physical facilities, including a furnished office and work space and *[insert number] OR [such]* examination room(s), for use by Physician to efficiently and effectively perform Physician's obligations under this Agreement. Such facilities shall be and remain equipped with such furniture, lighting, utilities, computers, computer lines, *[identify any necessary specialty medical equipment or other resources required]* medical equipment, telephones, medical records systems, medicines, and other supplies normally required for the performance of the Services. Employer shall seek the advice and input of Physician as to equipment and supply changes that directly impact the Services so as to avoid disruption of efficient delivery of Services. The Physician agrees to notify Employer of any perceived deficiencies in any facilities, equipment, technology, or supplies in the medical office or clinical space.

(h)   *Support Staff.* Employer, at its expense shall engage the services of *[insert number]OR [such]* trained physician assistants, clinical nursing staff, *[insert number]* trained medical technicians or assistants and other professional technicians, administrative clerical, scheduling, and billing and collection support staff services as necessary for Physician to efficiently and effectively perform the Services and other duties required under this Agreement and in accordance with accepted standards of medical practice. Physician shall provide direction to such employees or contractors insofar as they are employed to assist in connection with the performance of Physician's Services hereunder. All personnel furnished by Employer shall be administratively responsible to Employer and Employer shall be ultimately responsible for paying, hiring and firing of support personnel, with input from Physician with respect to those employees or contractors that Physician directly supervises. Physician shall have the right to interview and provide input for any personnel directly supervised by Physician.[1]

(i) *Participation in Managed Care Contracts.* Employer shall use its best commercial efforts to ensure that Physician is included as a provider in all managed care contracts, accountable care organizations, health maintenance organizations, physician-hospital organizations, independent practice associations, and any other managed care organizations with which Employer participates, so as to enable Physician to fulfill Physician's obligations under this Agreement.

(j) *Professional Liability Insurance.* Employer shall provide professional liability insurance for Physician in the minimum amount of [two] Million Dollars per occurrence and [five] Million Dollars in the aggregate annually (the "**Minimum Amount**"), and Employer shall be responsible for payment of any insurance deductibles. Upon expiration or termination of employment for any reason, Employer shall provide extended reporting endorsement coverage (tail coverage) in the Minimum Amount for Physician for claims that occur during the time the Physician was employed by the Employer. Such tail coverage shall be of unlimited duration and shall name Physician as a named Insured and Employer shall provide Physician, or shall cause its insurer to provide Physician, evidence of such tail coverage upon request. Furthermore, to the extent coverage is available through purchase of medical malpractice insurance Employer shall provide coverage for Physician's legal defense in administrative and disciplinary proceedings for medical staff or licensure proceedings, CMS audits, governmental inquiries, etc. The obligations described in this Subparagraph 3(j) *Professional Liability Insurance* shall survive the termination or expiration of this Agreement.

Employer shall not be responsible for and shall not provide liability insurance coverage for any occurrences, acts, activities, or services engaged in by Physician that are not within the scope

---

[1]If the physician employee requires specific or unusual items of support (such as a new piece or type of medical equipment or specially trained support personnel) to perform the Services, this should be explicitly stated in the Agreement.

of Physician's duties under this Agreement, or occurred prior to Physician's employment with Employer under this Agreement.

(k) *Medical Records, Fee Billing and Collection Responsibilities, Compliance with Laws.* Employer or its delegate shall have responsibility for keeping and maintaining patient medical records in connection with the Services, setting charges and fees for Services, and billing and collection and auditing of amounts owed for Services. All such activities shall be performed on a timely basis and in an accurate manner and in accordance with applicable laws, applicable policies and procedures of the Employer, applicable public and private payor requirements and any applicable Employer accreditation standards. The obligations described in this Subparagraph 3(k) *Medical Records, Fee Billing and Collection Responsibility, Compliance with Laws* shall survive the termination or expiration of this Agreement.

(l) *Indemnification of Physician for Employer Duties.* The Employer agrees to defend, indemnify and hold harmless Physician from any claim, loss, damage, cost, expense, liability, cause of action or judgment, including reasonable attorney's fees, costs and disbursements, arising out of or related to Employer's or parent or subsidiary companies, officers, directors, administrators, employees, physicians, representatives, staff, independent contractors, agents or designees: (i) failure to comply with applicable state, local or federal laws and Employer's guidelines and policies, or other applicable regulations in connection with performing medical record and billing keeping or auditing services, setting of medical fees and billing charges, billing or collection or auditing activities, or (ii) errors or defects in medical record and billing keeping or auditing activities, setting medical fees and billing charges, coding, billing or collection activities, or auditing activities, in each case related to Physician's Services and not due to Physician error. The obligations described in this Subparagraph (l) *Indemnification of Physician for Employer Duties* shall survive the termination or expiration of this Agreement.

(m) *Access to Patient Records.* Employer shall reasonably provide Physician, or shall cause the provision to the Physician, of the requisite patient records and documentation and other customary supporting information reasonably necessary for the Physician to render Services under this Agreement and to accurately code and bill for such Services.

(n) *Notice of Claim.* Employer shall immediately notify Physician of any professional liability or other claim made against the Physician or the Employer related to the Physician's provision of Services under this Agreement, including copies of any writings reflecting or discussing the same. The obligations described in this Subparagraph (n) shall survive the termination or expiration of this Agreement.

4. *Billing; Reassignment of Claims.* Physician hereby designates Employer as Physician's true and lawful agent and reassigns Physician's right to Employer to bill and collect monies due for all Services provided hereunder. All collections from such Services provided by Physician shall belong to Employer. Physician acknowledges that Employer shall determine the amount of fees charged to patients and payors and the use of such funds in its sole and reasonable discretion. So long as Physician's employment under this Agreement is in effect, Physician shall accept the compensation received from Employer pursuant to this Agreement as payment in full for all Services rendered to Employer's patients and shall not submit any separate or additional billings to patients, public or private third-party payors, or other responsible parties. Physician shall execute any necessary documents necessary to qualify and authorize Employer to directly bill the federal Medicare program, state Medicaid programs, or any other third-party payor for such Services. Physician shall abide by and cooperate with all billing policies and procedures established by Employer and the applicable payors. The obligations described in this Paragraph 4 *Billing; Reassignment of Claims* shall survive the termination or expiration of this Agreement.

5. *Outside Professional Activities.* Physician may engage in outside professional activities that do not compete or interfere with Physician's employment by Employer hereunder. Where Physician is a full time employee, Employment outside the Employer's physician practice must be approved by the Employer, which approval shall not be unreasonably conditioned, withheld or denied. Physician shall be entitled to retain any compensation for such outside activities so long as such activities are performed without the use of any equipment, supplies or other property of Employer or any other personnel of Employer. Physician shall be responsible for obtaining separate professional liability insurance for such outside activities.

6. *Physician Medical Judgment.* Notwithstanding anything to the contrary contained herein Physician shall have the sole and exclusive responsibility for making medical care judgments and determinations on behalf of patients to whom the Physician renders the Services. The Employer shall not exercise any control over or interfere with the independent professional judgment or determination of the appropriate health care to be rendered by the Physician to the patients receiving the Services.

7. *Medical Records.*

(a)   Medical records for Services shall be the sole and permanent property of Employer. Upon termination of this Agreement for any reason, Physician shall turn over to Employer all relevant records of patients for Services in Physician's possession. The medical records shall be kept and maintained by Employer in accordance with all relevant state and federal laws and regulations, including, but not limited to, the privacy and security standards of the Health Insurance Portability and Accountability Act of 1996 set forth at 45 CFR Parts 160, 162, and 164 (collectively, "HIPAA") and the Health Information Technology for Economic and Clinical Health Act of 2009 and its implementing regulations (collectively, the "HITECH Act"), and applicable policies and procedures of the Employer, applicable accreditation standards and public and private payor requirements and Employer agrees to take such actions as are necessary and appropriate in connection therewith.

(b)   Notwithstanding the forgoing, in the event that there is an audit, review, claim, dispute, lawsuit, inquiry, governmental investigation, governmental agency inquiry, medical licensing board inquiry, issue regarding the physician's medical license, which in any such event involves the care of a patient, then Physician may release the patient records and discuss the patient's health care subject to compliance with state and federal law. If requested in writing and at Physician's expense, the Employer shall ensure that a complete copy of the entire record of the relevant patient shall be promptly provided to Physician or his or her legal representative, in no less than ten business days after such written request has been received.

(c) The obligations described in this Paragraph 7 *Medical Records* shall survive the termination or expiration of this Agreement.

8. *Confidential Information, HIPAA Compliance, Exceptions to Confidentiality*

(a) All information, technology, records or data possessed by Physician relative to the activities of Employer of a confidential or proprietary nature, including without limitation, lists of patients, names of accounts, pricing information, business plans, strategic plans and other like information, is the property of Employer. During the term of this Agreement and for three (3) years after the termination or expiration of this Agreement, Physician shall not disclose to others (except for the benefit of Employer), or use for the benefit of others, any such information (with the exception of patient information reasonably required to treat patients or receive payment therefore and then such disclosure or use shall be only for such purposes) so long as such information is treated as secret or confidential by Employer or is not of common knowledge in the industry. Upon the termination or expiration of this Agreement, Physician shall return all of Employer's confidential information to Employer, and Physician shall not retain any such confidential information thereafter.

(b) Physician agrees to maintain the privacy and security of any individually identifiable patient health information received from or created for Employer in accordance with relevant state and federal laws and regulations, including, but not limited to, the privacy and security standards of HIPAA and the HITECH Act (each as defined above), and agrees to take such actions as are necessary and appropriate in connection therewith. To the extent permitted by law, Physician shall cooperate and communicate freely with other health care providers who provide professional services to patients of Employer.

(c) Notwithstanding anything to the contrary contained herein, information, technology, records or data shall *not* be considered to be secret or confidential or proprietary and Physician shall not be liable for the use and disclosure thereof if such information, technology, records or data (i) was in the public domain at the time of disclosure or thereafter comes into the public domain through no fault of the Physician, (ii) is otherwise available to the receiving party without restrictions on use or disclosure, (iii) was known to the receiving party at or before the receipt thereof from the Physician, (iv) is independently developed by the receiving party, (v) is disclosed after Physician's receipt of a governmental, medical board or health care agency request or investigative demand, (vi) is required to be disclosed to a court, governmental or regulatory authority of competent jurisdiction or by deposition, interrogatory, document production request, subpoena, or other similar legal demand, or (vii) is a patient's medical record or other thing for which Physician is entitled to copies upon a specific request in writing from a patient or patient's representative.

(d)   Additionally, Physician may disclose this Agreement (i) in confidence to Physician's attorneys, accountants, auditors, tax preparers, and financial advisors; (ii) upon request from any government entity or court of law; and (iii) insofar as such disclosure may be necessary to enforce its terms or as otherwise required by law.

(e)   The obligations described in this Paragraph 8 *Confidential Information, HIPAA Compliance, Exceptions to Confidentiality* shall survive the termination or expiration of this Agreement.

9.   *Termination*.

(a)   **[OPTIONAL:** *Termination Without Cause*. Either party may terminate this Agreement for any reason or no reason upon one hundred twenty (120) days prior written notice.]

(b)   *Termination With Cause*. Except as otherwise provided in this paragraph, either party shall have the right to terminate this Agreement with cause if the other party breaches a material provision of this Agreement and fails to cure such breach within ten (10) calendar days of the giving of written notice by the non-breaching party specifying such breach or default. This paragraph only relates to independent causes of breach and is not intended to provide for a cure period for any of the immediate causes for termination described in Paragraphs 9(c) and 9(d) below.

(c) *Immediate Termination by Employer With Cause.* Employer may immediately terminate this Agreement effective as of the date stated in a notice delivered to the Physician upon the occurrence of any of the following:

(i) Physician's death or, subject to compliance with all applicable state and federal (e.g., the Americans with Disabilities Act), Physician suffers a permanent disability or becomes impaired to such an extent that it renders Physician unable to perform the essential functions of Physician's job with reasonable accommodation, unless Physician qualifies for leave under any applicable leave policy of the Employer;

(ii) the suspension, termination, revocation, material restriction or limitation or voluntary or involuntary surrender of: (A) Physician's license to practice medicine in the State, or (B) Physician's registration or license to prescribe controlled substances by any federal or state regulatory agency, in each case following a hearing and any appeal, unless such hearing and appeal is waived by Physician;

(iii) the suspension, exclusion, debarment, or sanction of Physician by any federal or state sponsored health care program for which Physician provides Services, including, without limitation, Medicare or Medicaid, in each case following a hearing and any appeal, unless such hearing and appeal is waived by Physician;

(iv) if for reasons of patient quality of care or professional misconduct, Physician has his or her medical staff membership or clinical privileges revoked, or materially restricted by a hospital necessary for the performance of Services required under this Agreement, or if Physician voluntarily relinquishes his or her medical staff privileges in lieu of any action by a hospital necessary for the performance of Services required under this Agreement;

(v) Physician's failure to maintain board certification or board eligibility in the Specialty if board certification or board eligibility is required as a condition of employment, unless waived by Employer;

(vi)   Physician's conviction of, or plea of guilty or "no contest" / nolo contendere to, a crime involving the practice of medicine or moral turpitude (i.e., theft, fraud, embezzlement or similar crime of dishonesty), use or possession of illegal drugs, or of any felony, whether or not sentence is imposed;

(vii)   the inability of Employer to obtain or maintain on behalf of Physician the professional liability insurance coverage required under this Agreement after reasonable commercial efforts to do so; or

(viii)   if Physician enters into a business arrangement that materially restricts, limits or interferes with Physician's continued ability to provide Services under this Agreement.

(d)   *Immediate Termination by Physician With Cause.* Upon the occurrence of any of the following events, Physician may elect to terminate this Agreement effective as of the date stated in a notice delivered to the Employer:

(i)   if the Employer or any of its parent companies, or any of the hospitals where Physician provides Services are convicted of health care fraud or any other health care related crime, or are terminated, debarred or excluded from participation in any Medicare, Medicaid or any other federal or state health care program for any reason;

(ii)   if the Employer or any of its parent companies, or any of the hospitals where Physician provides Services have their accreditation or business license revoked, restricted, suspended, conditioned, denied or allowed to expire without renewal;

(iii)   if the Employer fails to rectify the taking of any action by Employer or any of its parent companies, or any of the hospitals where Physician provides Services, that restricts, limits or materially interferes with Physician's ability to provide Services under this Agreement within thirty (30) days of written notice thereof from Physician;

(iv)   the dissolution of Employer or the sale, transfer or assignment of all or substantially all of the assets or medical practice of Employer or any of its parent companies to any entity;

(v)   the commencement by Employer or any of its parent companies or a hospital where Physician provides Services, of a voluntary case under any applicable bankruptcy, insolvency or other similar law, now or hereafter in effect, or the entry of a decree or order for relief in a case under any such law, or appointing of a receiver, liquidator, assignee, custodian, trustee (or other similar official) or for any substantial part of such party's property, or ordering the wind-up or liquidation of affairs, or the filing and pendency for thirty (30) days without dismissal of a petition initiating an involuntary case under any such bankruptcy, insolvency or similar law, or the making of any general assignment for the benefit of creditor's or the failure of any such party to pay its debts as such debts become due, or the taking of action in furtherance of any of the foregoing; or

(vi)   upon occurrence of a Change of Control of Employer or any of its parent companies. "Change of Control" means the sale or transfer of all or substantially all the assets of Employer or any of its parent companies, however accomplished, including, without limitation, by merger, consolidation or acquisition of Employer or any of its parent companies, with, by or into another corporation, entity or person, or any change in the ownership of more than fifty percent (50%) of the voting capital stock of Employer or any of its parent companies in one or more related transactions. Upon the Change of Control, Physician shall have the right to terminate the Agreement upon 30 calendar days written notice.

(e)   *Return of Equipment and Records.* Upon the termination or expiration of Physician's employment for any reason, Physician agrees to promptly return to Employer all keys, equipment, medical and office supplies, cell phones, computers, parking or building entrance cards, prescription pads, documents, records, reports, computer discs, flash drives, files, books, correspondence, lists, including, but not limited to price and patient lists, or other written or electronic records, including originals and all copies, relating to Employer's business, which are or have been in Physician's possession or under Physician's control.

(f)   *Hospital Medical Staff Privileges Unaffected.* Termination or expiration of the Agreement shall not, in and of itself, be deemed to adversely affect Physicians medical staff appointment or clinical privileges or membership status in any hospitals or require Physician to resign the same, unless an independent action by the medical staff has called for such medical staff or clinical privileges resignation and Physician has been afforded full due process under the Medical Staff Bylaws.[2] This Subparagraph 9(f) *Hospital Medical Staff Privileges Unaffected* shall survive the termination or expiration of this Agreement.

(g)   *Notice to Patients.* Upon termination of this Agreement for any reason, Employer shall send a written notice to patients treated by Physician if and as required by applicable law and as recommended by AMA Code of Medical Ethics, Opinion 7.03. The obligations described in this Subparagraph 9(g) *Notice to Patients* shall survive the termination or expiration of this Agreement.

10. OPTIONAL: *Post-Employment Restrictive Covenants.*

(a)   *Non-solicitation of Patients.* Physician agrees that for a period of one (1) year from and after the termination of this Agreement, Physician shall not directly or indirectly solicit the business or care of any patient to whom Physician provided Services under this Agreement and had personal contact with while employed by Employer, except to the extent that such activities are unrelated to, and not competitive with, the business, products and/or medical services supplied or proposed to be supplied by Employer to such patients. The obligations described in this Paragraph 10(a) *Non-solicitation of Patients* shall survive the termination or expiration of this Agreement.

---

[2]Variation of this clause recommended in American Medical Association (AMA) *Annotated Model Physician-Hospital Employment Agreement* 2011 Edition, Updated March 2012, §9.6 *Effect of Termination,* p. 81.

(b) *Non-solicitation of Employees.* Physician agrees that for a period of one (1) year from and after the termination of this Agreement, Physician shall not directly or indirectly solicit, induce, or attempt to influence any employee or independent contractor of Employer to become Physician's employee or independent contractor or to terminate his or her relationship with Employer. The obligations described in this Paragraph 10(b) *Non-solicitation of Employees* shall survive the termination or expiration of this Agreement.

(c) *Restrictive Covenants Not Applicable.* The restrictive covenants described above shall not apply in the event Employer terminates Physician without cause pursuant to Paragraph 9(a) *Termination without Cause*, or Physician exercises Physician's right to terminate the Agreement due to breach by the Employer pursuant to Paragraphs 9(b) *Termination With Cause* or 9(d) *Immediate Termination by Physician With Cause* or Paragraph 12 *Amendment to Comply with Laws* below.

11. *Physician's Representations.* Except as previously disclosed to Employer in writing, Physician represents to Employer that Physician has never been the subject of any action or proceeding to restrict, suspend or revoke Physician's license to practice medicine in the State, has never been excluded from participation in the Medicare or Medicaid programs or other government-sponsored healthcare programs and that no proceedings or investigations are currently pending or to Physician's knowledge threatened by any federal or state agency seeking to exclude Physician from such programs or to sanction Physician for any violation of any rule or regulation of such programs. Throughout the term of this Agreement, Physician agrees to notify Employer immediately in the event any such proceedings are commenced against Physician.

12. *Amendment to Comply with Laws*. Although the parties believe that this Agreement and the intent of the parties embodied herein complies with applicable laws and regulations, in the event any material provision of the Agreement is determined to be in violation of state or federal law, rule or regulation, or governing judicial or regulatory interpretation, whether existing or newly promulgated, such provision shall be re-negotiated by the parties in good faith to render the provision in compliance with such law, regulation, or interpretation. If the parties cannot agree on such re-negotiated terms, this Agreement shall terminate upon reasonable written notice from one party to the other.

13.   *General Provisions.*

(a)   *Notices.* Any notice required or permitted to be given hereunder shall be sufficient if in writing and shall be deemed given on the date of delivery to that party personally or to that party's home or office by mail, facsimile or email. The date of delivery may be proved by any reasonable evidence, but if there is no evidence of the date of actual delivery, then delivery will be presumed (1) with respect to Physician, when personally delivered to Physician, or four (4) days after deposit in the U.S. mail, postage prepaid, and addressed to Physician at his or her last known address as shown in Employer's records; and (2) with respect to Employer, when personally delivered to an officer or director of Employer or four (4) days after deposit in the U.S. mail, postage prepaid, and addressed to Employer at its principal place of business, unless the party to whom the notice is addressed proves a later date.

(b)   *Entire Agreement.* This Agreement, including any attachments incorporated by reference herein, represents the entire agreement between the parties and supersedes all prior agreements, whether written or oral, between the parties with respect to the subject matter hereof.

(c)   *Amendments in Writing.* This Agreement may be amended only by a written instrument executed by Physician and a duly authorized representative of Employer.

(d)   *No Waiver of Breach.* The waiver by either party hereto of a breach of any provision of this Agreement shall not operate as or be construed to be a waiver of any subsequent breach by either party.

(e)   *Severability.* If any provision or portion of any provision of this Agreement is held to be unenforceable or invalid by a court of competent jurisdiction, the validity and enforceability of the remaining provisions of this Agreement shall not be affected thereby.

(f)   *Governing Law, Jurisdiction.* The parties acknowledge that this Agreement has been negotiated in the State of _____ for Services to be performed therein and, therefore, this Agreement shall be interpreted under and governed by the laws of the State of _____. Any controversy, dispute or claim arising out of or relating to this Agreement shall be litigated, if at all, in the appropriate court of jurisdiction in _____ County, State of _____. This Paragraph 13(f) shall survive the termination or expiration of this Agreement.

(g) *No Assignment of Agreement.* Physician acknowledges that the Services to be provided by Physician are personal to Physician and Physician may not, therefore, assign Physician's rights or duties under this Agreement. Likewise, Employer agrees that it shall not assign this Agreement without the prior written consent of Physician. Such assignment shall not relieve the Employer of its obligations hereunder unless agreed to in writing by Physician.

(h) *Counterparts.* This Agreement may be executed in two or more counterparts, all of which together shall constitute one and the same instrument.

(i) *Captions or Headings.* The captions or headings used herein are for convenience only and do not constitute part of this Agreement.

(j) *Survival.* Each provision of this Agreement that would by its nature or terms survive the expiration or any termination of this Agreement shall survive the expiration or termination of this Agreement.

IN WITNESS WHEREOF, the parties have duly executed and delivered this Agreement to be effective as of the Effective Date first above written.

[EMPLOYER NAME]

By:_____   Date:_____

Printed Name:_____

Title:_____

Address:

[PHYSICIAN NAME]

By:_____, M.D.   Date:_____

Printed Name:

Address:

BASIC LICENSES, PERMITS AND OTHER REQUIREMENTS OF WHICH TO BE AWARE WHEN OPENING A MEDICAL PRACTICE

In addition to establishing and registering a separate legal entity, counsel for a physician or physician group contemplating opening a medical practice needs to check the statutory and administrative requirements in the relevant state with respect to the licenses, permits and other requirements specific to opening a medical practice. The basic licenses, permits and other requirements for medical practices normally include:

➤ **Physician State Medical License:** A physician must be licensed by the medical board in the state in which he or she wishes to practice. The American Medical Association website has a link to each state's board at: *http://www.ama-assn.org/ama/pub/education-careers/becoming-physician/medical-licensure/state-medical-boards.page.*

➤ **Employer Identification Number / Tax Registration**: the physician will need to apply for an employer identification number, or EIN, which can be accomplished on the Internal Revenue Service website *http://www.irs.gov/Businesses/Small-Businesses-&-Self-Employed/Apply-for-an-Employer-Identification-Number-(EIN)-Online.* This number identifies the new business to the federal government for taxes.

➤ **State and Local Tax Registration Requirements:** Likewise the new business will also need to be registered for state and local taxes, which vary by state. Detailed information about each state's tax registration process can be found on the Small Business Administration website. *https://www.sba.gov/content/learn-about-your-state-and-local-tax-obligations.* State and Federal tax (Circular E) information is available at: *https://www.irs.gov/publications/p15/ar02.html.*

➤ **National Provider Identifier (NPI) Number**: All medical providers need a national provider identifier number, which can be applied for on the National Plan and Provider Enumeration System website, *https://nppes.cms.hhs.gov/ NPPES/Welcome.do* Medicare, Medicaid and private insurance companies use this number to keep track of and pay health providers as well as HIPAA transactions. Individual provider NPI's are called Type 1 NPI numbers; organization provider NPI's are called Type 2 NPI numbers. Do not use another entity's Medicare P.I.N. that it assigns to you. If the physician never had a prior Medicare PIN, the physician will not be able to get paid for any Medicare services until he or she is assigned his or her personal NPI number.

➤ **DEA Registration Number:** To prescribe medication, the physician will need to be registered with and have a unique number issued to the physician by the U.S. Drug Enforcement Administration (DEA). This can be accomplished online at the DEA website *http://www.deadiversion.usdoj.gov/drugreg/index.html.* Be aware that there are also states that require physicians who write prescriptions to be registered with the State Board of Pharmacy (or that state's equivalent thereof or perhaps even the state's equivalent of the DEA), so counsel for the physician is well advised to check with the individual state medical board to determine if such a state requirement is applicable.

➤ **Other Additional Federal and State Regulations:** The following are other federal regulations depending on the type of medicine practiced and the procedures provided in the physician's office or clinic. Often states have parallel regulations so it is important for the counsel to check for state requirements.

• **Laboratories**: There is a federal regulation requiring that all physicians' practice laboratories require a Clinical Laboratories Improvement Amendments (CLIA) license and certification according to the level of the tests performed.

The license and certification is issued through the U.S. Centers for Medicare and Medicaid Services. See *https://www.cms.gov/Regulations-and-Guidance/Legislation/CLIA/index.html?redirect=/clia/*.

- **X-rays**: If a physician has or plans on having in- office X-ray equipment, the physician will have to register with the particular state where the equipment is located, typically through the health department or Department of Environmental Resources.

- **Biomeds:** The Environmental Protection Agency (EPA) definition of medical waste is very expansive and means "all waste materials generated at health care facilities, such as hospitals, clinics, physician's offices, dental practices, blood banks, and veterinary hospitals/clinics, as well as medical research facilities and laboratories." OSHA (the Occupational Safety and Health Administration) has an established procedure for dealing with biomedical waste hazards that the Physician needs to follow, depending on the type of procedures that will be performed in the physician's office. See *https://www.epa.gov/rcra/medical-waste*.

- For state links to Hazardous Waste Programs and U.S. State Environmental Agencies see: *https://www.epa.gov/hwgenerators/links-hazardous-waste-programs-and-us-state-environmental-agencies*.

➢ **County and City Tax Registration and License Requirements.**

There are also county and city tax registrations and often occupational licenses that are required, so counsel needs to check with the tax collector of the county and city, as well as the department of licenses and permits for the county and city where the physician's practice is going to be located to make sure that the business entity has received all the necessary licenses and business permits necessary and completed all the inspections necessary before opening the practice. At a minimum, the local Fire Marshall usually has to make an inspection of the premises prior to occupancy. The county

Medical Association can be a remarkably useful first step in providing 'local' jurisdictional information and phone numbers.

➤ Hospital Medical Staff and Clinical Privileges

Submit applications for hospital and staff clinical privileges or change in provider status. This application information will come from the hospital medical staff office. This is often an internal political exercise as much as a professional administrative exercise.

NOTE: The above is included for illustrative purposes only to help assist the general attorney in considering the type of typical 'core' permit and license requirements that are usually applicable when opening a medical office. It is not meant to be a complete or all-inclusive list of every permit or action an attorney should consider on behalf of a client, because that is state law and fact dependent. Counsel should consult with an appropriately state licensed health law attorney and experienced state licensed corporate and tax law attorney to ensure the most appropriate advice for the local jurisdiction.

INDEX

References are to chapters and footnote numbers (e.g., 15: III.B; 18: VI.B refers to section III.B in Chapter 15 and to section VI.B in Chapter 18). Appendix material is indicated by the prefix App.

A

healthcare unit classification rules. *See*
Healthcare unit classification
rules
**National Practitioner Data Bank
(NPDB)**
generally, *12*: I
checking and contesting data entries,
12: III
confidentiality, *12*: IV
contents, *12*: II
disciplinary procedures, *4*: IV, VI
LEIE compared, *13*: IV
litigation use of, *12*: V
regulatory oversight, *13*: IV
reports, *Ch.* 12
state licensing boards, *12*: III
National provider identifiers (NPIs),
13: III; *App.* C
Negotiations
physician employment contracts, *9*: VI
strikes and lockouts as weapons,
17: III
**New Hampshire and restrictive
covenants**, *10*: V
New Mexico and restrictive covenants,
10: V
NLRA. *See* National Labor Relations
Act
NLRB. *See* National Labor Relations
Board
Noncompete covenants. *See* Restrictive
covenants
Nonemployee contract relationships,
Ch. 8
accountable care organization
agreements, *8*: II
administrative work, *8*: VIII
ambulatory surgical center joint
venture agreements, *8*: II
attorneys, *8*: III.B
business questions, *8*: VIII
compensation, *8*: VIII
conflicts of interest, *8*: III.C
controlled substances prescribing
rules, *8*: XIX
credentialing assistance, *8*: VIII
due diligence, *8*: VIII
equity and nonequity joint venture
agreements, *8*: II

exclusive and nonexclusive contracting
agreements, *8*: II
form agreements, *8*: III.A
hospital administration, *8*: VIII
hospital service line co-management
agreements, *8*: II
income assurances, *8*: VIII
indemnification, *8*: V–VI
independent physicians, *8*: I
initial considerations, *8*: III
joint and several liability, *8*: XIX
malpractice insurance, *8*: XIX
management services agreements,
8: II, VIII
market position, *8*: VIII
medical consulting services
agreements, *8*: II
medical directorship agreements, *8*: II
Medicare, *8*: III.B
on-call coverage agreements, *8*: II
outsourcing services, *8*: II
overview, *8*: I
patient assignment, *8*: VIII
payment terms, *8*: VIII
physician service agreements, *8*: III.B
for cause termination, *8*: XVI
change-of-control clauses, *8*: XII
compensation, *8*: XIV
covenants not to compete, *8*: XIV–
XV
future opportunities, *8*: XVIII
initial term, *8*: X
managed care considerations, *8*: IX
mergers and acquisitions, *8*: XII
network considerations, *8*: IX
nonassignment clauses, *8*: XII
renewal terms, *8*: XIII
termination provisions, *8*: XI
unwind provisions, *8*: XVII
walk away provisions, *8*: XIII
professional services agreements, *8*: II
arrangement benefits, *8*: IV.E
benefits, *8*: IV.H
billing and collection arrangements,
8: IV.F
compensation, *8*: IV.F
hospital hiring restrictions, *8*: IV.C
indemnification, *8*: V
insurance carrier advice, *8*: V